GERALD J.J. TULCHINSKY is a member of the Department of History at Queen's University, Kingston, Ontario.

The River Barons charts the development of the business community in Montreal through the crucial years between 1837 and 1853, when the small commercial fraternity of the 1830s, responding to the challenge of a transportation revolution, grew much more complex and diversified. This period saw the beginning of the railway age in Canada, and the rapid extension of lines out from Montreal ensured the city's economic expansion. This was also the era when large new plants, concentrated near the Lachine Canal, a newly available source of hydraulic power, suddenly intruded upon the original network of small workshops scattered about the city.

Professor Tulchinsky focuses on the entrepreneurs. He describes the business community's branches and groupings, its ethnic makeup — French and English, Scottish and American — and the reasons for its success. He explains how the city's merchants, professionals, and politicians embraced, utilized, and came themselves to be transformed by innovations in transportation and the possibilities for large-scale industrial development. And he devotes special attention to the Montreal businessmen themselves, their objectives and aspirations, their attitudes and ideas.

In this excursion into business and urban history, Professor Tulchinsky amplifies from a modern perspective the pioneering work of Creighton, Tucker, and Cooper.

GERALD J.J. TULCHINSKY

The River Barons

MONTREAL BUSINESSMEN AND
THE GROWTH OF INDUSTRY
AND TRANSPORTATION 1837-53

UNIVERSITY OF TORONTO PRESS

Toronto and Buffalo

© University of Toronto Press 1977
Toronto and Buffalo
Printed in Canada

Library of Congress Cataloging in Publication Data

Tulchinsky, Gerald J.J. 1933-
  The river barons.

  Bibliography: p.
  Includes Index.
  1. Businessmen – Montreal – History. 2. Montreal – Industries – History.
  3. Railroads – Canada – History. 4. Shipping – Canada – History. I. Title.
  HC118.M6T84   338'.09714'281   76-26019
  ISBN 0-8020-5339-4

This book has been published during the
Sesquicentennial year of the University of Toronto

This book is dedicated to
the memory of my father

ר׳ אריה הינך ב״ר יעקב יוסף

Contents

Preface

In recent years Canadian historians have become increasingly interested in the development of Canada's cities. More than ever before they have begun to study Montreal, Toronto, and Winnipeg, where, to a great degree, the economic, political, and cultural life of the country was shaped. Attention is now being focused upon social change within the urban context, as well as upon the metropolitan processes at work in these and other cities. Historians are now anxious to move beyond the concepts of Innis and Creighton, who stressed the function of Montreal in continental terms, to an understanding of what took place within the cities: physical expansion and population increase, social problems and class divisions, the rise of ethnic communities and cultural assimilation, politics and corruption, and wealth and poverty, in addition to many other urban themes.

Canadian cities have also begun to attract the attention of historians interested in economic development and in the business classes, whose activities in commercial, financial, industrial, and transportation ventures stimulated and directed urban growth. Business history has a strong connection with urban history because most major businessmen in Canada operated from an urban base. From the earliest years, Canadian merchants, although serving a relatively unsophisticated agricultural and timber economy, became increasingly dependent upon key port towns where manufactured goods from abroad were exchanged for upcountry produce. Historians have become more and more concerned with the growth of trade centres, the mobilization of capital, the fluctuations in the prices of Canadian staple commodities and, increasingly during the last few years, with the businessmen themselves. As merchants became steamboat-owners, real estate speculators, politicians, industrialists, bankers, and mining promoters they were acting as entrepreneurs – innovators in technology or business organization – in the successive eras of rapid economic change of the nineteenth century. The pursuit of profits took many forms which, though sometimes both complex and vague, were increasingly dominant in the urban business scene.

This present study is an attempt to examine certain aspects of the business history of Montreal in a crucial era of change from the late 1830s to the early 1850s. It follows the interaction of Montreal's business community with the ongoing 'transportation revolution' that was rapidly accelerating the pace of North American economic life in the mid-nineteenth century. Though it covers a period treated often before, this excursion into both business and urban history differs from its predecessors in focusing attention on the personnel of the Montreal business community. To probe beneath the drama of Montreal's pursuit of, and failure to achieve, the commercial empire of the St Lawrence described so vividly and compellingly by Professor Creighton, I have tried to piece together the composition of Montreal's business community, its branches and groupings, its ethnic makeup – French and English, Scottish and American – and the factors that made for its success. Above all, I have sought to explain how the city's merchants, professionals, and politicians embraced and utilized, and were themselves transformed by, the innovations in transportation and the possibilities for large-scale industrial development in Montreal during the 1840s.

To be sure, transportation and industry were only two aspects, albeit highly important ones, of the increasingly elaborate structure of economic services provided in Montreal during this era. Banks, insurance companies, warehouses, stock and commodity exchanges, and vast wholesale and retail houses were immensely significant ancillary commercial services, and a complete examination of the city's economy, would have to give more extensive treatment to these sectors than they have received here. It would be too simplistic, however, to see a close, well-developed integration of all these parts of Montreal's economic life during the 1840s and 1850s. My research has revealed little financial connection between the railway and industrial development discussed in these pages and the Montreal banks. Except for modest short-term loans and occasional acceptance of railway shares as collateral for personal loans, the city's banks did not support railway promotions, and I have seen no evidence that the banks purchased railway shares or bonds on their own account. The same holds true for manufacturing. Like their US and British counterparts, Montreal banks did not provide investment capital for such long-term ventures; they preferred instead the traditional and more profitable and reliable dealings in commercial paper, note issues, and foreign exchange. Consequently, there is little discussion of banking in the pages that follow.

Transportation and industry were the two leading sectors in the alterations of Montreal's economic and social life in the middle years of the century.

Transportation was selected not only because, of all the factors contributing to economic expansion, this one was vital and fundamental but also because of the important transition begun in Montreal by the inauguration of the railway age during these years. Montreal's industry is treated here because it, too, experienced an important transition during the late 1840s and early 1850s when the network of small scattered shops around Montreal was intruded upon by the sudden appearance of many large new plants concentrated near the newly available source of hydraulic power in the Lachine Canal. In both of these major sectors, then, the city of Montreal experienced significant growth, and it saw even more significant changes within the business community, now much more complex, more varied, and broader than the small, almost exclusively commercial fraternity of the 1830s. It is with that evolution and its implications that this study is concerned.

Professor Creighton has explained how Montreal's commercial leaders attempted to extend the city's metropolitan reach during the hundred years ending in 1850. Any student of Montreal's economic development must, therefore, begin with a heavy debt to his *Commercial Empire of the St Lawrence,* as well as to G.N. Tucker's *Canadian Commercial Revolution* and to Professor Ouellet's monumental *Histoire économique et sociale du Québec 1760-1850,* which is indispensable for an understanding of the provincial context in which Montreal developed during those years. Professor John Cooper's recent *Montreal: A Brief History* is enlightening, and his many earlier studies of some of the city's institutions and its social structure in the nineteenth century are highly important works on the flourishing English-speaking elements in Montreal of that time.

While studying with Professor Cooper, I was first introduced to the nineteenth-century economic history of Montreal and began to glimpse some of the many possibilities for research into the city's economic and social development. It seemed to me that the time between the late 1830s and 1853 was one of the most important in Montreal's economic growth. During those years a number of decisive transportation and industrial developments occurred. At the same time there was an efflorescence of new insurance, mining, banking, and telegraph companies established by Montrealers, who demonstrated keen awareness of the possibilities for profit in these enterprises. While the period was an intensely active one in a variety of ventures, it also encompassed several major landmarks in the development of transportation and industry in Montreal. 1837 was the first full year of operations of the Champlain and St Lawrence railway, and the following year the government commenced planning for a substantial commitment to transportation improvements in Lower Canada. 1845 marked the beginning of the important St Lawrence and Atlantic railway to Portland,

and 1846 the start of systematic exploitation of the Lachine Canal's hydraulic power. 1847 saw the completion of the Montreal and Lachine Railway, the first leg of a western rail system, and the beginning of a period of intensive railway promotion. 1851 brought the opening of through railway connections to Boston and New York. Finally, 1853 witnessed the start of regular steamship service between Montreal and Liverpool, the commencement of the Victoria Bridge between Montreal and the south shore of the St Lawrence, and of the Grand Trunk Railway. Still further, 1853 marked the end of the first stages in the city's industrialization.

The period between 1837 and 1853 saw also a proliferation of all kinds of new enterprises, corporate and private, and the enlargement of older ones. This was a time of optimism and buoyancy, which abated only briefly in the late 1840s. It was also an era of qualitative changes, for some members of the Montreal business community readily became accustomed to a new climate of enterprise in which large companies appeared and thrived as a result of large urban growth, year-round business activity, and industrial development during the 1850s.

In studying this expansion a number of questions arose concerning the enterprises of the time and how they were built. Who were the businessmen so often involved in the many Montreal companies chartered in these years? To what kinds of businesses did they belong? Was there a relationship between their national (ethnic) or religious affiliation and their business prominence? To what extent did established merchants invest in industrial enterprises? How was capital for these ventures raised, and how much of it came from domestic sources? Why were the city's first three railways built south to join United States lines? To what extent did the provincial government assist these developments and provide a generally favourable environment in which they and others like them might prosper?

Not all of these questions could be satisfactorily answered, partly because of the paucity of biographical information about many of the men who figured so prominently in Montreal's economic life in those years. Business records, company and private, are even more scarce. Giants such as Peter McGill, Hugh Allan, and John Young apparently left no records providing clues to how and why they and others like them conducted affairs the way they did. Thus it proved impossible to investigate this group of major entrepreneurs except by examining what they accomplished in transportation and industry, the two newest and most spirited and dramatic economic activities in Montreal in this period.

By examining the business community's involvement in shipping, railways, and manufacturing, however, certain conclusions can be reached about the general character of Montreal entrepreneurship in this period. Throughout these years it was cautiously venturesome, but clearly more audacious in the early fifties than it had been a decade earlier. Preferring diversity to total commitment to a single venture, most merchants were unwilling or unable to transfer sizable sums of capital from commerce for investment in transportation, or to seize new industrial opportunities opening at the end of the forties. From the beginning, promoters sought government assistance in transportation developments and their most ambitious schemes were founded, or soon came to depend, upon provincial and municipal support.

Transportation therefore encouraged the growth of co-operative as well as individual entrepreneurship in Montreal. It involved larger investors and directors, who comprised only a small group consisting mainly of established merchants as leaders, supported by many lesser merchants and by a government that, though collectively a large investor, also deferred to the larger merchants. The latter, a small group, along with a few of the new industrialists who emerged during the forties, had by the early fifties become experienced and more venturesome entrepreneurs. Accordingly, this study, after a general examination of commerce in Montreal, explores the changes in shipping enterprise, the growth of interest in railways among Montreal merchants and forwarders, and the rise of a new group of manufacturing entrepreneurs as the city entered the first stages of industrialization.

I have received generous and valuable assistance from the staff at the Douglas Library of Queen's University, the Public Archives of Canada, the Archives de la Province de Québec, the McGill University Archives, the McCord Museum, the Archives of the Superior Court at Montreal, the Château de Ramézy, the Archives of the City of Montreal, the Montreal Board of Trade, the Canada and Dominion Sugar Company, Dow Breweries Ltd, Canada Steamship Lines, and Molson Breweries Ltd. Mr. A.J.H. Richardson of Ottawa provided me with an immense amount of information about the Montreal business community in the late eighteenth and early nineteenth centuries. Mrs Isobel Dobell, curator of the McCord Museum, took great interest in this project and drew upon her extensive knowledge of Montreal families to provide me with many useful leads in my search for private papers. Professor John Cooper of McGill University kindly allowed me to consult his notes of some inaccessible private manuscripts and Professor Fred Armstrong provided invaluable assistance in securing copies of correspondence. Principal John Archer of the University of Regina, formerly chief librarian at McGill, attempted to secure access for me to several company archives. I had helpful discussions with E.A. Collard, former editor of the Montreal *Gazette,* Omer Lavallée, railway historian and Canadian Pacific Railway Company archivist, Paul McLeod, who produced a valuable thesis for the University of Rochester on Montreal's 'free trade' movement in the late forties, William Greening, a Montreal business historian, and Merrill Denison, who wrote the history of the Bank of Montreal. Other discussions with Professors Alfred Dubuc, whose forthcoming book on Thomas and William Molson promises to be a major contribution to Canadian entrepreneurial studies, Fernand Ouellet, Jean-Pierre Wallot, John Cooper, and the Rev. Jacques Monet SJ aided my research and perspective. At a later stage, in discussions with Professor Brian Young of the University of Vermont, I benefited from his insights into the Montreal railway promoters of the seventies and eighties. I am grateful to all these people, and to the many Montrealers who responded generously to my requests for biographical information published by Mr Collard in the Montreal *Gazette*. I must include a special note of thanks to Larry MacDonald, whose many helpful suggestions have greatly improved this book. My greatest debt is to Professor J.M.S. Careless, who acted as my adviser while these chapters were being prepared as a PH D thesis for the University of Toronto, for his kindness, patience, and very valuable advice.

I wish to thank the editors of *La revue d'histoire de l'amérique francaise* for permission to reprint here an article that appeared in the March 1973 issue, vol. 26, no. 4. Chapter 2 of this book first appeared in *Canadian Business History, Selected Studies, 1497-1971*, edited by D. Macmillan, McClelland and Stewart, 1971.

I am also happy to acknowledge fellowships from the Province of Ontario, the Province of Quebec, the J.S. Ewart Foundation, and the Maurice Cody Foundation at the University of Toronto, which made it financially possible for me to do the research for this study, and to Queen's University for sabbatical leave and the Canada Council for a Leave Fellowship during 1972-3, when this manuscript was completed.

This book has been published with the help of a grant from the Social Science Research Council of Canada, using funds provided by the Canada Council, and a grant to University of Toronto Press from the Andrew W. Mellon Foundation.

THE RIVER BARONS: MONTREAL BUSINESSMEN AND THE

GROWTH OF INDUSTRY AND TRANSPORTATION 1837-53

1

Introduction

In the old quarter of Montreal, along St Paul Street west from Place Jacques Cartier to McGill Street, a few commercial houses still survive, descendants of wholesale firms established in the late eighteenth and early nineteenth centuries. In the ancient, sombre, three- or four-storey stone buildings on this street and its short branches – St Gabriel, Ste Thérèse, Hospital – close to the harbour of Montreal, these few remaining trading firms, whose operations in commerce and in a variety of allied business operations began in the simpler era of a staple economy, suggest still the archaic flavour of Montreal's early mercantile activity. Dark wooden shelving, filled with items of hardware and crockery, spices and tea, and bolts of cloth along the walls and piled high on the huge counters, run the length of the premises on either side from the front of the building far back into its dim recesses.

Most of the buildings in this ancient commercial quarter once housed firms trading in commodities from the interior and manufactured goods from abroad. Still standing behind a few of them are long garage-like stone buildings with broad indented loading platforms along their entire length and large doors every few yards. These were warehouses for flour, wheat, and ashes reaching Montreal from Upper Canada or the American midwest, carried up by wagon from barges that drew into the quays and the beach, or from sloops anchored offshore.

Commerce was the lifeblood of Montreal. Almost since its beginnings in 1642 the small settlement on the island in the St Lawrence at the foot of the almost impassable Lachine rapids had been a place of trade for furs and a major depot of that business. The buying and selling of staple commodities and imports, and associated commercial activities such as shipping, handling, packing, and storing, the construction and maintenance of vessels of all types, as well as the management of these enterprises embraced an immense proportion of the working people of Montreal.

By the first year or two of Queen Victoria's reign, Montreal's business community had experienced continuous change since the late eighteenth century. While constantly absorbing new members and discarding those merchants who failed or retired, the business class had also periodically adjusted to new and challenging economic and political realities. The fur trade from Montreal was changing in scope and orientation during the late 1770s; by 1779 it had extended west to the rich Athabasca country. The distance to the new western grounds had given rise to the need for the more highly organized and integrated trading structure of the North West Company to cope with the higher transportation costs and lengthier credit requirements of the vastly more extended operations. This new structure, though weaker, was more flexible than its major competitor, the Hudson's Bay Company, and was evidence of the ability of Montreal merchants to adapt to new conditions in order to continue competing effectively in the volatile fur trade.

Another structural shift even more basic and far-reaching among the Montreal businessmen arose with the new staple trades of the early nineteenth century. The growing wheat trade of the St Lawrence valley in both Lower and Upper Canada and the rapidly expanding population of the region created an immense market for manufactured goods and elicited a vast expansion in the activities of Montreal's wholesalers. The downriver flow of ashes, wheat, and flour along with timber and other forest products greatly expanded the number and scale of Montreal firms handling these commodities. Exports and imports stimulated the growth of expanded auxiliary services as well. Among the most important was transportation, which was enlarged and dramatically changed during the first two decades of the nineteenth century. The numbers of barges, bateaux, and more capacious Durham boats increased, while the use of steamboats, introduced on the St Lawrence in 1809, was rapidly advancing.

Other new services arose as the city's essential commercial function was changing so rapidly from furs to other staples during these years. Banks were among the most important of the new facilities. Shortly after the Bank of Montreal was formed in 1817, the Bank of Canada was established by another Montreal group of businessmen. The City Bank was established in 1831, mainly by American residents in Montreal and with large inflows of Boston and New York capital, and La Banque du Peuple was founded in 1835 by French-Canadians and Americans living in Montreal and in the surrounding towns. All of these financial institutions were formed, as Merrill Denison has shown, because of a pressing shortage of commercial capital. They were intended to alleviate recurring seasonal crises in the money supply and to marshal commercial resources to facilitate trade.

Although substantial in the aggregate, these changes occurred slowly, almost imperceptibly, during the first two decades of the nineteenth century, while the fur trade, though declining in importance, appeared still to be one of the pre-eminent economic bases of the Montreal business community. Great fortunes amassed by the titans of the fur trade made them the richest men in the city. Their houses, clubs, and institutions overshadowed all else in English-speaking Montreal. The golden legend of Montreal consisted mainly of stories of the conquest of the western fur-producing territories. Yet the pre-eminence of the fur traders in the Montreal business community was rapidly fading. Though still deeply involved in furs during these two decades, many firms were becoming increasingly committed to the staple trades.

The transition was gradual. Since the beginnings of the British regime, Montreal's business community had been growing exuberantly, but in the shelter of a comforting continuity. The giants of the fur trade were powerful principally because they were the suppliers of manufactured goods and equipment for the upcountry trade. Importing these items, mainly from Britain, and assembling them at Montreal was their most vital function in the operation of the North West Company. Supply-importing, warehousing, shipping, and the connections abroad this meant for the firms engaged, was the activity that gave them dominance in the fur trade. Though oriented to the fur trade, they could, and increasingly did, provide supplies for the growing new upcountry settlements. Nearly every major member firm of the North West Company was developing mercantile contacts in Upper Canada in these years. Many also had links with French Canadian merchants along the lower St Lawrence, Ottawa, and Richelieu river valleys. Firms like Forsyth, Richardson and Company, Moffatt, Gillespie and Company, and Peter McGill and Company by 1821 were deeply involved in the export and import business to the St Lawrence Valley, particularly Upper Canada. Prescott, Brockville, Kingston, and York merchants were connected to these and to other old, and several new, mercantile firms by a chain of credit, shipping, and other service arrangements provided at Montreal.

In the handling of upcountry produce at Montreal certain mercantile houses dealt generally in all or most commodities. But general merchandising was rapidly becoming more complex as some traders began to specialize, to concentrate on specific items or on the provision of certain kinds of services for both the export and the import trades. By the early 1820s the specialized trades were becoming clearly delineated, as revealed in the correspondence of Stanley Bagg, a Montreal Yankee merchant, contractor, and landowner, who notwithstanding his diverse general financial interests concentrated heavily on wheat and flour in his commercial transactions. During winter buying trips in northwestern

New York and northern Ohio between 1824 and 1826, Bagg contracted with local merchants, warehousemen, millers, and forwarders to process thousands of bushels of wheat on his behalf. His correspondence is filled with details about variations in grades of wheat and flour and about problems of milling, spoilage, and shipping.

The fact that a number of Americans were very prominent in these lines of trade did not, of course, mean that no one else dealt in them. The American commercial influence in Montreal seems to have been concentrated in the handling of staple items through upcountry connections, with few and weak business links eastward to Britain. This trade in imported goods, mostly the manufactured commodities heavily in demand in the Canadian agricultural and timber communities dependent upon Montreal's entrepôt facilities, rested overwhelmingly in the hands of the merchants who formerly had participated in the fur trade. These firms, handling groceries, liquors, cloth, hats, glass, hardware, and other items were, with few exceptions, British, many of them Scottish, and they retained and increased their broad, continuous strength in almost all lines of trade through the mid-nineteenth century.

Through the same process by which the expanding commercial life of the early decades of the nineteenth century attracted new entrepreneurs into entirely new ventures, many of the older industries auxiliary to commerce also changed. In St Lawrence shipping the growing traffic in goods and commodities in both directions along the river and the opportunities provided by the invention of steamboats and the facilities of the Lachine Canal encouraged the growth of large shipping companies at Montreal. At the hub of three river systems, the St Lawrence, the Ottawa, and the Richelieu, Montreal became a shipping centre in many ways as important as Quebec. The distribution of imported manufactured goods, as organized at Montreal after 1809, came to be handled by specialized shipping companies heavily dependent upon the use of steamboats. From the 1810s onward the St Lawrence River traffic in premium goods – paying a high freight rate per weight and volume – was increasingly concentrated in the hands of large firms like Molson's St Lawrence Steamboat Company and Torrance's Towboat Company. Entirely new to shipping when they entered the business with new vessels in 1809 and 1816, both companies within a few years had become extensive firms, while as early as the twenties steamboats were operating from Montreal along the Richelieu and from Lachine, Montreal's western outport, along the upper St Lawrence and up the Ottawa and its tributaries. Not all of these ventures were focused on Montreal, to be sure, but many of the significant companies – such as Peter McGill's Union Towing Company, which monopolized shipping traffic on the Ottawa and Rideau – were financed in large measures by Montreal capital and directed by Montreal businessmen. Similar steamboat ventures on the Richelieu and smaller rivers were, to an increasing extent, financed and directed by Montrealers and oriented heavily to the Montreal market.

Although the St Lawrence Valley was of central importance to the city's commercial life, the Richelieu River Valley was also of substantial significance. Improving trade with this important wheat-growing region, and the possibility of increasing the trade with Vermont and New York to the south, attracted Montreal investment during the thirties in the form of mercantile credit, banking, steamboats, and railways. The ancient Richelieu-Lake Champlain-Hudson River route provided an outlet for some Lower Canadian production, a source of supply for certain goods, and, above all, the opportunity of securing an outlet to the sea alternative to and more expeditious than the St Lawrence. Attempts since the 1810s to improve navigation by building the Chambly Canal on the Richelieu showed a willingness to exploit the American connection for these purposes, and by the thirties iron and steam appeared about to realize those expectations.

Among the business community of the twenties and thirties were some of the most successful venturesome entrepreneurs ever to make a dollar in Montreal. Some were titans, of which Montreal produced only a few in each generation, such as fur traders James McGill, Simon McTavish, and the McGillivray brothers of the 1780s and 1790s, brewer, distiller, and real estate speculator William Molson, of the first two decades of the nineteenth century, and bankers and railway builders Shaughnessy, Stephen, and Smith at the end of it. The leading Montreal businessmen were rooted mostly in one of the branches of the staple trades or the services attached to them and dabbling in several other enterprises at the same time. Most of the giants of the twenties and thirties who remained prominent in the next three decades encompassed – very often simultaneously – several major business interests within their careers. Peter McGill was a fur trader, staple dealer, shipowner, forwarder, banker, and railway promoter; George Moffatt had almost the same spread of interests, while Joseph Masson and James Ferrier – perhaps the wealthiest Montrealers of their era – were also behind insurance and gas companies and involved in large-scale real estate speculation at the same time. In their multiple and simultaneous economic interests they were never committed, it seems, to only one business or even necessarily to any one place. Such diversity of interests and mobility is evidence of their remarkable astuteness and flexibility. New opportunities often came to their attention first and they had the capital or high credit ratings, as well as the experience in the management of substantial enterprises, to move with strength and confidence into these ventures. And because they were so sharply aware of the opportunity for the monopoly or innovator's profit that often accrued to entrepreneurs, they shrewdly understood the opportunities of banking and transportation developments. Even the giants, however, were, by no means infallible, as shown by the rates of entry and demise of firms in all areas of commerce and the financial distress and occasional failure of even some of the city's most important merchants.

Amongst these many changes in the economic life of Montreal in the years from the mid-teens to the late thirties, there was a small but important growth of industry. Much of it was stimulated by the growth of shipping and the rising demand for steamboats. The small Montreal shipbuilding industry was given a new and strong impetus by this demand. Engine foundries were established independent of the existing shipyards to adapt English steam engines for marine use. By the early twenties two foundries were producing their own marine engines in small but increasing numbers not only for the Montreal market but also for boats being constructed as far away as Niagara and Quebec. Demand for castings for stationary engines and a wide variety of marine engines greatly extended this industry, and by the forties it was one of the most important in Montreal.

Over twenty-five years from the mid-teens to the end of the forties, gradual changes in the economic life of Montreal had greatly expanded the range of its traditional commercial facilities and added a small but dynamic engineering industry to its industrial sector. The changes were, of course, not revolutionary; Montreal was still unquestionably dependent upon commerce, and every sector of the city's economic life was still affected directly by the vagaries of trade. The aspirations of businessmen for control, or for a preponderant share, of the midwestern staple trade, chiefly grain, had not been realized by the end of the thirties, but Montreal had nevertheless become a port of significance, particularly in the importation of manufactured goods. The city had also become a banking centre, with representatives in most of the major towns of the St Lawrence Valley, as well as an industrial centre. Montreal's growth was to quicken sharply during the forties, and in these early years of the age of steam and iron the city was almost transformed by the strength and versatility of its large and varied business community.

2

The business community:
the pattern of involvement

I

Between 1837 and 1853 the leading members of Montreal's business community built an impressive transportation system that included more than two hundred miles of railways extending from the city. At the same time they increased their investments in various shipping enterprises and created far-reaching new ones. Others seized the opportunity provided by the availability of Lachine Canal water power and a promising market to create new industrial and manufacturing ventures and to enlarge older establishments.

The rise of a new group of industrialists who broadened the business community without changing its fundamental commercial orientation was only one aspect of the constantly changing business scene. Some merchants left the city altogether, while others terminated their partnerships and regrouped in new firms. But there remained at the head a small group of leading businessmen who promoted and directed these transportation ventures and ran some of the leading industrial establishments. Through strengthening older financial institutions and setting up new ones as well, these entrepreneurs brought Montreal by 1853 to the threshold of an era of much more rapid and extensive railway and industrial development.[1]

Ethnic solidarity was everywhere a common feature of the world of business before the rise of joint-stock companies. David Landes has pointed out the importance of the ethnic and religious ties of Calvinists, Jews, Quakers, and Greeks in financial, mercantile, and industrial developments in western European countries during the nineteenth century.[2] The interdependence of members of these groups was based essentially upon trust, respect, and ethnic pride and was solidified by close business and family ties which helped to make them formidable business forces. By buying and selling to each other, often uniting in a common cause, endorsing each other's notes, extending loans, training one another's sons, establishing closer family and business connections through marriage, and by providing useful intelligence about potentially profitable ventures, the Protestant bankers of Paris and the Jewish bankers of Germany became extremely powerful.

Though the situation in Montreal in the middle years of the nineteenth century was by no means analogous to that in Europe, there are certain similarities in the fact that four clearly identifiable ethnic or national elements existed in the local business world: Scots, Americans, English, and French Canadians, with perhaps two minor groups, the Jews and the Irish, in roughly that order of prominence. The existence of these elements in local commerce does not suggest that they were mutually exclusive during the mid-nineteenth century. Although national, ethnic, and religious divisions kept Montreal socially and politically divided to some extent, there was considerable integration in the realm of business, especially among members of the English-speaking groups. Even apart from the joint-stock companies, there were a number of copartnerships in which Scots joined with Americans or French-Canadians for limited terms.

II

American-born merchants, almost all of whom were from neighbouring New England, became some of the most eminent men in their special branches of Montreal business. They included the Wards in the construction of steam engines and John Frothingham, Benjamin Brewster, J.T. Barrett, and Samuel Bonner in the hardware trade – described by antiquarian Edward Murphy in 1882 as a business sector 'in which Americans largely preponderated.'[3] Among staple dealers, Massachussetts-born Horatio Gates had been the recognized Montreal leader until his death in 1834,[4] but following him were several others, such as Harrison Stephens, who was of immense importance in this trade, Stanley Bagg, Jedediah H. Dorwin, and Orlin Bostwick, all of whom were very active until the mid-forties. In chemical and drug manufacturing and wholesaling there was the Lyman family, in private banking John E. Mills, in flour milling Ira Gould, in rope manufacturing John Converse: all American-born Montreal businessmen of significance. So, too, were Charles Seymour, an active commission merchant throughout the late forties and early fifties, Caufield Dorwin, an exchange and money broker, D.W. Eager and Charles L. Ogden, provision inspectors, Norman Froste, a general merchant, William F. Hagar, a hardware merchant, J.A. Perkins, a commission merchant, William Phillips, a wealthy grocer, George Warner, an exchange broker and commission merchant,[5] and Hannibal and N.S. Whitney, who operated a wholesale dry goods house in these years. There were many other members of the Montreal American community, which was strong in both the number of men engaged and their prominence in commercial and industrial pursuits.

It would be difficult to determine the exact number of American-born merchants or to quantify their prominence,[6] but they comprised probably the second most significant national group in the economic life of Montreal in the period from 1837 to 1853. Although they mixed with others somewhat more freely than in the days when steamboat-builder John Ward had first arrived from Vergennes, Vermont, in 1818 and wrote home complaining of discrimination against Americans, the Yankees, like the Montreal Irish, the Scotch, and the Jews, maintained national bonds in their own American Presbyterian Church and in the New England Society, keeping alive, perhaps, like Ward, fond hopes of returning home from their painful yet profitable exile in Canada.[7]

Several factors made for their success in Montreal during this era. The discrimination against Americans by merchants and officials after the wait of 1812 helped to isolate them as a distinct group within the city's business community.[8] They appear to have kept largely to themselves socially, and at the end of the twenties they were even moved to create their own separate Presbyterian church where they could worship more comfortably than among the dour and unfriendly Scots of the St Gabriel Street church. But in addition to the open hostility that in some ways may have helped to unify and strengthen them in business, there were other reasons why the Americans had become a formidable force in Montreal business. They were very active in the trade, both legal and illicit, which arose between Lower Canada and the neighbouring American states, particularly Vermont and New York, during the mid-1810s. According to the testimony of one self-confessed American dealer in contraband, each winter live cattle and sleigh-loads of packed pork, butter, and cheese were driven overland from Vermont for the Montreal market, especially to provision the British military and naval forces stationed there. At Montreal, tea and sugar loaf were purchased for smuggling back into the United States, where these items were more expensive. Abner Bagg, whose various business ventures included a brewery at Laprairie and who was one of the major contractors on the Lachine Canal, had a small hat factory in nearby Terrebonne County during the early twenties, for which he requested a business correspondent in upstate New York to send some materials to an agent in Champlain for smuggling into Canada and wrote another correspondent in Troy to send a trunk to the same agent who would forward it to Montreal 'by the first *safe opportunity*.'[9]

Americans may have had another advantage, though for only a brief period perhaps, in the burgeoning staples trade through Montreal. In the period before the completion of the Erie Canal, much produce from western New York State was sent down the St Lawrence to Montreal for export. This trade, which formed a substantial proportion of the total volume of commodities entering the port, appears to have been controlled by Montreal's American merchants. Surviving correspondence suggests that many of the people with whom these Montreal Yankees did business were their own kin or friends from New England. Massachusetts-born Horatio Gates, a founder of the Bank of Montreal and the city's biggest dealer in upcountry staples, handled mostly pork, flour, and potash from the Black River and Genesee area of New York. Other American merchants based in Montreal in the twenties, such as Abner Bagg and J.H. Dorwin, also bought large quantities of Genesee wheat and flour for shipment to Montreal. It is not clear why this small American sector of the Montreal business community dominated and nearly monopolized the portion of this New York trade that flowed through Montreal during the early years. But Montreal's Americans probably had certain distinct advantages over others in the legitimate and illegitimate commerce between the St Lawrence Valley and Vermont and southern New York. Generally sound knowledge of business conditions in the United States, an established line of credit or support from guarantors known to banks or creditors, and access to dependable information about current prices and prospects, processing, storage, and transportation in staple-producing regions would have helped give them a strong competitive advantage. They would also likely have had a network of reliable agents. Between 1819 and 1821, Abner Bagg sent instructions to trusted established agents in Rochester, Canandaigua, and Geneva, New York, to buy wheat and have it ground into flour, barrelled, stored over the winter, transported to the nearest ports, and sold.[10] (Sometimes the flour was sold to third parties even before it reached Montreal.)

A typical Montreal Yankee was John Frothingham, a native of Portland, Maine, who was the co-owner with William Workman of the largest hardware and iron wholesale outlet in Montreal. After the death of Horatio Gates in 1834, Frothingham was probably the most prominent and wealthiest New Englander in Montreal. His firm did a very large business and later even engaged in the manufacturing of hardware in its own large plant in Montreal's new industrial quarter along the Lachine Canal. Frothingham owned a substantial amount of real estate in Montreal, including two huge properties on the slopes of Mount Royal.[11] He was also an important early figure in the development of the City Bank, which had become since its establishment, mostly with American (non-resident) capital, in 1831 a major rival to the Bank of Montreal; he was its president from 1834 to 1848 and had a large personal investment in its stock. Frothingham was also a director of the Montreal Savings Bank and a member of the Montreal Newsroom, an early businessmen's gathering place. Like so many of his fellow New Englanders, he was a supporter of the American Presbyterian church in Montreal and a benefactor of such church institutions as the new Queen's College at Kingston.[12] He was also representative of most American Montrealers in the fact that he did not participate prominently, if at all, in public affairs. Though prejudice against them was clearly waning, Americans were, with very few exceptions, such as John Mills who was mayor of Montreal in 1847, not deeply involved in politics even at the municipal level nor, it seems, a significant element – even commensurate with their economic importance – in the city's social life. But neither Frothingham nor his fellow New Englanders, such as Connecticut-born John E. Mills, Harrison Stephens from Jamaica, Vermont, and Benjamin Brewster, to name the most prominent, were unaware or unresponsive to the new opportunities for profit in real estate, railways, shipping, and insurance ventures that emerged so strongly at the dawn of the forties.

III

Other immigrants who had become commercially prominent in Montreal by the forties included a small number of Irish, including the Workman brothers, William and Thomas, Edward Murphy, a dry goods merchant, and Henry Mulholland, who owned a large hardware firm. John and Thomas Ryan, general commission merchants, also operated their own ships between Montreal and Quebec. These businessmen, along with a few others, such as tavern owners, artisans, or operators of small shops of various types,[13] were the sole representatives in the business world of Montreal's huge Irish-born community, which by 1851 amounted to 11,736, or 20 per cent of the city's population, mostly working class and many of them common labourers.[14]

The small number of Jewish merchants in Montreal, however, were drawn from a community numbering less than two hundred.[15] Theodore Hart, Jesse Joseph, and Alexander Levy were in commerce, while the Moss family, as well as selling clothes, manufactured some of its own merchandise. Of these, only Theodore Hart had any connection with the shipping or railway companies.

The Jewish community of Montreal had been expanding rapidly during the forties, its composition becoming more complex. The German, Polish, and English Jewish immigrants gradually trickling into Montreal from the twenties onwards were suddenly augmented towards the end of the forties. Most Jewish immigrants were generally in very modest circumstances, and some were in need of the help supplied by the Hebrew Benevolent Society, hastily-formed in 1847, which included many from the original Spanish and Portuguese congregation begun in 1778. The Levys, the Harts, and the Josephs were members of this old, established, and comfortable community of merchants, landowners, and professionals which prided itself on the badge of suffering of the Spanish Jews and their generation-old fight in Lower Canada for political equality.[16] While many of the Polish and German newcomers toiled on the painful fringes of Montreal's commerce, as assorted pedlars, tailors, hawkers, retailers, and workers, some Spanish Jews, by contrast, were already wealthy and powerful men.

The Joseph brothers, Jesse and Jacob, were perhaps the most successful of the Montreal Sephardic Jews. Sons of Henry Joseph, a merchant who settled in Berthier about 1800, they had moved to Montreal.[17] Jacob became wealthy as a tobacco importer and manufacturer while Jesse became a commission merchant. Although by no means a large-scale merchant, Jesse was consignee of cargoes from Britain and grew wealthy. An active investor in a wide variety of enterprises, Jesse had extensive investments in real estate and in the Champlain and St Lawrence and the St Lawrence and Atlantic railways; he was one of the original promoters of the Montreal and Lachine Railway, the Montreal Telegraph Company, and the New City Gas Company, and later was an active promoter of other telegraph companies and of the Montreal Street Railway Company.[18]

There were some English-born among Montreal's prominent businessmen, but apparently fewer than either Scots, Americans, or French Canadians. Among the English was Joseph Shuter, who, as well as serving on the Board of the Champlain and St Lawrence Railway, was also a director of the Bank of Montreal from 1831 to 1847. Steamboat-builder William Parkyn and engineer John Bennet were leading English-born businessmen of Montreal, as was William Lunn, a director of the Bank of Montreal from 1828 to 1849, of the Provident Savings Bank, and of the Montreal Insurance Company from 1839 to 1849, and a promoter of the New City Gas Company. English, too, was brewer John Molson, whose sons, John, William, and Thomas (the former two in particular) were directors of the Bank of Montreal and partook of many other joint-stock ventures besides their railway and shipping interests.

IV

While French Canadians were not numerous as directors of or large investors in many joint-stock companies, they were nevertheless a significant element in the business community, though not all were themselves in commerce. Pierre Beaubien, a medical doctor, was a director of La Banque du Peuple and the Mutual Insurance Company, a promoter of the Montreal Mining Company, and the owner of considerable real estate in Outremont. Alexandre Maurice Delisle, a lawyer and politician, was a director and large investor in both the Champlain and St Lawrence and the Montreal and Bytown railways, besides owning valuable local property. Most French Canadian businessmen, however, even the wealthiest, kept aloof from extensive involvement in the major railway ventures, with the exception of the Montreal and Bytown. But they were committed heavily to other joint-stock companies. Olivier Berthelet, who held extensive real estate, was a backer of only the abortive Banque des Marchands,[19] while Jean-Baptiste Bruyère was a director of the Montreal Gas Company from 1842 to 1849. Augustin and Maurice Cuvillier took active roles in the Committee of Trade and the Bank of Montreal respectively. Edouard Raymond Fabre, publisher of *La Minerve* and a local bookseller, was active briefly as a director of La Banque du Peuple. Jacques Grenier, a dry goods merchant and an officer in the Montreal Board of Trade, was also a director of La Banque du Peuple, another director of which, Pierre Jodoin, held a £300 investment in the Montreal and Lachine Railway. Augustin Norbert Morin, a lawyer and politician, was active in the St Lawrence and Atlantic Railway Company and a director of the Montreal Mining Company. Joseph Vallée, a wholesale provision merchant, was a director of the City Bank, La Banque du Peuple, and the City and District Savings Bank. Amable Prevost and Jean Bruneau (both dry goods merchants) and Frédéric-Auguste Quesnel were all directors of La Banque du Peuple.[20] Louis Comte, a builder, and Joseph Bourret, a barrister, were directors of the Mutual Insurance Company of Montreal, while the latter was also a director of the Montreal Mining Company.

Hence, while few French Canadians were directors or heavy investors in the most important railways, some were active in the City Bank (besides dominating La Banque du Peuple), the Montreal Mining Company, and the Mutual Insurance Company. Aside from these concerns, a few French Canadians were active also in shipping and shipbuilding. Many of them were involved in various branches of commerce throughout the forties and early fifties. In some sectors they were less noteworthy than in others. Among commission merchants and agents, for example, there were practically no French Canadians. None were listed in a directory of 1845, and only one in 1852. This was true also of the hardware trade, wholesale and retail, and there was one French firm of brewers out of eight during these years. There were no French Canadian brokers, nor any firm of boot, shoe, or leather dealers that lasted for more than a few years. And out of seventeen auctioneers operating between 1845 and 1852, only three were French Canadian, one firm lasting only a few years.[21]

But in the dry goods trade, both wholesale and retail, especially the latter, many French Canadians were involved. They owned four of approximately twenty-five wholesale houses and eighteen of thirty-two retail firms operating between 1845 and 1852.[22] From this group came some of the most active

French Canadians to participate in joint-stock ventures, including the Hudons (shipping), Jean-Louis Beaudry, Jean-Baptiste Bruyère, Amable Prevost, Jean Bruneau, the Cuvilliers (also in auctioneering), and the Massons.

Nevertheless, though their businesses were small and short-lived in many instances, some of Montreal's most important traders and investors were drawn from the French Canadian community.[23] Joseph Masson was probably Montreal's leading French Canadian businessman; until his early death in 1847 he was connected with both traditional commerce and the new frontiers of enterprise of the forties.[24] Masson, the Montreal participant of Robertson, Masson and Company, a Montreal and Glasgow partnership, had an extensive importing and exporting business that dealt mostly with French Canadian merchants in Richelieu Valley and St Lawrence south shore villages, trading manufactured goods for produce, especially potash. Masson's business contacts on the south shore were probably aided by his marriage into the prominent Raymond family of Laprairie.[25] As his commercial success made him increasingly wealthy, Masson, like so many of his fellow merchants, sought the respectability and peace of a country estate. While many of the English-speaking merchants established residences in the western outskirts of the city or on the slopes of Mount Royal, Masson sought out the beautiful countryside of nearby Terrebonne seigneury, which he bought in 1832 for £25,150 stg in cash. Here he began the building of a vast manor house and spent more and more of his time.[26] In these comfortable years Masson performed substantial service in municipal and provincial politics: he was a member of the Special Court of Sessions, which conducted Montreal civic government from 1836 to 1840, was elected to a term as city alderman in 1843, and served as a member of the Legislative Council between October 1834 and March 1838.[27] Besides his trading firm, his investments in Montreal real estate, and his growing interest in the development of Terrebonne, Joseph Masson was deeply committed to certain aspects of the new economy of Montreal. Though not an exuberant railroader, he supported the St Lawrence and Atlantic scheme. Banking, however, had much more attraction for him; he was elected to the board of the Bank of Montreal in 1826 and remained a director until his death. The size of his investment in the bank is not known, but Masson was also a very large shareholder, though not a director, in the rival City Bank. He was a director of the Montreal Insurance Company and president of the Montreal Gas Company through most of the forties.

There was, nevertheless, a relatively small degree of joint-stock participation from the French-speaking community that in 1851 comprised 46 per cent of the city's total population.[28] Though joint-stock ventures were not the only channels of participation in Montreal's economy in this period, they were the newest and in some ways the most dramatic. They all required acceptance of the joint-stock structure as well as agreement with the purpose for which the companies were established. With the latter probably most French Canadian businessmen would have agreed, but the requirement that they relinquish control of their funds to an impersonal company may for some have been less acceptable.[29]

The problem of French Canadian economic participation is much more complex than this, however. The assertion that French Canadian businessmen and investors were reluctant to accept the joint-stock company system is called into question by the examples mentioned above. Nor can it easily be demonstrated that in this period French Canadian businessmen were averse to new ventures such as railways or to rapid expansion, and examples will be given below that entrepreneurial *élan* was present amongst them. What can be shown is that French Canadians were a disproportionately small segment of the Montreal business community, no matter how broadly (but reasonably) one might wish to define the term 'businessman.' Why this should have been so is a central question in an examination of the economic development of Lower Canada in this period and later. There is probably no single answer; at least those reasons that have been advanced so far are not convincing. Fernand Ouellet's notion of 'mentalité' is of limited use, because to suggest that it is in the 'nature' of the French Canadian to want to remain a small businessman is to imply further that the French Canadian businessman or farmer was not interested in the pursuit of maximum economic gain and lacked the necessary drive, flexibility, ingenuity, and ruthlessness of a real entrepreneur. His values were different from those of the *Anglais,* they were spiritual, rural, and familiar; he was a peasant, *tout simple.* Such a view is too exaggerated to be persuasive.

It might be possible to come a little closer to the truth by examining the broad social and political context of the St Lawrence economy of which Montreal was then the pivot. It must be remembered that the city derived its major importance from the trade with the upper St Lawrence and Great Lakes regions and, to a decreasing extent, the trade of Lower Canada. (Merchants in Lower Canadian towns were not dependent upon Montreal wholesalers to nearly the same degree as were Upper Canadian merchants; as production of wheat in the western sections of Lower Canada declined, the Montreal connection with them had weakened.) Montreal's French Canadian merchants, even the greatest of them, Joseph Masson, were exclusively oriented to this declining market, while their English confrères were almost as exclusively linked with the steadily expanding markets to the west. For the French Canadians to have made the switch to the west would have required the accumulation of practically a whole new set of business tools: an intimate knowledge of the staple-producing regions, the establishment of reliable agents there, and the creation of a substantial line of credit with banks and respect for their notes where they were hitherto unknown.

Credit from British manufacturers and suppliers would also have been indispensable, and there is no evidence that French Canadian merchants in Montreal other than Masson had established the necessary connections in Britain. Bank credit at Montreal was almost a prerequisite for successful trade, and in securing this there appear to have been some problems. The evidence is by no means conclusive, but there are hints that as early as 1817, the small *Anglais* mercantile community of Montreal were not united in the new bank. (The rival Bank of Canada was established in 1818, mainly by a group of American Montrealers including Gates, Frothingham, and Jacob DeWitt.)

Just as a number of American businessmen found it helpful, or necessary, to establish their own banks, the French Canadians appear to have felt the same compulsion. In 1835, Louis Michel Viger, at the head of a group of French Canadian merchants from Montreal and outlying towns – along with a number of Montreal Americans including Jacob DeWitt – set up La Banque du Peuple. Its prospectus, a printed circular which pointed out that the new bank's benefits would extend 'à toutes les classes de la Société indistinctivement,'[30] suggests that some discrimination had been experienced. Far from being a sign of weakness, the formation of the Banque du Peuple was evidence of strength, of the combativeness and resilience in the French Canadian mercantile group in Montreal and in nearby towns. The bank enjoyed widespread popularity, and large numbers of people subscribed to its shares; barely two years after the prospectus was issued the directors reported triumphantly that it had more shareholders than the other two Montreal banks put together. It was truly a peoples' bank. A few months later, in August 1837, directors Timothée Franchère and Hosea Ballou Smith, a very successful crockery merchant, reported that the bank was in a 'prosperous state of affairs.' After successfully riding out the accusations that it had financed the purchase of arms for the Patriotes in 1837, the Banque du Peuple entered the forties on a strong financial note.[31] By 1843 it had a capital stock worth £200,000.

Yet for all its strength in the Montreal region La Banque du Peuple was not utilized as an instrument for the creation of new commercial frontiers beyond Lower Canada. The lack of evidence that it established agents beyond the province or had any extensive dealings with Upper Canadian or Maritime banks is a strong indication that La Banque's customers were not involved in the Upper Canadian trade. As we shall see, even the most ambitious of the French Canadian shipping companies, La Compagnie du Richelieu, while fighting such competitors as the mighty Molson and Torrance companies for the lower St Lawrence traffic, refrained from engaging in the fragmented and apparently more competitive shipping business on the Ottawa and upper St Lawrence rivers, probably for much the same reasons. The point seems to be suggested by arguments advanced in the petition in 1846 for a second French Canadian bank in Montreal, La Banque des Marchands. A very large segment, perhaps a majority, of the city's French Canadian merchants, including many with impeccable credit ratings,[32] supported the bank because 'il est notoire qu'il devient de jour en jour plus difficile d'avoir l'aide des établissements financiers de cette ville, même avec le meilleur papier; Ce qui est une preuve incontestable des demandes considérable[s] qui leur sont fait tous les jours; D'où il résulte une gêne inouie jusqu'à présent dans toutes espece d'affaires, au grand détriment du Commerce, de l'Agriculture and de l'Industrie dans tout le District de Montréal.'[33] The focus of their attention was Montreal and its environs, whereas their *Anglais* competitors were oriented to the west, as their voluminous memoranda and petitions through the Board of Trade grandiloquently – almost poetically – announced.

Thus there was no absence of initiative among French Canadian merchants during this era. The examples of their entrepreneurial skill – of which only a few are mentioned in these pages – are numerous. Still, with few exceptions, they were confined to Lower Canada by factors over which they had no control and from which there seems to have been no escape. The comparative lack of prominence of French Canadians in the business affairs of Montreal must be seen in relation not just to Lower Canada but to the entire commercial system of which it was the central emporium. Further elaborations on this theme are needed before a definitive statement can be made, but it is doubtful whether a sociologist's stereotypes or a historian's clichés are of much further use.

v

The Scots, finally, comprised the dominant group in most forms of commerce and were often leaders in the enterprises examined in this study. Among brewers there was William Dow; among brokers, John and Robert Esdaile; and Robert Anderson owned a glass and china company. All of these were leading firms in their fields. In the dry goods trade during the forties and early fifties the Scottish-dominated firms were those of the Gillespies, the Gilmours, J.G. Mackenzie, Joseph Mackay, William Stephen, Henry Morgan, and Dougald Stewart. John Young was prominent as a commission merchant. The Gilmours and the Allans owned the chief ocean shipping establishments, while the Redpaths, prominent contractors, became leading Montreal industrialists during the fifties.

These were only the most famous of the Montreal Scottish merchants; others with Scottish names about whom little is known were legion. In the dry goods trade alone were Campbell, Douglas, Fraser, Reid, Galbraith, MacFarlane, and

Morrison, in brokerage Gairbairn, Geddes, and Macdougall, and among commission merchants and agents Dougall, McTavish, McGill, Anderson, Bell, Auld, Campbell, McDonald, McKay, McNaught, and Redpath.

Scots were the single most active group in the business ventures examined here. The exploits of William Dow, James Ferrier, William Edmonstone, David Macpherson, Peter McGill, Hugh Allan, and John Young in shipping and in railways — as well as in telegraphs, gas, mining, and insurance — will be outlined below. Others participated at lesser levels. Robert Anderson was a promoter of the Montreal and Bytown Railway and a director of the New City Gas Company, while Robert Armour, a bookseller, had directorships in the City Bank, the Montreal Insurance Company, the Montreal Gas Company, and the Montreal Provident and Savings Bank. Adam Ferrie, an Ayrshireman who emigrated to Canada in 1829 after a successful commercial career, helped to establish the City Bank to compete with the Bank of Montreal and was also a director of the Montreal Insurance Company, the Montreal Gas Company, and the Gore Bank in Hamilton.[34] John Jamieson, a director of the Bank of Montreal (1835-9), was a merchant who operated his own ship, the *Douglas*, in Montreal's ocean trade. James Leslie, a general merchant who had retired by the mid-forties, reappeared among the promoters of John Young's abortive scheme in 1849 to build a canal from the St Lawrence at Caughnawaga to Lake Champlain. Andrew Shaw, a general merchant, owned three large ocean-going barques and was one of the founders and early presidents of the Montreal Telegraph Company. John Smith, like Shaw, was a promoter of the Montreal Steamship Company and the Montreal Insurance Company and a director of the Montreal Mining Company. William Watson, the flour inspector whose wealth helped to establish the Ogilvie milling company, was a founder of the Montreal Insurance Company and the owner of real estate in the city. And William Macdonald served as a director of both the St Lawrence and Atlantic and the Montreal and New York railways.

The career of Peter McGill helps to explain why Scots were able to occupy the proud and profitable first place in the city's commercial life. Born Peter McCutcheon in 1789 at Wigtonshire, Scotland, he migrated to Canada in 1809 to serve as an employee of Parker, Gerrard and Ogilvy, a copartnership with a major interest in the North West Company.[35] The partnership was part of a London, Quebec, and Montreal firm which came gradually under the control of George Moffatt of Montreal and Peter Gillespie of Montreal and London, to emerge as Gillespie, Moffatt and Company, the largest importing house in Montreal. McGill's connection with that company likely helped him considerably when he went into business in 1820 with William Price, a Quebec timber merchant who was also in partnership with James Dowie and Nathaniel Gould of London and Kenneth Dowie of Liverpool, the latter a former partner to Moffatt. Heavily involved in the timber trade on the St Maurice, Rimouski, and Saguenay rivers, the new partnership (which lasted until 1843) also exported wheat and flour.[36] McGill's interests, however, were not confined to trade. Bolstered by the sizable resources of an estate inherited from his uncle, John McGill of York, he invested heavily in the Ottawa Valley, buying several saw mills at St Ignace near the Grenville Canal.[37] McGill also was one of the principal owners, among a small group of Montreal investors, of the Ottawa and Rideau Forwarding Company whose steamboats and barges plied the triangular river and canal system between Montreal, Bytown, and Kingston. He had other unspecified commercial interests in the Ottawa Valley, and in the thirties maintained large offices in Bytown to manage his affairs there.[38] McGill owned a number of farms to the southeast of Montreal in Ascot Township, and to the west between 1830 and 1849, the Marmora iron works, which included mining and substantial timber rights.

From all of these enterprises, Peter McGill became a rich and powerful man in the Montreal business community.[39] Honours were lavished upon him. He became a member of the Legislative Council of Lower Canada in 1832 and of the Executive Council of the Province of Canada in 1847. (Despite his strong constitutionalist position during the troubles of the mid-thirties in Montreal, McGill was not anathema to French Canadians.) He was president of the Montreal Board of Trade in 1848 and mayor of Montreal (by appointment) from 1840 to 1843. He served as president of a multitude of local associations, including the prestigious St Andrew's Society, the Lay Association of Montreal, the Montreal Auxiliary Bible Society, the British and Canadian School Society, and the Canadian Branch of the Colonial Life Assurance Company. Besides acting as a trustee of Queen's College, McGill served as governor of his namesake college and of the Montreal General Hospital.[40]

After 1853 bad times came upon Peter McGill. Although he was still a powerful man in the Bank of Montreal, his firm began to decline. Never free of huge debts to his former British partners, Gould and Dowie, McGill was forced in 1858 to transfer virtually his entire fortune to his creditors in order to secure release.

Yet of all his large and farflung business concerns, his connections with the Bank of Montreal were probably the most important, if not for himself then certainly for the community as a whole. A director of the bank since 1819, McGill became its president in 1834 and continued in this office until June 1860, only a few months before his death.[41] Presiding over the daily meetings of the directors, where decisions were made on discounting notes and extending loans, McGill had a significant role in conditioning the climate of enterprise in Montreal for more than a quarter of a century. The high regard in which he was held in the Montreal business community was based on a combination of awe at his wealth and success and respect for his business acumen. He was invited to share these attributes by acting as director in various companies, including the Champlain and St Lawrence Railway during the critical construction period between 1834 and 1836.

McGill's lengthy retention of the presidency of the Bank of Montreal was perhaps also based upon the strength of his associates. He was never really his own man even after inheriting his uncle's fortune. During his lengthy association with Gould and Dowie, McGill had accumulated a huge, indeed a staggering, debt of over £40,000, which he was not able to reduce after the partnership ended in 1843. McGill continued his business affairs, but he seems never to have come out from under his heavy obligations, and by 1853 he was effectively out of 'the Trade.'[42]

VI

Although a handful of leaders all but dominated developments in transportation, the pattern of participation in these years reveals that many other members of the Montreal business community, and some professional men besides, were recruited to back these and other joint stock or private ventures such as banks and insurance and gas companies, which have not been included in this study. Their participation may be described as consisting of either the investment of £500 or more, or the holding of a directorship in any one of the enterprises. Indeed, in some cases their business activities were much more extensive and included investments in, for example, real estate,[43] personal loans, and trade.

Nevertheless, though a great many merchants were promoters or directors of at least one company, it is also clear that they were only a minority of the city's total business community, which included, besides wholesalers and general merchants, shipowners, industrialists and lesser manufacturers, commission merchants and agents, auctioneers and brokers, and retailers in all branches of trade. For example, among the approximately thirty local shoe and leather store owners operating between 1845 and 1852,[44] many of them manufacturers and wholesalers as well as retailers, not one fits our particular category (of directors or promoters of our transportation and industrial enterprises). Excluded are a large number of very small shoemakers and the owners of large establishments such as Brown and Childs (which catered to the wholesale trade), J. and T. Bell, and W. Smyth and Company, each of whom might well have employed a significant proportion of the many local shoemakers.[45] And among the eight firms of brewers, only William Dow and William Molson shared in these ventures. But of the members of approximately thirty-five hardware firms in existence between 1845 and 1852 a larger proportion did participate, including Benjamin Brewster,

John Frothingham, William Workman, Joseph Barrett, James Ferrier, Henry Mulholland, and Charles Wilson.

Among brokers, general merchants, auctioneers, and commission merchants there was only slightly greater enthusiasm for railway and shipping companies. Out of more than fifty commission merchants and agents in Montreal during this period only four figured as promoters, directors, or large shareholders in transportation and industrial undertakings. Among general merchants, however, there was a much higher proportion of participants as directors and leading shareholders; of the forty-four firms of this sort existing in Montreal in 1843, twenty-two partners were active, including Adam Ferrie, George Moffatt, Peter McGill, John Torrance, and John Young.

One of the problems hindering accurate description and measurement of the Montreal business community arises from the overlapping of some of the kinds of commerce. One group described as general merchants included some who acted as importers, wholesalers, and retailers of imported goods, as well as brokers, commission agents, auctioneers, or in a few instances specialists in dry goods. Another difficulty lies in the high turnover of individuals and the frequent changes within firms during these years of shifting business conditions. For example, of the twenty-three commission merchants and agents, some of whom are also included among general merchants in 1845, ten were no longer in business in 1852, a decline of 43.5 per cent in six years.[46] Over ten years the decline was greater: out of twenty firms in this category in 1843, only six remained in business by 1852. Of twelve auctioneers and commission merchants (a single category) in 1843, six survived until 1852. But of fiteeen boot, shoe, and leather dealers, both wholesale and retail, only five continued to 1852, and of nineteen hardware firms eight had survived. The severe attrition, however, was even more pronounced in the dry goods trade: out of twenty-nine wholesalers in 1843, only eleven lasted until 1852, and of forty retailers, only one seems to have survived the decade.[47]

Individuals or firms sometimes moved to another branch of commerce, so that the decrease was more apparent than real. In the overwhelming majority of cases, however, those who did not remain appear to have left the business community altogether, though some stayed in Montreal, probably in retirement or as employees of others. Still, it is clear that there were comparatively few instances of commercial longevity in the city's business community during the period. This is demonstrated by the fact that such a small percentage of the firms in hardware, dry goods, general merchandising, auctioneering, or the commission trade lasted from 1843 through to 1852.

The number of firms – many of which had two or more partners – also fluctuated during the decade, the amount of change varying with the branch of trade. The number of general merchandising houses varied from thirty-nine in 1843, to fifty-five in 1845, to forty-five in 1849, and to thirty-five in 1852. In hardware the variation was not as great, but the same general tendency to fewer firms was in evidence at the end of the forties: nineteen in 1843, twenty-three in 1843, twelve in 1848, and nineteen in 1852.[48] The number of dry goods merchants also fluctuated throughout the decade, showing a decline in the late forties: there were twenty-nine wholesalers and forty-one retailers in 1843, forty-five in both branches in 1845, twenty-four wholesalers and thirty-three retailers in 1848, and thirty-one and forty-two respectively in 1852. Much the same pattern was in evidence among commission merchants, whose number changed from sixteen in 1843 to fifteen in 1845, to ten in 1848, and up sharply to twenty-one or twenty-two in 1852.[49] The variations in these four branches of Montreal commerce were very likely related to alterations in general business conditions in Montreal. The expansion early in the forties matched the increase in the city's trade, the growth of its own population, and the general prosperity in Canada West, while the contraction at the end of the decade reflected the reduction of commerce. Many marginal firms with limited capital and small turnover were forced out of business in these years of stringency, while most of the larger and stronger houses – whose partners supported the new transportation ventures – endured.

These figures have been compiled only for 1843, 1845, 1848, and 1852, and do not fully account for the brief entries and exits of probably many other merchants in these fields in intervening years. Nor do the statistics take account of the entry of firms after 1843, some of which remained in existence until 1852 and probably beyond. They provide, however, a glimpse of the rapidity of change and of the size and flexibility of the business community in Montreal during the forties and early fifties. It is also noteworthy that even from the general commercial community there was, at best, only a moderate participation in shipping, railway, and industrial enterprise.

The more than one hundred wealthy Montreal business leaders in banking and trade who were prominent as shipowners and directors of railway and other companies included members of all the city's ethnic, religious, and commercial groups, along with a small number of Montreal's professional men. The scale of their investments and evidence of the size of their commercial activities indicate that most were highly successful and wealthy merchants, many of whose careers long preceded the 1837-53 period. And some of the most prominent merchants, such as Hugh Allan, John Young, and William Workman, were just beginning lengthy careers as businessmen – entrepreneurs who seem to have exercised occasional strong influence in provincial and municipal politics. Yet the years from the late thirties to the early fifties comprised for them a highly productive and profitable era, when they broadened their interests extensively from commerce to a wide range of new enterprises that dealt in insurance, banking, mining, and gas works, besides the shipping, railway, and industrial firms examined in this study.

Although it is difficult to determine the precise financial worth of most Montreal merchants in this period, it is clear that some of the city's wealthiest merchants refrained from putting substantial sums in railway and shipping companies and limited themselves to investing in either the City Bank or La Banque du Peuple and in one or more of the gas, telegraph, and insurance companies. But they still constituted only a handful of exceptions to the general pattern of the established Montreal merchants supporting and directing the new shipping and railway ventures.

This group tended to concentrate its directorial activity and local corporate investments in railway companies and shipping, and in one of the commercial banks, usually the Bank of Montreal. The amount invested in any particular company need not have been very large for some of these merchants to be elected to the boards of directors. Commercial prominence, reputed wealth, and service in organizations like the Board of Trade or in provincial or municipal politics seem also to have been important criteria for election to directorships in the companies. The most active and successful leaders were men like Peter McGill or the Molsons and the Torrances, who had managed substantial shipping firms and had probably the keenest understanding of the profit potentials in innovations in the field of transportation. Their experience and enthusiasm helped to elevate them quickly to positions of leadership in the railway companies. Along with participants from older trading firms they understood better than others the need to improve Montreal's transportation network.

This cadre of leaders were not men of poor or modest beginnings. Accounts of their lives by late nineteenth-century eulogists (usually containing all that is known of the origins of these men) indicate that most of the prominent members of the Montreal commercial fraternity had been favoured with considerable advantages. Family business connections in Montreal, combined with some experience and often backed by grammar school (or collège classique) education, paved the way for their easy entry and accelerated advancement. They were also usually in command of or had access to substantial capital. Their recruitment to the largest or best established firms was not, then, a result of upward mobility — though this was true of a few — but of a transference of wealth and advantage within Montreal families, or the transmigration of capital and skills, entrepreneurial and technical, from Britain and the United States.

There was also a correlation between the involvement in new transportation enterprises and various kinds of commercial businesses. As general or commission merchants, most directors and heavy investors in railways and in shipping were dealers in imported goods or in exported commodities or both. Others specialized in certain kinds of items, hardware predominating. These were the branches of Montreal commerce most amenable to improvement by more efficient transportation, and that expectation provides one additional explanation of their practitioners' active and keen pursuit of improvements of this sort.

VII

Many of the same business leaders were prominent shareholders and directors of the insurance, telegraph, mining, and gas companies established in Montreal during these years. Moreover, the same men were connected with the commercial banks, most of which had branches throughout the Canadas,[50] and this participation increased bank capitalization during the forties. The Bank of Montreal went from £500,000 to £750,000 in 1842 to £1 million in 1853; the capital of the City Bank was raised from £300,000 to £500,000 in 1847; La Banque du Peuple was chartered in 1844 at £200,000.[51] As for new ventures, the Montreal Mining Company was incorporated in 1847 — one of several promoted by Montreal investors in that year — at a capital of £200,000, the Montreal Fire, Life and Inland Navigation Assurance Company (later the Montreal Insurance Company) at £200,000 in 1843, the New City Gas Company in 1847 at £25,000.[52] The older Montreal Gas Light Company increased its capital the same year to £50,000, while the Montreal Telegraph Company and the Montreal and Troy Telegraph Company were capitalized at £15,000 and £5,000 respectively.[53] Though not all of the capital was raised at once, these new companies are evidence of faith in the strength of the city's economy felt by contemporary Montrealers, who supplied most of the capital and direction for these enterprises.

In all the new ventures being established during the period from the late thirties to the early fifties a segment of the Montreal business community demonstrated impressive talent for mobilizing the capital resources of the community. Yet their interest was, with few exceptions, limited mainly to endeavours that would enhance the commercial power and extend the metropolitan reach of Montreal. Shipping, railways, insurance, banking, and even telegraphs all served this end. Fewer men were prepared to move into industrial ventures with the same degree of alacrity. A significant proportion, perhaps most, of the new industrial activity developed in Montreal from 1846 to 1853 was undertaken by foreigners, many of them Americans. Most of these entrepreneurs invested in concerns the same as, or similar to, the ones in which they were already involved, even though it was usually on a modest scale. On the other hand, extremely few of the leading industrialists participated actively in promoting railways or shipping enterprises, except for a few steamboat builders who briefly owned shares in the vessels they built.

The Montrealers who first took up the challenge of railways and of ocean-going steamships were above all attempting to solve the problems created by the inadequacies of lower St Lawrence River transportation, just as their predecessors had advocated the construction of the Lachine and other canals in the upper section of the river. There was hard economic reasoning behind their promotion of railways down to the northeastern United States, which they viewed as a short land bridge to the Atlantic. Supplemented by steamships, such railways, they hoped, would reduce transportation costs to a level that would make Montreal a greater entrepôt of trade. In short, these Montrealers were attempting to complete the last links in the transportation chain which they saw as vital to the city's continuity as a metropolitan centre. There was little economic nationalism in this, no hesitation in linking their own railways to American sister lines being eagerly thrust northward from New England. Nor were all Montreal business leaders convinced that railways, after all, provided the best solution to the city's transportation problems. Some were prepared to support John Young's dubious scheme of building a new canal between the St Lawrence River and Lake Champlain. But their main aim was still to improve transport to the sea.

Soon, however, many Montreal businessmen became convinced of the utility of railways as tools for opening up new hinterlands and ensuring the city's hegemony over its traditional ones. To this end other entrepreneurs were even prepared to build railways that would rival already existing or soon-to-be-completed lines. The abortive St Lawrence and Ottawa Grand Junction was one such attempt on the part of a small but influential group to develop a new hinterland. These ventures reflected optimism about both the future of Montreal's commerce and the availability of sufficient capital in the city.

Thus, between 1837 and 1853 the city's business community experienced not only general enlargement, consolidation in various branches of commerce, and the addition of significant groups of manufacturers, but also the rise of a group of aggressive entrepreneurs in transportation and industry. Gaining experience in joint-stock companies they were able to generate wealth and self-confidence for similar ventures during the later fifties and well beyond.

VIII

Though united by mid-century in many joint-stock companies as shareholders, directors, or customers, most Montreal businessmen would have considered themselves a community long before. Whether importer or exporter or both, whether wholesaler or retailer in hardware, clothing, or dry goods, there were strong bonds of unity between the members of Montreal's commercial houses notwithstanding their rivalry. The very imprecision of classification – the term 'general merchant' including specialists in hardware, or dry goods who also dealt in wheat – suggests the flexibility with which many businessmen crossed and recrossed each other's lines. Moreover, they signed for each other's notes and loans, and they formed numerous partnerships and acted as assignees for bankruptcies among themselves.

Symbolizing this broad unity of purpose were several flourishing institutions. Associations like the Montreal Board of Trade brought together virtually all the city's merchants in an active association that eagerly, often stridently, asserted commercial interests before provincial and imperial governments and, when necessary, before the rest of Montreal. Changes in tariff legislation, the usury and bankruptcy laws, navigation on the St Lawrence by vessels of United States registry, improvements to the navigation on Lake St Peter and the Ottawa River, enlargement of the Lachine Canal's locks and basin, and uniform postage rates were among the many requests addressed to the provincial and imperial governments in petitions. Numerous memoranda were dispatched to government on a host of matters affecting business conditions, conveying complaints, suggestions, accusations. With a minimum of obsequiousness, ostentation, circumlocution, these statements from the Board of Trade are indicative of the sense of power and habitual authority possessed by the Montreal business group, which felt itself the equal of politicians and officials and believed also that the satisfaction of its interests would benefit the whole province.

The Board of Trade was established in 1842 to succeed the Committee of Trade, 'a standing committee of Merchants to be authorized by their constituents to watch over the general interests of trade of the country' formed twenty years earlier by Montreal merchants who realized the inadequacy of 'the solitary exertions of individuals or ... occasional hasty and inadequate deliberations of public meetings.'[54] Horatio Gates, George Auldjo, George Moffatt, François Antoine Larocque, Peter McGill, John Forsyth, Charles L. Ogden, James Leslie, John Flemming, Henry McKenzie, Campbell Sweeny, and Samuel Gerrard had been elected to the committee to defend Montreal's trading interests by making representations to those in authority, to provide general assistance for and decide disputes between members, and to put down illicit trade. Fifty-four merchants, virtually the whole commercial community, had subscribed to this early association, which soon busied itself with petitions to the Lower Canadian legislature for aid in deepening the channel of the St Lawrence and other matters of common concern.[55]

For nine of the committee's seventeen-year existence (it ceased to function after June 1839) George Auldjo was its president, serving from 1825 to 1833 and in 1835-6. With his brother, Alexander, a partner in the firm of Auldjo and Maitland, George Auldjo personified the transitional entrepreneurship of Montreal in that era when one Canadian staple was rapidly delining and others were rising. Though connected by marriage to John Richardson, a leading partner in one of the firms dominant in the North West Company, and though his own firm (in operation as early as 1785 under John Auldjo, another brother[56]) had undoubtedly participated in the fur trade, George was deeply involved in Montreal's newer commercial affairs. He and George Garden, another partner, were both directors of the Bank of Montreal during the twenties and, as a sideline to their general merchandising business (specializing in wines, spirits, and dry goods), they acted as Montreal agents for two foreign insurance companies.[57] George Auldjo also owned a lot of real estate in Montreal. Similarly, the careers of other original members on the executive of the Committee of Trade, McGill, Gerrard, Moffatt, Larocque, and McKenzie, testified to the shift away from the fur trade to a new, more diversified, commercial orientation.[58]

Then, in 1842, the Montreal Board of Trade received a charter from the legislature of the new United Province of Canada.[59] Like its parent, the organization was primarily concerned with the health of Montreal's trade and with specific matters affecting the business climate. These concerns were reflected in the membership, which was drawn almost entirely from the commercial community, and in the issues deliberated at general and council meetings. The leading officers of the Board and the members of its subcommittees were the very elite of the trading fraternity.

The years 1845 and 1846 were especially busy and anxious ones for the Board. Besides its usual concerns that year about improvements to the city's commerce, including the St Lawrence and Atlantic railway, enlarging the port of Montreal, deepening Lake St Peter, improvements to the navigation of the Richelieu, and the establishment of uniform postal rates, the Board was faced with serious external threats to Montreal's established trade pattern. The American drawback legislation of 1845, allowing goods to pass duty-free through the United States by inland navigation to Canada, would increase the preference for importing via United States ports.[60] Thomas Cringan, the Board's vice-president, wrote gloomily that unless extra duties were placed on goods imported through the United States this trade 'will ... stop a most important trade, that of the direct trade to Cuba and Porto Rico; will injure the carrying trade both by sea, and the canals in Canada; will tend to divert a considerable amount of the Canada trade from Great Britain, to the United States, and by depriving vessels of their outward freights, raise the freight upon exports; as also by diminishing the upward freights of the Canal boats very much enhance the downward freights.'

The Board's reaction to the even more serious threat posed by the withdrawal of Imperial protection for Canadian wheat and flour was stronger and more protracted, and immediately took the form of recommendations for repeal of Imperial duties on American wheat imported into Canada and of the Navigation laws. Some Montreal merchants, however, led by John Young, found the Board's policy still too cautious and established the Free Trade Association to seek the adoption in the Province 'of Free Trade principles ... in all their comprehensiveness.'[61]

Throughout the forties and early fifties the Montreal Board of Trade remained pragmatic, defensive, and cautious. Though its council meetings and annual general sessions occasionally considered grand schemes to radically enhance Montreal's trade, such as John Young's proposed St Lawrence and Lake Champlain canal,[62] the members devoted their main attention to the more mundane concerns previously mentioned. The Board never did support Young's proposal, and only mildly endorsed railway projects, even during the latter part of this period when several such schemes were underway with many leading businessmen as backers. Restrained in endorsing newfangled transportation schemes, the Board worked actively to improve the river systems that had traditionally carried Montreal's trade and to change specific laws, provincial and municipal, in order to improve the climate of business enterprise in the city.

While the Montreal Board of Trade was the largest and most broadly representative of all sectors of the local business community, other organizations of businessmen also existed. Some were informal and small groupings, such as the Board of Brokers, an association of produce dealers through whom a large proportion of Montreal's export trade of staples was conducted by 1850.[63] After meeting each week to exchange information, the brokers published a circular listing prices and quantities of commodities, shares bought and sold at Montreal, as well as news of ship arrivals from sea and from inland ports, and ocean freight rates.[64] This publication helped to systematize commercial news for merchants in Montreal, upcountry centres, and Britain. A reorganization of the Board of Brokers took place in 1862, perhaps because of increasing specialization in the brokerage business. Its successor, the Montreal Corn Exchange, formed in 1863, included several of the men previously prominent in the earlier association.[65]A number of Montreal merchants who traded shares and securities had been meeting regularly since the forties and were probably the same group which had come together in 1849 to seek incorporation as the Merchants' Exchange and Reading Room of Montreal.

Another organization, the Mercantile Library Association, formed in 1841, was more than just a club for the city's commercial fraternity or a library and reading room with trade news publications from abroad.[66] The association was a kind of Mechanic's Institute for merchants, and it is noteworthy that in the early Victorian 'age of improvement' there was a search for self-improvement among many Montreal merchants who attended the annual winter series of lectures offered through the forties to explain the complexities of their commercial world. They listened to discourses by John Dougall on 'The principles and objects of commerce,'[67] by Augustin Norbert Morin on 'the importance to the inhabitants of cities of encouraging the production in the country of articles for importation.' by W.H. Sherwood on the usury laws, by Henry Driscoll QC on commercial law and 'Joint-stock companies and the law of principal and agent,' by T.S. Hunt on the discoveries of modern science, and by the Rev. Mr Cordner on the importance of shoes in history. The well-attended lectures provided the listeners with ideas and information through the long Montreal winters while commerce lagged, awaiting the spring cargoes of ships from sea and the vessels from upriver with produce from the West. Montreal's merchants were fortified also by assurances from Lord Elgin himself, who, in introducing the 1848-9 lecture series, spoke of 'the useful and honourable career of the British merchant ... which, when [followed] with diligence and circumspection, leads always to respectability, not unfrequently to high honour and distinction.'[68]

Though heterogeneous in racial composition, religion, and business affiliation, and constantly changing in personnel, the Montreal business community had an obvious unity of purpose – the pursuit of maximum profits – for which vice-regal blessings provided comforting, but unnecessary, justification. Yet most Montreal businessmen already realized the need for voluntary association in societies to lend collective strength to the aims they shared. The 1840s, therefore, was a period of transition, not in reshaping their purposes but in organizing the pursuit of those objectives during the concurrent series of crises caused by external forces and the challenges and opportunities of the North American transportation revolution.

In the period from 1837 to 1853 Montreal's successes and failures in meeting these circumstances were largely the result of the conjuncture of strengths and weaknesses arising from its location on the major artery of navigation, which, despite the construction of canals, could not match the advantages provided by alternative United States routes for the interior trade. Though it was the metropolis of the St Lawrence, its businessmen came to learn that this was not an advantage on which they could rely for success in the competition for commercial hegemony. The experiences of the city's merchant-entrepreneurs in shipping and railway enterprises would reveal both the vestiges of the old dreams and belief in the possibility of a masterstroke, along with a growing belief that limited objectives involving some continental integration were more realistic for the business interests of Montreal.

PART ONE / SHIPPING

3

Montreal forwarding firms on the upper St Lawrence

From 1838 onward there was a steadily mounting volume of trade between Montreal and the western interior. The Lachine Canal, which underwent enlargement from 1843 to 1848, accommodated much – though not all – of this up-river traffic, and the tolls collected on the tonnage and goods passing through its locks tell of continuous growth between 1837 and 1853.[1] It may be presumed that the many vessels, steamboats included, to avoid tolls by running the Lachine rapids at some risk, and whose cargoes and passengers are not included in these figures, increased in more or less the same proportion. These vessels brought down a huge variety of commodities from the upper country. As well as wheat, flour, and ashes, mostly destined for export, there were immense quantities of supplies for Lower Canada, and a good deal too for the timber camps in the Ottawa Valley. Among Montreal's many commercial functions was that of a depot for food, particularly packed beef and pork (from as far away as Cincinnati), and for a vast array of imported or – increasingly – Montreal-made hardware goods that were marshalled and shipped up to the timber shanties.

When the commodities poured into the port each spring and fall the news of their arrival and their fluctuating prices and general market conditions were reported by the *Gazette* and other newspapers. The arrival, or non-arrival, in town of notably large quantities of any item was a matter of vital importance to exporters and commission agents, as well as to owners of ocean going ships. Indications of quality of the Upper Canadian harvest expectations or unusually large single sales of wheat might entail the difference between profit and loss, between affluence and sudden ruin, for staple dealers. Who were the consignees of the major shipments of commodities this week? Are freights rising or holding steady? How many Upper Canadian merchants have booked into local hotels and how heavily are they buying? How friendly are the banks this week for discounting commercial paper? How much is the premium on first-rate bills of exchange? Facts, hints, guesses, prophecies, and warnings on all these matters were supplied in columns of the newspapers.[2] These, and a score of other considerations, were the ingredients of the Montreal commercial calculus that a merchant, whether established or newly arrived, had to understand and cope with in order to stay in business. Whether from interpreting newspaper reports, chatting with shipmasters on the quays, gossiping with competitors along St Paul Street, or gleaning intelligence from upcountry correspondents or overseas suppliers, the Montreal merchant had to manage his affairs so that he avoided heavy losses and, over a season of trade, or two seasons at most, made a profit on his transactions. Few managed this difficult balancing act. From among those who did emerged the entrepreneurs of the forties and fifties.

Auctions often told the story. At them the buyers and sellers, whether commission merchant, speculator, or dealer, sparred for margins of farthings as they carefully fingered the wheat and discussed the myriad markings on barrels of flour from upcountry millers or beef from Ohio packers. The price determined was registered and reported to all who wished the news, and those now owning the goods knew that, like the Upper Canadian merchants and farmers, their returns would be determined months later in Liverpool or Glasgow.

Shipping between Montreal and its interior hinterland had become a specialized trade by the early thirties. Called 'forwarders' or 'forwarding merchants,'[3] these shipping firms were large companies with several steamboats, numerous barges, and sloops to convey cargo up and down the St Lawrence, Ottawa, Rideau, and Great Lakes waterways. By no means were they in complete control of upper St Lawrence commerce; numerous private steamboat owners operated up and down the river successfully over many years, and a number of the bigger trading firms ran their own boats independently of forwarders or 'tramp' vessels. Yet an examination of the principal firms and their partners reveals the extent to which the upriver shipping industry provided a highly organized structure for Montreal's economic penetration of the interior. It also shows that Montreal forwarders depended upon support from partners in upriver towns, and that the interior transportation system was not so much dominated by Montrealers. It was a complex network requiring an exceptionally high degree of capitalization and organization, as well as participation from partners through the entire upper St Lawrence Valley and lower Great Lakes. Competing with its eastern seaboard rivals for this traffic, the St Lawrence forwarding network also anticipated competition from the railway mania of the early fifties. A number of Montreal's leading railway entrepreneurs of the fifties served their business apprenticeships in St Lawrence shipping firms, a fact which demonstrates the flexibility of some businessmen and their entrepreneurial exploitation of new business opportunities during this important period of transition and expansion.

II

The number of steamboats in use on the upper St Lawrence and on Lake Ontario increased rapidly during the early thirties, especially after the Ottawa-Rideau river system of canals was completed.[4] And as the St Lawrence canals were constructed during the forties, steamboats came into even more widespread use as the volume of shipping along the river increased. After 1845, to be sure, such factors as the United States Drawback Acts and the elimination of Imperial protection limited these expansive tendencies. And by the fifties the railways, which were planned to channel commerce more efficiently to and from the interior – especially the lines projected to run west from Montreal – were clearly affecting the pattern of enterprise in the forwarding business at Montreal. Nevertheless the forties were a period of expansion and general prosperity in Montreal shipping. The Montreal forwarders appear to have confined their activities exclusively to the shipping of goods upwards to and produce downwards from lower Great Lakes and upper St Lawrence River ports[5] in their steamboats and sailing vessels, which were either sloops or Durham boats (listed in the Ship Registers of the time as 'barges' of between 70 and 120 tons displacement).[6]

It has been observed that '1837-38 ushered in a new era' in Lake Ontario and upper St Lawrence navigation as the shipping business became consolidated in order to reduce costs and competition among the large number of vessels vying for freight and passengers.[7] This process of consolidation may have begun earlier, however, at the beginning of the thirties, when Montreal interests established a powerful steamboat line which quickly achieved an increasingly strong position in trade with the interior. Primarily because it was the furthest point that could be reached by ocean ships, Montreal was the centre of this forwarding business between the thirties and the early fifties, whether by the Ottawa-Rideau route or by the St Lawrence River. Because of the importance of this business it attracted the participation of many Montrealers, who invested substantial capital in steamboats and other vessels. The forwarding trade of the upper St Lawrence was important also because of its linkages with the Montreal steamboat construction industry, examined later in this study. Perhaps most important of all was the fact that forwarding was an enterprise in which some of Montreal's most aggressive and most successful railway promoters were involved at an early stage of their business careers. Just as the downriver steamboat companies produced the Molsons and the Torrances, who took such an active role in the promotion of railways to the Atlantic during the mid-forties in order to overcome the serious navigational problems of the lower St Lawrence, railway entrepreneurs Luther Holton and David L. Macpherson, who promoted western railways in the early fifties, emerged from among the forwarders to exploit the new transportation possibilities to the interior. Steamboating in Montreal then was only an aspect of what might be called a Canadian 'transportation revolution'[8] a sequential innovation of canals, steamboats, and railways in this region accompanied by the growth of manufacturing. At Montreal these elements were being marshalled not so much to create a new hinterland — though the quintessential commercial Montrealer, John Young, still wrote in those terms — but to defend the existing trade that Montreal might well soon entirely lose.

This chapter describes the pattern of participation, the personnel and groups in Montreal's forwarding trade, rather than the details of how their businesses were conducted. It is intended to provide a glimpse of one aspect of Montreal's business world and, in references to the forwarders' partners in upriver ports like Prescott and Kingston, to demonstrate the strength of Montreal's metropolitan reach in transportation.

III

Until the completion of the St Lawrence canals during the late forties, the use of the river for the transportation of goods and passengers was fraught with time-consuming delays and costly portages, especially on upriver trips. Rafts, bateaux, and Durham boats could make their way downriver, but passage upward was made difficult between Cornwall and Prescott by the Long Sault rapids and other navigational hazards. Not until the early thirties were steamboats, with sufficient power to overcome the rapids, put into service.[9] These steamboats towed other vessels through the rapids up to Prescott, but traffic by this route was limited, especially after 1832 when the Rideau Canal provided an excellent alternative route to the interior of Upper Canada from Montreal. But for the relatively narrow locks of the Grenville and Carillon canals on the Ottawa River, small steamboats could navigate this vast inland waterways system safely through to Kingston. Although it did not provide an adequate alternative to the improvement of the St Lawrence, whose towns like Prescott and Brockville were not served by the Rideau, the new backcountry route could be used for through traffic from Montreal to Kingston and other Lake Ontario ports, and for intermediate traffic to the Ottawa Valley and the communities along the canal.[10]

For more than a decade the Ottawa-Rideau system thrived on this trade. Until the mid-forties, it diverted much traffic from the St Lawrence. Despite the limitations of the Grenville Canal, which required trans-shipment of goods

because its locks were too small to allow passage of steamboats, Montreal for-
warders quickly invested in the new route by establishing the Ottawa and Rideau
Forwarding Company.[11] Not much is known about the structure of this firm or
its capitalization. Yet many of its backers were highly prominent in Montreal.
One major participant in the company soon after its formation in 1831, and its
dominant partner, was Peter McGill,[12] then at the height of his power. Other
Montreal investors in the Ottawa and Rideau Forwarding Company included
Horatio Gates, Montreal's major staple dealer of that era, J.D. Bernard, a Mon-
treal auctioneer and commission merchant, and Emery Cushing, another Montreal merchant. Ottawa Valley entrepreneurs Philemon Wright and Thomas
Mears of Hawkesbury were also part of the syndicate, while John Molson too
was a major investor.[13] By early 1837 the company, which was administered by
a committee consisting of McGill, Cushing, and Molson, along with John
Redpath and Thomas Phillips, two former contractors on the Rideau Canal, and
John Frothingham, one of the wealthiest of Montreal's merchants, was in serious
difficulties.[14] Only private loans from Frothingham to the extent of some
£9,000 had prevented the firm from going under. The crisis had developed
during the 1836 season as a result of organizational and navigation problems
along the canal, difficulties soon overcome, and, more seriously, the eruption of
a tough freight-rate war between competing forwarders. 'The latter part of the
season' Frothingham gloomily reported 'was passed in fruitless opposition
among the Forwarders, Us to regain our Customers & former position, & the
river [Forwarders] to retain them at any sacrifice.' Clearly, the only sensible
solution, he continued, was to eliminate costly competition by making

some arrangement for the ensuing year & the [Committee of Management],
being convinced from past experience that the present rates of freight do not
remunerate the [Forwarders], whose business is liable to so many contingencies,
gladly availed themselves of the favourable feeling to enter into arrangements ... to adopt a Tariff & other improvements in the system of carrying on
their business. The [Committee] considering the duty they owed to the stockholders whose interest they were bound to promote to the utmost of their
power readily agreed to embrace so favorable an opportunity of benefiting the
Co. & of extricating them from their present difficulties.[15]

Although further attempts to compete with the Ottawa and Rideau Forwarding
Company were made by other steamboat owners, the company was able to
dominate the Ottawa-Rideau system by means of this and subsequent arrangements to restrain competition. Their ownership of the most usable ingress to the
Ottawa River from the St Lawrence at St Anne's, where a privately owned lock

built in 1816 was enlarged, also helped to limit competition.[16] But control of the Ottawa-Rideau route by no means ensured those who were party to the 'arrangement' a monopoly of shipping westward from Montreal, for even though major carriers were in agreement, including the Jones, and Hooker and Henderson firms, there were mavericks ungentlemanly enough to ignore collusive arrangements or break them at will.

By 1839 the Forwarding Company had come under the control of Macpherson, Crane and Company, a Montreal and Kingston firm that operated along the St Lawrence as well. Its commitments on the Ottawa-Rideau system alone were very extensive, including a total of ten steamboats, six on the Rideau Canal and the rest on the Ottawa River. There were also twenty-six large decked barges from seventy-five to one hundred tons each and twenty-four smaller ones. Four major warehousing establishments were maintained at Montreal, Bytown, Kingston, and Prescott, besides smaller depots at Lachine, Grenville, and Carillon.[17] The total number of employees was more than 650, including 600 crew members alone. The firm had agencies in Toronto, Hamilton, Niagara, Amherstberg, and Cobourg and thus maintained contacts with merchants far into the interior. By the end of the thirties this company was apparently also planning to expand its operations because six schooners were then being built for Lakes Ontario and Erie.

Macpherson, Crane and Company was the largest forwarding firm in the Canadas until 1854.[18] In 1842 its three major partners were David L. Macpherson, of Montreal, his brother John, of Kingston, and Samuel Crane, of Prescott. Only that year David Macpherson became a senior partner in the firm, but since his arrival in Canada in 1835 he had been employed in the company's Montreal office, where he had come to learn the business. Born and raised in Inverness, Scotland, Macpherson had been educated at its Royal Academy, a grammar school. Although nothing more is known about his background, his attendance at a grammar school and the fact that not long after his arrival he became a partner in a large firm suggest a family of some means.

The scale of the firm's operations was, as noted, very large. At Portsmouth near Kingston, the Lake Ontario pivot of a rapidly increasing forwarding trade, the company by 1845 had constructed its major base for western operations. Extensive wharves, warehouses, and ship repair facilities were maintained.[19] At Prescott, where Samuel Crane was the resident partner, it had a major shipbuilding and ship repair yard and facilities for transferring premium freight from large lake steamboats to small river steamers and bulk freight from lake schooners to Durham boats and bateaux. The number of vessels maintained by the firm increased substantially during the forties with the construction of five more steamboats and numerous barges; by 1851 at Montreal alone eight steamboats were registered.[20] Several more were registered at other St Lawrence ports, chiefly Kingston and perhaps a few others elsewhere on the lower Great Lakes, where by the late forties the firm's ships called regularly. Their steamboats made scheduled runs to Port Stanley and Cleveland on Lake Erie and eastward as far as Whitehall, at the foot of Lake Champlain.[21] Besides ships on the upper St Lawrence and the lower Great Lakes, Macpherson, Crane and Company had a large road transportation system that included fleets of wagons ranging the roads in areas not served by waterways. Meanwhile operations on the Ottawa were continued, although in view of the new feasibility of the St Lawrence route and the eruption of competition in that area, the Ottawa branch probably accounted for a far smaller proportion of the firm's total business during the fifties than the thirties.

At Montreal, David Macpherson was at the heart of the firm's activities. Here, all cargoes, whether coming down from the interior, upbound from Lake Champlain, or occasionally inbound from Halifax, were trans-shipped or laid up in warehouses. At Montreal, vessels were serviced either at the company's own small yard, at Cantin's huge shipyard, or at other yards along the Lachine Canal or in the harbour area. In Montreal the volume and pace of shipping was increasing during the late forties and early fifties. More vessels were constructed by the company after 1846 than in any other short period in its history. Two schooners were built at Montreal in 1846 and another the following year. In 1849 a large steamboat, the *Phoenix*, was commissioned, and in 1851 two much larger steamers, the *Champion* and the *Reindeer,* were constructed at Montreal.

David Macpherson managed all these varied operations in those years of growth. Like many of his associates, he was also interested in railway ventures. Along with his father-in-law, William Molson, Macpherson was a director and large investor in the Montreal and Lachine Railway between 1847 and 1852; he also invested in the St Lawrence and Atlantic. By the early fifties Macpherson was deeply involved in the promotion of the St Lawrence and Ottawa Grand Junction Railway, a proposed western extension of the Montreal and Lachine, the potential value of which he was in an excellent position to appraise. A year later he was a leading member of the group that secured control of the renewed charter to build the Montreal and Kingston Railway. Indeed, Macpherson's advice might well have been heavily relied upon in the private negotiations for the establishment of the syndicate that bought control of that railway in 1852.[22] Unlike so many of his colleagues on the business scene in Montreal, he did not participate in most other local endeavours, whether financial, commercial, philanthropic, or social, with some or all of which most mid-Victorian Montreal bourgeois were associated. He seems to have eschewed the banking, commerce, insurance, mining, and real estate schemes that attracted others.

The entry of David Macpherson into railways at this point may explain his virtually complete departure from shipping in 1853. On 27 June 1853 the firm sold five of its eight Montreal-based steamboats to another group, consisting of John Jones of Montreal, Peter Robertson of Bytown, and Donald Thompson of Quebec, all of whom were unknown except Jones, the proprietor of Tatersall's Auction Mart in Montreal.[23] Although MacPherson, Crane and Company continued in business, the sale of so much of its carrying capacity strongly suggests that a large amount of capital was required to meet some emergency or other needs. While it is possible that financial difficulties overtook the firm, the disinvestment of 1853 coincides with David Macpherson's new commitment to railway contracting for the Grand Trunk Railway and his subsequent removal to Toronto. His requirements for capital and the growing faith in railways, apparent in Canada during that era, might have induced Macpherson to reduce and perhaps ultimately to liquidate his holdings in and associations with the forwarding business.

IV

Hooker, Holton and Company and H. Jones and Company were the other two major forwarding firms in the upper St Lawrence trade. Both were firmly based at Montreal and included partners at upper St Lawrence ports. Hooker, Holton and Company in the mid-forties consisted of the partners James Henderson and Luther Holton at Montreal, Francis Henderson at Kingston, and Alfred Hooker at Prescott; there was also a partner in Bytown. This old firm of forwarders and commission merchants had experienced a number of changes since 1831, when it was Willison and Hooker.[24] At that time, the Montreal partner, probably Willison, employed Luther Hamilton Holton as a clerk.

Holton was born in Lansdowne township of Leeds county in October 1817 and moved with his family to Montreal in 1826. Although little is known about his background, he appears to have come from a family of limited means.[25] Having received little formal education, Holton applied himself to business and advanced to a full partnership in the forwarding house probably in 1844.[26] Unlike his competitor Macpherson, Holton accepted a good deal of involvement in local and provincial public life. A founder of the Montreal City and District Savings Bank, he served as a director from 1846 to 1873. He was an active member of the Free Trade Association that was established in 1846 and became a Liberal member of Parliament in 1854. Holton developed a strong interest and an apparent competence in public economic policies, so that in 1863 he was appointed to the Macdonald-Dorion administration as minister of finance.[27]

Much of his interest and ability in these matters probably arose from his experience in forwarding, which for many years had been his principal business concern. When James Henderson, the firm's senior Montreal partner, retired in 1845, Holton appears to have succeeded to his position and to have become the manager of the firm's affairs there.[28] It was not a large business by comparison to Macpherson's, but it was a very active one with almost the same range, extending west as far as Hamilton and south to Lake Champlain, probably through agents or by leasing 'tramp' vessels rather than by means of its own ships. This company employed three of its own steamboats from Montreal during the late forties and two others from Prescott and Kingston, besides various schooners and barges, and other leased steamboats, including the *Grenville* from its owner, William Rodden. By 1853 the Hooker and Holton forwarding company was operating a total of their own seven steamboats on scheduled runs between Montreal and Hamilton.[29]

The firm changed form slightly in January 1850 when, after the expiration of the agreement between the Kingston and Montreal partners, Holton seems to have become even more important as the predominant Montreal member. He increased his interests in the firm by purchasing some shares from his late partner, Henderson. Now the firm was known as Hooker and Holton; apparently the only other major associate besides Holton was Alfred Hooker in Prescott, who was also a partner in another forwarding firm operated by George Jacques of Montreal and Elijah Hooker of Prescott. Although a separate concern, Hooker, Jacques and Company appears to have worked in conjunction with Holton's company.[30]

In early January 1854, Luther Holton sold his shares in three steamboats and six sailing vessels to Hooker, presumably his whole interest in the firm's assets.[31] By this time, he was deeply committed to railways, having participated, like Macpherson, in the Montreal and Kingston venture and having become involved with Macpherson and Gzowski as a contractor in the Toronto and Guelph Railway. Thus, again like Macpherson, Holton was faced with demanding practical commitments to railways. He withdrew from shipping perhaps with a growing belief in the efficacy of the new 'medium.' In any event, aside from politics, over the next several years Holton devoted himself almost exclusively to railroad contracting, two pursuits that everyone knew were not unrelated.

The Jones family of Montreal, Brockville, and Kingston, as H. Jones and Company, had been in the forwarding business since at least 1829[32] and were the third most important forwarding firm on the upper St Lawrence. Throughout the forties they operated at least two steamboats, two schooners, and a considerable number of barges between Montreal and the upper ports. One of their steamers, the *Dawn*, ran regularly between Montreal and Hamilton.[33] In carrying capacity and in geographical extent of business the Jones firm was as large as Holton's. The partners were Sydney Jones of Montreal and Henry Jones of Kingston. Although the Brockville partner is unknown, the firm's branch there was H. & S. Jones' and was an interest of the locally prominent family of the same name.[34] Sydney, the Montreal partner, is virtually unknown, apart from this firm; possibly he was only a temporary resident of the city. From this, and from the fact that the firm operated at least as many vessels at other ports as at Montreal, it might be concluded that their headquarters was elsewhere, probably Brockville.

The origins of the partnership are obscure, but it had not sprung suddenly into existence in the forties when its Montreal-based ships were constructed.[35] Unlike both Holton's and Macpherson's companies, the Jones firm did not witness the removal of Montreal participation in the early fifties. One of the group that purchased the five steamboats sold by Macpherson, Crane and Company in 1853 was John Jones of Montreal. Although apparently not in the Jones forwarding business earlier, he might well have become a member of the firm before forming a partnership with two other investors from Bytown and Quebec to buy the Macpherson interests.

V

There were, to be sure, other forwarders besides these three on the upper St Lawrence. A relatively small amount of capital was required to buy a boat and, judging from the large number of sailing vessels and steamboats operated by Montrealers on the upper St Lawrence, the large companies faced strong competition. But many of the owners of these boats might have been acting as investors rather than as forwarders. By the forties upper St Lawrence shipping may have become too specialized and demanding a business for amateurs; a vessel might have been more profitable hired out to the regular forwarding companies than competing with them. Since, however, many of these minor shipowners were also involved in commerce as commission agents, importers, or exporters, they probably also used the vessels in their own businesses most of the time, especially at peak periods of activity. Newspaper advertisements throughout the forties indicate that notwithstanding the clear dominance of the three large firms in upriver shipping many smaller independent forwarders continued to exist.

Although most smaller shipowners were far less important individually than the three large companies, they were not all weak or unambitious. A group calling itself the New Forwarding Company sprang into existence in the autumn of 1839 with the announcement that £50,000 was to be raised among supporters in Montreal, Brockville, Perth, Bytown, Gananoque, Picton, Belleville, and Niagara, most of them merchants incensed at the great increase in rates levied in 1837 by St Lawrence River forwarders following the collusive arrangement of that year.[36] Participation was invited from 'parties desirous of encouraging the reduction of Freights, and other necessary reforms in the methods of conducting the business.' Though the proposed company was apparently never established, the scale of dissatisfaction and the proposal to raise so much capital are indicative of strength and ambition in the mercantile community of the upper St Lawrence Valley. The Montrealers behind the project were T.B. Anderson, Joseph Shuter, James Scott, Charles Mittleberger, Theodore Hart, and J. Benjamin, all established merchants.

Theodore Hart, a Sephardic Jew of the local Spanish and Portugese connection, was the proprietor of a general merchandising house, Hart, Benjamin and Company, which seems to have included a member of the Benjamin family that owned a wholesale and retail drygoods outlet in the forties and early fifties. Hart was not entirely unfamiliar with shipping. Together with Benjamin and Samuel Hart and Jacob Joseph, of Montreal, Abraham Joseph of Quebec, Arthur Wellington Hart — all of them also Sephardic Jews — and Henry Bradford of Liverpool, and Mark Wolff of London, he was part owner of a medium-sized barque that was apparently used on the transatlantic run to Montreal or Quebec.[37] Among Hart's other business interests, mining promotion was very important; he was one of the Montrealers behind several companies that received charters in 1847 to open mines in the region north of lakes Superior and Huron. In particular he took a very active part in the formation of the Canada Mining Company and the Echo Lake Mining Company — he was the latter's first president — and apparently had substantial interests in the Montreal Mining Company.[38]

James Scott, another Montreal backer of the New Forwarding Company, had a stake in the transatlantic shipping business, while Joseph Shuter, a former crockery merchant, was vitally concerned, as a director of the Champlain and St Lawrence Railway, with cheaper freights from the interior.[39] T.B. Anderson was one of the principal partners of Forsyth, Richardson and Company, a large merchandising firm since the late eighteenth century.[40] Charles Mittleberger, like the other Montrealers, had for years been concerned with interior trade in the Ottawa Valley and the Niagara region, where his brothers William and Henry lived.[41]

Although the New Forwarding Company did not develop beyond the promotion stage, other smaller firms sprang up and carried on over a number of years.

One was Murray and Sanderson, which was active during the forties. The principal partners were Donald Murray of Montreal and George Sanderson of Brockville. Since 1840 they had operated two steamboats and several boats between Montreal and Kingston, upward by way of the Rideau Canal and downward by the St Lawrence.[42] In January 1846 the general merchandising firm of Tobin and Murison purchased a half-interest in both steamboats and became partners in the Murray and Sanderson firm. Perhaps the newcomers brought in badly needed capital. In any event, the new union did not last long, for in January 1847 John Tobin went into bankruptcy and two months later sold his share of the steamboats to George Sanderson.[43] Nearly three years afterwards, Murray and Sanderson also bacame bankrupt, an event which probably broke the partnership between them, but not their ability to continue in business. Sanderson retained ownership of the steamboats, and Donald Murray was soon back in the forwarding business.[44]

Another small and short-lived forwarding concern was the firm of Smith and Glassford. It seems to have begun in 1847 when George Smith of Montreal, a former steamboat agent, purchased a steamboat and one or two smaller vessels in partnership with James Glassford of Kingston. They may well have been the upper St Lawrence associates of the Gilmour timber company, whose Montreal agent, James Gilmour, supplied funds for the purchase of two steamboats and two sailing ships in 1847.[45] The same vessels were sold to George Smith in April 1849, and sold again one day later, to Gilmour. One of Smith's own ships was mortgaged to the Gilmours, and in this complicated way the Smith and Glassford and the Walker and Gilmour interests seem to have merged.

The last of the smaller Montreal forwarders in this era was Masson, Farlinger and Company, which, though active during the middle and late forties did not last after 1850. Its partners included Montrealers Paul T. Masson, John G. Kennedy, and Thomas Farlinger of Fort Covington, New York, a village near the St Lawrence River. The firm possessed only a few vessels, including a steamboat and two sailing ships.[46] In the early fifties the firm seems to have significantly scaled down its operations by selling its vessels to the main forwarding companies.

VI

Besides the large and small firms exclusively concerned with the forwarding trade, some Montreal merchants owned shares in ships plying the upper St Lawrence River. Their combined operations could not have amounted to much of a challenge to the forwarding companies, however, whose Montreal-based steamboats alone numbered fifteen, compared with the three operated by independents not connected with forwarders. Although some of these independent shipowners might well have hired their vessels to the companies, there is no evidence that any of them did; these merchants probably used their vessels for their own commercial purposes generally and perhaps occasionally rented spare space to other merchants.

These minor shipowners included George P. Dickson, a Montreal commission agent during the mid-forties, who purchased a schooner in 1845 along with Gordon Warren, another Montreal merchant, and George Bogg of Prescott; they advertised shipping space to interested parties in 1845.[47] Other small shippers included merchant Clement Kain and forwarders John McCuaig, Francis Clemow, and Edward Hackett.[48] Pierre Jodoin, a Montreal wholesale dry goods dealer and prominent director of La Banque du Peuple (See appendix A) appears to have worked his steamboat *Ste Hélène* on the upper St Lawrence between 1848 and 1853, when he sold it to a syndicate of Belleville, Kingston, Gananoque, and Montreal merchants, the latter including Maurice and Austin Cuvillier.[49]

Yet other Montrealers had interests in upper St Lawrence shipping. William Parkyn, engineer and foundry operator, owned a steamboat in 1849 and maintained partial financial interest in it even after the boat was sold to a group of Kingston merchants.[50] Jean Chaltré and Daniel Kehoe of Montreal, both 'master mariners,' might well have operated their two vessels on the upper St Lawrence. The Allans and Gilmours, whose interests lay primarily in Atlantic shipping, and the Tates, whose ships plied the lower St Lawrence, seem to have had connections, if not investments, in upriver shipping as well. The Tates's Royal Mail Line of Montreal-to-Quebec steamboats was connected in 1845 with the firm owning the steamboats *Canada, Henry Gildersleeve,* and *Highlander,* which ran between Kingston and Coteau du Lac.[51] Even as late as 1853, sailing vessels independent of the major upper St Lawrence forwarding firms were carrying cargoes from Montreal to Great Lakes ports.[52]

VII

Beyond the immediate confines of their city, Montreal forwarders also probably invested a substantial scale in vessels registered at other St Lawrence or Great Lakes ports. Very likely this extra-Montreal investment in ships was confined to the large forwarding firms that had direct contacts with upriver or lower Great Lakes businesses. Small investors, like those noted above, probably confined their participation to local opportunities.

It would be hazardous to attempt to make an estimate of the total investment in St Lawrence shipping in this period and difficult to determine what proportion of that capital was supplied by Montrealers. One of the barriers to such an estimate is the difficulty of determining precisely how far afield Montreal businessmen invested in shipping. Another is estimating the value of ships that varied in size, power, fittings, and date of construction. Therefore, what follows here is an attempt to determine the general level of investment made by the city's businessmen in shipping during the forties and early fifties, rather than specific investments in themselves.

Between 1838 and 1853 there were eighteen Montreal-registered upper St Lawrence steamboats in which Montrealers had whole or partial ownership. Because of the differences in the size and power of these ships, an approximate fifteen-year average value of £2,500 could be established on the basis of probable market value. While this might seem to be a conservative estimate, considering the fact that in 1845 a new, moderate-size steamboat for the Richelieu cost £5,000, some vessels sold for as little as £500.[53] On this basis Montrealers would have had an investment in these boats — in which they owned approximately one-half of the total shares — of £22,500. In sailing vessels, bateaux and Durham boats, of which there were an immense number in the possession of forwarding firms, the investment in those registered at Montreal alone probably exceeded £3,000, on the basis of an average value of £100 each.[54] Thus the total investment in Montreal-based vessels for the upriver trade was approximately £25,500. It is highly possible that Montrealers had half as much again invested in ships registered at Kingston, Picton, Brockville, Hamilton and other St Lawrence river and Lake Ontario ports.[55] Thus an aggregate figure for estimated Montreal investment in upper St Lawrence shipping might be about £38,000. While this may not appear to be a large amount, it excludes the larger sums invested in lower St Lawrence, ocean, and Richelieu River shipping.

Although this investment was made throughout the twelve years from 1839 to 1851, seven of the eighteen steamboats and eighteen of the twenty-four sailing ships at Montreal were registered in 1847 or later. This indicates that the completion of the St Lawrence canals acted as a stimulus to investment in shipping. But their effects were not sustained beyond the earliest years of the fifties,[56] despite the early success registered by the canals in the years immediately following their completion.[57]

It is not known how profitable this shipping was during these years, or precisely how the completion of St Lawrence canals and the increasing use of steamboats expedited movement, because of the paucity of information about rates on freight and passengers. Judgments about the shipping industry must be based, therefore, on circumstantial information. As for the pattern of entrepreneurship in upper St Lawrence shipping, with which this chapter is primarily concerned, it is apparent that a watershed had been reached by 1853. This is evident, first, from the fact that two Montrealers, Macpherson and Holton, whose firms were the most important in the industry, disinvested completely, a probable result of their sense that, compared to railways, shipping along the upper St Lawrence was not likely to be an effective, or profitable, competitor.[58] And their actions might well have set off sympathetic reactions among other Montrealers who owned both steamboats and sailing vessels for the Montreal-to-Kingston trade. After 1851 there was a sharp reduction in the number of steamboats built at Montreal specifically for the upriver trade, as the serious effect was felt of the entrepreneurial shift away from investment in shipping for this region.

The pattern of entrepreneurship in upper St Lawrence shipping reveals two features of the climate of enterprise that will receive further comment in later chapters. One is the fact that many Montreal merchants owned shares in steamboats, demonstrating the heavy commercial interest in transportation. Moreover, the forwarding firms great and small were intercity partnerships in which the Montreal interest, though large, was not overwhelming. Brockville, Prescott, and Kingston shares in these concerns were substantial, and it is by no means clear that the Montreal partner was the dominant one in each firm. Secondly, although the well-informed William Hamilton Merritt stated in 1845 that 'the whole trade of the [upper] country has been thrown into the hands of a few forwarders, who control this steampower,' there was some successful competition for the large companies from Montreal steamboat owners and others in upriver ports such as Kingston.[59] The opening of the St Lawrence river to American shipping in 1849 and the competition provided by United States steamboats for St Lawrence traffic reduced still further the possibility of near complete control by the three large firms.[60]

French Canadians were almost entirely absent from the upriver forwarding business, in part because very few of their firms traded with Upper Canada. French Canadian merchants were attracted instead to shipping ventures in the section of the St Lawrence between Montreal and Three Rivers and in the Richelieu River Valley.

VIII

Shipping along the upper St Lawrence was always hazardous, especially before the canals were completed. In 1833 a new Montreal shipping firm was established as both forwarder and insurer of 'boats, vessels and goods and produce on the waters of Upper Canada and Lower Canada.'[61] This was the Canada Inland Forwarding and Insurance Company, which was followed three years later by the Quebec-based Canada Marine Insurance Company, a venture strongly supported by Montreal investors who secured incorporation in 1839.[62] In 1838, the

Prescott-based St Lawrence Inland Marine Assurance Company began to insure vessels and cargo between Montreal and Quebec and within a year was ready 'to take risks on all property conveyed on the waters of the Canadas.'[63] Several similar companies were formed during the next few years, including the Inland Steam Transportation and Insurance Company, the Canada Inland Assurance Company, and, finally, the Montreal Fire, Life and Inland Assurance Company, which seems to have become the major Montreal firm in shipping insurance by the mid-forties.[64] Rates varied according to perceived hazards. In 1839, companies insured at five shillings per £100 'and in proportion elsewhere.'[65] The upper St Lawrence above Montreal still threatened navigation even after canals had overcome the most serious difficulties, and this probably explains why no policy was allowed to exceed £2000. Although companies typically disclaimed responsibility for losses on the St Lawrence rapids at Coteau, Cedar, Cascade, or Lachine 'unless there is on the steamboat or barge a competent pilot or master duly authorized by us to run those Rapids,' they were still forced to pay for substantial losses on damaged cargoes.[66] But marine insurance was nevertheless a highly profitable and growing business along the river, despite occasional heavy claims. Recognizing a wider insurance frontier in the elimination of the Navigation Acts, the Montreal Company petitioned the government in 1850 for permission to 'take Marine risks generally on vessels navigating within or without this Province to and from ports whether British or foreign.'[67] The leadership of this large insurance organization had long rested in the hands of some of Montreal's most powerful men; the promoters included John Molson, John Torrance, and Joseph Masson, and more than a dozen other leaders in commerce, industry, and the legal profession.

4

Shipping on the middle St Lawrence and Richelieu rivers

I

St Lawrence River shipping between Montreal and lower ports, mainly Quebec, was a busy and lucrative business. Sailing ships inbound to Montreal from overseas ports often required towage for at least part of the trip, immigrants who had disembarked at Quebec needed transportation into the interior, and the traffic in goods and passengers between the two cities and intermediate ports mounted steadily. Among a number of firms operating steamboats and sailing ships along the river below Montreal, the Molson and Torrance lines were the largest. Begun in 1809 as a sideline to their brewery, at the start of the steamboat era, the Molson shipping business grew rapidly into the biggest on the Montreal-Quebec run. Their *Accommodation* was followed by larger and much more powerful tugs, which enjoyed a virtual monopoly of the intercity business. A separate firm, the St Lawrence Steamboat Company, which remained under Molson family control, was established in 1822 to manage the rapidly increasing business in freight, passengers, and towing. The Molson's shipping business went from strength to strength; during the thirties they added the *Canadian Eagle*, in 1841 the *Queen*, and in 1852 the *Ocean Wave*,[1] while ten large sailing ships were based in Montreal.

The Torrance line, or the Montreal Towboat Company, emerged in 1824 when John Torrance launched the *Hercules* specifically for towing sailing ships upriver from Quebec to Montreal.[2] By the early thirties the Torrances had at least two of their own large and powerful steamboats on this run, the *Britannia* and the *St George*, in addition to the *Canada*, which they owned jointly with the Molsons. After the addition of the *British America* in 1837, the *Britannia* was sold to a French Canadian group led by Hypolite Denault, a Laprairie merchant and shipowner, for service between Montreal and Chambly.[3] But so sensitive were the Torrances to possible competition that they made Denault agree, on pain of a £100 fine for each violation, to stay off the Montreal-Quebec run. In addition to steamboats, the Torrances had a fleet of seven schooners at Montreal to carry cargo along the river.[4] In 1851 they added the *Ontario* to their steamboat service.[5]

While they were clearly the dominant shipping firms on the middle St Lawrence and were able to fend off some parvenus, the Molsons and Torrances were not able to eliminate competition altogether. So large and lucrative was the Montreal-Quebec traffic that several smaller companies were able to keep a steamboat or two in business. One of these was the firm owned by the brothers William and George Tate, Montreal shipbuilders who were able to compete successfully against the giants through the forties. Beginning apparently in 1840 with the *Lady Colborne,* the Tates quickly added the *Lord Sydenham* in 1841 and the *North America* and three sloops in 1842; the *Lady Elgin* was added in 1848 and the *Crescent* in 1850.[6] The Tates, however, may have been little more than agents for the powerful Pollock and Gilmour timber and shipping interests that stretched from Bytown through Montreal, Quebec, and Chatham, New Brunswick, to Liverpool and Glasgow. The Pollock-Gilmour connection held mortgages on all but one of the Tate ships through the forties, although by the end of the decade the Tates were apparently free of this control. In 1850 they launched another steamer and by 1853 had two more on the intercity run.[7]

The People's Line, owned by John Ryan and a group of Quebec merchants, maintained a precarious competition on the same route during the forties. After boldly underbidding all others in 1847, Ryan was awarded the contract to transport mail between Montreal and Quebec for the next three years, but was unable to meet his obligations and defaulted to Torrance and shipowner John Munn.[8] Ryan bid again for the mail contract in October 1849, but by the spring he faced serious financial barriers that again prevented him from meeting his contractual obligations; after trying unsuccessfully to negotiate with Torrance for assistance he defaulted.[9] In May 1850, the deputy postmaster general, Thomas Stayner, confided to the provincial secretary, James Leslie, that 'any further reliance upon Mr Ryan would ... tend to subject us in an aggravated degree to the power of the Steam Boat Proprietors.'[10] After that date, no more was heard from the People's Line, and aside from minor competition from the Tates and from the Quebec Forwarding Company, a small firm that began in business in 1843, the Molsons and Torrances appear to have had the unchallenged run of the river until a new and much more powerful challenge emerged in the early fifties.[11]

By the mid-forties these two Montreal firms were no longer really competing against each other, except superficially. Not only were they collaborating to fix freight and mail carrying rates at high levels but they had in fact begun to merge their operations.[12] Since 1833 they had jointly owned the steamboat *Canada,* and in 1842 they bought the *Montreal,* followed five years later by the *Lord Sydenham,* as well as numerous barges and other craft in which they had combined interests.[13]

II

Although shipping on the upper and lower St Lawrence was dominated by large companies whose owners were entirely English, the shipping trade in the middle section of the river between Montreal and Three Rivers and in the Richelieu Valley attracted small firms whose members were largely French Canadian. While these areas were seriously afflicted by the setbacks to wheat cultivation during the early nineteenth century, and experienced severe distress during the mid-thirties, there were small clusters of minor but active French Canadian entrepreneurs with capital, foresight, and ingenuity in some of the villages along the south shore of the St Lawrence and along the Richelieu.[14] They were attracted to sail and steamboat ventures during the thirties, and they expanded their interests in the early forties, stimulated perhaps by the completion of the Chambly Canal, which facilitated the shipment of an increasing volume of exports to the American market. The expanded use of steamboats on Canadian waterways and the general quickening of economic activity following the building of railways through the region also encouraged the steamboat business along the Richelieu between Montreal and Lake Champlain.

During this period a number of French Canadian businessmen in Montreal also became entrepreneurs in shipping, and in 1845 both groups, the metropolitan and the local, came together to create La Société de Navigation du Richelieu, the earliest ancestor of Canada Steamship Lines.[15] The company (renamed La Compagnie du Richelieu in 1847) became the largest and probably the most successful shipping enterprise in the region and was the focus of temporarily successful efforts to unite the several steamboat companies serving the Richelieu and middle St Lawrence into one firm. These efforts were spurred on by a growing realization among the shipowners that the reduction of competition would help them to maintain profits in the face of rivalry from railways. By 1853 the agreement between the company and the other major steamboat operators on the Richelieu made three years earlier to limit competition between them was ended. The company then had to decide whether to renew arrangements with rivals, to return to open rivalry and to probable ruin, or to withdraw from the Richelieu trade altogether. It was the last option that was adopted.

Notwithstanding its name, La Compagnie du Richelieu did not confine its operations to that river. After 1850 the firm moved slowly into the St Lawrence to expand its freight, passenger, and raft-and-barge towing business between Montreal and other St Lawrence points and the Richelieu. The transfer to the St Lawrence trade was completed by the end of the 1853 shipping season, for that was the last year that the company operated any of its vessels on the Richelieu. Even with the formation of the shipowners' cartel of 1850 profits were modest, because the volume of shipping on the Richelieu declined significantly each year thereafter. Therefore the company's decision of 1853 to withdraw from the Richelieu and enter the lower St Lawrence was less a thrust to new frontiers than a flight from a declining commercial waterway.

Thus 1853 was a decisive year in the shipping trade of the Richelieu and middle St Lawrence rivers. It marks the exit from one and the entry into the other of a medium-sized firm with eight years' experience in a highly competitive field. The landmark is significant because the company, though smaller than the Molson and Torrance lines that dominated the intercity trade on the lower St Lawrence, was able to compete successfully with them for a share of the river traffic between Montreal and Quebec after 1854. Thus the growth of the company to that point demonstrates the ability of a group of French Canadian businessmen to build a successful enterprise. And the entry of La Compagnie du Richelieu into the St Lawrence, and the growing strength within the company of a group of Montrealers, illustrates the increasing domination by Montreal of transportation in its immediate hinterland.

III

The Richelieu river was a major channel of trade for Canadian lumber exports to the United States since 1827. During the late thirties and early forties, traffic through St John's mounted to significant figures, and this major Richelieu river entrepôt increased rapidly in size.[16] Much of the lumber dispatched to this American market was trans-shipped at Montreal. Though secondary to Quebec as a timber-exporting centre, Montreal received large quantities of forest products for its own urban needs as well as for export.[17] By the early thirties many sawmills in the Montreal district were producing lumber for house construction and the shipbuilding industry. At Chambly the large-scale production of lumber for the American market was a major industry.[18]

Stimulated by favorable conditions during the thirties and forties, a number of shipping ventures, large and small, were launched to carry this traffic between Montreal and river ports.[19] It was established practice for a number of entrepreneurs to band together in a company to buy an existing steamboat or commission a new one. As early as 1832, following a similar venture initiated in 1825, local investors established the Ferry Boat Company, under the leadership of S.H. Carlou, Flavien Amelin (Hamelin), a Montreal river pilot, and Paul Kauntz, to operate the *Canadian Patriot,* a steamboat of 196 tons, in the cross-river service between Montreal and Longueuil on the south side ·of the St Lawrence.[20] Two years later another group, calling itself the Source de Varennes Steamboat Company, built an even larger vessel for the lower St Lawrence trade, operating it under the management of Paul and Pierre Eustache Lussier and François-Antoine Larocque. In the same year the Union Canadienne Joint Stock Company built the steamboat *Union Canadienne,* with Andrew Achim, Victor Choniy, and Joseph Vincent, all of Longueuil, leading the enterprise.

The three companies were similar in structure. Each had sixty-four shares, most of which were held in units of one or two by a dozen or more unnamed investors. Each was managed by trustees or directors drawn from among the largest shareholders. Their leaders, and very likely most of the shareholders, were French Canadians, and they concentrated on the trade between Montreal and Longueuil.[21] Finally, except for François-Antoine Larocque, a prominent Montreal merchant and former fur trader (whose activities will be discussed later in this study), the owners of these vessels were apparently of minor economic importance in the region.

Most of the promoters of these enterprises might well have come from the class of shipowners, captains, and part-owners of small sailing craft operating along the river. The activities of these entrepreneurs were growing considerably during the thirties and forties as local and through (Montreal-Three Rivers-Quebec) traffic mounted. The ship registers of Montreal show a substantial increase during these decades in the number of small ships built for river traffic, and an active trade in these vessels.[22] While the operations of the big steamboat companies on the St Lawrence seem to have been concentrated mainly on the through-passenger and premium freight traffic between large river towns, the sloop and schooner owners had an open field in transport between the many small villages along the St Lawrence and lower Richelieu. Although the volume of traffic may not have been large, and perhaps not considerable enough to have remunerated steamboat companies, it was sufficiently substantial to have paid 'tramp' operators whose investment and costs were lower.

This smaller business, though perhaps not booming, was moderately thriving and expanding and consequently attracting further investment. The small craft were owned mostly by French Canadians, probably because of the virtual absence of English in the small river-front villages and the strong orientation of the Montreal commercial community as a whole to the upcountry trade. French Canadian merchants like Joseph Masson, on the other hand, had strong business connections in these St Lawrence and Richelieu villages.[23]

The small entrepreneurs were usually, though not invariably, sailors. The sole owners of the steamboat *Charlevoix* in 1837, however, were a sculptor, a tanner, and a physician. But these were exceptions to the general rule that almost all the sailing vessels built and registered at Montreal during the forties were owned by sailors, generally listed as 'master mariners.'[24] Of the fourteen schooners and sloops of fifty tons or more thus registered between 1841 and 1851, eleven had shipmaster-owners while another belonged to boat-builders.[25] Plying the St Lawrence and the Richelieu, they were mainly based in Montreal, because the bulk of their business was likely export staples and manufactured goods, both of which, particularly the latter, were handled there.

Although these mariner-entrepreneurs commonly built sailing ships, hundred-ton schooners or fifty-ton sloops, they were clearly capable of financing and managing steamboats. The formation of the three Montreal-Longueuil ferry boat companies, as well as the commissioning of the *Charlevoix* in 1837, show financial and managerial strength among the French Canadian shipmasters and small bourgeoisie in Montreal. A group of them had in 1845 formed La Société de Navigation du Richelieu, a successful and long-lived business. During its growth to a major St Lawrence river shipping firm by 1853 there was considerable evidence of adroit management.

IV

In all, there were thirty-five shareholders in the venture led by Jacques Felix Sincennes, Augustin St Louis, and Louis St Louis, who together bought sixty of the company's 130 shares valued at twenty-five pounds each.[26] There was in addition a large group of investors – all but five of them French Canadians – drawn mostly from the Richelieu Valley. Pierre Edouard Leclerc, Victor Hudon, and the prominent lawyer-politician Lewis Thomas Drummond, were the only Montrealers in the enterprise at the outset. Although Leclerc's business career is unknown, Hudon was a fairly prominent local businessman primarily involved at that time with his cousin Ephraim in a Montreal dry goods and groceries retail establishment. Fifteen years later Hudon went into the importing business on his own and, in the early seventies, into cotton manufacturing at Hochelaga outside Montreal.[27] As well as participating in the Richelieu venture, the Hudons bought a few sailing craft and probably operated them along the St Lawrence, serving small villages like St Césaire, St Dominique, and St Pie, where Victor Hudon had served his commercial apprenticeship.[28] In these little ports the firm might have conducted some trade of its own and very likely also carried consignments of cargo for other merchants. In 1849 a consignment consisting mainly of flour, pork and butter was sent to Halifax, occasioning comment in *Le*

Moniteur as the first attempt by a French Canadian firm to ship goods to Halifax.[29] Ventures of this sort occurred, of course, after the Société de Navigation du Richelieu was formed, but they indicate the degree of Hudon's interest in, and experience with, the management of a small shipping business further afield.

Sincennes was a Sorel merchant of considerable means. In the *Richelieu* venture alone he invested £1000 of the total cost of £3220. Although the St Louis family had shares in other shipping ventures, then and later, Jacques Sincennes appears to have confined his shipping interests to the Société de Navigation du Richelieu, whose affairs he came to dominate.[30]

Like various other concerns, the Société was formed to own and operate a steamboat that constituted its sole major asset, the *Richelieu*, built by Montreal shipbuilder William Parkyn. As new vessels were added, new shares were sold both to established shareholders and to new ones. And as an older vessel was sold off or retired, the shareholders in it were effectively out of the company unless they had invested in a newer steamboat. Hence the company's associates changed in this way as well as by the normal transfer of shares. While bookkeeping was complicated by the necessity to keep separate accounts for each vessel, the firm was able to function successfully under this system. Investors expected all profits after operating expenses to be divided among them without provision for building up reserves. In its early years the company had few of the features of the modern company; until 1857[31] it operated under articles of association that provided looseness and flexibility.

Its purpose was to exploit the through and intermediate passenger, premium freight, and towage business between Montreal, the Richelieu River and Lake Champlain. With the completion of the Chambly Canal in 1843, it became possible to establish uninterrupted steamboat communications between the St Lawrence and St John's. Indeed, the whole upper Richelieu-Lake Champlain region beckoned more enticingly than ever before, especially since the eastern United States market for Ottawa Valley lumber was beginning to increase.[32] Although there was potential future competition from railways, in this region such as the St Lawrence and Atlantic and the already extant Champlain and St Lawrence, their competitive advantage over steamboats was not yet established. And steamboats could serve the riverfront villages, which the railways would not reach.

With these inviting prospects the company was able to begin operations soon after its three trustees took delivery of the *Richelieu* on 7 October 1845. Not much could be accomplished during what remained of the 1845 navigation season, but the firm was in a position to begin next year's work strongly by seeking contracts with merchants along its route and announcing its forthcoming service. The 1846 season proved to be a very busy one, and the year ended with the company showing a large net profit of £1295, permitting a dividend of £8 per share.[33] This was a yield of 32 per cent. Timothé Franchère, the company president, was understating the achievement when he summed up the year's progress by saying that affairs were satisfactory.[34]

The Société de Navigation du Richelieu had an even better year in 1847. Although no new vessels were added to its fleet in the interval, profits were considerably higher; though operating expenses had increased, net profit stood at more than £2000. The company was able to pay £14, a return of 56 per cent to each shareholder, and still retain a modest surplus for contingencies.

Not surprisingly, other companies arose to exploit the traffic in this region. One was the Société de Navigation du St Laurent et du Richelieu, formed in September 1847 with a capital of £6500. This sum was raised from 260 shareholders[35] in order to commission the *Jacques Cartier,* a large steamboat built at Sorel. While a number of the supporters of this new company were also shareholders in the senior firm, many were new. And like the older firm, owned in large measure by non-Montrealers, the new one included many residents of St Lawrence and Richelieu villages like St Denis, St Antoine, St Mathias, Berthier, St Simon, St Charles, Chambly, Beloeil, St Ours, La Présentation, and Sorel. Indeed, Montrealers held only a total of thirty shares in this new venture, which was dominated by large shareholders like Jacques Félix Sincennes and George Cairns, who held forty each, and Timothé Franchère, P.E. Leclerc, and L. Guéront, each with twenty.

The fact that these men were also prominent in the more senior company may explain the proposals for the union of the two concerns almost as soon as the new firm's steamboat was ready in 1848. Indeed, the speed of the merger suggests a prearranged union. Accomplished early in March 1848, 'sur des Bases justes et équitables pour les deux Sociétés,' the merger promised a division of profits roughly according to the value of each steamboat, or in proportions of one-third and two-thirds to *Richelieu* and *Jacques Cartier* owners respectively.[36] The two steamboats, operated by the united company so that traffic was shared rationally between them, would have offered more effective service to prospective users along the route served. It was the first many mergers.

It was fortunate that the new Compagnie du Richelieu, as it was called, had the competitive strength of two steamboats and a larger body of shareholders than before, because more competition was being threatened. The 1848 navigation season brought serious rivalry from several other steamboats. And on the horizon was the threat of an even more severe contest for South Shore-Richelieu River traffic from the Champlain and St Lawrence Railway, whose owners were now planning their southward extension from St John's along the Richelieu to the United States border. Returns from the 1848 season showed the effect of steamboat rivalry. Profits for the Compagnie that year fell to less than one-half the 1847 figures, the dividends were down proportionately. Thus, when shareholders met in St Charles for the annual meeting in late February 1849 the results of heightened competition were explained to them, Louis Marchand, a Montreal merchant, sometime alderman, and member of the Harbour Commission, also explained that because the new ship had cost nearly £400 more than originally estimated more capital was required.[37]

During the navigation season of 1849 competition reduced the company's profits even further. Because of 'l'opposition acharnée contre laquelle nous avons eu à lutter ... nous avons été dans la nécessité de transporter les passagers de pont de Sorel, Berthier et autres ports intermediaires à Montréal pour la modique somme de dix sols et les contres produits et effets à des taux très reduits.'[38] Shareholders were reminded too that the general commercial depression had reduced the volume of goods shipped, while a cholera epidemic in Lower Canada had sharply reduced freight and passenger traffic. As a result profits were a mere £763/9, and only a small dividend of slightly more than 7 per cent was paid, a poor showing to investors who had enjoyed such high returns in 1846 and 1847. These high profits could be restored only by reducing or completely eliminating competition. A merger with one more major firm would soon force others into line. Independent owners of steamboats operating on the Richelieu would be ill-advised to continue on their own, because they would be likelier to succumb to the potentially more severe rivalry of railways. 1850 was therefore an appropriate year for the steamboat companies to face the question of their short-range profits and long-run viability, because the extension to the Champlain and St Lawrence was nearing completion and the St Lawrence and Atlantic's track was approaching Sherbrooke. Doubly vulnerable, the steamboat owners were being driven towards some form of fusion.

One of the major competitors was former shareholder Augustin St Louis, a Sorel merchant. Together with relatives he had bought twenty shares in the *Richelieu*, but had never become involved in the management of the concern and possibly had not held the shares for long. Despite the profitability of the venture St Louis might have objected to some features of its management and the increasing prominence in it of Jacques Félix Sincennes, who continued to buy shares whenever he could and was apparently intent upon dominating the company.[39] Although he did not have any recorded ownership of vessels before investing in the *Richelieu*, St Louis was now interested in running his own steamboat; in November 1847 he purchased the steamboat *Oregon*, apparently in conjunction with Thomas Stuart Mears, a Hawkesbury lumber merchant, who maintained a silent partnership in the vessel.[40] At approximately the same time,

St Louis purchased the steamboat *Vulcan* for the St Lawrence and the Richelieu run, cutting deeply into the Compagnie du Richelieu's business. In addition to these two vessels, St Louis seems to have been operating a third steamboat, the *St Louis,* which he owned exclusively, in the same areas.[41] Thus his carrying and towing capacity was probably as large as that of Compagnie du Richelieu.

There is no apparent explanation for St Louis's success in his shipping enterprise. It is probable that much of his freight was upper St Lawrence lumber shipped by Mears, his partner. In any event his firm was a menace which the Compagnie du Richelieu could well do without. At their annual meeting in February 1850 the shareholders quickly agreed to a proposal to appoint a committee to meet with St Louis and discuss suitable means for eliminating the competition which threatened to ruin them both.

At the same time other measures were taken to improve company efficiency. One was the allocation of one steamboat specifically to tow rafts and boats destined for the United States, presumably to facilitate their speedy movement along the Richelieu by ending the delays caused by stops to embark and discharge passengers.[42] Moreover, a schedule of rates for towing according to tonnage and size of vessel was published in local newspapers. Finally, the company petitioned the provincial Board of Works for the reduction of tolls on the Chambly Canal to the level of those in effect on the St Lawrence canals.

Although he was the most important rival, Augustin St Louis was not the only competitor to the Compagnie du Richelieu. Small sailing vessels also plied the Richelieu.[43] Some steamboats, owned by entrepreneurs in one of the river villages or in Montreal, worked along the Richelieu on scheduled runs picking up traffic and passengers. Other vessels devoted themselves almost exclusively to carrying lumber between Bytown and Whitehall, New York, at the foot of Lake Champlain. Some evidence of the extent of this business was revealed in February 1850 when Sincennes, himself an officer of the company, confessed that he and William McNaughton, a merchant and 'master mariner' of St Ours, had purchased the steamer *Lord Stanley* and five barges 'dans la vue de continuer la ligne de Transport de Bois de sciage entre Bytown et Whitehall'[44] Sincennes wanted to inform his colleagues because he had known for several years 'comme cette association de ma part pouvait peut etre porter ombrages à quelques membres de notre compagnie.'[45] But the shareholders could hardly have left without feelings of considerable suspicion of one who, while still an officer in the company had become one of its competitors. Still, there was hope that some of the most menacing competition could be contained, or eliminated altogether, if St Louis could be brought to terms.

Negotiations between him and the company less than one month later produced a set of proposals for an association with St Louis (who was represented by George-Etienne Cartier).[46] P.E. Leclerc of St Hyacinthe, the Richelieu company's president, announced that from the start of the 1850 shipping season the two firms' total carrying capacity would be combined, as had been accomplished in 1848 between the owners of the *Jacques Cartier* and the *Richelieu*. Eleven-eighteenths of the profits from the joint venture were to go to the company, and the remainder to Augustin St Louis and his son Augustin. The three-year agreement also stipulated that even though the Compagnie du Richelieu was to operate St Louis's ships as part of its own fleet, Augustin St Louis, fils and Félix St Louis, another of the senior partner's sons, were to be hired as captains on the *St Louis* and *Richelieu*.[47] Thus, in return for giving up their separate business, the St Louis were to be given a fixed proportion of slightly more than one-third of the new combine's total profits and to receive salaried positions as company employees. The company, on the other hand, had the advantage of controlling what must have been most of the steamboat carrying capacity between Montreal and Lake Champlain. Yet it had also the added responsibility and expense of maintaining three additional vessels. No attempt was made to bring other shipping companies, such as the Macpherson or Holton lines, which ran some vessels on this route, into the arrangement, probably because they offered no serious competition.

For the time being, at least, the syndicate, comprising five steamboats altogether, resisted the opportunity to extend their interests to the St Lawrence. In March 1850 the Ryan brothers of the Peoples' Line, who were unable to complete their mail contract, were trying to interest the Compagnie du Richelieu in assuming some of their obligations. The company, however, wisely refused to consider further the Ryans' proposal 'vues les circonstances actuel [sic] dans les Quelles se trouve la Compagnie du Richelieu.'[48] It would have been extremely hazardous for them to have ventured into the St Lawrence against the powerful Molson-Torrance combine, even had competition on the Richelieu been completely eliminated. In the spring of 1850 they could not even be sure that the recently made arrangements with St Louis would be free of disruptions. Yet perhaps the suggestion that their operations be widened to include the St Lawrence planted itself deeply in the company's memory, to be retrieved for consideration at a future date.

While the 1850 navigation season brought the firm some satisfaction, profits were disappointingly less than expected. Assessing the year's activities for the shareholders, J.B.E. Durocher of St Charles told shareholders that out of £3969/3/1 total profits, £2425/11/10 remained to the company after the St Louis were paid their proportion. Since this sum was spread over a capital of £18,000 (the value of the five steamboats) he announced that this year's dividend would be only 16 per cent and that the company would have to borrow

£1500 in order to pay them.[49] In effect, however, real profits were much larger, approximately 23 per cent, because the acquisition of St Louis's steamboats had cost the company nothing (except a fixed proportion of the annual profits). Thus, realistically speaking, the capital over which dividend was to be spread was only about £11,000, the total investment in the *Richelieu* and the *Jacques Cartier* and some small additions of equipment.

Profits were down for several reasons. Running costs of the five vessels was high[50]; and returns on passenger traffic from Montreal were unprofitable, probably because of competition from other steamboats and railways. Moreover, the company had entered into what proved to be unrewarding contracts to carry sawn lumber from Quebec and Three Rivers to Lake Champlain. An enormous disbursement for the rent of barges on which the lumber was carried resulted in little or no profit. In an apparent effort to avoid meeting the high rental charges the executive was authorized to buy five barges at a maximum cost of £500.

Despite these problems, the end of the 1850 season marked an important turning point in the history of the Compagnie du Richelieu. It had achieved five years of successfully profitable existence in the highly competitive Richelieu shipping trade. The effective and promising temporary union with St Louis had provided for two more years of control over most of the traffic on the Richelieu and middle St Lawrence, limiting costs and expanding profits. And the change of the firm's meeting place and offices from the Richelieu to Montreal, 'l'endroit le plus convenable pour y renuir le plus grand nombre d'actionnaires."[51] was of considerable symbolic importance. It pointed up the fact that the most lucrative traffic, chiefly lumber destined for Lake Champlain, was marshalled at Montreal and other points above it on the Ottawa or St Lawrence. Moreover, though changes in the ownership of shares were not systematically recorded, it was clear that most of the shareholders were by now Montrealers.

By early 1851, therefore, the Compagnie du Richelieu had reached a stage of both maturity and transition. It was no longer small, although competition was by no means obviated because of its enlarged size, and no longer a purely local Richelieu river enterprise. It had come some distance since its beginnings five years earlier in the tiny Richelieu River towns where subscriptions had been sold in the *Richelieu.* It had been absorbed by the metropolis, just as the Richelieu and middle St Lawrence economies were becoming increasingly unified with that of Montreal through the greater use of steamboats and railways, which bound regions together. Between 1851 and 1853, the transition from Richelieu to St Lawrence and from local entrepreneurship to metropolitan control continued. By the end of the 1853 season the process was complete.

V

Between 1850 and 1854 the volume of shipping on the Richelieu River fell drastically. Between 1848 and 1849 the number of ships passing through the Chambly Canal had mounted rapidly by nearly 600 per cent and the tonnage of goods carried by more than 400 per cent, from 18,835 tons to 77,216.[52] But the rate of increase itself fell during 1850 by 41.2 and 11.3 per cent in tonnage of goods and shipping. And for the next four years there were no significant increases in the volume of goods moved, while in 1852 there was a decrease of 20.9 per cent. At the same time shipping declined from 143,194 tons in 1850 to 90,691 tons in 1851 to 82,618 tons in 1852. Although tonnage of both vessels and goods rose in 1853 over the 1852 figures, they had merely returned to 1849-50 levels.

Any expectations that the 1853 revival of trade would continue were shattered by the drastic reduction in activity during the 1854 season, when tonnage of goods moving through the canal decreased by 26.7 per cent, while shipping capacity fell by 34.6 per cent.[53] This decline in the fortunes of the shipping industry along the Richelieu was not matched by similar decreases in shipping along other major Canadian waterways during the early fifties. The St Lawrence canals carried a rapidly accelerating volume of goods and shipping after 1849. Tonnages of commodities carried in 1851 increased by 56.3 per cent over 1850, and the following years saw increases of 9.3 (1852), 32.2 (1853), and 31.8 (1854) per cent.[54] Although Welland Canal traffic declined in 1854 by 15.3 per cent, it had been increasing every year from 1848 until 1853.[55] The same was true of both the Burlington Canal and the St Anne's lock on the Ottawa. Thus, the decline of shipping along the Richelieu contrasts sharply with the pattern of moderate growth of traffic along other major waterways. The decline was reflected at St John's, where the value of the export and import trade with the United States reached its apogee in 1850-1 and fell off sharply thereafter.[56] Thus, the Compagnie du Richelieu and its competitors were rivals for a shrinking volume of traffic during the early fifties, and this slow decline in the local shipping market largely explains the shippers' urgent drive for consolidation and ultimately their flight from the Richelieu altogether.

Sensitive to the beginnings of this traffic decline, the company's executive made further efforts to reduce costs during the few months following the annual meeting in February 1851. They decided that the practice of towing rafts on regular passenger trips would be continued, 'en autant que la compagnie éprouverait des pertes considérables en discontinuant les towages.'[57] It was agreed that the aging *Richelieu* would not be used any longer for towing but would be confined to two passenger trips weekly along the Richelieu and between Vercheres, Varennes, and Boucherville. Yet these and the earlier measures to improve efficiency failed to make the 1851 season more profitable than the previous one. A dividend of less than 14 per cent was paid, calculated on the basis of £16,000 capital, reduced from £18,000 due to the withdrawal of St Louis's steamboat *Vulcan* at the end of the 1850 season.[58] Although this represented a higher real return, because the St Louis steamboats were not a company investment, shareholders were crestfallen nonetheless. Perhaps the exciting returns of 1846 and 1847 would never again be reached, and the directors themselves may have begun to believe this.

For some years past, virtually the same men had filled positions on the company's executive. When shareholders chose their leaders in February 1851, they again selected P.E. Leclerc as president and Jacques-Félix Sincennes as secretary treasurer. But that year there were several additions to the board, which now included four Montrealers whose presence reflected the increasing orientation of the company to the metropolis.

For the first three years only one Montrealer, the merchant N.B. Desmarteau, had sat on the Board. He operated two dry goods stores, one by himself and another with Louis Marchand, who by 1852 had his own sturdy business.[59] Desmarteau and Marchand had jointly bought twelve shares in the *Jacques Cartier* in 1848 and were thus among the larger investors in the company. Marchand joined the board in 1850, as did J.M. Lamothe. The next year two more Montrealers, Victor Hudon and J.B. Boulanget, were recruited. Lamothe was a Montreal bookseller and stationer with a small but apparently prosperous business, while Boulanget was a merchant tailor.[60] These directors were all relatively unimportant businessmen in Montreal, except for Victor Hudon, whose affairs were probably of a somewhat larger order. However, they were all prospering in the late forties and acquiring sufficient experience and finance to be able to expand their entrepreneurial interests beyond the confines of their business bases, just as their English-speaking counterparts had been doing for some time. In adverse circumstances they had directed the growth of what was now a large and moderately successful shipping enterprise. With this achievement behind them and with the *élan* developed during the same years in their respective businesses in Montreal, they were prepared for the new prospects of the fifties. Among these prospects were both severe disappointments and beckoning possibilities.

It was probably with some chagrin that most shareholders heard of the St Louis family's intention, announced in February 1852, to withdraw the *St Louis* and the *Vulcan* from the syndicate at the expiration of its term.[61] It is not clear what the family intended to do with their liberated ships, but the precaution was taken to require the St Louis's to protect and maintain the rights of the company by refraining from competing with them. Even though the agreement had only one more year to run – for the 1852 navigation season – the company wanted to prevent the recurrence of open competition on the Richelieu-middle St Lawrence trade.

A new and inviting business prospect now arising was the establishment of connections with the St Lawrence and Industry Village railway, which had been completed in May 1850.[62] This was a short twelve-mile line running from Lanoraie, on the north shore of the St Lawrence some fifty miles downstream from Montreal, to Industry Village on the L'Assomption River in Berthier County. Preliminary contacts with the railway were made in 1852 through Montreal businessman Jedediah Hubbell Dorwin, the president of the Industry Village and Rawdon Railroad, a northward extension of the St Lawrence and Industry Village completed the same year.[63] In return for the purchase of £1000 of the railway's shares the shipping company was given 'le privilège exclusif de faire accoster les vaisseaux à vapeur à l'exclusion de tous autres au quai de la dite Compagnie du Chemin de Fer tout pour y prendre et débarquer seuls des voyageurs et des Marchandises et effets transportés ou a être par le dit Chemin de Fer.'[64] Further arrangements necessary for the establishment of efficient service between the two companies were approved in advance.

1852 had been a somewhat more profitable year for the company, bringing a dividend of 25 per cent. Yet even with this favourable turn the future was highly uncertain because of the impending withdrawal of the St Louis boats from the syndicate and the possibility of renewed uncontrolled competition, assurances to the contrary notwithstanding. Thus the link to the St Lawrence and Industry Village Railway might have presented itself to the shareholders as a means of compensating for profits reduced because of renewed rivalry and avoiding sole reliance on the Richelieu trade. It was an inviting prospect for the Compagnie du Richelieu to have the monopoly of the promising new railway's shipping business. Although that line was only twelve miles long, there were prospects of further extensions into a fast-growing, productive area on the north shore of the St Lawrence.[65] The *Jacques Cartier,* the company's newer and more efficient steamboat, was assigned to this route, the aged *Richelieu* being left to serve the Richelieu River. But, by the end of the 1853 navigation season, the once thriving steamboat traffic on the Richelieu had so much diminished that it was no longer felt profitable to keep a steamboat running on the river at all. 'Vu la diminution du Commerce, transport des passagers etc. qui s'est opéré sur la Rivière Chambly [Richelieu] surtout depuis la Confection du Chemin de fer du St Laurent et de l'Atlantique,'[66] the company decided to discontinue the operations of the *Richelieu* and to sell the vessel, 'pourvu que sa mise à prix ne soit pas moin de

Deux mille quatre louis Courant.' A month later the shareholders heard that the eight-year-old steamboat had been sold for £2500 and the proceeds would be distributed in proportion to shares.[67]

With the sale of the *Richelieu* and the assignment of the *Jacques Cartier* solely to the St Lawrence trade, an era in the history of the Compagnie du Richelieu, whose name was now strikingly inappropriate, had come to an end. The transition to the St Lawrence, begun in 1850-1, was now complete. With Montreal businessmen like Marchand, Lamothe, Boulanget, and Hudon still comprising the overwhelming majority of the company's officers, as had been the case since 1851, the company's character as a Montreal-owned and Montreal-based enterprise was strongly confirmed. Its management was in the hands of Montrealers, and its prosperity was affected by the metropolis, where other entrepreneurs were finally bringing the St Lawrence and Atlantic Railway to completion. Drawn completely to Montreal, the company after 1853 concentrated its attention exclusively to shipping along the St Lawrence. During the next three years the Compagnie du Richelieu demonstrated not only that it could survive the rigorous competition of four other steamboat companies for the traffic between Montreal and Three Rivers but also that it could provide the necessary leadership to unite with three of these rival firms, La Compagnie du Lac St Pierre, La Compagnie du Cultivateur, and La Compagnie de Traverse de Laprairie, to form La Compagnie de Navigation de Montréal à Trois Rivières in March 1856.[68]

The new company would consist of three steamboats for the Montreal-Three Rivers trade, and two new vessels, still on the stocks at Cantin's Montreal shipyard, for the Montreal-Quebec run. Hence, on the verge of the 1856 shipping season, barely ten years after the company began operations on the Richelieu and the middle St Lawrence, it had become an important part of a large syndicate formed to service the shipping trade on the lower St Lawrence between the major centres of Montreal, Three Rivers, and Quebec. This subsequent growth of the firm will not be discussed further; it is mentioned to show that 1853 marked not just the end of one stage but also the beginning of another in the company's development.

VI

Along the Richelieu and the middle St Lawrence a great many of the steamboats, perhaps most, were owned by groups or single individuals, almost all of whom were French Canadians. Virtually all shares of La Compagnie du Richelieu, and the vessels with which the company competed, were owned by French Canadian merchants, some from St Lawrence or Richelieu river ports and an increasing number from Montreal. That French Canadians clearly dominated this business and that the Montreal element became predominant within La Compagnie du Richelieu are important facts. But even more significant is the fact that these French Canadian enterprises were characterized by a verve and resilience, by an unwavering pursuit of profits sometimes attributed to 'the Protestant ethic,' that enabled them to survive against each other.

This discovery calls in question some popular generalizations about French Canadian business and entrepreneurial *élan*. Fernand Ouellet has asserted that French Canadians were not equal to the challenges of the modern commercial economy as it emerged in Quebec. As early as the late eighteenth century, for example, in the fur trade 'l'entreprise canadienne-française n'a pas été suffisamment sensible a l'appel de la conjoncture ... [des] exigences du temps.'[69] The failure of French Canadians to participate fully in business was attributed in the forties by Etienne Parent mainly to their 'mad passion for the professions.'[70] The sociologist Norman Taylor has recently argued, moreover, that resistance to change and inflexibility before altering business circumstances has remained characteristic of many present-day French Canadian businessmen.[71] The subject of French Canadian entrepreneurship obviously requires much more detailed examination, particularly of small-scale businesses, such as the early Compagnie du Richelieu, and the business affairs of many bourgeois. The discovery of other successful enterprises, though comparatively small but nevertheless of substantially larger wealth than realized, would force such generalizations to be revised. Still not known is the extent to which French Canadian entrepreneurs were forced to accept alien values, in Alfred Dubuc's words, 'to participate, in some way, in the values and behaviour of the main group of entrepreneurs.'[72] As we have seen, French-Canadians appear to have been as aggressive and flexible in business as other Montreal businessmen, and that many of them were fully capable of adjusting successfully to the mid-nineteenth century challenges in transportation.

5

Ocean shipping and trade

Between the late thirties and the early fifties the number and capacity of vessels engaged in ocean shipping between Montreal and outside ports expanded markedly as a result of the rapidly mounting volume of exports and imports passing through the port of Montreal.

Inbound from Liverpool, Glasgow, and London each spring, the barques slowly eased up the St Lawrence past Quebec towards Montreal, heavy with their loads of general cargo consigned to the city's importers. Woollen and cotton goods, manufactured hardware, pig iron, bar iron, and steel, fine clothing and hats, and hundreds of items meticulously selected by British agents, or by some Montreal merchants themselves on their annual buying trips, were unloaded during these busy April and May days. Hastily carted from dockside to warehouses, display rooms, and auction rooms and advertised in newspapers, they were sold to country merchants from Upper Canada and the towns and villages neighbouring Montreal. For several almost frantic weeks the waterfront bustled with teamsters, longshoremen, and sailors, watched over by nervous merchants and their clerks.

Despite the shallows of Lake St Peter – simply a widening in the river just below Montreal – Montreal's ocean shipping trade grew immensely during the forties as trade to British ports mounted. Yet the city's ocean trade was by no means exclusively with Britain. By 1849 an impressively large number of ships – though only a small proportion of the total – ran between Montreal and lower ports in the Gulf of St Lawrence and the Maritimes. A few ships even arrived each year from the West Indies with sugar and molasses. From the Magdalen Islands came barrels of fish and whale oil, and from Arichat, St John's, Saint John, Halifax, and Canso came fish, and from the West Indies sugar, molasses, and whale oil. Much of this substantial trade was conducted by a small but important group of French Canadian merchants, including Ephraim and Victor Hudon who as noted above were interested also in the Richelieu trade. Hubert Paré, later a promoter of the Montreal and Bytown Railway, and Alexis Painchaud, a local shipowner whose fleet of sloops and schooners for years plied regularly to the Magdalen Islands and occasionally to Antigonish.[1] Besides these, cargoes of sugar, coffee, and molasses arrived from Havana, wine and brandy from Oporto, Spain, and vinegar from Bordeaux, while ships from St Ubes with salt and coal from Hartlepool, and plaster from Antigonish, came into the crowded harbour of Montreal.

All incoming ships from sea — some arriving with coal ballast — stood round the harbour area and up into the Lachine Canal waiting to be loaded with the produce coming down from the interior. Flour, wheat, lumber, ashes, and staves destined for Liverpool, Glasgow, and London made up the cargoes most commonly loaded at Montreal, but there was also salt and flour bound for Halifax or St John's, and butter, pork, peas, beef, oatmeal, oars, and even live animals consigned for Liverpool.[2]

The availability of powerful steam tugs to pull sailing ships through the strong St Mary's current into the harbour and the establishment of Montreal as an official port of entry in 1832 greatly aided the advancement of the city's ocean traffic and the increase in commerce. But in order to reduce delays and to lessen the cost of this traffic, it was necessary to improve the navigability of the river between Montreal and Quebec to allow ocean-going vessels to ascend the St Lawrence unimpeded to Montreal. The Montreal businessmen most deeply affected by these matters were members of the commercial houses that processed exports and imports. Although these firms remained essentially unchanged in this period, particularly in their mode of operation, some of the large British houses were developing stronger Canadian partners. Merchants were taking an active role in government commissions to improve the shipping facilities to Montreal. Foundations were being laid for the expansion of shipping generally and, at the end of the period, for the introduction of steamships. And at this time the Allan Line, based in Montreal and the major shipping firm serving the city, was founded and strengthened.

The increase in the volume of shipping and the amount of trade at Montreal between 1837 and 1853 was substantial. The number of ocean-going vessels coming upriver to Montreal increased from sixty-five in 1838 to 208 in 1841, and, after a decrease to 151 in 1843, rose again to a plateau of two hundred ships or more annually from 1844 to 1847, a level to which the figures returned in 1850 following the downturn of 1848 and 1849. After 1850 shipping activity in the port remained at an annual average of two hundred ships or more for the

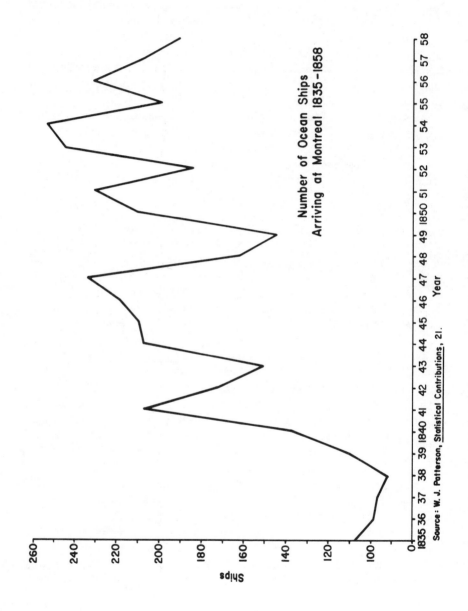

Number of Ocean Ships
Arriving at Montreal 1835-1858

Source: W. J. Patterson, Statistical Contributions, 21.

Year

Ships

rest of the decade[3] (see figure). The ship tonnage shows approximately the same proportional fluctuations.[4]

While the fortunes of the city's import and export trade explain the changing demand for shipping at Montreal, the value of imports was normally several times that of exports in any one year (see Table 1). In 1841, for example, the figures were £2.1 million for imports and £0.7 million for exports at Montreal, and in 1848 the figures were £1.5 million and £0.4 million.[5] Between 1838 and 1845 imports rose sharply, followed by a steep decline of approximately 40 per cent over the next four years. In 1850 began a substantial upturn in imports and in the following year figures were nearly up to the 1847 level. Between 1852 and 1853 imports skyrocketed, increasing by 60 per cent in one year.[6] Although there were subsequent fluctuations, imports during the remainder of the fifties were at a much higher average annual value than in the previous decade.

The sources of the imported goods were changing. Although the chief supplier of Montreal's imports was still Britain, during the forties the value of imported goods from the United States expanded significantly, increasing from £558 in 1842 to £143,219 in 1844; imports held at approximately that figure for the remainder of the decade. Indeed, while the fluctuations in British imports followed almost perfectly the pattern for total Montreal imports, after 1845, when imports were falling off sharply, the inflow of goods from the United States did not decline. The decrease of 10 per cent between 1845 and 1846 was more than offset by the 20 per cent increase in volume during the following year.[7]

Generally, exports from Montreal followed the same pattern as imports, decreasing or increasing commensurately with them. There were only minor variations in this correlation, as in 1841-2 and 1849-50, when imports rose while exports fell, and in 1846-7, when exports rose as imports dropped.[8] Although the proportion of exports to imports varied between 1:3 and 1:4 according to official figures, exports from Montreal might have been greater than that. Contemporaries noted that export items were frequently loaded on ships at Montreal, but not assigned to that port because the vessels picked up other cargo at Quebec which, for the sake of convenience, was given credit for all cargo on board.

Statistics of exports of individual items for the years 1845 to 1850 show that, with some exceptions, approximately the same pattern obtained as with aggregate exports, as in the case of the major commodities ashes, wheat, butter, peas, and flour. Declines after 1845 to lows in 1848 were followed by upturns thereafter. But several deviations occurred. For example, beef exports rose sharply after 1849 by nearly 600 per cent, while pork and barley exports, after

TABLE 1
Imports and exports at Montreal 1841-8 (£ stg)

Imports

Years	British colonies			United States	Other foreign states	Totals	
	Great Britain	West Indies	North America			Sterling	Currency
1841	1,632,489	–	38,615	10,763	17,978	1,699,837	2,068,135
1842	1,614,981	1,072	32,686	558	12,570	1,661,868	2,021,106
1843	911,828	1,255	54,576	58,509	33,751	1,059,921	1,289,571
1844	1,803,226	367	55,578	143,219	30,922	2,034,315	2,475,084
1845	1,990,864	8,329	33,876	100,114	20,446	2,153,631	2,620,252
1846	1,734,760	31	37,111	90,513	31,205	1,893,623	2,303,908
1847	1,491,877	270	49,487	126,557	27,785	1,695,978	2,063,440
1848	1,062,948	–	29,522	107,873	17,138	1,217,604	1,481,418

Exports

Years	British colonies			United States	Other foreign states	Totals	
	Great Britain*	West Indies	North America			Sterling	Currency
1841	526,064	11,782	35,543	–	–	575,400	700,070
1842	565,681	5,137	28,137	–	–	598,955	728,729
1843	285,876	5,720	27,470	–	–	319,067	388,199
1844	597,276	3,444	16,766	–	450	617,916	754,231
1845	571,096	–	21,339	–	–	592,436	720,797
1846	517,021	–	18,784	5,293	–	541,100	658,338
1847	641,928	–	32,878	22,587	400	697,794	848,982
1848	283,104	–	27,474	11,124	358	322,061	391,841

SOURCE: JLA (1949), App. B
* Includes Ireland

declining to record lows in 1848 for the half-decade 1845-50, levelled off in 1849 and fell again by more than 50 per cent in 1850.[9]

II

The ships that carried these commodities to and from Montreal were relatively large vessels, brigs, barques, and 'ships' up to 400 tons, the size that could safely navigate the St Lawrence river up to Montreal before the channel through Lake St Peter was deepened. While relevant statistics are very meagre for this period, newspaper summaries of the 1837 and 1844 seasons give information on ownership of the vessels calling at Montreal. Only two of the eighty-four vessels arriving at Montreal in 1837 (seven made two trips, so that total arrivals that year were ninety-one) were listed as 'belonging to' (which one assumes means registry or ownership at) Montreal.[10] Aside from Quebec and the Maritimes ports of Sydney, Halifax, and Saint John, which together accounted for twelve vessels, the remaining seventy were based at British ports. Although registry did not necessarily mean that the owners resided in the same port, or even in the same country, that was a strong presumption. There were also intraimperial partnerships. The Allan ships, for example, were usually owned jointly by several members of the family, including Hugh in Montreal and his brothers in either Glasgow or Liverpool.[11] Both ownership and port of registry of these vessels changed often enough to make it difficult to pinpoint them under these headings. But even with these qualifications it is clear that the overwhelming majority of ocean-going vessels calling at Montreal were owned as well as registered in Britain.

Perhaps the major reason for British command over the city's ocean shipping was that a ship based in Montreal would not have been fully utilized, because it was not a year-round port – being busy only from the beginning of May until the end of October. There might also have been a problem with respect to insurance at Montreal of both vessels and cargo. Montreal insurance companies appear to have specialized mainly in fire and inland shipping insurance, while British and American companies with Montreal agencies seem to have been solely interested in fire insurance.[12] British registry would perhaps have made it easier to secure necessary insurance coverage and the fullest utilization of the vessel at the same time. Although registry of ocean-going ships in Montreal seems to have increased somewhat during the forties, mainly because of the Allan interests, British predominance did not change significantly.

Montreal newspapers of the thirties and forties abounded with notices advertising the availability of shipping space in Liverpool- and Glasgow-bound vessels, and the names of certain ships and owners occur with regularity. The

John Bell and the *Great Britain* were well-known trading ships on the London-Montreal run, and the *Great Britain* was frequently the first vessel into the harbour in spring.[13] Both vessels were owned by the London firm of Temperley, Carter and Darke, from which the Temperley-Ross line later emerged. The Gilmour-Pollock ships from Glasgow and Liverpool were also frequent callers at Montreal carrying imports from Britain; but since these vessels were apparently utilized solely for the timber trade they could be said to belong more properly to Quebec, a much more important timber-exporting port than Montreal.[14]

The importing business was conducted by a considerable number of firms that acted as the consignees of the ships. Some firms were outstandingly busy in this period. In 1837, for example, several were consignees of three or more ships. These concerns were described in Montreal directories either as auctioneers or, more usually, as general merchants. Among the busiest firms that year were three: LeMesurier, Routh and Company, Millar, Edmonstone and Company, and Peter McGill, each of which received twelve ships. Six vessels were consigned to Gillespie, Moffatt and Company that year, and five each went to the firms of Robertson, Masson and Company, and R. Froste. The three concerns of Cunningham and Buchanan, Tobin and Murison, and J. Torrance received four ships each, while four other firms, Atkinson and Company, R.F. Maitland and Company, Andrew Shaw, and Molson, Davies and Company received three.[15]

Seven years later, during the 1844 navigation season, when the total number of ships arriving from sea was 171, these same firms were consignees of many cargoes,[16] but their relative importance had declined. Peter McGill received nine, Millar, Edmonstone and Company six, and LeMesurier, Routh and Company six, while only Gillespie, Moffatt and Company had increased its business to fifteen cargoes. Other houses increased their trade considerably: Andrew Shaw received eight ships' cargoes, S. Greenshields and Son six, John Torrance five, and Augustin Cuvillier and Sons fifteen. The latter specialized in selling goods at auction on commission and during the late thirties appear to have been the most active firms in this business.[17] Moreover, firms new to Montreal were doing as large a business as older establishments: J. and A. Burns took in six cargoes, Thorne and Heward eight, Knapp and Noad six, and Dinning and Senior seven. At the same time, many other firms received fewer consignments, and the majority of the much larger number of houses in this business — out of a total of fifty-three in 1844 — were consigned only one or two cargoes that season.

LeMesurier, Routh and Company seems to have been able to maintain its position as a major consignee of ocean ships coming up to Montreal from 1837 through 1853.[18] In 1848 many vessels were consigned to them. The firm was composed of two principal partners, H.L. Routh and H. LeMesurier, of Quebec.

Routh was a Montrealer who, besides his commercial activities, was for many years the Montreal agent for the Royal Fire and Life Assurance Company as well as an active member of the Montreal Board of Trade and a director of the Bank of Montreal (1834-5).[19] While Routh's firm was one of the largest general merchandising establishments in the city, he was also active, until 1855, in the lumber trade,[20] living for a short while in New York. But, his main interest was commerce and, as if to underline the fact, in the late forties he became a warden of the Montreal Trinity Board, a government-appointed body that administered navigation on the St Lawrence between Montreal and Quebec.[21]

Another major importing general merchandising firm was Peter McGill's, which, like LeMesurier, Routh and Company, seems to have remained essentially unchanged from the late thirties to the early fifties. Other aspects of McGill's career will be discussed at length, especially his railway interests, but these should not obscure the important commercial side to his business interests. McGill seems to have reorganized his commercial affairs after 1838, when the partnership between himself, William Price of Quebec, Kenneth Dowie of Liverpool, and James Dowie of London in a vast lumber business broke up. McGill, together with the Dowies and Nathaniel Gould of London, continued their commercial activity of importing British manufactured goods and exporting Canadian timber.[22] While McGill's business arrangements are not easy to unravel, it appears that he was much less an independent entrepreneur than an agent of his London and Liverpool partners. The partnership was dissolved in January 1843, and from that time on the business was carried on in liquidation, with McGill very heavily in debt to Gould and Dowie.[23]

His ability to continue a solvent business was seriously impaired by severe reverses during the downturn in business activity after 1847. Although he was still able to meet all claims against him, McGill was apparently losing what commercial vitality he once possessed. By 1851 he had no more desire to expand his general merchandising business, and, though he remained moderately active, his major concern was to wind up his commercial affairs.[24] From the late forties onward, McGill devoted himself to the Bank of Montreal and to a lesser degree to public affairs, including a brief membership in the provincial Executive Council in 1847-8 and the presidency of the Montreal Board of Trade in 1848. His once-great trading house, however, slowly withered away.

The third, and in some ways the most dynamic, general merchandising firm active in importing was Millar, Edmonstone and Company. This was an old partnership that had become one of Montreal's most important commercial houses as early as 1816 under the name of Millar, Parlane and Company.[25] At that early date their company was not only a wholesale importer but also a retailer of silks and fancy goods, a diversity typical of general merchants. James

Millar, one of the founders, was a native of Ayrshire, Scotland. While he was building a strong business, he was also active in a number of associated Montreal institutions such as the Bank of Montreal, the Montreal Insurance Company, and the Committee of Trade.[26] Millar died in the summer of 1838; Parlane, of whom nothing is known, appears to have passed out of the partnership well before Millar's death.

William Edmonstone joined the old firm around 1831, and for some years before 1837 it had been known as Millar, Edmonstone and Company.[27] In 1831 Hugh Allan, then only twenty-one, arrived from Ayrshire to apprentice in the firm. He was the second son of Captain Alexander Allan, who had been sailing ships between the Clyde and Montreal since the early years of the century.[28] Becoming a full partner in 1835, Allan significantly expanded the operations of Millar, Edmonstone. While remaining a large general merchandising establishment importing considerable quantities of goods, the firm began in 1836 to make the transition to ship-owning with the acquisition of its first vessel, the 214-ton barque *Thistle*.[29] Although still attentive to trading, the firm thus laid the foundations for its own shipping business.

Other important importers included Gillespie, Moffatt and Company. The Montreal partner was George Moffatt, who was busily involved in Montreal railway promotions during the late forties. Like Peter McGill, however, Moffatt's prime business concerns were essentially in commerce, where his business base was the firm he had entered as a clerk in 1811 after a few years of service with McTavish, McGillivray and Company followed by a very brief partnership with Alexander Dowie.[30] The partnership evolved over many years. When Moffatt entered it was Parker, Gerrard and Ogilvy, of which the major Montreal partner was apparently Samuel Gerrard. It changed to Gerrard, Yeoward, Gillespie and Company, then to Gerrard, Gillespie, Moffatt and Company.[31] The latter partnership illustrates the complexities typical of these associations. It was formed in 1816 and was to last for five years from the spring of 1817. By the agreement, Robert and George Gillespie, Jasper Tough, and George Moffatt were each to hold two shares, while William Finlay and W. Stevens would each have one until 1 May, 1819, when their shares would be doubled. Alexander Gillespie of London was to be persuaded to participate as was a Mr Strachan, also of London. Moreover, Robert Gillespie was to have the option of pulling out altogether should his brother, Alexander, refuse to participate; but if Robert remained he had the option of bringing in John Jamieson as of 1 May 1819. To recount the detailed changes in the partnership thereafter would be tedious, but they were numerous during the five years.[32]

By 1821 Moffatt was evidently the leading Montrealer in the firm, Samuel Gerrard having retired that year. Further changes occurred between then and the late thirties when the firm became Gillespie, Moffatt and Company, including as principal partners Moffatt in Montreal and the brothers Gillespie in London. Other partners between 1837 and 1842 were the Montrealers James Blackwood Greenshields and Robert Paterson, Lewis Moffatt and Alexander Murray of Toronto, James Gillespie of Quebec, and Robert Gillespie jr, of London.[33] The Toronto participation by Moffatt's son Lewis marks a strengthening of the firm's Canadian connections.

In its general merchandising business, Gillespie, Moffatt and Company was one of the largest Montreal houses handling groceries, dry goods, and hardware; it was dealing in staples as well. In 1848 the firm's relative importance was at least as great as it had been ten years earlier. Its warehouse was one of the biggest in Montreal and had a capacity of 25,000 barrels of flour. The partners were never seriously interested in developing shipping as a sideline business, and the only gesture they made in that direction was the purchase in 1835 of a 376-ton sailing vessel, the *Douglas,* for the transatlantic run.[34]

Another major import and export house was Robertson, Masson and Company, which included as the major Montreal partner Joseph Masson, whose business interests were by no means confined to commerce, although, as with his colleagues in other general merchandising houses, that was his essential interest. Founded by Hugh Robertson in the early nineteenth century, the firm had come, at the Montreal end, into Masson's own control in 1828. Since at least the mid-twenties he had apparently been in charge of its dealings with French Canadian merchants in nearby villages, especially on the south shore, where he purchased wheat and potash and sold manufactured goods.[35]

While relatively substantial information exists on the larger mercantile houses, such as the first three discussed here, and on companies of secondary importance like Masson's, very little is known of smaller firms engaged in export and import and, in a minor way, in shipping. Consignees of only one to four cargoes of imported goods annually, these houses nonetheless operated over many years and, in cases, continuously over the years from 1837 to 1853. In 1837, they included many firms whose principal partners are now largely unknown.

One exception is Andrew Shaw, a minor merchant but a prominent local figure because of his participation in Montreal public and social affairs. His career helps to illustrate the diversity of the business community. Born in Glasgow in 1775, Shaw moved to Canada in 1810 to enter the well-established mercantile firm of James Dunlop. In 1815 he began business on his own and, according to Dorwin, Montreal's omniscient commercial observer, became 'a large West India merchant.'[36] At some point, however, Shaw shifted his commercial attention almost entirely to trade with Scotland. Although he had other interests, including the Montreal Telegraph Company, of which he was a very active promoter and, in 1847, the first president,[37] his prime business concern, aside from trade itself, was shipping. In 1847 he had built two large ships at Quebec, the *Liverpool* of 918 tons and the *Jane* of 700 tons. The latter was sold to John Molson only three months later, but the *Liverpool,* although reregistered in London shortly after completion, seems to have remained in Shaw's possession.[38] He purchased the barque *Sarah* from John Molson in 1842, and he may well have owned other ships at that time because he was reputed to have been an extensive shipowner. Shaw went bankrupt in 1849, but he recovered sufficiently to remain in business. His firm was still in operation in 1853, although perhaps not as actively as before, and he took a leading part in the establishment of the Canadian Ocean Steam Navigation Company in 1854.[39]

Transatlantic partnerships, while still a feature of Montreal commerce, were therefore beginning to change. Although generalizations are hazardous because of the shortage of information, the transition to Canadian-based firms for the export-import trade was most certainly not complete by the early fifties. But in a number of instances the Montreal-based partner was becoming as important as the British. It was by no means evident in every case that dependence on British connections was lessening, or that the beginnings of the shift were entirely salutary for the firms involved. Peter McGill seems to have paid a price for his quasi-independence, while George Moffatt was able to maintain London participation and expand the Canadian operations of his firm at the same time. In the case of Robertson, Masson the Canadian partner appears to have become the principal one in a Montreal and Glasgow firm. In others, such as Millar, Edmonstone and Company and LeMesurier, Routh and Company, the firm's major partners were apparently all Montrealers likely retaining only London, Liverpool, or Glasgow connections.

The reasons for this subtle beginning of a shift in control are far from clear. Very likely the uncertainty in Montreal in the late forties about the future of commercial relations with Britain ruptured some transatlantic partnerships and strained others. While legal bankruptcy was not, to be sure, a convincing indication of real insolvency, large numbers of them occurred during this period, and evidence in one or two cases suggests that the Montreal merchant involved did not suffer permanent, or perhaps any, damage.[40] If the loss was incurred in Britain, it probably undermined British confidence in Canada, at least temporarily. The longstanding British ties with most mercantile houses in Montreal may also have been weakened by the growing Canadian orientation towards the United States in the late forties as a market and as a point of departure to Europe. While exports to Britain from Montreal declined after 1847, they were increasing to the United States, and after the mid-forties the value of goods legally imported to Montreal from the United States increased markedly.[41] The railways being planned and built by Montrealers in those years were all designed to channel this growing north-south commerce as well as the overseas trade with the mother country. Thus, while the American trade amounted to only a very small fraction of Montreal's trade with Britain, it was more than just a minor distraction in the established pattern of commercial relationships.

III

While these alterations were gradually taking shape during the late forties they were likely not evident to most Montrealers, because the largest shipping and commercial firms in the city benefited from large-scale British investment. The outstanding example was Edmonstone, Allan and Company, an instructive case study of the role of British capital in Montreal's commercial houses and of the diversification of a business in trade and shipping.

The Allan shipping firm's affiliations with the St Lawrence were probably the most longstanding of any of the companies whose vessels sailed regularly to Montreal. In the mid-twenties Alexander Allan had decided to establish one of his five sons in Montreal both as Canadian agent of his expanding St Lawrence operations and, perhaps, as a potential family entrepreneur in the promising business of North American staples and the limitless economic opportunity of the New World. Hugh was chosen for this role. After preliminary training in the family's Greenock office, Allan, Kerr and Company, he came to Montreal in 1826 on the *Favourite,* a Montreal-built ship.[42] There he was placed in the care of William Kerr, a Montreal merchant who, as the Greenock firm's name implies, was perhaps linked with the Allans in a partnership or other business arrangement. After three years of training in Canada, Allan returned to Scotland, and then was sent out again in 1831 apparently to apprentice with Millar, Parlane and Company, a firm probably associated with the Greenock Allan firm in a partnership or co-operative arrangement because Hugh Allan rose rapidly in four years to become a full partner in 1835.[43]

Allan was trained in both the commercial and shipping branches of the business. Until 1835 he had been a wheat buyer on the south shore of the St Lawrence near Montreal, but he seems to have begun early to concentrate on shipping and shipbuilding for which his family connections and training suited him. In 1836 the firm began constructing several ships in its own Montreal yard, under the direction of master builder E.D. Merritt. All were sailing ships but one, the *Alliance,* an immense 434-ton steamer, for the Montreal-Quebec run, perhaps built primarily for the purpose of towing the firm's ships upriver.[44] The construction of these ships says much, of course, for Allan's *élan* and experience, as well as for the substantial existing Montreal shipbuilding industry, which also produced a large number of steamboats. Allan, however, added administrative skill, entrepreneurial aggressiveness, and the strength of the transatlantic Allans, whose experience and resources suggested the power and promise of the age of steam.

The ships built at Montreal for the company from 1836 onward were of two types. Several large vessels were built for the firm between 1836 and 1841, the *Thistle* in 1836, the *Gypsy* in 1838, and the *Blonde* and the *Brunette* in 1841.[45] Although all were commissioned for Hugh Allan and his colleagues in the Montreal firm, the Glasgow and Greenock Allans soon acquired shares, a clear indication of the Allan family's strength within the partnership. The other ships built for the firm were of the much smaller schooner class, and were probably used to carry river traffic for the firm's local business. These were the first ships operated by the Edmonstone, Allan firm. Among others in use regularly in the late forties were the *Albion*, the *Caledonia*, the *Montreal*, the *Amy Anne*, the *Toronto* and the venerable *Canada* and *Favourite*.[46] Neither of the last two were registered in Montreal, although the others were; but from both sides of the Atlantic the Allans were operating ten vessels more or less regularly between Montreal, Glasgow, and Liverpool, and several schooners between Montreal and Quebec. Assuming that each ship made only one return trip during a season, the Allans controlled between about 5 and 12 per cent of the total ocean-going shipping at Montreal, during the forties.[47] Though ships other than those of the Allan Line carried goods regularly between British ports and Montreal, the Allans were probably the single most important firm in the business. It was certainly the only major ocean shipping line with a Montreal base.

Although few details concerning the operations of the Edmonstone, Allan company — or of other shipping companies — are known, they suggest the scope and complexity of shipping. Millar, Edmonstone and Allan in the early forties were acting as commission agents in the sale of pig iron and soap for Glasgow companies.[48] In exporting, Edmonstone and Allan did not simply pick up cargo from Montreal staple dealers and forwarders. They used widely dispersed buying agents to ensure sufficient cargo for the holds of their outgoing ships or, more likely, to profit from the staple trades. The partners received regular reports of the markets as far west as Brantford and London, at least until the early fifties.[49] With the firm's apparent pre-eminence in the Montreal transatlantic trade and with the capital resources and skill of Hugh Allan's family (he was joined by his younger brother Andrew in 1839) the firm was in a strong position to take advantage of new opportunities. Given their aggressive personalities, it would have been surprising if they had not accepted the challenge of establishing the first Montreal-Liverpool steamship service.

During the decline of the pace of commercial life of the late forties in Montreal because of the lessened demand for Canadian-exported wheat and flour, as mentioned above, shipping activity in the port of Montreal was considerably reduced. From 221 ocean-going ships totalling 62,710 tons calling at Montreal during 1847, the number dropped nearly 30 per cent to 164 vessels totalling 42,157 tons the following year and declined by a further 10 per cent to 149 ships, or 37,703 tons, during the 1849 navigation season.[50] The value of imports declined 25 per cent in 1848 and remained at approximately the same level until 1851. Average annual Montreal-Liverpool freight rates fell drastically on all commodities after August 1847; the average rate on flour declined from 5/4 per barrel in 1847 to 4/2 in 1848, to 3/6 in 1849, and to only 3/ in 1850. The decline in ashes freight began in 1849 and fell in the same proportion, but the wheat freight decline was cataclysmic, from 12/7¾ per quarter in 1847 to 4/2 in 1848, 6/11½ in 1849, and 6/2 in 1850.[51] Moreover, the volume of receipts of all major staples from upcountry except ashes declined after 1847, and the number of river vessels also fell, but less drastically. In such circumstances the activities of shipowners were bound to be affected adversely, and Allan's expansion, pursued so actively in the early forties, was thereafter temporarily halted. Between 1845 and 1850 the Allan line added only one ship to its fleet of fourteen.

The upturn in shipping activity at Montreal in 1850 by more than 35 per cent over 1849 gave Allan's business a new stimulus. By 1851, when the increase in shipping was almost 25 per cent over 1850, his firm began an ambitious expansion involving the introduction of ocean-going steamships.

IV

It is true that the development of navigational facilities in the St Lawrence and at the port of Montreal were the responsibility of public bodies, and thus not the direct functions of entrepreneurship with which this study is specifically concerned. Nonetheless the condition of the harbour directly affected commerce, in which most businessmen in the city were deeply involved. The commercial community had laboured to improve the harbour during the late twenties and in 1832 had succeeded in having Montreal declared an official port of entry. These achievements, they were well aware, had to be augmented by others in order to advance Montreal's status as a major ocean port. A number of merchants participated on the Board of Harbour Commissioners with an obvious keenness born at least as much of personal or group business interests of 'public spirit.' To be sure, not every member of the Montreal business community would have been enthusiastic about river improvements. Although steamboat interests would not likely have welcomed measures that would threaten their business of towing vessels or lighters upriver, they would nevertheless have welcomed an increase in river traffic. But, in the main, the business community strongly supported the deepening of Lake St Peter below Montreal.[52]

Harbour and river developments also illustrated the close ties between business and government. The government helped to condition the climate of enterprise by stimulating and encouraging both general economic development and specific institutions designed to advance growth – of trade in particular. Although it is clear that some ministries were less inclined than others to implement particular economic measures, all governments after the Union seem to have shared the broad assumption that the needs of the Canadian commercial community were those of the whole province. Indeed, even during the period of the Special Council of Lower Canada's administration many laws designed to foster economic growth were passed.

The shallowness of Lake St Peter, a wide section of the St Lawrence River between Montreal and Three Rivers, was one of the major barriers to the development of Montreal's ocean shipping trade. Whereas the river was generally thirty feet deep or more between Montreal and Quebec, quite enough to allow ocean vessels to navigate the channel without serious difficulties, Lake St Peter was an obstacle. In the section through which the river's main channel passed there was an average depth of from eighteen to twenty feet, which was only just sufficient. But at the eastern end of the channel the depth was only fourteen feet, a major hazard. In midsummer and autumn, when river levels were low, the depth fell to eleven and one-half feet, and vessels going up or down were required to have virtually their entire cargoes removed in order to get over the shoal. Such transfers meant substantial delays and high costs for lighterage. In 1840, forty-two vessels required lighterage at a cost of £5,084/0/3.[53] Moreover, the existence of the shallows and the somewhat restricted natural channel made it necessary for most ocean vessels travelling that section of the river also to require towage, in addition to what was normally needed to overcome the St Mary's current in the St Lawrence a few miles below Montreal.

Unless Lake St Peter were made completely navigable by ocean ships, so that delays and extra costs were removed, Montreal could obviously never hope to become an unhampered ocean port. A considerable quantity of goods, especially some classes of timber, observers noted, would have been loaded onto ships at or near Montreal had it only been possible to get the vessels up to the harbour and downriver again unimpeded.[54] While the St Lawrence canals were being constructed during the forties the *Canadian Economist* pointed out that unless Lake St Peter were deepened to allow large ocean ships to reach the port the larger vessels from upriver ports might bypass Montreal and head straight for

Quebec.[55] Agitation by Montreal merchants to have the government of Lower Canada improve the river went back at least as far as 1826. Serious efforts to enhance the navigability of Lake St Peter were undertaken in 1844 by the Province of Canada, under the Board of Works, after repeated urging by the Montreal Board of Trade. However, instead of improving the existing channel, which was judged to be hazardous because of its crookedness, the Board of Works tried unsuccessfully to dig a new one through the shallow section. By 1846, despite the expenditure of £70,000 the work was still incomplete, and in Montreal opinion was growing that the attempt to dig a new channel rather than improve the old one was a serious error. On hearing it estimated that another £400,000 would be required to complete the new channel, the government ordered work to be suspended.[56]

Before 1850 the Montreal harbour commissioners were concerned only with the improvements to the harbour authorized by the legislature of Lower Canada in 1830.[57] Over the next decade extensive modifications to the port were made under the direction of George Moffatt, Jules Quesnel, and Captain Robert S. Piper (who supplied technical advice), who urged that work be proceeded with quickly lest the city's trade be grievously injured.

Besides the powerful and prestigious George Moffatt, a commercial patriarch whose career had begun in the ancient days of the fur trade, a number of lesser-known business figures served on the Harbour Commission. Jules Quesnel was an old Nor'Wester who after 1811 had spent some years in Upper Canada before entering business in Montreal in the early twenties.[58] Until 1839 he maintained an importing business, through which he developed business connections with Toronto merchant John Spread Baldwin. After leaving his job as harbour commissioner, Quesnel served briefly on the Special Council of Lower Canada and subsequently on the provincial Legislative Council.[59] It is not known whether Quesnel had any personal interest in shipping that would help to explain his desire to improve Montreal's harbour. His name does not appear on the Montreal shipping registers of that period. Possibly his participation on the Harbour Commission was simply a reflection of his general prominence in the business community.

P.L. LeTourneaux, who joined the Commission in 1836, does not appear to have been prominent in Montreal's commercial life at this time. Nothing is known about him except that along with Alfred LaRocque, Jean Bruneau, Damase Masson, and Olivier Berthelet, among many others, LeTourneaux attempted to secure incorporation in 1846 for the Banque des Marchands.[60] Thomas Cringan, another harbour commissioner from 1836 to 1839, was much better known in Montreal's commercial life, participating in railways and other enterprises that aided the city's trading activity. Turton Penn, though perhaps less prominent than Cringan, had been involved in commercial affairs for many years. Dorwin mentioned that Penn was a partner in what was already a large Montreal auction house in 1816.[61] Of unknown origins, Penn subsequently became active in such institutions as the Committee of Trade, the Montreal Newsroom, the Montreal Library, and the Board of Directors of the Bank of Montreal.

William Lunn was a harbour commissioner briefly in 1839 and 1840. An Admiralty official at Montreal in charge of naval stores from 1819 to 1834, Lunn became a minor figure in Montreal business circles, managing his wife's investments.[62] From 1838 to 1849 he served on the Board of the Bank of Montreal, and from time to time he participated in other commercial institutions such as the Provident and Savings Bank, the Montreal Fire, Life and Inland Navigation Assurance Company, and the New City Gas Company.[63] He was also very active in the Anglican Church and the Montreal Bible Society, and he supported the Montreal Lunatic Asylum and the Montreal General Hospital.

From 1840 to 1850 the Harbour Commission, which administered the port and continued to make improvements, consisted of the same three men: John Gordon Mackenzie, John Try, and Charles Seraphim Rodier.[64] A native of Dingwall in northern Scotland, Mackenzie immigrated to Canada in 1811, served an apprenticeship with Forsyth, Richardson and Company, and formed a most useful business connection by marrying the daughter of Horatio Gates.[65] He began a wholesale dry goods firm in 1829, and by the end of the forties had become one of the leading general importers and exporters in the city. Active also in local insurance and railway projects and banking, he served for years as a director of the Bank of Montreal. Mackenzie was an active member of the Board of Trade and had been associated with the Committee of Trade since 1822. He served on the government-appointed Montreal City Council from 1840 to 1843, but achieved no other prominence in public affairs.[66]

John Try was less well known, but he was commercially prominent or wealthy enough to be elected for four years to the Board of the Bank of Montreal. His commercial connections, if any, cannot be traced, but Try was the owner of some valuable properties in central Montreal.[67] Charles Séraphim Rodier, however, was better known, perhaps largely because of his successes in municipal politics. He was a Montrealer, born in 1796 and attended the Collège de Montréal and, subsequently unlike most of his fellow graduates – went into business, in which he succeeded as a wholesale merchant.[68] At age forty-one he left commerce temporarily to study law, which apparently added to his ability as an entrepreneur and perhaps to his prestige. He was elected to the Montreal City Council annually from 1833 to 1836, and then was appointed to the Special Court of Sessions which governed the city until 1840, when he was reappointed for another three years.[69] An officer in one of the local militia battalions, the Seventh, at the same time, he was obviously considered loyal to the government. Following his ten-year membership in the Harbour Commission, Rodier was elected Mayor of Montreal three times between 1857 and 1860. In 1867 he was appointed to the Legislative Council of Quebec for the district of Lorimier and remained a member until his death in February 1876.[70] While mayor, Rodier returned to the Harbour Commission as the representative of the City of Montreal. But his appointment to that body earlier suggests his importance in the business community. It is unlikely that the presence of one French Canadian on the three-member Harbour Commission since its beginnings, except for a year in 1839-40, was strictly fortuitous. It was clearly politically desirable to have a French Canadian on the Commission, preferably one with business interests. If the government had sought to appoint French Canadian commissioners according to some objective criteria of wealth, range of commercial interests, and general prominence in the business community, it cannot now be determined whether Quesnel, LeTourneaux and Rodier were the obvious choices. Yet objective criteria would have been next to impossible to establish, and although these three may not have been as prominent as English-speaking merchants, they were clearly businessmen with a personal stake in advancing the cause of commerce in Montreal.

During the four years after 1850, the Harbour Commission of Montreal was much more closely involved in the deepening of the channel of Lake St Peter than it had been during the forties because the works were put directly under its charge.[71] Succeeding John Try as chairman was John Young, who had been on the Commission since 1850. Young had arrived in Canada in 1826 from Scotland, where he was born in 1811 of parents 'in the humble walks of life.'[72] After living a few years in Kingston he moved in 1829 to Montreal where he started as a clerk in John Torrance's wholesale business and quickly moved ahead in the firm. In 1835 he and David Torrance took over a branch of the business in Quebec, where Young remained for five years. When he returned to Montreal in 1840, he was an experienced businessman. He then went into partnership with Harrison Stephens, a well-established merchant who specialized in importing American rice, tobacco, and other goods.[73] The new firm began a thriving trade with the Canadian and American west.

When that arrangement lapsed in 1845, Young formed a partnership with Benjamin Holmes, until then the cashier of the Bank of Montreal, and Joseph Knapp, not a Montrealer but perhaps related to James Knapp of Knapp and Noad, Montreal general merchants.[74] This partnership lasted until 1849, when Young left the firm possibly over a disagreement with Knapp, who favoured the Annexation movement.[75] After 1846, on the other hand, Young strongly favoured free trade, including the immediate removal of the navigation laws, in order to improve the city's prospect of becoming an entrepôt of both British and American trade. Since 1846 Young and his tiny Free Trade Association laboured strenuously to promote their cause in the short-lived Montreal newspaper, the *Canadian Economist,* and in the Montreal Board of Trade.[76]

Simultaneously Young began a lengthy and successful career improving Montreal's harbour. He was responsible for carrying through the Lake St Peter improvements and pursued this task with enthusiasm until he left the chairmanship in 1859. Moreover, he continued as a member of the Commission from 1850 to his death in 1878, a period broken only by his absence for three years, from 1867 to 1870.[77] Although Young seemed to be the quintessential commercial Montrealer in his vigorous efforts to improve the St Lawrence below Montreal, he was already relentlessly pursuing his project of a St Lawrence River to Lake Champlain canal, to connect Montreal and New York, as the only viable solution to Montreal's inferior connections with European ports.[78]

The group of which John Young was a member was in charge of the improvements to Lake St Peter as well as the management of the harbour. They were permitted to borrow £30,000 to accomplish the necessary improvements. A board of three engineers, including Casimir S. Gzowski, was appointed in October 1850 'to examine fully into the whole matter and report to us the best means of effectually opening a channel of 16 feet in low water between this place and Quebec, as well as the cost of opening a channel of 13 feet, 14 feet and 15 feet.'[79] They recommended that the old, or natural, channel through Lake St Peter be improved where necessary, since it would cost less than taking up where the Board of Works had left off a few years earlier with the new cut. 'We think,' they wrote, 'that the greatly diminished cost of improving the old channel more than compensates for its few curves and slightly increased distance.'[80] They further recommended that the channel throughout be deepened to sixteen feet and to a width of 450 feet. 'It does not consist with right or reason or the enlightened spirit of the age,' they concluded their report, 'that obstacles be permitted to exist against the will and interests of the commercial world.'

Young and his two fellow commissioners accepted these recommendations. Work was begun in June 1851, and by November the channel had been deepened to fourteen feet and widened to seventy-five. By August 1852 the channel had been doubled in width and was two feet deeper.[81] Thus, fully laden 500-ton vessels drawing sixteen feet of water could safely traverse the flats or shallows of Lake St Peter, which before were only eleven to twelve feet deep at low water. Work continued during the next two years. By November 1853 the channel had been deepened to sixteen and one-half feet and widened to two hundred and fifty to three hundred feet. Although work on the channel continued during the later fifties, the end of the 1853 season marked an important plateau in the development of St Lawrence River transportation. These works made possible the unimpeded arrival of ocean vessels to Montreal, a most important landmark in the development of the city's status as an ocean port. Without the deepening and widening of the channel, the growth of steam navigation between Montreal and other ports would have been impossible.

v

The period from 1837 to 1853 witnessed several notable changes in Montreal's business scene. The growth in the absolute volume of trade in this period made it imperative, by the early fifties, that the navigability of the St Lawrence River be improved. The achievement of that object became a function of Montreal's commercial class, which by slow and subtle degrees was showing increasing strength, even some autonomy, in the still existing pattern of strong relationships with British commercial houses. Rising American trade, imports as well as exports, and shipments in bond under the Drawback Acts reflected this shift. On the other hand, trade with Britain remained the overwhelming proportion of the total, and better facilities for this British trade were increasingly needed. At the same time some firms were not only expanding traditional British connections but also extending into new ventures like shipping.

Yet in shipping and in trade this was generally a period of unspectacular growth. Entrepreneurship was dormant, reflecting the fact that, unless conditions were deemed to be advantageous, businessmen's courage faltered. Notwithstanding that, however, this period saw the emergence of two major entrepreneurs, Hugh Allan and John Young, both of whom contributed in different ways to these developments. Although Hugh Allan at this stage was barely more than an agent of his overseas shipping family's operations, he was successfully managing their interest in Canada and laying the foundation for new shipping ventures.

As for Young, he rose through a general merchandising firm to the Board of Harbour Commissioners and to the Board of Works, where he was instrumental in making the St Lawrence usable below Montreal. He helped to mould government policy in response to the demand for improvement, and he helped to implement the policy. He was one of the new men of politics and business, who saw that within the generally favourable climate of enterprise then existing in the Province of Canada, the infrastructure permitting growth had to be created. While Young was more of a businessman and much less of a politician than his contemporary Francis Hincks, they were alike in juxtaposing assumptions about the desirability of economic growth and the indispensability of government aid to that end.

6

John Young, Hugh Allan, and the advent of ocean steamshipping

I

Steamships came into wide use on the North Atlantic in the late thirties. Liverpool and Halifax were served by the Cunard Line, which provided scheduled, year-round runs after 1840.[1] By that time most of the major ports along the Atlantic seaboard had at least one such service, which was very attractive for passengers and premium freight.[2] In the tense atmosphere of rivalry between North American cities, Montrealers were decidedly slow in getting similar steamship lines running regularly to British ports; such runs commenced in 1853. Until the spring of that year only one steamship had come up from the sea to Montreal. In a voyage that was not repeated, the *Q.E.D.*, an iron-hulled barque with auxiliary steam power, arrived from Newcastle in May 1845.[3]

Offsetting the obvious benefits Montreal would derive from regular steamship service with British ports were clear disadvantages to certain interests or persons and one positively prohibiting factor: until the channel in Lake St Peter was deepened, not even large sailing vessels, let alone the much heavier steamships, could navigate the river to Montreal with safety and economy. There might well be considerable concern and opposition – selfish but powerful – from such steamboat owners as the Molsons and Torrances whose companies specialized in towing helpless sailing ships past the St Mary's current. The investment required for an ocean-going steamship – at least ten times the sum needed for a St Lawrence River steamboat – would also have been a deterrent to investors, Canadian or British.[4]

After 1850, with the improvements to the channel below the port and the beginning of construction on the St Lawrence and Atlantic Railway, Montreal's economic prospects seemed decidedly brighter. At that point it was not a

Montrealer but a Hamilton merchant, Isaac Buchanan, who investigated the idea of running a line of steamers between Glasgow and Montreal (to Portland in the winter).[5] Buchanan had a huge wholesale outlet in Montreal, and with his extensive commercial interests in Canada West he quickly saw the potential of a combined steamship and railway connection to Britain. John Poor, Portland's indefatigable, irrepressible, and omnipresent railway booster, who was primarily responsible for the St Lawrence and Atlantic Railway between his city and Montreal, personally conducted Buchanan over the completed section of the track. Buchanan left Portland enthusiastically announcing a plan to build three iron steamers of 1600 tons, each capable of carrying 6,000 barrels of flour and 150 passengers. He proposed to invest a total of £90,000 in the ships and to seek support from New York investors.[6] Nothing came of the scheme but news of it may have had a galvanic effect upon the Montreal Board of Trade, which until then had never taken up this cause although it had vigorously urged the government to implement numerous other measures to improve shipping.[7] The presidents of the Board since its establishment in 1822 had always been among the most prominent businessmen in the city, but none of them were primarily concerned with ocean shipping until 1851. In that year Hugh Allan was elected president, and he soon began to use his office to elicit support from the government for St Lawrence-Britain steamship connections. On 5 August, 1851 Allan brought several resolutions on the subject before the regular monthly meeting of the Board of Trade. The resolutions pointed out that Montreal, unlike Boston and New York, did not have steamship service, and that the advantages of the St Lawrence as a channel of trade between the mid-continent and Europe were 'unqualified.' Canada would gain substantially by such a service because of an increased flow of immigrants and an enlarged direct import and export trade – probably a reference to the unfortunate effects of the American Drawback Acts. Thus it was 'essential to the progress and prosperity of Canada' that a regular line be established and that the government offer 'some reasonable pecuniary assistance' – about £10,000 annually, for up to ten years – to anyone willing and demonstrably able to maintain such a service. The Board members endorsed these assertions, and empowered Allan to petition the government and to enlist the support of Montreal MPs.[8] This appeal to the government over Hugh Allan's signature drew the disturbing reply, however, that the subject had been raised in the Assembly the year before and had not been pursued.

The Montreal English press, despite a general enthusiasm for 'progress' did not immediately commit itself strongly to the idea of steamships. A sampling of editorial opinion in the most commercially oriented newspaper in the city, the Montreal *Gazette*, reveals no discussion of steamships in 1849 or 1850, and very little in 1851. It was not so much disapproval, or lack of interest, as a preoccupation with other concerns: the commercial depression, which lasted until 1850,[9] the appeal of the railway, which only began to make an important impact on Montreal after 1847 with the completion of the Montreal and Lachine Railway.

John Young must have been one of the first Montrealers to see the opportunities that transatlantic steam connections held out for the city. Although keenly appreciative of the importance of railways, especially the St Lawrence and Atlantic, Young's major attention was focused on Montreal's waterways and the necessity of improving them. His valuable work as harbour commissioner, discussed in the previous chapter, was only one aspect of his wide-ranging participation in the city's improvement as a shipping centre. He became commissioner of public works in the Hincks-Morin government in October 1851,[10] probably because he keenly felt the need to prosecute vigorously the St Lawrence River improvements, as well as other public works. After his appointment, Young was in a position to try to implement some of his ideas. One of these was to offset some of the damage done to the St Lawrence trade by the availability to American ports of steamship service assisted generously by British government mail subsidies. After attempts failed in the late forties to have the British government subsidize steamship lines to Canadian as well as to United States ports, Young began to encourage the Canadian government to provide the necessary help.[11] He was also aware of other advantages of American ports over the St Lawrence route, among them cheaper transatlantic rates; since 1845 those ports had been more available to Canadian importers than ever before as a result of the passage of United States Drawback Acts.

During the eleven months he served as commissioner of public works, Young was able to convince the Canadian government to provide a subsidy to a steamship line for regular service to Montreal. Of course he had the support of the Montreal Board of Trade, whose president, Hugh Allan, had gone up to Toronto (then the capital) in late August 1851 especially to urge the government to establish a line of steamers between the St Lawrence and Britain.[12] Francis Hincks, inspector general in the Baldwin-Lafontaine government, had then informed Allan that although he was personally in favour of the idea, the time was not appropriate for the proposal to be brought forward, in view of the prospect of an early prorogation of the legislature and the resignation of several members of the administration. At least the idea had been planted, however, and soon after Young became an MLA for Montreal and a member of the new ministry formed by Hincks and Morin on 28 October he began to urge the project on his colleagues. Most of them were not convinced (he wrote later) of the value of spending £20,000 annually for this service.[13] However, the idea did appeal to Lord Elgin as well as to Hincks; and in February 1852 Samuel Cunard, the eminently successful Atlantic shipping magnate, indicated to the Canadian government that he would be prepared to establish the St Lawrence steamship service for an annual subsidy of £10,000.[14] Apparently convinced by this of the viability of the project, the cabinet permitted Young to explore the possibilities of getting the service started – with government support limited to £10,000 annually – by advertising in Canada and Britain for tenders in the spring of 1852.

There were numerous inquiries, but only three tenders for the service. Hugh Allan of Montreal offered at £36,000; a British group headed by McKean and McLarty of Liverpool and assisted by a number of Montrealers tendered at £24,000; and a London consortium bid at £52,000 annually. Ironically, Samuel Cunard did not tender, perhaps because he had not been serious in the first place or because he considered the attached conditions too restrictive. In providing the service the contractor initially had an option of operating on either a fortnightly or a monthly basis for a reduced subsidy between Liverpool and Montreal, but the administration soon decided that fortnightly service would be required.[15] Moreover, limits were set on passenger fares and freight rates, and the ships were to be of at least 1500 tons displacement (later amended to 1200 tons) and have no less than 1000-ton cargo capacity. The agreement, to last for seven years, was to come into effect in the spring of 1853, when the first ship would sail from Liverpool.

It is not surprising that Hugh Allan was interested in this project. The possibility of government support, the upturn of business conditions, and increased shipping activity in the port of Montreal during 1851, all would have helped to make him interested in establishing a potentially highly profitable steamship service. Up to that time his transatlantic shipping business had been entirely dependent on fifteen sailing vessels, eight of them apparently owned entirely by his father and brothers, whose operations were based on Glasgow and Liverpool. This co-operation was beneficial and probably necessary for efficiency, but the Allan brothers may have found it increasingly inhibiting, especially as the head of the firm, Alexander Allan, grew older and probably exercised less central management over the family shipping enterprise.[16] The Allans were by no means in control even of the Montreal firm, which was still Edmonstone, Allan and Company; and Edmonstone still held substantial proportions, varying in each case, of the shares of the firm's Montreal-based ships. George Burns Symes, a Quebec timber merchant, held smaller proportions of shares in a few of the ships, and in others the British Allans were partial shareholders.

In this complex structure of ownership and control Hugh Allan may have felt increasingly constricted and frustrated. Possibly the impending advent of steam navigation offered him not only the possibility of entrepreneurial gain but also the chance of at least partial escape from confinement in the family firm. But the new venture, demanding sizable investment and the adoption of the newest marine technology by a firm that had until then relied entirely upon sailing ships, was probably made possible by a realignment of power within the old family concern. By the early fifties the head of the business, Alexander Allan senior, entered his seventies. Then, if not earlier, he must have somewhat lessened his involvement in the business and have left to his sons not only the daily management of affairs but also the central direction of policy, hitherto concentrated in his hands. The Allan sons, Hugh and Andrew in Montreal, James in Glasgow, and Bryce at Greenock, were ready to make the leap to steam. They had probably been waiting half a decade for the opportune moment. They had not added to the number of sailing ships in their transatlantic ocean fleet since the mid-forties, even after the return of prosperity to the Canada trade and the mounting volume of freight.

Yet even with quasi-independence from paternal control, a deep fund of rich experience, substantial resources, and the clannish mutual support of brothers in the same business enterprise, the Allans were not able to move as individuals. In any case, each was probably unwilling to shoulder the entire risk. Although not public shareholders, the British Allans were closely connected with the new venture in every way. James and Alexander oversaw the construction of the ships on the Clyde; they advanced payments to the builders, insured the ships, and outfitted them.[17] They may well have been silent partners to Hugh or other shareholders, and they were almost certain to be the British agents for the new steamship service; but they put no money into the company itself. Hugh found it necessary to recruit a number of Montreal capitalists to join him in forming the Montreal Ocean Steamship Company in 1852.[18] When they secured incorporation in 1854 the company then comprised nine shareholders who agreed to raise the authorized £500,000, which could be expanded to £1 million at the discretion of the company.[19] Hugh subscribed for eight shares out of sixty-four, and his partner Symes, an old associate from Quebec, also took eight.[20] Allan's partner Edmonstone took four shares, as did Sir George Simpson, governor of the Hudson's Bay Company, while William Dow, a wealthy Montreal brewer and large property owner with interests in banking and insurance, took two. Harbour Commissioner John Gordon Mackenzie took six, Allan's brother Andrew, Robert Anderson, a Glaswegian who had moved to Montreal in 1840 and became a successful merchant and banker,[21] and John Watkins, a Kingston merchant, each subscribed for two shares. The rest of the shares possibly were sold to Allan's relatives in Britain.

It would perhaps appear odd that these Montrealers, none of whom aside from the Allans and Edmonstone were major shipowners, should become shareholders in an ambitious and complex enterprise to build and operate steamships on the North Atlantic. Yet most had more than just a nodding acquaintance with shipping: Simpson was a shareholder in several steamboats plying the upper St Lawrence,[22] and it is highly possible that other participants in this venture, such as J.G. Mackenzie, had at least small investments in shipping. Thus the involvement of merchants and bankers in a highly promising new shipping venture is not surprising. Whether experienced in shipping or not, they were probably investing with the same detachment they might have shown for railways, and since the project held very considerable promise, they were participating as entrepreneurs with expectations of high initial profits.

The new Montreal Ocean Steamship Company immediately contracted for the construction of two large steamships with the reputable Clydeside builder, William Denning of Dumbarton. They were to be iron-hulled craft of 1700 tons displacement each, with 350 horsepower engines and a speed of eleven knots. Named the *Canadian* and the *Indian,* they were to have stateroom and steerage accommodation for several hundred people and ample room for cargo.[23] With a mixture of pride and expectant ambition the Allans and their new associates awaited the provincial government's answer to their tender.

The Allans' tender, however, had not been the lowest, yet in making all of these preparations they clearly expected the contract. But the government, or John Young who was the minister responsible, had not opted for the Allans. In fact during the summer of 1852 Young had clearly decided to accept the tender from McKean and McLarty with some modifications.[24] It was only after some months of negotiations between them and Young completed in August 1852, that an agreement was finally reached.[25] He secured the support of the Montreal to Portland railway companies, the St Lawrence and Atlantic and the Atlantic and St Lawrence, both of which agreed to pay £2,000 annually as part of the subsidy to the steamship line. This amount, together with £1,000 each year from the city of Portland − which would benefit substantially from the new service as its terminus during the winter − would leave £19,000 to be raised from the provincial government, if the McKean and McLarty tender was accepted. The authorities finally and somewhat reluctantly agreed to this commitment in July 1852, and John Young communicated these financial terms to the Montreal agent of McKean and McLarty, David Bellhouse.[26]

Hugh Allan's outrage must have resounded through Montreal counting houses. Had he not gone to the trouble of forming a company and commissioning the construction of special ships for this service? To be sure, no one had asked him to do so, and no one could have guaranteed that his tender would be accepted, but he was, after all, a Montrealer, a Canadian surely, and an experienced shipper who had served the mercantile community well. It was monstrous that the contract should be given to Liverpool intruders — and he made up his mind that the decision must be undone. Allan had friends and influence in the vast concourse of Montreal merchants. Only a year before he had been elected president of Montreal's prestigious Board of Trade. He was a wealthy shipowner with impressive connections in Britain, a director of the Bank of Montreal, and a promoter of the Merchants' Bank; he was president of the Montreal Telegraph Company; he was the son-in-law of John Smith, a very wealthy retired grocery merchant of Montreal.[27] Even at this relatively early stage of his career, Hugh Allan was a powerful man who would expect to get his own way.

Allan's competitors for the contract, however, were at least as influential and as wealthy. In 1852 and 1853 the victorious McKean and McLarty were really the business agents, or the managers, of a syndicate that a year later became incorporated in Canada under the name of the Canadian Steam Navigation Company.[28] Among the members of the group were a number of rich and powerful British capitalists and shipowners, led by a group of merchants that included Robert Gillespie a partner in Gillespie, Moffatt and Company, and London merchants Thomas Holdsworth Brooking, Robert Garter, and Matthew Hutton Chator. Besides Robert McKean, Donald McLarty, and Robert Lamont of Liverpool, there were other investors from the same city, including John Carmichael, John Holme, a timber merchant, John Laird, a shipbuilder of Liverpool and Birkenhead, and Patrick Henderson, a Glasgow merchant.[29] Although none of the Liverpool participants in this venture were among the twenty most important timber-importing firms operating in the port at that time, they were clearly merchants of wealth and experience.[30]

The capital of the group was £300,000, which might be enlarged to £1 million. As well as British entrepreneurs, the syndicate included a number of Montrealers who, unlike the Montreal partners in the Allan group, all had considerable shipping experience. There was Thomas Ryan, a native of Ballinakill, Ireland, who, along with his brothers Edward and John, had been prominent in the Montreal-Quebec shipping trade for a decade or more and was a merchant in Montreal. There was Luther Holton. And there was James Greenshields, also a partner in Gillespie, Moffatt and Company and an important shareholder of the Union Towing Company, which operated on the Montreal-

Quebec run.[31] Greenshields and Ryan were directors of the Bank of Montreal during the forties; Holton was a prominent director of the second most important Montreal financial institution, the City Bank, and, as noted above, the owner of a major Montreal forwarding company. Ryan had been president of the Montreal Board of Trade in 1849-50, immediately preceding Hugh Allan's three-year term of office.[32] Together with their Liverpool associates, these men seemed to be at least as impressively efeective as Allan and his confederates.

Canadian participation in this venture would have seemed highly desirable to the Liverpool-London group. It would be necessary to have a number of knowledgeable and influential men at the Montreal end to ensure efficient management and to establish necessary contacts there. All had investments in internal shipping along the St Lawrence and were connected with merchants further west. Thus they would be in an excellent position to supply the volume of freight that should make the new company a financial success. There might also have been a strictly political reason for the inclusion of Canadians in the association. Luther Holton was a known Liberal, and although he became a member of the Legislative Assembly only in 1854 his affiliations during the previous tenure of a Liberal administration might well have helped his group to secure the contract. (On the other hand, it should be noted that Holton's political connections had not helped his cause in negotiations during the same period with the same government for the contract to build the Grand Trunk Railway.) In any case the McKean and McLarty bid had been the lowest of three by a substantial amount, and to the government which had initially set its own participatory limit at £10,000, this factor was very likely decisive. Thus, whatever the original intentions of the English capitalists in seeking Canadian participation in the venture, the result seems to have been no more than the useful recruitment of experienced local businessmen.

The contract called for the shipping company within ten months to begin regularly scheduled runs fortnightly to the St Lawrence, for the seven months during which it was open, and monthly trips to Portland when the river was closed to navigation. In June 1852 McKean and McLarty proposed to begin the service in the spring of 1853 on a monthly basis and commence fortnightly service as soon afterwards as possible, certainly within the year.[33] For the Board of Works, John Young accepted these alterations, because the contractors in offering to begin in the spring were starting the service earlier than the time stipulated in the contract.[34] At the same time Young asserted that the contractors were themselves responsible for securing formal agreement from the other parties to the subsidy arrangements, the railways and the city of Portland. Since this process took until the early autumn to complete, the contract was not signed until October, and a few weeks later it was ratified by the legislature.

Hugh Allan did not wait long to begin attacking both the contract and the contractors. Taking advantage of his supposed impartiality as president of the Montreal Board of Trade, in December 1852 he sniped at several soft spots, real and imaginary, in the arrangements. Applauding the legislation of November 1852 permitting the government to subsidize a steamship line, he asserted that 'your Memorialists expected the steamers in question to be in operation in the ensuing spring.' Indeed, some merchants had already made 'arrangements for the transmission of merchandise by them.' Thus, he implied that they would suffer losses or inconvenience.[35] This accusation is unconvincing; not only does it indicate an unlikely naiveté among Montreal merchants, but also Allan himself, as late as the previous March, in correspondence with the Board of Works over the specifications of the service, had strongly implied that if awarded the contract he might not himself have begun in the spring of 1853.[36] In any case Allan objected too soon, because his competitors did start the service, albeit inadequately, in May of that year.

Allan's second allegation was that the contractors McKean and McLarty were unable to fulfil the conditions of the arrangements and were evading their obligations by offering the contract to another company that would probably not honour the original agreement. He was referring to the formation of the Canadian Steam Navigation Company, which had naturally and predictably evolved from a contracting partnership to a limited liability company.[37] It is true that the securing of a charter from the British government for this company had been delayed, mainly because of opposition by Cunard, but that would not impede the performance of the steamship service, since the group was already incorporated under Canadian law. Certainly these organizational manipulations were no indication of bad faith, and Allan was guilty either of stupidity, which was unlikely, or of dishonesty in this charge. It is not surprising that Allan should have lashed out, for a thwarted entrepreneur, like a jilted lover, is chagrined, but it is surprising that he should have had the audacity to use the Board of Trade to make these accusations.

The allegations were not without effect, however. Immediately the Board of Works – headed by Jean Chabot since Young's sudden resignation in late September 1852 – required assurances from the contractors through their Montreal agent, David Bellhouse, that his principals certainly would be able to meet the terms of the agreement.[38] (The irony of one of Allan's own relatives by marriage representing the firm he was so zealously attempting to undermine should not be lost. Bellhouse, like both Allan brothers, was married to a daughter of John Smith.)[39] Bellhouse felt it necessary at the end of March again to offer assurances that the service would indeed commence as planned at the appointed time and that the delay in securing incorporation in Britain would offer no impediment.[40] But the persistent Hugh Allan, still wearing his Board of Trade hat, complained again in April, now alleging that the contractors were remiss in their obligations because the ship *Genova*, sent to inaugurate the service, was probably only about half the size stipulated in the agreement, being perhaps six hundred tons rather than twelve hundred. D. McLarty Jr admitted that this was so, but he also pointed out that since the service was begun early, according to the contract, its stipulations were inoparative until ten months after final ratification of the agreement. For the time being the Board of Works was satisfied by this explanation, and even the grumpy Hugh Allan was temporarily silenced by the excitement over the impending arrival of the *Genova*. The Board of Trade did, however, pass a resolution that, while lauding the new service, recommended that the 'same privileges and facilities' be granted to other steamship companies with the same object.[41]

The Allan brothers were understandably absent from the well-attended banquet held on 12 May 1853 to honour the arrival that day of the *Genova*, the first transatlantic steamship to arrive in the city. Young, appropriately, gave the evening's keynote speech. With the usual mid-Victorian windy eloquence, he expressed his credo of progress for his beloved city. It was the old message of Montreal's rightful place as entrepôt of the Great Lakes basin. In the era of imperial protection, the St Lawrence trade had been oriented entirely to Britain, he asserted, but now Canada could export wherever she liked; the advent of free trade thus opened larger vistas.[42] The natural advantages of export and import by way of the St Lawrence route, closer to Liverpool than either Boston or New York, together with the new canals, would soon draw increased traffic to the river and hence reduce freight rates. He suggested that an enlarged foreign trade from Montreal with Cuba and even China would soon follow. The speech was not John Young's best. Nevertheless, it did embody the central theme for most of his public career: that Montreal's waterway position was the most important factor in its prosperity, and through the adoption of correct measures the city could become an even greater continental trading centre than it then was.

Young's words and thoughts were echoed by the other speakers that evening, as the toasts followed profusely from other dignitaries, including the *Genova's* captain, the mayor, and Thomas Coltrin Keefer, noteworthy engineer and publicist. Keefer, too, eulogized Montreal's advantageous position with some vigour. Interestingly enough, although a well-known propagandist for railways through his pamphlet of 1850, *The Philosophy of Railroads*, he deprecated them in favour of canals, which 'had the priority over railroads in point of birth, and in Canada ... in point of importance.'[43] The products of the American midwest, in time perhaps even cotton from the southern states, would flow through the port of Montreal. These were some of the rhapsodic utterances of those who spoke on that significant occasion, the beginning of regular transatlantic steamship connections from Montreal.

II

Years later, John Young, perhaps not an entirely impartial observer in this matter, wrote that Allan had scarcely waited until the service was in operation before he began to mount an attack upon the contractors for alleged inefficiencies of their vessels. While it was true that Allan at the time was still the president of the Montreal Board of Trade, and could seem to be the impartial protector of Montreal's commercial well-being, he was hardly a disinterested judge. Yet Young had good grounds for his charges in 1877 that the 'manner in which the contract has hitherto been managed has been exceedingly unsatisfactory to the whole community, not one of the provisions in it having been ever properly observed.'[44]

In fact, the performance of McKean and McLarty (who had come to represent the whole syndicate of contractors) during the 1853 navigation season had been far short of what the agreement stipulated. Instead of 1200-ton ships, their vessels on the Montreal run continued to be, like the *Genova*, only about 600 tons. Vessels had not kept to their schedules, and they had not made the required number of trips. During 1853 their ships had made six voyages to Portland and only three of what were to have been fortnightly visits to Montreal.[45] To be sure, the Canadian Steam Navigation Company had had serious difficulties to contend with: a delay in securing incorporation in Britain and unusually severe winter sailing conditions. Indeed, during 1854, they performed far better and brought vessels to the St Lawrence fortnightly from mid-April to mid-September. But their ships were still slightly smaller than the required size. Besides, the company had not lived up to its commitment to charge a maximum freight rate of only sixty shillings a ton.

The government was insisting upon strict performance of the contract, and since McKean and McLarty had, on their own admission, not done so, the continuation of the subsidy to them was in jeopardy. The government's strictness on the subject, notwithstanding substantial improvement in one year and the company's apparent desire to fully honour the contract, is somewhat puzzling. In view of the fact that Hugh Allan still obviously yearned for the subsidy, it is possible that he was making representations to members of the administration that he could perform the service better. Young, who, at least in retrospect, was not partial to the Allans,[46] had resigned from the administration in September 1852. Allan's hectoring as president of the Board of Trade and, possibly, as a competitor and highly-available replacement, might have injected the necessary sternness into the administration.

Following protracted correspondence and a spirited defence of its performance by the Canadian Steam Navigation Company, the government annulled the contract as of the end of the 1855 navigation season. Robert Lamont, who had come from Liverpool to present the contractors' case, was tersely told in March 1855 that 'the Commissioners of Public Works do not see any reason for your deferring your departure for England.'[47] Several months later, Allan, who had been waiting expectantly all this time, was given a contract with the government to maintain the same service, beginning in 1856, for a subsidy of £24,000, the exact sum paid to his former competitors.[48]

While nothing is known of the negotiations between Allan and the Taché-Macdonald administration, or the then chief commissioner of public works, François Lemieux, it is unlikely that there were any other stronger contenders for the subsidy than Allan, in part, at least, because his group already had an established Liverpool-Montreal connection and steamships ready for use. Allan's shipping firm – the Allan Line – was to become the largest of all transatlantic shipping companies based at Montreal.[49]

III

Another steamship venture originating in Montreal was the Canada Ocean Steam Navigation Company, chartered in 1854. Though this concern was not intended to serve the transatlantic trade, it provides another example of Montreal entrepreneurship in shipping. The company also shows that trade with the maritime provinces was sufficiently promising in the opinion of a number of Montreal businessmen to require the services of steamships. The Canada Ocean Steam Navigation Company was established to operate steamships on the lower St Lawrence River, in the Gulf of St Lawrence, and to ports in the Maritime provinces.[50] Already in existence under articles of association before incorporation, the company had contracted for the steamship *Oneida,* then under construction in Scotland.

Imports to Montreal from other British North American colonies, chiefly Nova Scotia and New Brunswick, while generally less than half the value of American goods, had fluctuated during the forties with little tendency to increase over the decade.[51] The overwhelming bulk of the commodities imported from the Maritimes came from Halifax, including considerable quantities of sugar, molasses, fish, and small quantities of 'wearing apparel' between 1847 and 1851. Imports of sugar increased markedly from 1849 to 1851, while fish jumped 300 per cent from 1847 to 1848 and fluctuated around that level between 1848 and 1851.[52] Shipping activity between Montreal and Maritime ports experienced a sharp increase in 1853 and the prospects for an increase the next year would have encouraged Montreal merchants who looked also to more trade with lower St Lawrence ports.[53] Besides Halifax, Montreal imported large quantities of fish from Arichat, Cape Breton, in some years nearly as much or more than the amounts brought from Halifax. In return, Montreal exported sizable quantities of flour to various Maritimes ports, including Halifax, Saint John, Canso, Miramichi, Bathurst, Pictou, and Arichat. To Halifax, Saint John, and Canso, flour shipments increased sharply after 1848, and to Halifax, which was by far the largest recipient of Montreal exports in the Maritimes, the quantity leaped from 13,298 barrels in 1848, to 22,498 in 1849, to 45,413 in 1850.[54]

Therefore the prospects for the new steamship venture serving British North America were moderately promising. Although the annual volume of trade in 1848 between Montreal and Quebec and other British North American ports was slightly lower than for 1841, there had been a considerable decline in the middle of the decade. The return to 1841 figures seemed to augur well for the Canada-Maritimes trade, and the availability of efficient steamship transportation might well stimulate more of it, or at least draw heavily upon what did exist. Until then, the trade had apparently been carried entirely in sailing vessels. And Montreal's trade to these other British North American ports was only one-third that of Quebec's.

A few Montreal commercial houses seem to have specialized in Maritimes trade in this period, although more than a decade earlier at least one Montreal merchant, Jedediah Hubbell Dorwin, had traded with Nova Scotia, Labrador, and even the West Indies.[55] One such firm was Tobin and Murison, a lengthy partnership between John M. Tobin of Montreal and a merchant named Murison – possibly in Halifax from where the concern brought four cargoes of sugar and rum in 1837.[56] The firm might have suspended its Maritimes trading by 1844 when the partners were perhaps more involved in trading and shipping along the upper St Lawrence. In conjunction with George Sanderson of Brockville they purchased two steamboats in 1846, the *Ericson* and the *Propeller.*[57] After bankruptcy in 1847 Tobin recovered and re-established himself as a Montreal auctioneer and commission merchant.[58] By 1853 he was specializing in selling the cargoes of fish, sugar, and rum from vessels in from Halifax, Canso, and Saint John consigned to James Mitchell whose commission house handled many Maritimes cargoes.[59]

An impressive group of prominent Montrealers came together to form this new shipping company. They were headed by trustees William Workman, David

Torrance, Andrew Shaw, Ira Gould, and John Kershaw, all of whom except Kershaw were connected with one or more of the most important transportation and industrial enterprises in Montreal in this period.

While David Torrance, Andrew Shaw, and John Kershaw had knowledge of ships and had invested in them in the past, both William Workman and Ira Gould were neither engaged in shipping nor in the general merchandising that was often allied to it. Although Workman's interests were extremely wide and varied, including railways, banking, and land speculation,[60] Gould's were apparently limited to a large flour mill on the Lachine Canal and the sale of hydraulic power to industrial users at the St Gabriel lock. The fact that they were now not only investing in shipping, but also taking the lead in directing the venture is further evidence of the mobility of capital and entrepreneurial drive of members of the Montreal business community. Since, under the Act of Incorporation, each trustee was required to have an investment of at least £1,000 in the company, each of the five had made a substantial commitment. John Kershaw's previous experience in the shipping business had apparently been very indirect, the brief ownership of the mortgage on a schooner.[61] Indeed, Kershaw's large investment and sudden prominence in the Canada Ocean Steam Navigation Company is surprising in view of his apparent business insignificance.

There were forty-two other shareholders in the concern, most of them highly important local businessmen. One was William Watson, city flour inspector and the uncle of Alexander and John Ogilvie who founded the Ogilvie flour milling company.[62] William Murray, the secretary of the Montreal Insurance Company and at one time a local merchant, was also a supporter, as was Ferdinand McCulloch, the cashier of the City Bank and secretary of the Montreal and Lachine Railway.[63] William Cowan and William Carter, partners in a ship-chandling business,[64] as well as several partners in Montreal hardware firms were also behind the scheme. Representing two of the largest houses were Harrison Stephens, and John Frothingham, along with the latter's partners, Thomas and William Workman. Benjamin Brewster and Henry Mulholland, also large hardware merchants, supported the project, along with James Hutton, Montreal agent for a number of English steel and edge tool manufacturers.[65] There were Amable Prevost and Louis Renaud, both dry goods merchants, both interested in banking: Prevost in La Banque du Peuple and Renaud in La Banque des Marchands.[66]

The largest number of backers came from the large community of Montreal's brokers and commission and general merchants, who dealt directly with the large volume of export and imported commodities. Included were the commission merchants James Scott (who, like many, was also an auctioneer), Philip Holland, James Mitchell, Henry Chapman, Thomas Kay, H.L. Routh, Hector Russell,

John Smith, George D. Watson, Augustus Heward (a general broker), and John and Robert Esdaile, grain and produce dealers.[67] These men not only were prominent in Montreal's commerce but were also active participants in many other company promotions during the forties and early fifties. Dow, Holton, Brewster, Holmes, Mulholland, Russell, Shaw, Stephens, and Frothingham put considerable money and directorial effort into railways, shipping, insurance, gas, and other enterprises. Their support for this company reflected the importance they attached to maritime and lower St Lawrence trade and their belief in steamships.

The history of the Canada Ocean Steam Navigation Company after 1854 is not known. The venture is not mentioned at all in the works of Atherton and Croil. Perhaps it came to fruition. The company's first vessel, the *Oneida* — already under construction in 1854 — was sold.

IV

The advent of steamship navigation to Montreal in 1853 revealed not only technical advance but also diversity of entrepreneurship. A number of Montreal businessmen besides Allan were keenly interested in developing steamship connections between Montreal and Britain, preferably with the provincial government's subsidy. The fact that they and the Allans still relied upon the participation of British entrepreneurs may show a lack of self-assurance in management as much as a need for capital. But the international partnerships established in steamships were a continuation of the old pattern of co-operation in ocean shipping and commerce of sailing days.

Although the would-be entrepreneurs from Montreal were almost all traders, there were a few significant exceptions, among them Ira Gould, miller, and William Dow, brewer. William Workman, though a wholesaler of iron goods, was not a staple exporter; before 1853, he had had no financial interests in shipping. While the others had been involved in ocean shipping previously, these three had not. Nor had Thomas Ryan, a St Lawrence River shipper and, with his brother John, owner of the People's Line of lower St Lawrence steamboats.

Thus the inauguration of steamshipping from Montreal to ocean ports was to a great extent a mixture of old patterns in new technological garb. Usually the businessmen of the earlier era were one; yet the exceptions to this pattern, the newcomers, are worthy of attention because their presence underlines a newly emerging aspect of Montreal's business life, the growth of an investor class. While this form of investment had already been noticeable in Montreal's railway development in the forties and early fifties, it had now spread to shipping. Its emergence suggests not only the mobility and diversity of entrepreneurial behaviour in Montreal by this time but also the existence of sufficient surplus capital available locally to enable Montrealers to take a large share of the total investment.

Hugh Allan's victory was in some ways a landmark in the development of Montreal entrepreneurship. The shareholders in his company were all Canadians, although perhaps much capital had been borrowed by Allan personally from his brothers in Britain. The entrepreneurs – those who stood to gain the huge profits which commonly go to innovators – were Canadians, however. And though details of share distribution in the ill-fated McKean-McLarty scheme are not known, it apparently had also included very substantial Canadian investment, though controlled from London and Liverpool. Besides, the Canadian Allan-led group proved to be more successful in meeting the government's requirements for regular fortnightly service to Montreal. By 1854, Allan had laid the basis for a large transatlantic shipping company and was also, in some ways, the embodiment of the transition from sail to steam in Montreal ocean shipping. Both Allan's company and its competitor demonstrate also the strength and resources of the Montreal business community. The capital seems to have been mobilized by the individual shareholders themselves from their private resources; it is very doubtful if banks supported these enterprises, except through personal loans to individual promoters on good security.

Although a full examination of the impact of steamships upon the economy of Montreal is outside the scope of this study, a brief sketch of some salient facts is instructive. Steamship arrivals at the port increased slowly over the next few years, until, during the 1859 navigation season, thirty-five ships came to Montreal. Cargoes increased from 5,545 tons in 1854 to 43,704 tons in 1859, almost exactly the tonnage carried by ocean-going sailing ships.[68] Thus, in five short years, steamships had come to equal the carrying capacity of sailing vessels. Their regularity, speed, and novelty attracted a growing passenger traffic for both immigrant and luxury accommodations, while they also drew freight.

The role of government in shaping the framework, or conditioning the climate, in which entrepreneurs operated is perhaps nowhere more plainly illustrated than in this case. The provincial government had made it physically possible for large ships of ocean-going size to reach Montreal without lighterage, and it had now been persuaded by John Young to help finance a regular steamship service. Steamships would not have come to Montreal so soon had the subsidy not been paid, and government funds continued to be of fundamental importance in the Canadian ocean shipping business for at least another decade.[69] Professor Aitken has emphasized government involvement in the interstices of the economy in the nineteenth and twentieth centuries in terms of 'defensive expansionism' against the United States. It is possible in the light of the specific instances cited here to detect another aspect of Canadian government participation. This is the sharing of an assumption by governments — and by most of the men who composed them — that the general role of the state was to stimulate economic development, not necessarily because of the need to fight a competitor, but because it was desirable and right. The government shared an ideal of economic 'progress' through the efforts of businessmen operating in a favourable climate, a point of view not discouraged by the fact that businessmen had a respected place in government circles. Since the advent of responsible government, the influence of businessmen in government was no doubt greater than ever. Among them, in addition to Francis Hincks after 1851, were John Young and A.N. Morin, who served as president of the St Lawrence and Atlantic Railway. The prevalence of the interests of businessmen in government, the assumption that what was good for them, their enterprises, and the world of business in general was at the same time right for the country, is markedly evident.

PART TWO / RAILWAYS

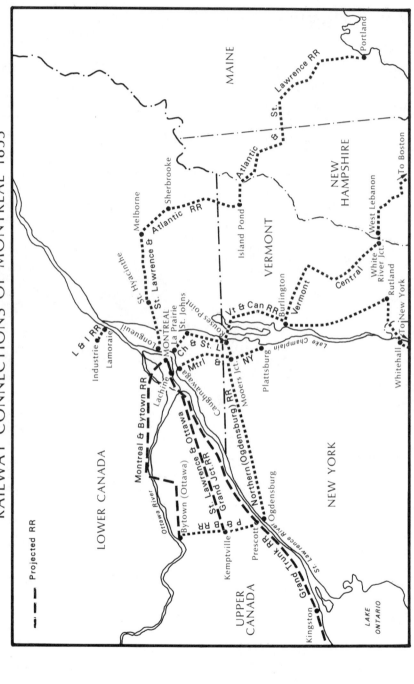

RAILWAY CONNECTIONS OF MONTREAL 1853

Projected RR

7

The Champlain and St Lawrence: Montreal's pioneer railway

For more than ten years following its completion in 1836, the Champlain and St Lawrence was the only railway extending from Montreal. Canada's first railway, it was a short fourteen-mile line from Laprairie, across the St Lawrence from Montreal, to St John's, on the Richelieu. It was designed to overcome the long-standing barriers to efficient transport between the St Lawrence River, Lake Champlain, and the Hudson River, to improve land communications between Montreal, the Richelieu, and the Eastern Townships, and to provide a more efficient mode of transporting lumber to the American market.[1] However, although the Champlain and St Lawrence signalled the beginning of Montreal's increasing reliance upon railways to supplement waterway transportation, the conversion to faith in the new medium was slow and incomplete. Montreal businessmen seem never to have lost the unquestioned key assumption that the St Lawrence River was the vital factor in their own, and their city's, economic well-being. Nevertheless, many Montreal merchants possessed enough entrepreneurial daring and flexibility to gamble on steam railways before they had been proven an efficient mode of transportation for North America.

Although much of the original impetus to build the Champlain and St Lawrence had come from Jason Pierce, an American-born merchant and forwarder at St John's,[2] Montrealers predominated in the company from the beginning. Many of them were veterans of the fur trade. In the thirties Peter McGill, George Moffatt, and François Antoine Larocque, and others, including Joseph Masson and Horatio Gates, who were prominent figures in the St Lawrence wheat trade, were increasingly connected with banking, shipping and other speculative activities in Montreal and in its hinterlands beyond. Included also were John Molson's sons, John and William, who were broadening the scope of the family's business interests beyond brewing, shipping, and real estate. John Molson jr was the Champlain railway's first president and a director for many years.[3] Peter McGill headed the group of Montrealers who petitioned in 1831 for a charter to build a railway from the St Lawrence 'to the navigable water communication with Lake Champlain.'[4] William Molson, no longer a company director after 1840, became involved in other Montreal railway ventures.

Also on the roster of promoters was George Moffatt, who was not only a former fur trader but also a winterer of many years, first for the XY Company, which he entered as a clerk at the age of fourteen, and later for the North West Company. Born in Durham, England, Moffatt was educated in London and, after his arrival in Lower Canada, at the Sorel school conducted by William Nelson.[5] This was followed by business training as a clerk in the firm of Parker, Gerrard and Ogilvy, the principal Montreal and London house supplying the XY Company. Moffatt left to join McTavish, McGillivray and Company for a brief period, and then formed a partnership with Kenneth Dowie, a former business associate of Peter McGill.[6] Dowie and Moffatt were in general merchandising, mainly engaged in supplying the fur trade but trading in some staples as well. There were a number of changes in the partnership over the next several years until it became Gillespie, Moffatt and Company, with Moffatt as the principal Canadian partner and Robert Gillespie of London as his English counterpart.[7]

Moffatt went on to great prominence in Montreal. His firm engaged heavily in wholesale merchandising, and he became very active in Montreal business affairs. In 1822 he helped to organize the Montreal Committee of Trade and was later one of the early presidents of its successor organization, the Montreal Board of Trade.[8] He was an early member of the Board appointed to inspect ashes, an important commodity in the city's trade in the early nineteenth century.[9] Moffatt's private business included minor investments in shipping and an abortive scheme to develop an island in the St Lawrence close to Montreal.[10] At the same time he became prominent in politics. He served as a member of the Lower Canada Legislative Council, the Special Council (from 1838 to 1841), the Legislative Assembly of the United Province of Canada and – perhaps the capstone of his Tory inclinations – became the president of the British American League.[11] Like John Richardson and other Montreal businessmen who became involved in political life, Moffatt probably welcomed the opportunities provided there to shape business institutions and conditions. His political and business prominence were often found useful in the advancement of major undertakings in the province.

Another early supporter of the railway was Horatio Gates. Though he died in 1834, two years before the completion of the line, he was, like McGill and Moffatt, a man of great importance in Montreal affairs and, like them, keenly interested personally in improving channels of commerce from the city. A well-established Montreal merchant since the early 1800s, by the twenties and early thirties he dominated the pork, flour, and ashes trade from the upper midwest of the United States through Montreal.[12] He was therefore interested in maintaining that trade by improving Montreal's comparative position in competition with New York, a result expected from the Champlain and St Lawrence Railway, which would help shift towards Montreal the trade balance that had favoured New York since the completion of the Erie canal in 1825. Through the Great Lakes states Gates distributed printed circulars advising his correspondents of the prices of commodities at Montreal and overseas markets.[13] His firm handled large quantities of produce from the United States side of the lower Great Lakes, notably packed pork from Ohio, of which, in 1833-4 alone, he purchased from but one of his agents some $44,000 worth.[14] He was one of the founders of the Bank of Montreal and the Montreal Committee of Trade, and a member of the boards to inspect ashes and flour at Montreal.[15] Notwithstanding these interests, and a brief involvement in politics as a member of the Legislative Council of Lower Canada in 1833-4, Gates was primarily a Montreal produce trader committed to the St Lawrence commercial system.[16]

Also among the early promoters of the Champlain railway were four French Canadian merchants from Montreal. One was François Antoine Larocque, who dealt in both the export and import trades following an earlier career in the northwest fur trade.[17] Another was Pierre Rastel de Rocheblave, a former wintering partner of both the XY and North West Companies and a partner in McTavish, McGillivray and Company from 1816 to 1821. Following the collapse of the latter in 1825, de Rocheblave became a partner in Larocque, Bernard and Company.[18] Jean Bouthilier, de Rocheblave's father-in-law, was also an early supporter of the railway. The fourth in this group of *Canadien* merchants was Joseph Masson, probably the wealthiest French Canadian of his time and the chief Montreal partner in the firm of Robertson, Masson and Company, importers of manufactured goods and staple exporters.

John Redpath was another leading Montrealer who supported the Champlain and St Lawrence. A native of Earlston, Scotland, he moved to Montreal in 1816 and became one of the city's major contractors. Between 1821 and 1825, together with Thomas McKay, he constructed a large segment of the Lachine Canal and then went on to build sections of the Rideau.[19] Redpath's secondary business concerns included the Bank of Montreal – of which he was a director between 1833 and 1869 – the Montreal Telegraph Company, and various shipping and mining ventures in the Eastern Townships. His only known public service was as an alderman for three years from 1840 to 1843, but he also helped to establish the Presbyterian college in Montreal. Interest in the Champlain railway might well have arisen from Redpath's contracting interests and from the expectation of receiving at least part of the work to be done.

These eight prominent Montreal merchants with investments in virtually all other phases of economic activity in the city and its hinterlands were joined by twice as many others in the Champlain and St Lawrence Railway Company.[20] There were Jason Pierce, a St John's merchant and shipowner,[21] and Lebbeus B. Ward, the operator of a Montreal foundry. Among them also was James Logan, a member of the Montreal-Liverpool firm Hart, Logan and Company, and Joseph Shuter, an importer specializing in crockery. Shuter dealt extensively in lumber from Upper Canada and was appointed by the government in 1829 to inspect shipments passing through Montreal.[22] Since some lumber deposited at Montreal was sent to Lake Champlain, Shuter, who handled substantial quantities of it, had an interest in facilitating its movement. The Montreal Committee of Trade, the improvement to navigation of the St Lawrence, the Montreal News Room (a place where commercial information from Canadian and foreign publications was available), all attracted his participation, as did the Bank of Montreal, of which he was a director from 1831 to 1847.[23]

As well, John Mills, an American-born Montreal merchant and property-owner, was keenly interested in the Champlain railway.[24] He was subsequently an active member of the Board of Trade, a founder of the City and District Savings Bank, and mayor of Montreal in 1847. Also prominent in municipal affairs was another charter member of the Champlain and St Lawrence Railway Company, John Boston, a lawyer and after 1839 sheriff of the County of Montreal. Briefly a director of the Bank of Montreal, Boston was also seigneur of St James in Lacadie County.[25] Benjamin Holmes, who then held the highly important position of cashier (general manager) of the Bank of Montreal, was also included.[26]

All of these Montreal businessmen were behind the Champlain and St Lawrence Railway project because it would, if successful, foster the economic well-being of Montreal and, directly or indirectly, their own personal profit. Importers, general traders, potash and other staple merchants, industrialists and bankers, veterans of the fur trade, and relative newcomers – Scots, Englishmen, French Canadians, and Americans – were all drawn together to promote this railway scheme, just as they had united from time to time in the past to build institutions for stimulating Montreal's growth.

Since stock registers of the Company have not survived, it is not known how much each of these putative railway promoters put up in the way of commitments to buy shares in the railway, which was capitalized at £50,000 in 1832. It is unlikely, however, that many deviated far from what was swiftly becoming the generally accepted maximum purchase of twenty shares of £50, or

£1,000, beyond which very few local merchants bought equity in any of Montreal's joint stock ventures.[27] In the Champlain and St Lawrence Company, the only significant exception to this norm was John Molson sr, who invested £9,000 and provided nearly 20 per cent of its original capital.[28] Little can be said also about dealing in the Company's shares or about the prices and amounts traded locally following the completion of the railway in 1836. Some evidence of considerable trading is provided in an 1851 list of shareholders, which shows that, despite many years of excellent profits and high dividends, many of the original promoters were no longer shareholders.[29]

Absent from the shareholders' list in that later year were earlier figures like Benjamin Holmes, James Logan, Tancrède Bouthilier, Lebbeus Ward, Joseph Shuter, Jason Pierce, John Redpath, and George Moffatt. And of the few original promoters who remained in 1851, Peter McGill held only eleven shares and John Boston three.[30] Joseph Masson and François Antoine Larocque were both dead by that time, but their shares were no longer in the family. John Molson sr had probably bequeathed his huge holdings to his son John, while John Mills's shares were also in his estate. By 1851, then, most of the original supporters of the Champlain and St Lawrence Railway no longer had an interest in the company. Normal trading in securities, though primitive and not on record in detail, would explain the absence of many of the original names. Probably an even more important factor, however, was the railway's growth in the fifteen years since it had opened. Between 1836 and 1851 the Champlain and St Lawrence changed from a fragile, spring-to-autumn, wooden-railed, short-portage railway to a year-round, iron-railed line between St Lambert, immediately opposite Montreal, and Rouses' Point, Vermont. There had been a virtual metamorphosis in the railway's orientation, for during the forties it became an adjunct of the northern New England railway network pushing up from Massachusetts toward the St Lawrence in an effort to draw to Boston the interior trade enjoyed by its rival, New York. With the drive towards American connections came increasing American investment in the company. Moreover, at Montreal the Champlain and St Lawrence had witnessed the growth of competitors. During the late forties the advent of two other lines seeking essentially the same traffic forced the Champlain and St Lawrence to extend the line southward and to gird itself for tough battles.

II

From 1836 to the mid-forties, the Champlain and St Lawrence Railway Company enjoyed abundant prosperity. Initial construction costs had been within the capital limit, so that the company did not find it necessary to sell large quantities of bonds to finance construction of the line. Early problems, such as those caused by snow and the snaking of strap-iron and wooden rails, were solved.[31] Gross income of the Company in 1836 amounted to £6042; it increased rapidly to £15,496 in 1839, declined slowly over the next few years to £11,800 in 1843, and returned to near the 1839 figure in 1844.[32] The following year receipts jumped to £20,100 and remained at approximately that level until 1850, when revenue again improved markedly for several years.

It is clear that the railway's revenue was closely related to the volume of lumber it carried. After 1839 there was a sharp decline in the value of wood products exported through St John's: in 1840 their worth was down by approximately 30 per cent, and though there was a brief upturn in 1841, the next year wood exports fell by a further 50 per cent. By 1843 wood exports through St John's were worth only £6,000, only one-sixth of the 1839 figure.[33] But the railway also carried a large passenger traffic, which increased during the forties.[34] This helped to offset declines in wood until the United States bonding legislation of 1845 accelerated all freight volumes on the line. Moreover, between 1839 and 1843, the year of the completion of the Chambly Canal (which bypassed the rapids on the Richelieu between Chambly and St John's), the Champlain and St Lawrence Railway was blessed with the absence of viable competition for the traffic between the St Lawrence and Lake Champlain.

Because of its fluctuating revenues and commensurate changes in net profits, the Company paid only modest dividends for most years down to 1850.[35] More might have been paid but for the insistence of the directors upon improvements in the rolling stock and in the road itself, efficiently administered by the Company's manager, William Dobie Lindsay.[36] A successful St John's steamboat owner, Lindsay also leased his vessels periodically to the railway. He bought a new engine in 1845 and the same year put down iron rails throughout; he acquired new boxcars and repaired much of the Company's run-down equipment.[37] Lindsay's refurbishing of the railway from 1845 to 1847 was dictated by the need to improve equipment but also by the directors' increasing awareness that there would soon be at least two new competitors to the hitherto unchallenged hegemony of the railway over the St Lawrence-Lake Champlain trade.

One threat was the new Compagnie de Navigation du Richelieu and other shipping concerns that intended to utilize the Chambly Canal route to Lake Champlain. A second and perhaps more serious menace lay in a Boston project to build the Northern or Ogdensburg railway from Burlington, Vermont, around the northern part of Lake Champlain and through upper New York State to the St Lawrence at Ogdensburg. Although this particular scheme was, in 1845, only a grandiose idea, the serious discussion of it in newspapers and the ominous surveying of its route gave Montrealers and directors of the Champlain railway some cause for alarm.[38]

More serious still to the future profitability of the Champlain and St Lawrence was the scheme proposed in 1844 to connect Portland to Montreal, or more accurately to the St Lawrence River at a point immediately opposite the city. This railway, the St Lawrence and Atlantic, was to become a major carrier of exports and imports from Montreal. Current rhetoric held that the traffic in lumber from the whole of the Upper Canadian lumber-producing areas to the American market on the eastern seaboard would be attracted to this route. That would leave the Champlain railway with only poorly-paying local traffic from the immediately adjacent areas of the Richelieu Valley and Lake Champlain, an unhappy outlook for the owners of what was a moderately prosperous railway. Until 1844-5 they apparently had been content to maintain the Champlain and St Lawrence as a portage railway, but there were thus suddenly compelling reasons why it should be joined up with Boston's lines. The impending availability of the latter made the prospect all the more pressing, and resistance to this extension put up by shipping interests of St John's, such as Jason Pierce, were swept away.[39]

Extending the line south from St John's to the United States involved more than just the addition of track mileage; a change in metropolitan alignment was also implied. The connection had previously been with New York, by the Richelieu River to Lake Champlain, through Lake George, the Champlain Canal, and the Hudson River. But the pending railway network in the region, at least in the immediate future, meant connections with Boston, the most aggressive railway centre in the northeastern United States at that time.

As E.C. Kirkland has so amply demonstrated, the immediate success after 1843 of Boston's railway westward to Albany, where it was intended to siphon off some of the New York-bound traffic from the Erie Canal, sparked Boston capitalists into further railway promotion. In October 1843 the Vermont Central Railroad Company received a charter to build a railway from Burlington east to the Connecticut River.[40] In June 1844 the legislature of New Hampshire chartered the Northern, which was to join the Vermont Central at its eastern terminus and run to Concord, New Hampshire, where it would link up with the Concord Railway, an extension of the line from Boston to Lawrence and Manchester. Thus, by 1843, possibilities were opening for tying the Champlain and St Lawrence into a network that, when completed, would disgorge at Boston.

A short time later, during the summer and autumn of 1844, debate opened in Montreal on the subject of connections with either Boston or Portland. The shareholders and directors of the Champlain and St Lawrence Railway Company were looking more favourably on a southern connection with the United States. This change in outlook was no doubt assisted by the changing pattern of share ownership in the company. Many shares had been falling into the hands of non-Montrealers and other men who, if not Bostonians, were probably connected with that city's railway network. Although there is no clear evidence of a 'takeover,' it might well have been at this point that some of the original promoters of the railway, such as Jason Pierce of St John's, among others, began to sell off shares to outsiders. The transition was far advanced by 1851, when so many of the originals were noticeably absent from the list of shareholders. Boston control over the Champlain and St Lawrence, alleged in 1850 and 1851, might well have begun at least five years earlier, when influence over decisions about Montreal railways was most crucial. One representative of Boston interests was almost certainly H.R. Campbell, an American contractor who had undertaken to build the extension to Rouses' Point. In 1851, he held 562 of the company's shares, more than one-quarter of the total.[41] Other non-Montrealers on the 1851 shareholders list might well have represented Boston interests.

It is clear that a new group, whether Bostonian or not, had begun to emerge as directors of the Champlain and St Lawrence Railway in the early forties. In 1842, in addition to continuing directors John E. Mills, John Molson, and Joseph Shuter, several new men were suddenly elected to the board. Included were Mr Justice Gale,[42] John Bleakley, a Montreal lawyer,[43] James Keith, Dr William Robertson, and Alexandre Maurice Delisle, a member of the Legislative Assembly for the County of Montreal (between 1841 and 1843) and a founder, later the president, of the Montreal City and District Savings Bank. Delisle had an abiding interest in railways. He served the Champlain and St Lawrence faithfully into the fifties as a director and a promoter of its proposed northern branch, the Montreal and Bytown.[44]

Another newcomer to the directorate in 1842 was William Workman, who remained on the Board annually into the fifties. Although he was later a director of the rival St Lawrence and Atlantic, up to 1852 Workman's railway interests favoured the Champlain and St Lawrence in which he held the large number of forty-seven shares. He was also involved in the Montreal and Bytown project of the early fifties.[45] Benjamin Brewster joined the directors in 1844; although not conspicuous as a prominent local businessman, he was important in his special branch, wholesale hardware. His firm, Brewster and Mulholland, was a large and busy establishment selling large quantities of goods to Ottawa Valley lumber camps during the forties. Brewster, an American, was connected with Montreal's City Bank, an institution among whose shareholders there was a surprisingly large concentration of American-born residents of Montreal. He was also associated with the City and District Savings Bank, of which he and his partner, Mulholland, were among the first directors. Although Brewster was not a large shareholder of the Champlain and St Lawrence – he held only eighteen shares in 1851 – he was a valuable member of the board and became chairman of the company in 1852.[46]

Joining the directors at the same time as Brewster was Sir George Simpson of the Hudson's Bay Company. Aside from his principal tasks of managing his employers' fur empire, Simpson had important connections in the Montreal business world and large personal investments in such enterprises as shipping. He also acted as a kind of broker for some of his fellow employees at the Hudson's Bay Company, putting "the money out ... in Canada, in bank stock and carefully chosen real estate.'[47] Personally owning twenty shares, Simpson remained on the railway's board until 1849.

These were the men who directed the Champlain and St Lawrence through a period of expansion down to 1851, through vigorous and nearly ruinous competition in 1853 and 1854, and finally into amalgamation with the rival Montreal and New York Railway, which ran between Montreal and Plattsburg on the west side of Lake Champlain. Although within the small world of railway entrepreneurship in the city they were a distinctly identifiable group, they were generally representative of the Montreal business community. The railway investors and managers were drawn from all areas of the local business community: general merchandising, shipping, banking, industry, former fur traders, and the legal and medical professions. Moreover, it is evident that support for the project came from all the main ethnic segments of the community, although in this respect participation of French Canadians was small and short-lived. Larocque, de Rocheblave, Bouthilier, and Masson were gone by the 1850s; only Delisle remained as a French Canadian of any prominence in the company, and only a few others with French names held shares.

Another distinctive feature of railway entrepreneurs (defined as the largest shareholders and the directors with the longest service on the Board) was their strong inclination to confine their interest exclusively to one railway. Because of the absence of complete records of railway share purchases and sales in this period, it would be impossible to say with finality that directors of one railway never held significant numbers of shares (more than twenty) in other railways, yet the available evidence suggests that conclusion. John Molson, the second largest shareholder in the Champlain and St Lawrence, had not a farthing invested in the competing St Lawrence and Atlantic, nor in the Montreal and New York, in which his brother William was very active. The same was true of Mr Justice Gale or William Workman (the fact that the latter was a director of the St Lawrence and Atlantic in 1852 but not, in 1851, a shareholder suggests that he may have been representing the City of Montreal on the Board).

Directors Thomas Cringan, Benjamin Brewster and William S. Phillips, had no financial interests in the Portland line, and it is a good bet that they were equally chary of supporting the other rival railway, the Montreal and New York. This is not to say, of course, that many comparatively minor shareholders in the Champlain and St Lawrence did not at the same time support competing companies.

Occasionally, directors of the Champlain railway would hold a few shares in the Portland line; for example, George Simpson, John Mills, A.M. Delisle and Peter Dease. But only Delisle maintained both a directorship in the Champlain and St Lawrence and a substantial investment in the St Lawrence and Atlantic. With few exceptions, directors in the three competing railways confined their directorial activities to one line at any one time even though they sometimes owned shares in one of the rivals and, in a few cases, after shifting, became directors in the rival. A few directors of the St Lawrence and Atlantic, including John Torrance and T.A. Stayner, had briefly also been directors of the Montreal and Lachine Railway, but this was in 1847 and 1848, before the Montreal and Lachine's own ambition to become a competitor for Atlantic traffic had become clear.

III

By the late 1845 the Champlain and St Lawrence was planning to expand, – whether because of the *élan* injected by the new personnel on the board, fear of rivals, or enthusiasm engendered by newspaper coverage of railway building in neighbouring Vermont.[48] In November 1845, a group including the company's directors and a few others gave notice of its intention to apply for a charter to build a line onward from St John's to Mississquoi Bay on Lake Champlain. Although the extension was to be financed and constructed by another company, it was to be an integral part of the Champlain and St Lawrence system. A clear reference was made to New England's railway interests in a petition to the legislature of March 1846, which noted that not only Lower Canadians, but also 'inhabitants ... of the neighbouring States' were interested in the project.[49] Having registered its principal request for permission to extend southward, and a secondary application also to build a branch into the Eastern Townships – perhaps to thwart the St Lawrence and Atlantic's potential drawing power in that area – company officials awaited legislative approval.

The Draper administration of the day was faced just then with a number of railway petitions from Lower Canada, including a Lake St Louis and Province Line and a Quebec-to-Melbourne scheme, both of which required scrutiny by the newly-struck committee of the Legislative Assembly on railroad petitions and bills.[50] That committee, which considered general railway policy as well as specific bills, would probably have wished to refrain from recommending on the Champlain extension. Moreover, the Draper administration, which followed a cautiously restrained policy on public development projects, refused the company's request for 'such aid as possible' from the government, replying on this point that they were 'of the opinion that the initiation in the above cases rests with the respective parties and not with the Government.'[51]

Forced to wait for a decision, the company conceived a supplementary plan in June 1847 to further confound their rival, the St Lawrence and Atlantic, whose first thirty miles was then under construction, by building a bridge across the St Lawrence in order to bring their own line right into Montreal.[52] This idea was apparently not pursued, nor is there any evidence that it was discussed by the government. In any event, there was no provision for a bridge when, at last, the Champlain's southern extension was incorporated as the Montreal and Province Line Junction Railway Company in 1847.[53] But the charter was followed by two years of inaction on the project. The delay was probably a combination of economic uncertainty in Montreal between 1847 and 1849 and a lack of complete assurance about the location of the southern terminus of the line in view of the fact that its southern connections were not fully under construction until 1848-9.[54]

This delay required some changes in the company's charter to allow it more time to complete its surveys. Further amendments permitted enlargement of capital of the Montreal and Province Line Railway Company and enabled it to merge formally with the parent firm.[55] This may not have been an entirely welcome acquisition to the Champlain and St Lawrence owners, who were themselves in the midst of raising capital for modifications in their own line. And they might also have seen distinct advantages in having the two lines separate, to limit liabilities and to retain for themselves the profits and dividends previously enjoyed.

Formal amalgamation of the two companies took place, however, in 1850; but no construction was undertaken until plans to finance it were completed. A northern branch to St Lambert, the longer southern extension, expanded wharf facilities, and new rolling stock were all required. Hence, an increase of capital to £160,000 was deemed necessary. The only opposition to the Champlain and St Lawrence scheme to this point came from some residents of Ste Athanase in Rouville County, where it was felt that the company's frequent freight rate changes were injurious.[56] Similar complaints were heard from various St John's residents, but these grievances, perhaps real though minor, were not sufficient to convince the legislature to withold its permission for the company's expansion of capital. Under new legislation passed in 1850 share capital was expansible to £185,000; moreover, the company had authority to borrow a further £75,000.[57]

Contracts with H.R. Campbell, a noted American railroad engineer and experienced contractor, were completed in August 1850. He undertook to complete the extension from St John's to the Great Northern railway by July 1851 for £75,000: £28,125 in shares, an equal amount in bonds, and the remainder in iron rails.[58] The northern works were not undertaken at that point. The company's superintendent, A.H. Brainerd, informed the shareholders that these would cost a total of £78,750.[59] He did point out, however, that all the contemplated enlargements and improvements, including some more badly needed rolling stock, would increase the company's revenue by some £46,512 annually. Income would improve over existing business for passenger traffic by an estimated £16,775 for freight by £15,360. Increased traffic would result from the extended track, new wharf facilities, and improved capacity to sustain year-round operations efficiently, so that, over-all, business over the next two years would grow by about twenty-five per cent. The 'most sanguine expectations of shareholders will be more than realized' Brainerd predicted. The new railway, fully integrated with its southern connections, would speed trains to Boston or New York in twelve hours; and not only would the company prosper, but Montreal would benefit greatly too.

Some Montrealers were somewhat sceptical of the rosy predictions in Brainerd's report, and alarm was expressed by an anonymous letter writer in the Montreal *Gazette* over the implications of the American connections of the Champlain and St Lawrence. The extension south to Rouses' Point to join the Northern and the Vermont and Canada, the writer alleged, would put the Champlain railway at the disposal and the mercy of these American railways.[60] After committing itself to them, the Champlain and St Lawrence might well be abandoned by American lines arranging other link-ups with competing Canadian ones. Already there were plans to build two north-south lines that would cut heavily into the Champlain's traffic. One would link Plattsburg to Lachine, and the other Highgate, Vermont, to Ste Athanase, east of the Richelieu. The same American interests were seen to be behind moves that would almost certainly injure the Champlain and St Lawrence very seriously.

There was no immediate follow-up, however, to these imputations. Somewhat later, in 1851, came evidence that the Champlain and St Lawrence was indeed the tail of an American dog, wagging as its master wished. This, at least, was the conclusion reached by some observers at the sudden and startling proposal by the company to bridge the Richelieu at Ash Island, a place in the river approximately half-way between St John's and Rouses' Point.[61] Why should the company's directors have decided that they wanted a bridge across the Richelieu in order to construct the main line on the east side of the river? The main line was at the moment under construction on the west side. If the east side had been more desirable, why was that choice, which must have been clearly visible long before, not made earlier? Obviously some change of thinking had taken place since the annual meeting of January 1851, where not a whisper of this idea had been heard.

William A. Merry, the secretary of the Champlain and St Lawrence Railway Company, explained to members of the Legislative Assembly's committee on railways in September 1851 that the sole reason for the route change was to allow the company 'to compete with the Ogdensburg Railroad for a large carrying trade, which the Champlain and St Lawrence Railroad Company established and held previous to the opening of the Ogdensburg Road, but which that road has taken from them and now monopolizes — namely, the transport of the produce of the Western States and Canada West from the River St Lawrence to Lake Champlain for consumption in the Eastern States, and for shipment from the Atlantic ports.'[62]

He argued further that although the Champlain railway had been able hitherto to deliver goods from the St Lawrence River to Rouses' Point at cheaper rates than could the Ogdensburg railway, the latter had recently acquired a potential advantage in the floating bridge, only recently allowed by the New York state legislature, which the company was soon to build, so that its trains could pass readily to the east side of Lake Champlain, where they would reach the tracks of the Vermont and Canada railway at Alburg, Vermont. Thus the long-sought goal of a through railway system between Boston and the St Lawrence river would become a reality, Merry informed the legislators, implying that the Champlain and St Lawrence was about to be bested by a rival. The Canadian railway and, by implication, Montreal were soon to be outflanked by a seizure of their trade by Boston.

The weakness of this case should have been apparent. If the two railways, the Champlain and the Ogdensburg were truly competitors for the same St Lawrence to Boston or New York traffic, why did the Canadian company not try long before to avoid being outmanoeuvred by adopting a different route for the extension south from St John's, perhaps a route similar to the one being proposed to the railway committee? Instead they had put themselves completely in the hands of their supposed competitor by building directly to its eastern terminus, where the Boston-based Vermont railways would join up. Moreover, it appears that most of the Champlain railway's freight business had consisted, up till then, of lumber destined for the Lake Champlain and, ultimately, the New York market. Steamboats from Lake Champlain had come up to St John's to pick up the lumber brought by rail, which was then taken south through the upper New York waterway system. Besides this lumber, the Champlain railway carried a large passenger traffic, most of which apparently was drawn exclusively from the Montreal area and the region through which its tracks passed. Thus, in at least these two respects, there was no apparent rivalry between the Champlain and the Northern. They were complementary instead.

Nor is it clear that the latter had seriously damaged the former railway's traffic in flour, as the Champlain company alleged before the railway committee. William Merry, in testifying there, asserted that the Champlain and St Lawrence had carried forty thousand barrels of flour in the autumn of 1849 for the New England market and an equal quantity early the next year to Lake Champlain.[63] But in 1851, he claimed, the whole carrying trade of western produce, including flour, for these same markets went down by way of the Ogdensburg route, so that scarcely any descended the St Lawrence past Ogdensburg itself. Obviously meant to be taken literally, this statement was a clear misrepresentation of facts which any of the legislators who heard these allegations could have discovered easily. Receipts on the Champlain and St Lawrence were actually higher in 1850 than in 1849, and in 1851 were up by another 25 per cent.[64] Moreover, between 1850 and 1851 there was an increase of nearly 60 per cent in St Lawrence canal traffic;[65] and though there is no certainty that flour shipments increased by a similar percentage, they can hardly have decreased as Merry suggested.

Thus it is questionable whether the Ogdensburg and the Champlain and St Lawrence were in fact serious competitors. The orientation of the latter was heavily to Montreal, to the lumber trade, and, increasingly, to the Ottawa Valley. Furthermore, there is some evidence to support the contemporary opinion that there were close connections or mutual associations between the two supposedly competing railways and that both were controlled by the same Boston interests that had financed the chain of railways through Massachusetts, New Hampshire, Vermont, and New York – the 'Great Northern Route' to the Lakes.[66] Not only was H.R. Campbell, the contractor for the southern extension, also the engineer of the Vermont and Canada but Governor Charles Paine of Vermont, a 'paladin' of the connecting Vermont Central, was also on the board of the Vermont and Canada and, in 1852, became a director of the Champlain railway too.[67]

Thus there is some reason to believe that the proposals of the Champlain and St Lawrence to build a bridge across the Richelieu were not so much a result of competition as an apparently pressing necessity of the railway system as a whole.[68] A bridge across the Richelieu at Ash Island, not too far from the border, might serve the interests of all three lines as a substitute, if the 'floating bridge' across Lake Champlain linking the Vermont and the New York lines was not technically successful or was interfered with by the legislatures of Vermont and New York, where there was still considerable opposition to the project. A more pressing reason for the Richelieu bridge, at least according to the river's shipping interests, was the railway's hope of closing off as much as possible of the river traffic which competed with the extended Champlain and St Lawrence.

Notwithstanding the demise of the Richelieu River bridge scheme, which was simply dropped because the floating bridge project made it unnecessary. 1851 was a year of great accomplishments. There were some new concerns as well. The Champlain railway's contracts to build both extensions – the southern for £75,000 and the northern for £37,500 – along with £50,000 in improvements to wharf facilities,[69] had resulted in the accumulation of immense burdens. Directors revealed that by the end of 1852 the company's debts amounted to £217,523, almost all of it consisting of short-term bank loans, including £20,000 from the Bank of Montreal.[70]

The Champlain's directors had apparently not attempted to finance this growth by quickly calling in instalments on new shares which the company had been allowed to sell under recent legislation. By 1851 some 1100 (£55,600 worth) of these new shares had been sold, mostly to owners of the old issue, many of whom doubled their holdings, as did Hugh Allan, Edwin Atwater, A.M. Delisle, William Macdonald, John Molson, J.G. Mackenzie, Sir George Simpson, and the Workman brothers, Thomas and William, and many others.[71] In spite of the demonstration of great faith in the project by these Montrealers who doubled their investments, and by others who went beyond that, many original subscribers did not support the new issue. Perhaps to increase its marketability, the directors decided to extend payments on these new shares out over ten years, in annual instalments of five pounds each. This meant that only one, or at most two, instalments, totalling perhaps a little more than £11,000, had been received, hardly enough to cover expansion costs.

Clearly, then, the company was laying up potentially serious economic trouble for itself by going ahead strictly on borrowed capital. With mounting debts to banks for short-term loans at high interest, bankruptcy was distinctly possible unless the company's revenue on operations increased markedly. Instead of building up some cash reserves, the company over previous years had paid out dividends which included nearly the whole annual net profits. A decision by the proprietors in January 1852 to forgo dividends that year in order to improve the company's finances can not have had much effect on its debt position.[72]

IV

All troubles, actual and potential, were forgotten in the autumn of 1851 when the Champlain and St Lawrence, its extensions completed, stood at the entry of a new period in its history. No longer a portage line from Laprairie to St John's, the railway was forty-two miles long, connecting Montreal with New England's rail network through to Boston and New York. Yet, while there were clear reasons for Montreal to celebrate the occasion of the link-up, Boston was clearly the major beneficiary. Therefore it was most appropriate that large celebrations should take place in the Massachusetts metropolis. While Montreal's citizens had fostered three railways to the seaboard, including the St Lawrence and Atlantic and the Montreal and New York, Bostonians were united in their railway thrusts north and west and were interested in only one line to Montreal, as part of their expanding New England-Upper New York network.

The preparations in Boston for the commemoration of this achievement coincided with the finishing stages of work on the Champlain and St Lawrence and the Northern, two lines that were designed to tap the Canadian trade. The special booklet prepared for the celebrations emphasized the Canadian orientation of Boston's *drang nach norden*.[73] Statistical tables told of rapidly increasing imports from Canada down to 1850, and the publication ended with a comforting rhetorical question: 'If this remarkable increase took place before our Railway system reached the Canadas, what may not be expected now that it is completed and in operation both to Montreal and to Ogdensburg?'

An important prelude to the observances, soon dubbed the Boston Jubilee, was a much publicized perambulation of some prominent citizens throughout Canada to invite Canadian worthies to visit Boston for three days of festivities in mid-September 1851.[74] Obviously, the whole of Canada now was thought to be Boston's new economic fiefdom, the native chieftains being summoned to pay homage to the potentates in the counting houses of the new metropolis. Everywhere they went in Canada, Boston's emissaries were warmly welcomed. At Toronto, Governor General Elgin received them and accepted their invitation along with a group of businessmen and politicians from that part of the province. Montrealers too were invited when the New Englanders arrived on August 16 when the Montreal *Gazette* applauded the forthcoming jubilee which 'promis[ed] to be Americo-Canadian in its style and character ... and ... we gladly extend the hand of fellowship to our American brethren, trusting that this will prove the harbinger of many days of mutually profitable intercourse, both commercial and social, between the two countries.'[75]

In the late summer of 1851 it must have seemed to many that the battle begun six years before between Boston and Portland for Montreal's favours had at last been won by the former. Attendance at its Jubilee by so many prominent Canadians as well as the governor general seemed to symbolize Canadian recognition that Boston had won. From Montreal went Benjamin Holmes and A. Jobin, members of the Assembly for Montreal city and county respectively,

Justices Mondelet and McCord, Mayor Charles Wilson, a number of city aldermen and councillors, and John Molson, who still had an immense personal financial stake in the Champlain and St Lawrence Railway. Also attending were many from Toronto and small towns in Canada West, along with some Maritimers. Governor General Elgin, joined later by President Fillmore, attended only reluctantly out of duty to what appeared to be an auspicious harbinger of closer Canadian-American commercial relations.[76]

Montrealers seemed overjoyed with the omens. The Montreal city council sent a handsome gift and profuse thanks on behalf of all citizens to Mayor J.H. Daley of Boston.[77] Expectations of tangible financial benefits from the extensions and improvements to the Champlain and St Lawrence were justified when shareholders were told in January 1852 that 1851 had been an excellent year.[78] Receipts soared by 25 per cent, a good sign, and when the returns for 1852 were tallied gross income had jumped a further 30 per cent and the rise in profits, from £8480 to £14,078, was even more impressive. Passenger traffic, in the same year, grew by 33 per cent, freight by 56 per cent.[79] It was not surprising that traffic, revenues, and profits should have increased so swiftly. Until the completion of the rival St Lawrence and Atlantic in 1853 and the Montreal and New York Railway shortly thereafter, the Champlain railway, newly extended and refurbished, offered Montreal its only rail outlet to the sea. Even after its putative competitors came into operation the Champlain and St Lawrence was far busier, and presumably more profitable, than either of the other two lines.

Yet though the railway was an operational success, its finances were in a perilous state. The sizable debts accumulated during recent construction were becoming annoyingly oppressive by late 1852, when the repayment of short-term bank loans was due. At this point the company's directors decided to seek longer-term financing by selling shares and bonds. In March 1853 the company was authorized by an Act of the legislature to sell £175,000 worth of bonds and an additional £225,000 worth of shares.[80] It is unlikely, in view of incomplete sale of shares authorized under the provisions of 1849, that the company would soon be able to sell many shares of an even newer issue.

Other changes in the company's powers suggest alterations in the control of the railway. Whereas in the original Act no proprietor had been entitled to more than twenty-five votes, there was now to be one vote per share regardless of numbers; in the original, one could act as proxy for a maximum of 150 shares, but there were now to be unlimited proxies. These changes would facilitate centralization of the railway's control, which, though well advanced, was not complete. Under its amended charter, the Champlain and St Lawrence received permission to buy into Canadian and American railway and steamboat companies and bridge companies. These amendments were more than just tidying-up details; they helped to clear the way for meeting future exigencies. Though the absence of the company's minutes and letter books make it difficult to determine the reasoning, it is probable that the company was preparing for its battle with the Montreal and New York railway line, its major rival.

The conflict with the Montreal and New York Railway Company was to further weaken the finances of the Champlain and St Lawrence. During the rate war the former suffered a reduction of income. Though still able to pay operating expenses and interest on its bonded debt, the company suffered considerably, if not as much as its rival. Unfortunately the annual reports of the Montreal and New York are not available for 1853 and 1854, when the competition was at its height, and the newspapers seem to have refrained from commenting on the battles. One historian, R.R. Brown, wrote that the Montreal and New York's directors began buying up shares of the Champlain railway in the autumn of 1853 in an attempt to gain control. Their plan, he asserted, was purposely to wreck both companies so that they, as bondholders, could get possession of both railways at a fraction of their value.[81] However, there is little evidence that these designs were held, or that they succeeded.

During 1854 and 1855, the strain on the Champlain and St Lawrence's finances worsened. Sizable loans had still to be negotiated with Montreal banks in 1855.[82] Then, in 1855, the two contending companies merged as the Champlain and New York Railway Company.[83] The merger, however, did not arrest the decline of the combined system, for while one competitor was eliminated, another old rival, the St Lawrence and Atlantic, actively emerged in 1853. The latter was energized now through its absorption into the Grand Trunk, and later by the completion of the Victoria Bridge across the St Lawrence at Montreal in 1860. In 1863, the failing Champlain and New York was leased, and in 1872 sold, to the Grand Trunk.[84]

v

The Champlain railway declined after 1853, not only because of competition both east and west but also because of internal weaknesses. Through May, June, and July 1854 the lines' freight and passenger traffic grew, probably because of its excellent connections with Boston and New York. The railway must have been potentially profitable at least until the opening of the Victoria Bridge in 1860. The costly rate war with the Montreal and New York sapped much of its strength, but that was more a symptom of its troubles than a prime cause. Although the decline of the Champlain and St Lawrence might in the long run have been inevitable, the company could well have survived in a healthy state for some time had it entered the fifties in a financially sound condition. The failure of the company to build up a reserve of funds to provide a financial cushion for the period of extension, the failure to sell a sufficient number of new issue shares, and the borrowing of large amounts of money from banks on short-term, high interest loans, in this period introduced serious weaknesses that, when stress did come, proved to be very severe. The demise of the company demonstrated a failure of management, in an enterprise, moreover, which benefited from some of the most competent local managerial skill.

The experience of the Champlain and St Lawrence Railway between 1836 and 1853 shows the effects of the growing spread of American railways into the Montreal area at this early stage of the Canadian railway era. The decision by the owners of the Champlain and St Lawrence to extend their line southwards was the first of a series of similar decisions by other Montreal railway companies and an expression of the city's need for year-round transportation links with overseas markets. In this case Boston became the entrepôt for Montreal and, conversely, Montreal and the St Lawrence system became, to some extent, Boston's railway frontier. Furthermore, the development of the Champlain and St Lawrence showed a high degree of dependence on the United States, which provided its contractor, its locomotives, substantial capital, and, perhaps most important, its inspiration and entrepreneurial *élan*. These features, as we shall see, were not unique to the Champlain and St Lawrence Railway. What is remarkable is not that the Canadian railways were 'taken over' by Americans at a certain stage, but that they were from their very beginnings specifically and unequivocally designed to feed traffic into (and later to lock into) the northeastern United States railway system.

The Champlain and St Lawrence Railway, moreover, is an interesting example of Montreal entrepreneurship. Its conception in the early thirties and completion in 1836 with local capital demonstrated that Montrealers were alive to the possibilities of railways practically at the dawn of the railroad age. Montreal businessmen, despite their different national groups and the immense diversity in the length of their connections with the city and in their commercial activities, together recognized the value of a speedier system of communications with Lake Champlain. Also noteworthy was the speedy mustering of the necessary capital locally, mostly in Montreal, to build the railway. The assumptions that local capital was in short supply or that it was entirely commercial are called into question by the involvement of Montreal entrepreneurs in the financing of this railway. It was one of the first capital ventures in which they participated that was not only somewhat speculative, in view of its novelty, but also 'long range' in the sense that it required a longer period than they were used to accepting for the gestation of an enterprise. This factor may help to explain the reticence of many Montreal businessmen to become entrepreneurs in this venture. Yet, it also is suggestive of the size and mobility of domestic capital. While the institutions that stimulated and channelled mobile capital were not yet well developed in Montreal, there is evidence that after their original investments were made in the railway, many early investors moved their capital out again with relative ease.

It would probably be easy to exaggerate the significance of the Champlain and St Lawrence railway by saying that it brought Canada into the age of railways; that age, in fact, did not arrive until the late fifties. It would also be incorrect to say that it marked a beginning of the age of iron and steam, which was already well developed in the steamboat yards of the Montreal waterfront. Nor did the Champlain and St Lawrence mark the beginnings of an 'industrial revolution' by promoting secondary manufacturing for an enlarged market. Industrialization came to Montreal in rapidly accelerated, almost 'boom' conditions, during the late forties, when the Lachine Canal's hydraulic power was made available for industrial uses. The Champlain railway was less an end or a beginning than a stage in the transition to all of these things, to the age of railways, iron and steam, and industrialization. Perhaps the line's greatest value lay in providing for merchants a schooling in entrepreneurship in a new venture in transportation. By 1853, the Champlain railway seems to have supplied its owners with at least one more major lesson which was seldom lost to the view of subsequent Canadian entrepreneurs: that railways were not simply vehicles for improving transportation; they were instruments of financial manipulation in stocks and bonds, and of enrichment through construction contracts. Finally, the railway emphasized Montreal's dependence upon the eastern seaboard of the United States for markets and for a winter outlet to Britain. And, not least important, it was part of Montreal's historic endeavour to strengthen its competitive power over an elusive hinterland.

8

The St Lawrence and Atlantic Railway: the first stage 1844-6

The outstanding railway project in Montreal in the forties and early fifties was the St Lawrence and Atlantic, the Canadian section of an international railway between Longueuil and Portland, Maine. It was important not only because of its very length, some 120 miles from Longueuil to the United States border, but also because it provided the stimulus for other railway proposals during that era and elicited the most local comment and the broadest public support of any Montreal railway scheme. Between 1845 and 1853, the Montreal and Plattsburg and the extensions to the Champlain and St Lawrence were built — while several other schemes that never came to fruition were promoted — in response to, and in competition with, the St Lawrence and Atlantic. This plan of John Poor of Portland, Maine, to join his city to a point on the St Lawrence River opposite Montreal had profound effects on the Montreal business community, whose members were drawn through this company, or by opposition to it, into various other railway construction schemes. Thus, a study of the St Lawrence and Atlantic provides more than just an examination of an interesting international railway enterprise; it is also a point of departure for viewing the response of a large segment of the Montreal business community to the challenge of the railway.

Montrealers came slowly and hesitatingly to accept the religion of railways, despite local urgings and several examples of highly beneficial results from railway promotion by ambitious boosters elsewhere. The eminently successful Champlain and St Lawrence, the sole achievement in Montreal railway enterprise until the mid-forties, attracted relatively few local businessmen to the ranks of its shareholders. Until then there seems to have been little local interest in the latter, or in other railway ventures. When, from time to time, railway projects were mentioned in Montreal they were received with only mild interest in local newspapers rather than with the grandiloquent rhetoric with which they would have been welcomed elsewhere. The chief reason for the absence of receptivity to the 'philosophy of railways' was the tradition of the city as a port and the riverine psychology it bred.

The economic viability of railways was not yet part of the conventional wisdom of Montreal businessmen, who were, on the whole, still strongly oriented to shipping. This custom-bound thinking was never completely broken in the nineteenth-century, and even some of the city's most aggressive railway promoters, such as John Young and Hugh Allan, were primarily and essentially attached to the St Lawrence. While Young was no doubt aware of what railways had done for Boston and of what they might accomplish for Montreal, he never advocated the railway as the sole panacea for the city's nagging problem of contending unsuccessfully with New York for North American commercial dominion. The relative lack of enthusiasm for railways on the part of Young and other leading Montreal entrepreneurs until late in the forties was a factor in the delay in building major railway lines out of Montreal. Because large amounts of capital were required to build these projects, the leadership of the most important businessmen was needed to rally local capital and to impress foreign investors. This entrepreneurial hesitancy was much more important in delaying Montreal's entry into the railway age than the alleged obstruction of the French Canadian majority in the Legislative Assembly of Lower Canada before 1838.[1]

What was it that suddenly drew Montrealers to John Poor's grandiose scheme to connect the St Lawrence opposite the city to Portland by a 200-mile tramway? The United States Drawback legislation of 1845, seen by O.D. Skelton as the major explanation for Montreal's sudden conversion, is perhaps not as important a factor as others.[2] What drew Montrealers to the St Lawrence and Atlantic in the late forties more than to any other similar project was the route, terminus, and, perhaps, the uniqueness of this particular scheme. Whereas a railway connection with Boston could be seen to have harmful long-run implications for Montreal's trading position – and for its profitability, not to mention its *amour propre* as an independent entrepôt and colonial metropolis – there could be no fear that Portland would ever upstage Montreal. For sound economic reasons Montrealers would not want their city to play Buffalo to Boston's New York, or St Louis to Boston's New Orleans. They had laboured too long, and invested too much of their resources and rhetoric in a pursuit of continental commercial hegemony, to allow themselves to be relegated to the position of a secondary outpost like Kingston or, until recently, Toronto. Montrealers knew their city's past and looked hopefully to its future.

Another reason why the city's leading businessmen, and later their fellow citizens at lower levels of industry and commerce, suddenly embraced the St Lawrence and Atlantic railway scheme between 1844 and 1846 was the threatened loss of Montreal's western trade. Boston's Northern railway between Lake Champlain and Ogdensburg threatened Montreal's very commercial jugular. This dire menace could be met only by a railway from Montreal to an ice-free port, and the creation of a transportation system in which freight costs from the interior to tidewater would be lower than by Boston railways or New York canals. Since Boston might have been too overpowering an ally, Portland's offer was accepted. In the main, Montrealers preferred the lesser of the two possible Atlantic outlets, the better to preserve their own future. The railway to Portland, moreover, provided also the opportunity to bisect the Eastern Townships, to bring that developing region of the Province of Canada fully within Montreal's economic orbit.

Thus the promotion and development of the St Lawrence and Atlantic railway between 1844 and 1853 was, in the first two years of the scheme, a matter of the reluctant – and only partial – conversion of many Montreal businessmen to the new religion of railways. And perhaps unique in the history of the generally warm endorsement of the railway as an ideal transportation medium, the garnering of souls for this faith was in Montreal an arduous process conducted by foreign missionaries. The indoctrination was hasty and incomplete, while the baptism was indiscriminate and totally immersive. For a time the ruling potentates were obviously unconvinced; the apathy and backsliding among them and the masses enfeebled the prospects of the railway's success. The St Lawrence and Atlantic was not brought to Montreal with ease, but neither was its advent accompanied by lamentations. It was rather with suspicion and hesitation – along with considerable indifference – that most Montrealers witnessed the promotion of this railway. Since the St Lawrence and Atlantic at that time epitomized the railway age to Montreal, mainly because of the magnitude of the scheme and because it was the inspiration for others, the reception which it received is suggestive of the commitment to the city's ancient faith in the river system of which Montreal was the focus.

II

The initial Canadian impetus to build the St Lawrence and Atlantic railway came from Sherbrooke, the centre of the British American Land Company's settlement and industrial ventures in the Eastern Townships. For decades, residents of the region had felt isolated from the mainstream of economic life of the province by the lack of adequate transportation facilities.[3] The railway initially was of greater interest in Sherbrooke than in Montreal because it offered a highly promising solution to the Townships' isolation. Earlier in the forties, some Sherbrooke promoters, who were joined by others from adjoining settlements, had proposed to construct a railway from Sherbrooke west to the Richelieu to connect with the Champlain and St Lawrence at St John's. This eighty-five-mile railway scheme originated about 1840; its promoters secured a charter from the Special Council of Lower Canada the following year and some amendments to the bill in 1842 from the united Canadian legislature.[4] Although the line was never built, its advancement so early in the decade was evidence of the strong interest in railways and the venturesome independence in Sherbrooke and vicinity. The possibility that the Eastern Townships would build their own railway system, either to the Richelieu or south to connect with Vermont lines, goaded Montrealers to co-operate with Sherbrooke promoters on the St Lawrence and Atlantic lest they lose whatever chance there was to attach the region as an economic hinterland.

While Sherbrooke was thus the Canadian springboard for the St Lawrence and Atlantic, the chief source of inspiration for it was Portland, the ambitious city in Maine that was stimulated by John A. Poor into herculean and grandiose efforts at railway development. The St Lawrence and Atlantic was only one-half of a Portland-based railway system that included the proposed European and North American railway to traverse southern New Brunswick and make Portland the pivot of communications between the Canadas and the Maritimes.[5] This chapter, and the one that follows, are concerned with the Canadian half of the international railway between Montreal and Portland, the St Lawrence and Atlantic itself.

Poor's ambitions to build a railway to Canada was inspired by a proposal, under discussion in the thirties, to construct a railway from the Maine coast to the Canadian border. But he was also stirred by Boston's efforts in 1843 and 1844 to extend its railway connections north to Montreal.[6] His first proposal was to build a road from Portland to Sherbrooke, but realizing its greater potential he soon opted for a railway and began to campaign vigorously in Maine and in Canada. In order to convince Canadians of the viability of his scheme, and perhaps to demonstrate his own physical stamina, he traversed the St Lawrence Valley to Montreal and from there overland to Portland.[7]

Shortly thereafter, on 5 September 1844, he opened his railway promotion campaign with a letter in the *Sherbrooke Gazette*.[8] In a lengthy discussion of the comparative routes and distances of railways from Montreal either to Boston or to Portland, Poor informed readers that Portland was one hundred miles closer. Notwithstanding his presentation of this interesting information, Poor's comments were unaccented and perhaps intended as a test of Canadian reaction to the idea of a tramway to Portland. For him to begin his campaign in Sherbrooke rather than in Montreal was a response to the great enthusiasm for a railway in Sherbrooke and possibly a shrewd understanding that a commitment by the latter would ultimately draw Montrealers in behind the scheme. However, to secure their immediate participation, Montrealers would have to be courted carefully not only because of the high cost of Poor's scheme but also because there seems to have been little initial interest in railway projects in general.

While plans were being made for securing broad support in Montreal, the Board of Trade and probably some leading members of the city's commercial élite were being approached for support. This activity and the formulation of tentative plans for route and financing consumed the next two months, and it was not until November 1844 that petitions were presented to the legislature for incorporation of a railway company (in that era petitions normally preceded the incorporation of a railway). The first petition originated in the Eastern Townships and bore the signatures of hundreds of its residents.[9] These applications enumerated the old complaint of the Townships that poor communications isolated the region from the markets in Montreal and Quebec. One entreaty argued that a railway from the United States border at Stanstead through Sherbrooke to the St Lawrence River opposite Montreal would open up that whole region to more active commerce, and incidentally contribute to provincial revenues through increased consumption of dutiable articles. Another petition from the Townships included an eloquent appeal for some form of government assistance to the project; the petitioners felt 'that having at their own cost demonstrated [the railway's] practicality, they may now seek at the hands of a paternal government that aid and encouragement which is required to warrant a poor community in embarking its all in an undertaking of such extent.'[10] So far, the campaign for the St Lawrence and Atlantic expressed two related themes which were to be repeated and re-emphasized numerous times before the railway was completed: belief in the new medium as a solution to transportation problems and the need for government assistance. And behind these two points, which were made explicit, was the implied recognition of this proposed railway as an international endeavour and of the role of Portland as the new Canadian window on the Atlantic.

Up to this point Montreal was somewhat coyly non-committal on the Portland project. Though the Montreal *Gazette* – whose view reflected the general climate of opinion in commercial circles – spoke of 'our Railway to Boston or to Portland,' it warmly endorsed the idea of a rail connection to a year-round Atlantic port, because 'great as are the natural advantages of our position, they may be lost if not improved.'[11] Early in February, however, the

Gazette began to support Poor's proposals. Arguing that a rail link to Boston would make Montreal subsidiary either to Boston or New York, the newspaper stated that Montreal's prime interest lay in being the northern terminus of a railway that went directly to the Atlantic coast through the Townships.[12]

Notwithstanding the fact that the most important local newspaper was behind the Portland scheme, and unimpressed by Sherbrooke boosterism led by A.T. Galt, John Moore, and Samuel Brooks, the Montreal commercial élite remained unenthusiastic as late as the end of February 1845.[13] In a petition on behalf of the railway, the Board of Trade merely applauded the idea in general terms, pointing out that one of its specific benefits would be 'the political importance of cementing a good understanding between this Province and the frontier States of the American Union.'[14] Adding that local capital resources would be insufficient unless British support was forthcoming, the Board requested a government guarantee of 3 per cent dividend on the capital stock of the railway for twenty years.

In view of only moderate support in Montreal for the Portland connection, it seemed possible that Boston would steal a march on her putative rival in Maine. In January 1845, Boston agents were actually in Montreal attempting to influence the Board of Trade to favour the Boston route. Many Montrealers – shareholders in the Champlain and St Lawrence among them – would have been attracted to the idea of such a connection largely because of Boston's prominence as a port and because the Boston-based railway system would soon reach Burlington, only twenty miles from the border. As late as March 1845 an impressive array of Bostonians were still attempting to convince Montrealers that 'the Portland route, so-called, is not the one calculated to promote the interest of the Canadas.'[15]

John Poor, believing that overtures such as this could swing Montreal in favour of the Boston route, made a dramatic overland journey from Portland to Montreal in five days from 5 to 10 February 1845 in order to prevent what he believed was the imminent ruin of his efforts to win over the merchants of Montreal.[16] Even if the Board of Trade had supported the Boston linkage, however, it is unlikely, in view of the time it took to extend the Champlain line, that it would have been built any more swiftly than the St Lawrence and Atlantic. The Champlain and St Lawrence railway took five years to build the thirty-mile stretch connecting with Boston's railways in Vermont.

Poor might well have completed his historic journey in five days in order to convince Montreal's Board of Trade not to listen to Boston's siren song. It is likely, however, that he came up also to ensure the success of the St Lawrence and Atlantic in a more tangible, and even then traditional, way, by lobbying in the provincial legislature. He was an experienced hand at influencing legislators; not long before leaving Portland, he had successfully steered through the Maine

House of Representatives a bill setting up the complementary Atlantic and St Lawrence railway. Without the Canadian section, the American railway would be totally useless. Therefore Poor had to secure both parts of the international project. In the immediate future, of course, it would greatly assist him in raising capital for the American half, and help him to influence the legislatures of New Hampshire and Vermont, whose permission had not yet been secured, if he could arrange a charter for the 120-mile Canadian section.

The bill to charter the St Lawrence and Atlantic Railway came up for discussion in the Canadian Legislative Assembly on 7 March 1845.[17] Poor, who was in Montreal, undoubtedly held lengthy and earnest discussions with many members of the House and the administration, while the bill was under discussion. Another probability is that Poor appeared before the committee that reported on the legislation. And no doubt he was assisted by others, including George Moffatt, member of the Assembly from Montreal, who could be relied upon to be almost as persuasive as Poor himself. Because of Moffatt's eminence as a senior member of the Montreal business fraternity, and his long-standing conservative political affiliations, which would have provided him with some influence in the Draper administration then in power in the Province, he was chosen to pilot the bill through the Assembly.[18]

Moffatt's interests in the St Lawrence and Atlantic railway were more personal than sympathetic to the particular interests of his business constituency. Although an original promoter of the Champlain and St Lawrence railway, he was no longer active in its affairs, so that he had no conflict of interest in strongly supporting the newer and, to him, more promising railway. The St Lawrence and Atlantic would traverse the Eastern Township holdings of the British American Land Company of which he and the Gillespies, Moffatt's London partners, were directors.

The railway would serve not only the interests of the Eastern Townships generally but also the ambitions of particular centres within the region. The St Lawrence and Atlantic bill, which secured Royal Assent on 17 March 1845, included among its provisions a requirement that the railway pass through St Hyacinthe and Sherbrooke.[19] This proviso, which one member of the Legislative Assembly dubbed 'a very peculiar zigzagification,' required the railway to follow a circuitous route.[20] An additional indication that the company was intent on satisfying local needs was the permission to build a branch from the main line south to Stanstead to link up with a future railway in northern Vermont – a curious provision in view of the intended exclusiveness of the railway. Another spur would extend northeast to reach the St Lawrence opposite Quebec. Thus the interests of the major centres in the region – including St Hyacinthe, a relatively obscure Yamaska river town – would be served by the line.

III

Among the large number of promoters named in the bill which chartered the St Lawrence and Atlantic was a sizable group of Montreal businessmen. Prominent among them was John Frothingham, who had been born in Portland but who had lived for many years in Montreal. As the owner of 'no doubt the largest hardware and iron house in British America,'[21] Frothingham was probably much less interested in linking his new home to his old than in the value of the railway to Montreal's economic life, or perhaps in having his firm supply some of the needed hardware. Harrison Stephens, born in Jamaica, Vermont, and a resident of Montreal since 1828, was also on the list of supporters.[22] Like Frothingham, Stephens was a prominent merchant; according to Dorwin he was 'the most successful merchant of Montreal ... and made the most rapid fortune of any merchant in Canada.'[23] Stephens's Vermont background and early Canadian business experience, at Bedford on Missisquoi Bay, made him appreciate the utility of a railway through that region. Likely motivated by tangible business interests, he was in partnership with John Young in the importation of specialized goods, including tobacco and rice, from the United States.[24] Their firm also dealt heavily in trade with the Great Lakes region, so that they were concerned both with importing and exporting, and would have seen the railway as valuable. Although Young was not actively associated with the railway at this early stage, he became involved a year later, and was a key figure in negotiations for raising vitally needed capital through bond sales in 1851.

Other Montrealers who were original shareholders in the St Lawrence and Atlantic included Joseph Shuter,[25] American-born Joseph Barrett, a local hardware merchant and manufacturer,[26] and William Lyman, a drug and chemical manufacturer. None of these three subscribed for many shares in the company, nor did any of them become directors.

Not so perfunctory, however, was the involvement of Peter McGill in the enterprise. While Poor provided the idea, Galt the impetus, and Moffatt the legislative leadership for the St Lawrence and Atlantic Railway, Peter McGill added the indispensable association with the highest levels of the Montreal business community. If the railway were to be built, the resources of the whole business community and the assistance of its major financial institutions, including the Bank of Montreal, of which McGill was president from 1834 to 1860,[27] would have to be effectively marshalled. Frothingham, Stephens, Barrett, and Shuter, even acting in unison, could not have provided this leadership as effectively as McGill. Despite their personal respectability, none of them were among the city's moguls who, if anyone, might 'deliver' the support of the broadest possible segment of the Montreal business community. Such a potentate was McGill, whose wealth, prestige, and power were probably unrivalled in Montreal in this era. He was one of the earliest Montreal advocates of railways and one of the few in the city who did not need to be converted to them.

Although McGill may have been reluctant to back this new railway that would likely damage the Champlain and St Lawrence, which he had supported in the thirties, his concern for the safety of Montreal commerce overrode old loyalties. Enclosed in an early petition – one of several – sent in by a number of Township men in February 1845,[28] was a revealing report entitled 'Estimate of Traffic on the St Lawrence and Atlantic Railroad,' and signed by McGill, along with Galt, Charles Grant (seigneur of Longueuil – across the St Lawrence from Montreal), and two able officers of the Montreal board of Trade, Thomas Cringan and John T. Brondgeest.[29] The report revealed the chief concerns and aspirations of its influential signatories. Along with the litany of expectations unfulfilled and hope resurgent – the belief that 'next year' Montreal would overcome its more successful rival, New York – was an examination of the new US bonding legislation, the Drawback Act of 1845, which allowed goods exported from Canada to pass through the United States in bond. By this measure, they warned, the already substantial competitive advantages of American ports as export centres would be accentuated; even Montreal's vital import trade would be endangered.[30] Upper Canadian merchants, till then served mainly by Montreal import houses in various lines, would soon purchase their needs in New York where their exports would be sent. Thus Montreal's hinterland would be usurped and incalculable harm inflicted upon the city's whole economic structure. Also in jeopardy would be the St Lawrence canals, then under construction, to which the government had committed huge sums borrowed on the credit of the province.

An effective answer to this dire threat was required now, declared McGill and his associates; to place Montreal on the same footing as New York a winter outlet was needed. The St Lawrence and Atlantic would complement and complete the St Lawrence canals by creating a new Lake Erie-to-tidewater route which could compete effectively with the New York canals because of lower freight costs, estimated at eleven cents less on a barrel of flour. The Canadian canal and Portland railway system would also be able to thwart the menace posed by Boston's lengthening network of northern railways. At Portland, Montreal would have a year-round port much closer to Britain than either Boston or New York.

Montreal, the report concluded, could easily attract about 25 per cent of the wheat shipped from United States' Great Lakes ports to the Atlantic, as well as approximately 400,000 barrels of flour, and 100,000 barrels of packed meat for the Canadian, Maritime, and New England 'coasting, fishing and lumbering establishments.'[31]

The unmentioned but strongly implied suggestion was that Montreal would remain a metropolis of Canadian trade. In an address to the government on behalf of the St Lawrence and Atlantic it was not necessary to be explicit on that point. Indeed, a forthright statement on the comparative value of a connection with either Boston or Portland might have opened up a controversy in the legislature on the subject, and that question were better settled by Montrealers than by legislators. The report also omitted any discussion of the comparative advantages of Portland and Boston — or New York — as ocean shipping centres. Although Portland was certainly closer than Boston to Liverpool, it was doubtful whether its relatively undeveloped harbour could handle ocean shipping as efficiently as the emporium of Massachusetts.[32]

Though the ideas contained in the document were not new, they were stated with a forcefulness born of the growing uneasiness felt by Montreal businessmen. Peter McGill's endorsement of the St Lawrence and Atlantic seemed to epitomize the increasing fear in the commercial community that Montreal's very future as a city of trade was at stake. Although ten years earlier McGill had been among the most active in the affairs of the Champlain and St Lawrence, now — like Moffatt, his colleague in that venture — he was neither a director nor a leading shareholder. While reducing his investment in the Champlain railway, he subscribed for £1,000 worth of shares in the St Lawrence and Atlantic soon after the subscription books were opened.[33] For McGill to have done so when the former was showing profits, and paying good dividends, was unbusinesslike. Yet it was a measure of his faith in this bold new railway venture.

IV

The Boston assault upon Montreal, however, was by no means spent, for despite the fact that the St Lawrence and Atlantic had received its charter, Bostonians attempted to win Montrealers away from the idea. Shortly after Poor had left Montreal in March, once the bill had passed the legislature, partisans of the Boston route, mostly Americans, began to regale Montrealers with arguments in favour of a Boston terminus for an Atlantic railway.[34] The very day of Poor's departure Erastus Fairbanks arrived in town from Boston to conduct a campaign to win over the Montreal business community, which — in the light of early share subscriptions — was not yet enthusiastic for the Portland connection.

The Montreal *Gazette,* which generally reflected merchant opinions, was only a modest supporter of the scheme and announced that it was open to argument on the subject.[35] Fairbanks therefore had hopes of winning the battle for

Montreal's favour. He reminded Montrealers of their need to attract sufficient capital, and that, to a great extent, would depend upon the estimates of how profitable the railway was likely to be. Profits, he pointed out, would depend not so much on the termini of the line as on the traffic it would carry. A railway through a productive and populated region like the western Townships, which Boston hoped to tap by a line to Stanstead, would be more successful. With this debate going on about the Atlantic connection, the provisional committee of the Montreal-to-Portland company was spurred to strong efforts at getting the project underway as soon as possible.

Their campaign depended on the successful sale of the 12,000 fifty-pound shares in the company, which was capitalized at £600,000. Once the first five hundred shares were sold the company was allowed to come into formal existence under the terms of the enabling legislation.[36] The provisional committee was replaced by a Board of Directors, which consisted of George Moffatt as President, A.N. Morin as vice-president, Peter McGill, Thomas Stayner, John Torrance, Thomas Cringan, John Frothingham, A.T. Galt, and Samuel Brooks.[37] All were Montrealers except Morin, Galt, and Brooks. This eminent body, which represented most of the major subgroups in the city's commerce, aided by an eloquent prospectus, began to promote the subscription of shares in the St Lawrence and Atlantic railway company.[38] Starting in May 1845 the campaign showed considerable early success. By the end of that month, nearly £100,000 worth of shares had been subscribed as dozens of people signed their names in the registers in Montreal and Sherbrooke, where an enthusiastic drive was under way.[39] Plans were being made to carry the quest for financial support to Britain.

Although commitments for one-sixth of the company's estimated required capital had been received, it would be several years before this sum could be converted into cash. In fact, since the whole capital sum would be required to build the railway, the directors could regard the subscriptions as a bare beginning. And though, in a June editorial, the *Gazette* stated that 'the wealthiest and most intelligent merchants of Montreal have entered into it with spirit and good faith.'[40] the company had some distance to go before construction could begin with the assurance of sufficient revenue to pay for it. The paper claimed that 'considering the very restricted capital of the Province, the large amount of the sum already subscribed indicates the confidence felt in it as a remunerative investment.' But the amount committed by Montrealers to the enterprise thus far was not really very much – some two-thirds of the total – and the question was why so little was forthcoming from them and, more immediately important, how much more could be raised in the city.

The modest response was more a result of general doubt about the practicality of the enterprise than of meagre resources, as asserted by the

Gazette. Financial resources in Montreal, though not plentiful, were more abundant in this period of relative prosperity and general buoyancy than support for the St Lawrence and Atlantic suggests. Montrealers at this time found money to invest in essential and demonstrably profitable enterprises, as attested by the recent expansion of the Bank of Montreal's capital stock and other joint-stock ventures.[41] In any event, even if capital was not available in large amounts, subscription to shares required an immediate outlay of only a fraction — usually one-tenth — of the shares' total value. The point was that the merchants of Montreal were not convinced that they should depart from the established pattern of not investing large sums in any one venture. There were few exceptions to this habit, which came from caution and, more important, from the trader's need to keep capital as fluid as possible.

Although the response was initially only lukewarm, it came from a wide cross-section of the city's commercial community; and the shareholders lists soon began to resemble the membership rolls of the Board of Trade. They included not only the promoters of the scheme, McGill, Moffatt, and Frothingham, but also David Hart, George Desbarats, Thomas Stayner, James Logan, Thomas Cringan, William Edmonstone, William McCulloch, Samuel Gerrard, John Leeming, John Torrance, Thomas Kay, Joseph Shuter, William Dow, Thomas and William Molson, and a host of others.[42] Indeed, nearly the whole commercial fraternity was included as purchasers of ten or, at most, twenty shares. Whether they bought in because they believed in the efficacy of the venture cannot be determined, for the written testimony of Montreal's merchants on this railway has not survived. Yet the modesty of their support suggests that they were buying this railway stock not so much because they wanted to but because it was expected of them.

While subscriptions trickled in during the summer of 1845 — by September, 1542 shares had been taken by Montrealers — it became clear that the St Lawrence and Atlantic was drawing very little support from the non-commercial classes in the city or from French Canadians. Of the latter, the only significant subscribers to date were Joseph Masson and Benjamin Delisle. The absence of both of these important elements of Montreal's population from the company was a result partly of unaggressive salesmanship by the directors but partly also of their inability to develop very much enthusiasm for the project themselves.

Subscription from the Eastern Townships by early March 1846 amounted in 681.[43] Thus, together with Montreal's support, the company had sold a total of 2223 shares for £111,150, only slightly more than one-sixth of the authorized capital and not much of an improvement over total sales several months earlier. As it became clear to directors that more local capital was not likely to be forthcoming, other previously identified avenues of support, either from the government of the province or from British investors, were now seen as indispensable to the railway. The gentle calls in early petitions for aid soon became desperate shrieks for help.

The promoters had sought British participation in the company from the beginning. As soon as it was formally established in June 1845 after five hundred shares had been sold, the directors prepared to send A.T. Galt and William Hamilton Merritt (who declined) to London, where they hoped to float their scheme on the wave of enthusiasm for railway shares in Britain in the early forties.[44] 'We trust,' editorialized the *Gazette* just before Galt's departure, 'that the English capitalists will see that the railway ... is no fictitious speculation, but a safe and sound project, based on clear views of the necessities and capabilities of the country.'[45] Because of his associations with the London financiers behind the British American Land Company, Galt was an excellent choice. Soon after his arrival Galt formed a 'London Committee,' including Edward 'Bear' Ellice, Alexander Gillespie, and Robert McCalmont (later one of the promoters of the Montreal Ocean Steam Navigation Company) to assist him in selling St Lawrence and Atlantic shares.[46] So successful was Galt that within months 2633 shares were taken up in Britain: some four hundred more than had been sold in Canada.[47] Interested and favourable notices of the St Lawrence and Atlantic were appearing in a few English newspapers, and there seemed every hope that more support would flow in from Leeds, Manchester, Liverpool, Glasgow, and Edinburgh, which Galt intended to include in a promotion tour.[48]

v

Despite the early success of the sale of shares in Britain, and the more modest response in Canada, the company soon learned that it could not proceed with construction even though more than one-third of all shares had been sold. After the sudden collapse of the railway boom in Britain in the autumn of 1845, railway shares were anathema to investors and many British subscribers refused to pay instalments, while others boldly demanded the refund of the money they already had paid in.[49]

Faced with this news, the annual shareholders meeting held in Montreal in January 1846 was a gloomy occasion.[50] Given sales resistance in Montreal and the unlikelihood that the government of the province would come to the railway's rescue, it seemed highly doubtful whether the project could proceed. The shareholders decided to hold back from making any commitments until the company's financial state became more promising. And any further discussions would have to include representatives of the British shareholders. Meanwhile the St Lawrence and Atlantic railway was in limbo.

But John Poor would not allow his pet project to be put in abeyance. In the months since March 1845 when he had triumphantly departed Montreal with the St Lawrence and Atlantic bill in hand, he had been concerned with the Portland half of the project, the Atlantic and St Lawrence. The sale of many shares, securing of charters from Maine, New Hampshire, and Vermont and the letting of the contract for the first section of the line had all been accomplished by the spring of 1846.[51] Poor had not come all this distance to let the railway collapse as a result of fumbling or last-minute trepidation. If Portland was prepared to go ahead 'on a wing and a prayer,' then, he assumed, so should Montreal. With the practised hand of the experienced manipulator of legislatures and the skill of a successful stock promoter, he set about putting Montreal straight.

Poor had some assistance from A.T. Galt in winning back the Montrealers. Notwithstanding the partial withdrawal of British support, Galt had been insisting since his return from England that the project should go forward.[52] And it was perhaps Galt who arranged the agreement by which his colleagues were committed to proceed with the railway. On 17 April 1846, George Moffatt, A.N. Morin, and Samuel Brooks for the St Lawrence and Atlantic signed a 'convention and fundamental articles of agreement' with the representatives of the Atlantic and St Lawrence railway. Subject to ratification of the Board of Directors, and with the specific proviso that 'in the event of war between Great Britain and the United States this agreement shall be in abeyance' (an interesting reflection of the Oregon crisis), the agreement committed the St Lawrence and Atlantic Company to complete the railway within five years.[53] The Canadian line was to build according to construction and route specifications drawn up by A.C. Morton, the Atlantic and St Lawrence engineer. Another stipulation required that the whole Canadian contract be given to Wood, Black and Company of Portland who had undertaken the first section of the American side. The signing and ratification of this agreement was more than a simple breach of the promise made by the directors to the shareholders in the preceding January not to make commitments; it was a legally binding, penalty-risking agreement to build the line according to unknown specifications. It was a *carte blanche* for Poor and the Portland planners, and its consequences would soon become painfully apparent to the directors and shareholders, to the provincial government, and to the press. Moreover, if the agreement were honoured, this major Canadian railway would have an unfortunate technical legacy of an anomalous gauge which might well result in serious problems in the establishment of connections with other lines.[54]

Why the Canadians signed such an agreement is not known. There is no evidence that the representatives of the St Lawrence and Atlantic were induced in any way to accept these terms. The only compulsion which they might have felt would have stemmed from the news of Britain's decision to repeal the Corn Laws and put an end to colonial preferences. These events would have forced them to look upon the railway with greater urgency than before, as a new route out to enlarged markets. But whatever the real reason – perhaps a naïve faith in Poor, whom they had no reason to distrust – they agreed in haste to enormous concessions that, even allowing for inexperience, they could hardly have failed to understand. They and the shareholders who later confirmed the undertaking may have been acting in the belief that they were advancing the railway and Montreal's now pressing strategic interests with realistic dispatch, but they failed to say this in so many words. And the absence of any public discussion when the agreement was concluded leaves room for plausible, though unprovable, scepticism.

The special meeting of the shareholders called for July 1846 was not convened to secure approval for what the directors had committed them to in April. It was not until one year later that Montrealers learned of the portentous agreement, published in the lengthy report by A.C. Morton, on the wide gauge of five feet, six inches, that had been determined for the St Lawrence and Atlantic tracks. This meeting was less an explanatory session than a pep rally presided over by George Moffatt, whose dramatic oratory proved extremely effective in rallying enthusiastic support for the railway at last. 'There never have existed such imperative reasons for completion of this enterprise than now' he proclaimed.[55] The abandonment of free trade by Great Britain and the American Drawback Acts, he continued, 'sufficiently indicate the importance of emulating the enterprise of our republican neighbours, and of opening new channels for that commerce which otherwise must be driven from the St Lawrence, that the merchants of Montreal cannot possibly maintain a competition with those of the United States, unless they possess equal facilities of intercourse, which this Railroad will afford.' The assembled Montrealers loved it. Though they had been exhorted in this fashion for many years, there was now a timeliness to the message and a course of action open to them, which made many believe that to a greater extent than ever before their destiny was in their own hands.

Moffatt reprimanded Montrealers for their apathy and timidity. Many shares were in default as shareholders resisted paying even the first instalments. 'In justice to such of the English Subscribers as intended their stock to be *bona fide* investments in the work,' he continued, 'the apathy evinced in Canada might well warrant their belief in the inexpediency of its prosecution.'[56] Another meeting would be held on 17 August only a little more than two weeks from then; and, Moffatt warned, if the directors 'have [not] received that additional support which they conceive to be necessary, that so far as it can be legally effected, the enterprise [may] be abandoned for want of sufficient means to carry it out.' But if the new appeal were to afford evidence of determination to build the road, the directors would be prepared to recommend letting the contracts for the first section, the thirty miles from the south shore to St Hyacinthe.

If Montreal was ever seized with railway fever, not to say mania, it was on that July evening. After Moffatt's expostulations were finished, resolution after resolution was passed supporting the actions of the directors, lauding the engineer's report that the railroad be immediately proceeded with, expressing regret at the actions of some of the English shareholders, and finally declaring that the Canadian shareholders had eminent faith in the project. Most of the same points that had been previously made were restated, but one resolution spoke of another threat: 'without this work the depreciated value of real estate in Montreal, from its ceasing to be the commercial emporium of Canada, will probably exceed any limit that our worst apprehensions would at present assign to it.'[57] A decline in the value of local real estate might well affect a substantial cross-section of the population, certainly more than just the mercantile community, and this possibility was probably an argument strongly used by many Montrealers to draw money into the scheme.

The engineer Morton, who since April had been making surveys and estimating grades and costs, had presented a highly encouraging report to the meeting. He told the shareholders – and he showed in elaborately detailed figures in the appendices to his report, which each shareholder could examine at leisure – that the Montreal-Portland railway would be even more efficient than Boston's highly-touted Western Line to Albany. Morton predicted that the net income on the estimated $2 million investment would be nearly 10 per cent, and in addition to opening up new vistas of trade for Montreal the new railway would yield a handsome profit for investors.

Excited by rhetoric and assurances of success, the meeting adopted Moffatt's plan that a committee of five be appointed to arouse more local interest and solicit subscriptions. It remained to be seen whether the threat of calling off the project and the enthusiasm of the meeting could produce a large increase in the number of share subscriptions. The new committee detailed to stimulate support now began an aggressive share promotion campaign. It resembled the vigorous door-to-door subscription canvassing that had proven to be so successful in Portland, and it is possible that Poor suggested that Montreal use the Portland model. Subscription lists were opened for each city ward; where special ward subcommittees were appointed to bring in more support.[58] Each committee was to 'go in a Body to solicit subscriptions' and to visit every house in its ward. At daily meetings held to register results committees were instructed to make note of the 'names of parties refusing to subscribe ... with their reasons for doing so,'[59] a suggestion that heavy pressure, possibly through employers or business associates, was being used.

The renewed fears of merchants and property owners, combined with aggressive salesmanship, spelled success for the new drive.[60] Prospects for the success of the St Lawrence and Atlantic Railway suddenly took an encouraging turn. Not only were delinquent shareholders convinced to pay overdue instalments, but many new subscribers were brought into the company as the ward committees diligently and effectively scoured the city like commercial press gangs, and English and French Montrealers were induced to support the railway. The tradesmen and workers of St Mary's Ward bought shares in ones and twos to a total of eighty-four.[61] In St Antoine similar small amounts were subscribed, except for Charles Phillips, son of the former real estate developer Thomas Phillips,[62] who bought ten, and John E. Mills, American-born merchant, later mayor of Montreal, and currently chairman of the board of the rival Champlain and St Lawrence railway, who also bought ten shares. In St Louis Ward it was the same pattern; here only a fraction of the 354 shares sold were in substantial blocks.[63] William Lunn, long-time director of the Bank of Montreal, city alderman from 1840 to 1850, and an investor in other local enterprises, bought twenty shares. Louis Hippolyte LaFontaine bought ten, as did Pierre Beaubien, who had for many years been associated with La Banque du Peuple and later with the Montreal City and District Savings Bank.[64]

Shares sold in small numbers totalling 119 in St James Ward and fifty-five in the East Ward, while in St Lawrence 110 were subscribed.[65] William Dow manfully took ten more besides his original twenty. So did James Logan, Montreal manager for the interests of his uncle Hart Logan of Liverpool and a general merchant in partnership with Thomas Cringan.[66] The latter was a long-time director of the Bank of Montreal who was once, in 1840, a director of the Champlain and St Lawrence railway and had also been an associate of the Torrances in the Montreal Tow Boat Company.[67] In the West Ward 221 shares were subscribed,[68] at first the only large purchase being that of ten shares by Alexander Murphy – possibly a relation of Daniel Murphy, since 1824 a resident of Montreal and beforehand an extensive corn factor and miller in Ballyellen Mills, County Carlow, in southern Ireland.[69] A.M. Delisle tardily took ten shares and Thomas Nye, a lawyer and author, took eight.[70] Finally, in St Ann's Ward eight-three shares were sold in amounts of ones and twos.[71]

The new sales, then, were overwhelmingly to the 'lesser people' of Montreal, who had not likely been approached before for any public project, nor ever would be afterward in quite the same way as they were in the summer of 1846. The response was by no means unanimous. Many objected to being dragooned and others resisted for a variety of reasons. One complained of 'being badly used' by another railway; many, it was noted, said they 'will see,' 'can't,' or 'likely will.' Phillip Brady in the West Ward said he had 'no interest in the

Country' and Sam Price held railroads to be an 'abomination.'[72] But the generally warm response was probably as generous as it was mainly because the artisans and workers had been approached by well-known people in their own wards. Many might well have thought the railway to be a good thing, a sound investment, or a necessity for their own prosperity. On others some fairly heavy-handed pressure might have been exerted by employers. More likely, however, most purchasers acted out of a belief that it was expected of them, a sense of awe for the mighty men of the city who were now vigorously behind the railway, a certain self-flattery in being a shareholder in a large enterprise — and poor sales resistance.

As this campaign mounted, towards the end of August, it became clear that the St Lawrence and Atlantic Railway Company was in a far better financial position that at the beginning of the month to commit itself to a programme of construction. Shareholders who met on 22 August were told that more than fourteen hundred new shares had been taken up during the recent campaign in the city.[73] Thus, despite the threatened revolt of English subscribers, enough money would be coming in (a total of 5364 shares, worth £268,200, had firm backing, and of these 3964 were held in Canada, 650 in England, and 750 by contractors), Moffatt reported, to construct approximately fifty to sixty miles of the line, which would prove its efficiency and thereby elicit further support. His recommendation was accepted unanimously, and with the contract arranged work was soon underway on the roadbed of the first thirty-mile section of the line, from St Lambert opposite Montreal to St Hyacinthe. Perhaps the most important phase of the St Lawrence and Atlantic Railway was past.

In retrospect the promoters could compliment themselves on a very substantial achievement. During the previous two years the Montreal business community had been brought into the railway age. True, their line was not yet built, but the commitment had been made in unmistakable terms by a wide cross-section of the community, not just by the commercial élite. If the latter had not embraced the project with enthusiastic zest and generous support, they had at least decided that the railway must be built. This marked a substantial change from the attitudes of the earlier forties when Montreal, like New York, was largely indifferent to the new medium of transportation. To be sure, the promoters had been assisted in their salesmanship by fortuitous events; but much of the credit for securing support for the new railway was theirs alone. The modest backing they received, they knew well, was all they could expect. After all, despite the grandiloquent verbiage, the St Lawrence and Atlantic was essentially a portage railway, only part of a more complete transportation system the major basis of which was the river. Montrealers had done their duty. Now, perhaps, with a few shouts of 'on to Portland' the St Lawrence and

Atlantic would join the Atlantic and St Lawrence; they sat back to await the arrival of their line.

Several features of this initial stage of the St Lawrence and Atlantic railway scheme are worthy of recall in conclusion. The first is the relatively quick change from indifference or reluctance of many Montreal businessmen to general endorsement of the project in 1845 and 1846. Of the reasons for this conversion to the railway faith, the most important was fear in the business community for the loss of its western trade. Hence, the tracks to Portland were a defensive measure designed to offset the expected effects of Boston's railway drive to the St Lawrence west of Montreal. A second feature of this period is the fact that, though there were a number of leading promoters of the line, including several important Montrealers like McGill, Moffatt, and Young, as well as Sherbrookers like Galt, the St Lawrence and Atlantic was not yet an entrepreneurial venture of a few individuals or of a small group. Rather it was a project supported, practically without exception, by the whole commercial community of Montreal. The campaign of August 1846 further broadened local support by bringing into the ranks of shareholders many Montrealers who were not in the city's commercial group.

One further point of significance is that the overwhelming bulk of the capital committed thus far was to come from Montreal. Of 5364 shares considered to be reliably supported, 3964 were held in Canada; of these, approximately 700 were owned by residents of the Eastern Townships. Thus, Montrealers had committed themselves for some 3260 shares worth approximately £163,000, more than 60 per cent of the total amount of dependable share value. Although by no means sufficient to finance the construction of the Canadian half of the line, this was more than 25 per cent of the estimated total amount required. It was a substantial commitment by the community to a venture which, though touted as a guaranteed success, could hardly have been considered by local businessmen as a sure bet. More important, however, was the significance of this investment as a sufficient amount with which to commence the project. It engendered optimism that more local and British support would follow.

It is also important to note that capital formation for this railway did not directly involve the Bank of Montreal or any other bank. Aside from extending occasional temporary accommodation to the railway companies and acting as commissioned agents in bond transactions, there is no evidence that the banks were directly involved in the financing of this line or of other Montreal railways. They held no shares or bonds in any of the lines that came into operation during these years, nor did they extend lengthy loans. What kept them from doing so? Essentially it was conservatism. It is unlikely that bank directors would have wanted to put anything into highly speculative ventures such as railways, which were usually a long time abuilding. After all, early Canadian banks were created by merchants whose prime goal was to profit from handling commercial paper. Through this and associated endeavours, such as foreign exchange transactions in New York, immense profits were being made by the Bank of Montreal, the major financial institution in the city. For the shrewd directors of that bank to invest funds in unproven ventures would be simply out of character. And no matter how the directors might exaggerate the prospects of the St Lawrence and Atlantic for the general public, and no matter how vital the project, in fact, might be, the same men as bankers would carefully weigh the risks and the possible returns against what they knew they could get for the same money from commercial transactions. It was another matter, however, for the banks to extend personal loans for this and other purposes, or to worthy customers with rock-hard collateral. Should Peter McGill, the Molson brothers, Joseph Masson, George Moffat, Augustin Cuvillier, or John Redpath, to name only a few of the local tycoons, should such men borrow from their banks in order to buy railway shares, that of course was not an investment by the bank itself. And it is entirely possible that the commercial banks extended substantial individual loans for this purpose and even took railway shares as collateral. Evidence, however, is unfortunately lacking on the specific loans made by any of the Montreal commercial banks at this time. [74]

Even the local savings banks, the Montreal Savings, the Montreal Provident and Savings (which foundered in 1848 due to mismanagement) and the City and District Savings, which did not deal in commercial paper or make large personal loans and were required by law to hold their funds in secure bonds or stock, put virtually nothing in railway ventures (though they loaned small amounts on the security of railway shares). Of the few trust and loan and insurance companies with Montreal head offices, none put more than token amounts into railway ventures during those years. In short, Montreal's financial institutions, even the few relatively powerful banks, the Montreal, the City, the Bank of British North America, and La Banque du Peuple, were not directly involved in the promotion and development of these railways. And even the signs of indirect connection by personal loans to railway promoters is next to impossible to trace through the Bank of Montreal records, the only ones that seem to have survived. Indeed, even dealings in government bonds proved risky. Believing that debentures issued by the Montreal Harbour Commission could be sold in London at a tidy profit, the City Bank invested more than £90,000 in them, almost a quarter of its total assets. In the bank's serious crisis of March 1849 it was revealed that these debentures could not, in fact, be sold except at a probable discount of 20 per cent. The more shrewdly managed Bank of Montreal, however, had a mere £51,000 in provincial and other bonds in 1844, and by 1853 this had been reduced to £12,000.

The fact that the banks remained aloof from the financing of railway ventures — except occasionally to provide short-term loans by allowing over-drafts or other forms of brief accommodation — was also true of the United States and Great Britain during this period. Finance for the railway development in Britain was provided essentially by widespread sales of shares to small investors — just as the St Lawrence and Atlantic was floated — and, for industrial development, by the personal finances of the manufacturers themselves. Shares held by Montreal banks in railway companies seem to have been acquired as forfeited collateral for loans in default. The Montreal banks were commercial institutions, not investment banks.

Somewhat belatedly, Montreal was utilizing the railway to develop a new hinterland, the Eastern Townships. Although the St Lawrence and Atlantic was seen primarily as a portage railway between Montreal and Portland, part of its benefit to the city would be a greater flow of commodities, including cheaper firewood, and the enlargement of commercial outlets in an area which has been largely inaccessible. This sudden consciousness of the Eastern Townships as an attractive hinterland was probably a result of Montrealers realizing that unless they acted quickly the northern Vermont and New Hampshire railways reaching into the region would pre-empt a profitable opportunity.

9

The completion of the
St Lawrence and Atlantic 1846-53

I

The successful sale of shares during the summer of 1846 injected vigour into the St Lawrence and Atlantic Railway. Until then it was little more than a grandiose plan, enthusiastically pursued by promoters in Portland, the Eastern Townships, and some leading members of Montreal's business community. Without the spurt of energy in 1846 the project might well have proved abortive and Poor's great scheme would have gone the way of so many other railway ventures that never advanced beyond the promotion stage. Montrealers, indeed, would perhaps have returned to comfortable faith in the river's water transportation, or those with interests in railways might have directed their attention to extending the Champlain and St Lawrence or the Montreal and Lachine.

Although safely past its initial crises, the railway was by no means in the clear. The chief difficulty remained the question of amassing adequate financial resources. Others included the gauge and route of the railway and, in the closing stages, the question of its southern terminus. There were labour troubles, and a serious financial problem that arose because of the dishonesty or incompetence of one of the company's employees.[1] But these were comparatively minor problems that emerged briefly while the railway was being built, whereas the task of obtaining adequate finances dogged the company for years.

By the summer of 1846 the St Lawrence and Atlantic Railway was an adopted child of the Montreal business community. Leading merchants were selling shares throughout the city and continued to sit on the Board of Directors of the company. Peter McGill, T.A. Stayner, John Torrance, George Desbarats, A.T. Galt and William Molson remained active members of the company and were elected to the board of directors each year down to the completion of the railway in 1853. Also an active promoter of the Montreal and Lachine line after

1847, his participation in the company as a shareholder increased markedly from 1846 onwards, and by 1851 he possessed 208 St Lawrence and Atlantic shares, the second largest number then owned by a single person.[2] Other early promoters dropped out of active participation.[3]

Thomas Cringan was another early director not on the Board after 1849; indeed, by 1851 he was no longer even a shareholder. But although he was a large investor in the rival Champlain and St Lawrence,[4] on whose Board he had served in 1840, he devoted his most serious railway attention to the St Lawrence and Atlantic. In 1849, he acted as agent for the company in London.[5] Cringan's name was a weighty one in Montreal. An associate of James Logan, Cringan was an active member of the Montreal Board of Trade, serving as its president in 1847, and he had been briefly a member of the Board of Harbour Commissioners in 1839. John Young, another early member of the Board of Directors, dropped out in 1849 but remained very active in the company's affairs, and re-emerged in 1851 to perform vital work for the railway.

Thomas Stayner, deputy postmaster general of British North America between 1827 and 1851, and an independently wealthy man and a somewhat less prominent director, remained on the Board for a number of years.[6] John Torrance, another Montreal director, was one of the most important shipowners in the city during this period. His Montreal Tow Boat Company rivalled Molson's St Lawrence Steamboat Company in vessels. It might seem slightly odd that Torrance, a shipowner, would have been interested in a railroad line competing with his business, steamboating on the St Lawrence. However, the Portland line was intended chiefly as a winter outlet to the Atlantic for Montreal commerce, so that Montreal shipowners were as anxious as anyone else in the city to support the project. Indeed, it was not unreasonable for the Torrances and the Molsons to have believed that the railway, by increasing the annual volume of traffic to Montreal, would benefit their steamboat businesses on the St Lawrence during the ice-free months from May to November.

Other directors filled the places of those who withdrew from the St Lawrence and Atlantic, and some changes were made among the officers. There is no clear pattern to these additions and changes, but since the railway in 1849 became a beneficiary of government support politics probably played a part in the selection of some officers. A.N. Morin, a prominent member of the Board since its inception, became president of the company, succeeding George Moffatt in 1848. It was not likely a simple coincidence that a LaFontaine Reformer should succeed a high Tory to this office in the very year of the formation of the Baldwin-LaFontaine ministry. The fact that the provincial elections took place before the annual general meeting of the company and some of the results would have been known may have encouraged shareholders to decide for Morin. If the railway was to request some kind of government aid, it might be embarrassing, and possible damaging for negotiations between the company and the administration to be carried on by the irascible George Moffatt, who might well have found it difficult to hide his virulent contempt for Reformers. While most people would heartily have agreed with MacNab's assertion that railways were now the name of the political game, it would not have been wise to test Reform tolerance with yesterday's enemy. Morin was a happy alternative, for the member for Bellechasse was a known Reformer and had just recently been appointed Speaker of the Legislative Assembly.[7] He was a colleague of LaFontaine's from the days of the first Reform ministry in 1842-3, and was obviously an important figure in the party. To honour him with the presidency of the railway, and the substantial annual honorarium attached to the job, was a tactful change.

It is not known whether Morin's presidency was of any material assistance in the development of the administration's railway policy, which culminated in the Guarantee Act of 1849; but having served two years during that crucial period, Morin retired from the presidency in 1850 to be replaced by A.T. Galt, under whom the company secured the completion of the line three years later. Galt, of course, had been associated with the project since the beginning, but there were others on the Board in the early fifties who were entirely new to the St Lawrence and Atlantic. One was Benjamin Holmes, like Morin a Liberal politician, who had been a member of the Legislative Assembly between 1841 and 1844, before being elected again in 1848 for Montreal.[8] While perhaps not as important politically as Morin, he was an extremely useful acquisition for the directorship of the railway because of his experience over twenty years as cashier of the Bank of Montreal. After retiring from that position, Holmes had been considered for president of the seriously ailing City Bank, to help it recover or to administer its liquidation.[9] Besides commercial banking, Holmes was deeply concerned with savings banks as well, and in 1841 he introduced legislation to regulate them in the interests of depositors;[10] he later became one of the honourary directors of the Montreal City and District Savings Bank after it was formed in 1846. He was an active Anglican churchman and a participating member of the Montreal St Patrick's Society in the years when it served both Protestant and Catholic Irishmen. Like many other prominent Montrealers, Holmes was associated with the annexation movement in 1849, in which he took a very active part.[11]

Another newcomer was William Dow, a Perthshire-born Montreal brewer who was later an associate of Hugh Allan in the Montreal Ocean Steamship Company.[12] In 1851, when he joined the Board of the St Lawrence and Atlantic, he held sixty shares in the company and owned substantial amounts of Montreal

real estate. Dow was a director of the Montreal Provident and Savings Bank and Montreal Fire Assurance Company in 1848, and at one time had been a member of the Montreal Board of the Bank of British North America.[13] Charles Wilson's presence on the Board of the railway was not the result of a heavy financial stake in the company, for he held, in 1851, only a modest six shares. Wilson was then mayor of Montreal, the first to be elected by popular vote to that office, and he was immensely popular, being returned for three annual terms by acclamation. A Canadian from Côteau du Lac, he was head of a Montreal hardware firm before becoming mayor. Part way through his term of office, he was also appointed to the Legislative Council.[14] No doubt Wilson was in the railway's directorate to represent the city's interests in a project to which £125,000 of the municipality's money had been committed in 1849. As for George Desbarats, a local publisher who joined the board in 1850, there seems no apparent reason why he should have been included, other than because of his ownership of fifty shares in the railway.[15]

William Workman was another newcomer to the directorship of the railway, joining the board in 1852. Also a director of the Champlain and St Lawrence at this time, he appears to have thought the Portland railway a comparable investment. Workman took great interest in Montreal railways in the fifties. Although not a shareholder in the St Lawrence and Atlantic in 1851,[16] he later became a very heavy investor in the company, and at the time of its absorption by the Grand Trunk he was one of its major stockholders.

Another addition to the directorship in 1852 was François-Alfred-Chartier Larocque, a Montreal alderman between 1843 and 1850 and, like Workman, interested in promoting savings banks to encourage thrift among Montreal workingmen. He was an officer of the City and District Savings Bank from its foundation. Larocque was not a businessman, but a lawyer who never practised his profession. As the son of François Antoine Larocque, an old Nor'Wester, Alfred was perhaps well provided for. Following the demise of the North West Company, Larocque senior had established a commission business in Montreal and like other former fur merchants tried to make the transition to the new economy in this way. He seems to have succeeded, for soon he became a very large shareholder in the Bank of Montreal, a charter member in 1822 of the Montreal Committee of Trade, the forerunner of the Board of Trade, a life governor of the Montreal General Hospital, and an investor in steamboats.[17] His commission house was Larocque, Bernard and Company, with corresponding partners throughout the vicinity at L'Assomption, St Mathias, Chambly, Rivière du Nord, Maskinongé, and St Charles. Larocque's firm, which dissolved in 1838, had several Montreal partners, including Pierre de Rocheblave, Pascal Lachapelle, J.B. Demers, F. Moruchand, E.M. Leprohon, and E.R. Fabre.[18] What his son

Alfred added to the Board of the St Lawrence and Atlantic is difficult to discern, in view of his family background and personal interests. More of a *rentier* than a businessman, Alfred dabbled in a variety of time-consuming but unpaid public causes, including the Providence Asylum; he served as a school commissioner and later was a member of the Papal Zouaves. The railway was perhaps just another cause in which he was interested, and he served on the Board through the early fifties.

These new men who came into the directorship of the St Lawrence and Atlantic railway to aid Molson, McGill, Torrance, and Moffatt were highly similar to them in their fundamental identity with the Montreal commercial class. Each had a large stake in the city's economy, mostly in one or more of the various branches of its commercial life; wholesale trade, exporting, banking, shipping, insurance, or real estate. They all shared aspirations to enhance Montreal's commerce, and the prospective railway from Longueuil to Portland was clearly for them the vehicle to a bright future. Easily the most vital function they performed was the marshalling of financial resources to build the line and furnish rolling stock. Whether or not the private resources of Montrealers, if fully mobilized, would have been adequate cannot now be determined because their combined assets are not known. But, as we have seen, a Montreal businessman would not usually invest more than one or two thousand pounds in a railway. And the most obvious potential sources of support, outside the Montreal and Sherbrooke business communities, were British capital and the Canadian government. Both had been sought from the beginning, since the first acceptance of the St Lawrence and Atlantic idea by Galt. In the end, public aid from both provincial and municipal governments proved much more significant than the sale of shares in Britain.

II

By the end of 1846 it was clear that London support had collapsed. At the annual general meeting of the company to report on developments during the year, there was both favourable and unfavourable news. Forty-five miles of the line had been surveyed, from Longueuil to about fifteen miles beyond St Hyacinthe, and rails were soon to be laid.[19] Though the contractors, Wood, Black and Company, a well-known Pennsylvania firm, had agreed to accept one-quarter payment in St Lawrence and Atlantic shares (£35,000 of £140,000), more funds were needed. To seek them, and to buy iron rails, Galt had returned to England in December.[20]

Galt's prime purpose was to shore up the sagging financial support from English shareholders, who were standing firm in their previously announced withdrawal of support. Since they held almost one-third of the total of 7,676 shares subscribed, the company decided to take strong and quick action. The London Committee had already begun to make refunds to disgruntled shareholders on the grounds that their Canadian counterparts were not honouring commitments to pay instalments on their own shares, and the Londoners felt that while this continued they could have no confidence in the railway company. How many others would default was a question that must have occasioned some worried speculation among the directors. Now that a firm commitment had been made to the contractors, the company had to be able to rely upon the income from regular payments of instalments.

Galt's mission in 1847, therefore, was of crucial importance to the project, and his failure to convince the majority of English supporters to retain their shares was not from lack of strenuous efforts to rebuild their confidence in the prospects of the railway. Perhaps he had no reasonable hope of success in this time of British disenchantment with railways.[21] Nonetheless he importuned the investing public through his contacts in the British American Land Company, and perhaps through other agencies such as the North American Colonial Association, to whose shareholders he directed a strong appeal.[22] Failing to halt the stampede, Galt subsequently concentrated his efforts on convincing London financiers to invest in St Lawrence and Atlantic bonds, but apparently without notable success.[23]

In 1846 London investors were not yet fully recovered from the shock of King Hudson's ventures, which had resulted in immense losses on the paper value of stock. They were exceedingly wary of any railway promotion schemes, regardless of their origin. North American railways were soon to attract large quantities of British capital, and even in the mid-forties large sums were invested in American railway bonds at London. It would have been very difficult for the St Lawrence and Atlantic project, even with Poor's rhetoric, to have competed with the many American railway companies putting prospectuses before British investors. The *Economist* in this period seems to have paid far less attention to Canadian economic developments, including railways, than to similar American news.[24] By contrast to the United States, British North America was not seen to be as promising a field for investment, and Montreal was not as dynamic a city as New York or, in railway promotion, Boston.

Checked in London in the effort to revive confidence in the St Lawrence and Atlantic, and clearly having exhausted, temporarily at least, the readily available venture capital in Montreal, the directors turned to government. There were, of course, precedents for government participation in transportation development in the Canadas, and since the Union the St Lawrence canals were being built as public works.

Government aid for the St Lawrence and Atlantic had continually been sought. In 1844, the Sherbrooke promoters included in their petition for the incorporation of a company to build the railway, an appeal to 'a paternal government [for] that aid and encouragement which is required to warrant a poor community in embarking its all in an undertaking of such extent.'[25] They suggested that the government adopt one of three possible methods of providing financial aid: a grant of £5,000 annually for an unspecified period of years, the purchase of 20 per cent of the company's share capital, or a loan to the company of the same amount. Subsequent petitions usually included pleas for similar kinds of support, so that the company would have at least a core of guaranteed funds to encourage local and British private investors. The Montreal Board of Trade in February 1845 petitioned the government that the province should guarantee for twenty years the capital shares of the company, and a month later the committee appointed by the Act of Incorporation to manage the affairs of the railway made a similar request.[26]

Once construction began, the question of finance became even more pressing. Commitments to contractors and suppliers had to be met. Thus in the winter of 1846-7, in the financial crisis resulting from the withdrawal of much London backing and the failure to induce interest in new share issues, the directors were brought up against the possibility of the line failing for lack of funds. They again turned to government with importunate appeals for assistance. In June 1847 they petitioned the government for aid in the form either of share purchases, a loan with a mortgage on future revenue, or a guarantee of interest on a loan to be secured from private capitalists.[27] Possibly the railway had received an intimation from one or more of the London banking houses approached by Galt that loans were possible if the province guaranteed interest. The petition went on to suggest that the provincial government's apparent apathy had discouraged prospective investors in Britain. But, despite this petition and others in February and August of 1848, the government declined to give aid.

III

The province did become involved in the debate over the track gauge. This was indeed an important question. John Poor wanted the Montreal and Portland system built on a gauge different from that which was then standard for northeastern United States lines, four feet, eight and one-half inches, between the rails.[28] He conceived the railway as a completely exclusive and self-contained transportation system and wished to prevent it from becoming integrated with other New England railways because of the danger that traffic on the St Lawrence and Atlantic would be siphoned off to Boston, leaving Portland to languish. Since, to Poor, the whole purpose of the line was to energize Portland into major importance as an Atlantic port, he felt it necessary to protect the lifeline from 'raiding' by making it costly to tap,[29] and he secured the agreement of a small group of directors of the St Lawrence and Atlantic in April 1845 to the Portland plan of building the line on a five foot, six and one-half inch, gauge.[30]

Precisely when the shareholders were informed of this agreement is not certain. The Board of Directors must have ratified it a short time after it was signed, but the decision does not appear to have been reported to the shareholders before the annual general meeting of January 1847.[31] The usually well-informed Montreal *Gazette* did not comment on the topic of the gauge between January and mid-September 1847. But the subject was thereafter a matter of open and lively debate. The railway committee of the Canadian Legislative Assembly had been discussing the question and was of the opinion that though there were advantages to the broad gauge, uniformity with the northeastern American railway system was more important.[32] But the officers of the St Lawrence and Atlantic argued vigorously for the broad gauge. A.C. Morton, the company's engineer, forcefully put their case in a special pamphlet. Since a wider gauge made for lower costs per ton-mile because of the increased carrying capacity of such a railway, he argued that the St Lawrence and Atlantic would be able to offer lower freight rates and hence would be in a stronger competitive position for carrying western trade.[33]

Various amendments to the original Act of Incorporation were being sought at this time, but the most important question pertaining to the railway was still the gauge. Shareholders joined the debate; more than forty of them petitioned the legislature early in July against the adoption of the wide gauge.[34] They argued that the building of the railway on that basis would be a costly mistake because, unless it were uniform with other lines, a third rail would be required. Otherwise transhipment at junctions would be necessary. However, none of the complainants except Lewis T. Drummond was a major shareholder in the company, and their collective weight was not enough to sway the directors. A majority of the general body of shareholders attending a special general meeting of the company on 20 September 1847, ratified the wider gauge.[35] Most of the objectors probably withdrew their support shortly after the decision went against their view, because very few were listed as shareholders in 1851.

Perhaps it was in response to their protest that the railway committee recommended to the legislature that the St Lawrence and Atlantic be required to build on the narrower standard gauge. And the assembly, without debate, incorporated into the amendments to the Act of Incorporation a stipulation that the gauge be four feet, eight and one-half inches, rather than five feet, six inches.[36] The proponents of the wide gauge were quick to attack this measure. In September, Morin petitioned for the removal of the gauge requirement, and Portland's Judge W. Preble, the president of the Atlantic and St Lawrence, pointed out that the adoption of the narrow gauge would have very serious consequences, since the 1846 agreement between the two companies laid down a penalty of the forfeiture of the entire stock for failure to comply.[37]

The question was settled by an order-in-council authorizing the railway to build on the wide gauge.[38] The decision reflects the presence in the existing Sherwood administration of two prominent Montrealers, William Badgley and Peter McGill, both of whom, especially McGill, were sympathetic to protestations for the wide gauge. McGill was an officer in the company and a holder of forty shares, and he would have represented its interests strongly and effectively in cabinet.[39] An administration as weakly supported as Sherwood's was would not have been able to risk even one resignation.[40] And apparently to assist McGill in presenting his case, Judge Preble arrived in Montreal with John Poor in mid-September.[41] Poor's previous success in swaying the Maine and Canadian legislators was put to use and was probably an important factor in the decision. The views of the newly-arrived governor general, Lord Elgin, who took an interest in railways, might have helped to settle the question.

In retrospect it is unfortunate that more of a public issue was not made on the question of the gauge. The construction of the St Lawrence and Atlantic on a gauge different from all other railways in the region was no more defensible then than now. The mistake was perpetuated in the construction of the Grand Trunk, and it was a costly one. This was perhaps part of the price the country had to pay for the failure of government to formulate a specific railway policy. From this example of government involvement in economic development, one might conclude tentatively that the prevailing 'hands-off' philosophy of stimulating growth only by providing a favourable socioeconomic climate, while generally adequate, permitted the occurrence of serious anomalies and errors which might have been prevented.

IV

Once the gauge question was finally settled in the autumn of 1847, the construction of the first section of the St Lawrence and Atlantic could at last go forward. Much of the roadbed had already been completed, so that for the first thirty miles between Longueuil and St Hyacinthe it was merely a matter of putting down ties and rails. Though still severely plagued by financial worries, the directors decided to go ahead with this construction. Throughout the warm months of 1848, work proceeded with some fifteen hundred men under Black,

Wood and Company. By late December 1848, the first section was complete and it was opened for public use on the 27th, with two trains running daily between Montreal and St Hyacinthe.[42] A formal opening of the railway was held early in the new year, when the governor general, with an entourage of members of the legislature, made a grand excursion to St Hyacinthe for a celebration in honour of the occasion.[43] Between 1848 and 1853, when the St Lawrence and Atlantic was finally completed, there were three more occasions when Montrealers celebrated milestones in the construction of the railway. In October 1851, the line was finished as far as Richmond, seventy-one miles from Longueuil, and less than a year later to Sherbrooke, twenty miles further.[44] Some fourteen months later, the railway was complete to Island Pond, the agreed junction of the Canadian and American sections of the system.

With the opening of the first section, Montreal was at last connected by rail to the southern hinterland, the thriving agricultural region in the St Hyacinthe district. To enlarge the line's drawing power for traffic in this area, the directors invested in twenty shares of a steamboat to ply the Yamaska River between St Hyacinthe and St Césaire.[45] But the completion of thirty miles of the railway was still less than one-quarter of the proposed full length of the line. Although the directors reported to shareholders at the annual general meeting in January that much of the rest was surveyed and 'located,' they were clearly unable to muster more than a fraction of the funds for the remainder. The directors frankly told shareholders that they had no money to continue work beyond St Hyacinthe. Though Montrealers had been willing to subscribe for shares during the great drive of August 1846, many had not kept up payment of the instalments periodically called in by the directors. The directors reported that the section just opened would cost, with rolling stock, £198,000 to build, and the company's total receipts fell some £5,300 short of that figure. Shareholders would have to honour their commitments or forfeit stock; but though the directors voiced confidence that the 'majority of stockholders participate with them in their anxiety to complete the undertaking,' they must have known that they would continue to experience difficulty with defaulters.[46] Generous assistance provided by the Bank of Montreal in the form of loans was, of course, only an interim measure; a more reliable and well-founded basis of support was necessary.

The company again petitioned the legislature for aid. But in addition to government support in one form or another some changes in the legislation governing the line were desired, so that the officers could issue bonds — a point which had not been sufficiently clarified in the original, or subsequent acts of incorporation.[47] The Montreal *Gazette* favoured the railway's petition. 'It is not too much,' wrote its editor in early January 1849, 'to expect the Legislature of the Province to do what the East India Company and the enterprising States of the Union have done before it, in aid of such important national undertakings.'[48] But while most people were apparently of the opinion that government should subsidize railways, at least one person believed that they ought to be undertaken as public works.

This anonymous 'philosopher' of the railways argued in a letter to the Montreal *Courier* that companies such as the St Lawrence and Atlantic had demonstrated their inability to command sufficient credit in London to finance their railway: 'if the construction of railways be left to Private companies, such sections only will be undertaken as offer a prospect of large interest on the outlay when finished; while other sections, less promising would be neglected; whereas, if the Government undertook the work, the whole line would be completed, and those portions, which are much travelled over, and consequently yield good returns, would make up the loss on sections less used.'[49] If the province waited for private entrepreneurs to project, commence, and complete such works, 'it may wait till doomsday.' This interesting argument for government planning of railways does not appear to have had any support, but it is noteworthy as one of the few evidences of public debate about the most desirable relationship between government and railways. It is clear that the Guarantee Act that followed was not a matter of popular interest, and the public seemed unconcerned about the fortunes of the St Lawrence and Atlantic, or of any other railway in financial trouble. T.C. Keefer commented on this point a year later in his *Philosophy of Railroads.*[50]

Yet a measure to provide necessary government support for faltering railway schemes was of the deepest interest to the business community of Montreal. They had strongly expressed their views on that two months earlier at a large public meeting. It was no coincidence that Francis Hincks, the inspector general, discussed the St Lawrence and Atlantic at some length during his speech in support of the measure.[51] He pointed out that the company had experienced difficulties in financing the project, which, he also noted, would greatly facilitate the movement of commodities from the western to the eastern American states. Without the St Lawrence and Atlantic line it was unlikely that this commerce would pass through Canada East. By guaranteeing the interest on loans for railways over seventy-five miles long, the Guarantee Act of 1849 greatly aided the St Lawrence and Atlantic.[52] And another very important piece of accompanying legislation widened considerably the railway's potential basis of financial support. This was the bill passed in May 1849 to allow both the City of Montreal and the Sulpician seminary to invest in company shares.[53] This legislation must have required prior consultations with both the city and the Sulpicians, but in published reports of the meetings of the Montreal City Council there is no mention of the subject before the enabling legislation came into effect. It was later claimed that no formal discussions had been held between the city, the company, and the government, probably a true enough statement in a strict sense. But it is not difficult to see that the city council must have been easily convinced to support the St Lawrence and Atlantic. A project so highly touted to improve Montreal's flagging commerce would require the municipality to extend some support, if only as a matter of political expediency. Many local businessmen who served on the city council were shareholders in the company and would therefore be keenly interested in bringing the municipality into the venture: six aldermen held a total of thirty-four shares, while thirty shares were held by five councillors.[54]

The Montreal *Morning Courier,* probably reflecting the opinion of most city journals, came out strongly in favour of municipal aid for the railway in July 1849, arguing that 'in order ... that the Directors of the St Lawrence and Atlantic Railroad may be put in a position to demand of the Provincial Government a guarantee of the interest on the capital necessary to complete the remaining half of the entire Road, thirty-four additional miles must be constructed.'[55] This was a most auspicious time to complete the railway because reports from London suggested that since investors were looking for securities the rate of interest had fallen considerably, which should make it possible to sell St Lawrence and Atlantic 6 per cent bonds at par. Moreover, there was a report that the price of iron just then was one-third less than in 1846, and thus the cost of construction would be substantially reduced. Montreal, and perhaps other municipal corporations, as well as the Sulpician order and various ecclesiastical bodies, in the *Courier*'s view, were to be the financial salvation of the railway, because no further funds could be expected from private Canadian investors.

The finance committee of the Montreal City Council had agreed to recommend that the city purchase five thousand shares at twenty-five pounds by issuing bonds to the amount of £125,000, which would be paid to the St Lawrence and Atlantic Railway. Moreover, negotiations with the Sulpicians, the British American Land Company, and the contractors had produced a tentative agreement that each of the three would purchase one thousand shares.[56] This would produce a total of £200,000, enough to complete the remaining thirty miles and enable the company to qualify under the Guarantee Act provisions. Indeed, such aid in the form of share purchases would undoubtedly result in the sale of more of the company's stock to private investors and induce the backsliders among the earlier backers to pay the share instalments on which they were delinquent.

On 28 July 1849, some three hundred people petitioned Mayor E.R. Fabre to hold a public meeting of the citizens of Montreal to consider the proposal that the city support the St Lawrence and Atlantic Railway.[57] The meeting took place three days later in Bonsecours Market. Hundreds of citizens were present, and the mayor himself chaired the proceedings. Fabre opened by saying that the Council was convinced that the city should take shares in the railway, but he believed that the citizenry should be consulted before a commitment was made, especially in view of the amount of money involved. He pointed out that Montreal's total debt then stood at nearly £196,000, of which £80,000 was now due, and this heavy obligation should be kept in mind. Rising next, A.N. Morin brushed aside the mayor's warning and moved 'that the speedy completion of the St Lawrence and Atlantic Railway is of paramount importance to Montreal, and that it is alike the duty and interest of all the citizens cordially and zealously to co-operate in adopting such means as shall accomplish so desirable an object.'[58] John Shuter seconded the motion, stating that unless Montrealers did something to improve their trade 'the city would go to decay.' Benjamin Holmes and David Torrance moved a resolution stating that the Montrealers should avail themselves of the liberal provisions of the recently enacted Guarantee Act. They were followed by George Etienne Cartier, who apparently for the first time became involved in the affairs of the St Lawrence and Atlantic. He moved the critical resolution that the meeting urge the corporation to accept the finance committee's recommendation that Montreal purchase £125,000 worth of stock in the railway. The shares would be purchased by the sale of debentures which the city would redeem in instalments from seven to fifteen years.

John Rose seconded this resolution, but before it could be put to an open vote two gadflies, John Molson jr and Benaiah Gibb jr, interrupted the virtually unanimous approval of the resolution. John Molson had never shared his brother William's enthusiasm for the St Lawrence and Atlantic Railway and even though he dutifully subscribed for ten shares he remained a firm supporter of the Champlain and St Lawrence. Molson was a wealthy and prominent industrialist, and when he stood up to oppose the motion then before the meeting, he stood with the authority and wealth of the head of the Molson family enterprises, which put him on the same level as Peter McGill, John Young, or Hugh Allan. Benaiah Gibb, though not nearly as prominent a businessman, was a well-known tailor of considerable means,[59] and since he held only ten shares he was probably more concerned about the dangers to the municipal finances which a commitment to the railway would involve. Gibb and Molson argued that the level of taxation required to support repayment of the debentures would be onerous. The city would be destroyed, in Molson's view, since municipal taxation was already very high. Interrupted frequently by laughter, groans, and hisses, they were finally forced to sit down.

Although the meeting was obviously not in a mood to listen to such counsels of caution, Olivier Berthelet rose to administer a more polite refutation to the Gibb and Molson admonitions. 'What was the debt of Montreal,' he asked, 'compared to the enormous debt of New York City, which stood at $25,000,000? Indeed in comparison to any city's, Montreal's debt was so trifling that they need not fear of increasing it a little.' After urging everyone to get behind the railway, Berthelet criticized the great number of Montrealers who had not subscribed to it. It was perhaps fortunate for his reputation that those present did not know that Berthelet's own name did not appear in the original shareholder's lists.[60] He might well have been a shareholder in 1849, but not two years later.[61]

Though Berthelet was hardly the right person to admonish others, nonetheless, he was a Montrealer of considerable means and prominence. Born into a well-to-do family, he was a graduate of the Sulpician Collège de Montréal after which he went into business, and briefly entered provincial politics, when he sat in the Legislative Assembly as member for Montreal East between 1832 and 1834.[62] Further efforts to get him back into political life was unsuccessful.[63] Precisely what business Berthelet carried on is a mystery, but he was a wealthy man if his generous gifts to religious and welfare institutions are a valid indication. Despite his burst of enthusiasm on the afternoon of the meeting, however, he was never again active in the affairs of the St Lawrence and Atlantic Railway. Molson made one more unsuccessful attempt to talk fiscal sense to the gathering. But the motion was passed nevertheless and was accepted easily by the City Council. The City of Montreal subsequently purchased £125,000 of preferred shares.[64]

Both the seminary of St Sulpice and the British American Land Company stood to benefit substantially from the railway, the land company because the line would pass through some of its lands and through Sherbrooke, the company's ambitious administrative centre in the Eastern Townships, thus enhancing property values. Equally interested in the increased value of their own lands were the Sulpicians, still seigneurs of the Island of Montreal, which would benefit considerably from the prosperity the railway would bring. The British American Land Company duly purchased £25,000 worth of shares, and the Seminary promised a like amount.[65]

Although the company thus received a total of £175,000 from the City of Montreal, the Seminary, and the British American Land Company, its money worries were not over. The shares continued to sell at substantial discounts in Montreal as holders sold them for as low as 82 per cent of their face value. The gloomy commercial outlook of 1849 probably induced many of little faith to sell out. In the face of the declining support, while obligations to new construction contracts mounted, the company's directors decided to withhold the payment of dividends on common shares until the line was completed. Certificates for the value of the dividends were issued to shareholders in an attempt to bolster the value of the common shares.[66]

v

Construction on the line had apparently stopped while the financial problems were being settled. With new funds forthcoming, the company could finally look forward with some assurance to the completion of the work. Final arrangements took some months to complete, but on 30 November a contract was signed with Black, Wood and Company to complete the remainder of the railway within three years.[67] The agreed price was £6,550 per mile, three-quarters in cash and one-quarter in stock, and the company engineer, A.C. Morton, was to scrutinize the completed sections before they were to be accepted. By late January 1849 the roadbed was again under vigorous preparation and the contractors began purchasing iron rails in anticipation of a quick completion.[68] By the terms of the contract Black, Wood and Company leased running rights over the completed Longueuil-St Hyacinthe section, presumably mostly for their supply trains. They were sending firewood to Montreal, however, which on one occasion led to allegations of profiteering. But the contractors, for some reason, were not proceeding satisfactorily. When the section between St Hyacinthe and Melbourne was not completed on time, according to the agreement that portion of the work was taken out of their hands and finished by the company at the contractor's expense.[69]

Black, Wood and Company soon afterward withdrew from all their contracts with the St Lawrence and Atlantic, and the remainder of the railway was finished by the company.[70] Not much is known of the abandonment of the project by the contractors or the reasons; perhaps they experienced serious reverses of some kind. A deeper and more tantalizing mystery is the question why the company's directors agreed to let them out of the contract; questions to the directors on the topic in 1852, went unanswered.[71] Not long after they were relieved of their obligations under the 1849 contract, Black, Wood and Company sold back to the railway company, all, or most, of the shares they had received in payment for the sections completed. They had accepted the shares at par and in the resale took back only 50 per cent of the face value, or considerably less than the market price.[72]

The sundering of relations between Black, Wood and the railway company raised serious problems that John Young helped to solve. Though not still a director of the company, Young had remained active in the railway's affairs since 1846. In 1850 and 1851, he emerged as a key figure in the company, with A.T. Galt, who, even before he became president of the company in 1852, was its most active director. Both were instrumental in solving the financial crisis caused by the removal of the contract. Bonds and stocks to have been paid to the contractors came back into the company's hands. These securities, to the amount of £425,000, had to be sold in order to pay the cost of construction, which was now under the company's control. Young laboured arduously on the company's behalf to sell the bonds – backed by the provincial guarantee – on the best possible terms. After corresponding at length with Barings of London, Young, designated as the railway's agent, succeeded in placing £400,000 worth of bonds on the London market.[73] In order to make them marketable there, the railway company's directors were advised by Barings that the provincial guarantee should be extended to the principal as well as the interest of the bonds. The provincial inspector general, Francis Hincks, who took great interest in the sale, approved of the change, which was secured by an amendment to the Guarantee Act. Young was paid a commission of 1 per cent, or a sum of some £4,200 for his services.[74] This is the only evidence of substantial personal gains made from the railway by Montreal businessmen up till this time.[75] Although a sizable sum, Young's commission was modest compared to entrepreneurial gains made later in Canadian railway promotion.

The St Hyacinthe–Melbourne section of the St Lawrence and Atlantic was completed during the summer of 1851 and opened in August. Only two months later the railway was complete to Richmond, the junction with the proposed branch to Quebec.[76] Now, with more than seventy miles opened, the line was over half finished, so that the provincial guarantee for the interest on its bonds came into effect.

From Richmond the tracks swung south to Sherbrooke, and from there the intention was to build south to Coaticook and across the border to Island Pond in Vermont. Although the question of the route of the railway had not received any publicity in Montreal newspapers – and in the company's annual reports few details were ever given about it – there had been some discussion on the subject from the beginning. Following a straight line from Longueuil to Portland was obviously out of the question, because of difficult terrain in parts of the Canadian section, not to mention the Maine and New Hampshire mountain regions. It was impractical, also, from the point of view of the necessary participation in the scheme of both St Hyacinthe and Sherbrooke, which might have been excluded had brevity and directness been the sole criteria. From the beginning both towns had wanted to share in the project because of the obvious benefits the railway would bring. Other would-be metropolitan centres in the Eastern Townships hoped that the St Lawrence and Atlantic, or branches of it, would traverse their regions.

One such hopeful was Stanstead in the most southwestern section of the Townships, some forty miles from Sherbrooke. It had attempted since the late thirties to establish rail links with the outside.[77] In 1841 a group of Township men received a charter to build a railway from Sherbrooke through Stanstead to the Richelieu River. Throughout the forties and early fifties, the Stansteaders continued to advance this railway, named the St Lawrence and Atlantic Grand Junction, and were supported briefly by A.T. Galt and others later associated with the Portland scheme. According to an 1845 plan, this Township tramway was to pass through St Hyacinthe, Sherbrooke, and Stanstead, thus tapping the most populous parts of the Townships, and the threat that it might be pursued was one of the factors that led to the decision by the St Lawrence and Atlantic's directors to construct the line through Stanstead township. Nevertheless, discussion continued in the area during the early fifties on the subject of a railway from Stanstead to Boston.[78]

From the start of the Montreal-Portland project, the connecting Atlantic and St Lawrence Company was apparently even more interested in a short line than was its Canadian counterpart. Poor had intended to run the American railway northwest to the Connecticut River in northern New Hampshire and along the northernmost reaches of the river across the border into Canada.[79] Having in mind the shortest possible line in that sparsely settled and relatively unpromising White Mountain region of northern New Hampshire, Poor intended the Atlantic and St Lawrence to cross into Canada at the earliest opportunity. But this would pass on to the Canadians the cost of bridging the Connecticut River and building extra miles of track. However, the St Lawrence and Atlantic successfully prevailed upon their American colleagues to build west to Island Pond, still some fifteen miles inside Vermont. They agreed also to compensate the Atlantic and St Lawrence company for the additional costs of construction. For the Canadians, it was a worthwhile arrangement because not only did their railway thus traverse a potentially good area in West Coaticook, but they also had the advantage of excellent grades in that vicinity.[80] Moreover, the West Coaticook route made it easier for the St Lawrence and Atlantic to connect with a proposed northern Vermont line, the Passumpsic railway, at St Johnsbury.

There were some further questions about the route, but no serious challenges. In 1852 the promoters of a more westerly route from Sherbrooke proposed that the railway proceed to Lennoxville, through the town of Stanstead, to Island Pond. The directors agreed to consider this proposal, and even took the trouble and expense of a survey; but later decided against the idea because Stanstead was too close to Rouses' Point, the southern terminus of the rival Champlain and St Lawrence. Proximity was to be avoided because of the serious danger of traffic being siphoned off from the St Lawrence and Atlantic. As the westerly route through the town would bring the railway fifteen miles closer to Rouses' Point, it was rejected. The West Coaticook route was finally agreed upon by the two companies in early August 1852 and the line finally located.

VI

A historian of railways should attempt, so far as the available data allows, to answer the question of the utility of this railway, and of the Montreal lines generally. What saving did the St Lawrence and Atlantic provide to Montrealers? How was it able to compete with the other two lines that, by 1853, claimed to be offering similar service? Was the St Lawrence and Atlantic the most efficient, by reason of its gauge, its directness to the seaboard, or otherwise, as its promoters claimed during the early stages of its development? The crude returns of rail traffic entering Montreal, published daily during 1854, are one strong indication of the relative efficiency of the railways. During the spring and summer of 1854, the St Lawrence and Atlantic was clearly in second place in comparison to the Champlain and St Lawrence, in the volume of cargo carried.[81] In the total dollar receipts of the St Lawrence and Atlantic, freight was the most important producing almost one-half of total revenue. Against total receipts of $338,000 for the first six months of 1854 freight amounted to $165,000, more than double the second-best earner, which was first-class passenger traffic.[82] Second-class passenger receipts were about one-sixth the latter; returns for lumber were $31,000, and for firewood $27,000.[83] It is curious that there was no category for wheat and flour, which one would expect to have been carried, unless it was included under merchandise, which is unlikely. Most of the merchandise would have been manufactured goods from Britain destined for Montreal.

In the absence of comparable figures in these categories for the Champlain and St Lawrence Railway, only the most tentative comparisons can be attempted. From the 1854 returns it seems clear that the Champlain and St Lawrence was still the premier railway running from Montreal to the eastern United States. Its volume of merchandise was three times that of the St Lawrence and Atlantic, conservatively estimated, and the passenger traffic must have been even more. In contrast to the Montreal-Portland system, which passed through only a few major centres along its 250-mile route, the Champlain and St Lawrence went through St John's, an important navigation centre of the Richelieu River-Lake Champlain system and the centre of a comparatively populous hinterland. Moreover, the Champlain and St Lawrence connected with a railway network that covered much of the upper New England area and ultimately led to Boston and New York.

Most, if not all, of the firewood carried by rail was in all likelihood brought into Montreal. Vast quantities were consumed, and local supplies were practically non-existent. Here the St Lawrence and Atlantic could have perceived a real need, for its competitor was likely not a large supplier. There is some evidence, however, that the opening of the St Lawrence and Atlantic did not result in substantially lower firewood prices for the Montreal consumers, at least initially.[84] Thus, if the early pattern was followed, there was little social saving for Montreal in having the railway as a conveyor of firewood, and in any event, since revenue from that service was about 6 per cent of total receipts, the utility of the railway could hardly be justified from that standpoint alone. Nor could it be if just lumber traffic were considered, for the revenue from that item was only 25 per cent higher than returns from firewood, or £26,575, still a very small fraction of the total revenue. It is doubtful if much of the lumber carried on the railway went to Montreal, or indeed, whether most of it was Canadian in origin; but available evidence does not permit certainty on this point. Canadian lumber passing through Montreal and destined for the American eastern market might more readily be sent by the Champlain and St Lawrence to either New York or Boston. While it might have been more economical to send lumber by the St Lawrence and Atlantic to the Atlantic seacoast, delays and costs of trans-shipment to coastal vessels would probably have offset that advantage, despite early hopes to the contrary.

Thus the St Lawrence and Atlantic Railway was clearly not of great utility to Montreal for several reasons. First, the Atlantic terminus was not a major centre either for exporting or importing, much less for banking, insurance, and shipping, which are the hallmarks of an entrepôt. While it is true that just after the completion of the railway there were beginnings, of regular transatlantic steamship service to Portland, this was only seasonal and depended upon large subsidies from the Canadian government. These inconveniences probably offset whatever cost advantages the St Lawrence and Atlantic had over its competitors. Another disadvantage was the fact that it was completed seven years after it was first announced and nearly three years after its chief competitor for the St Lawrence-seaboard traffic. Montrealers had had to be very nearly dragged to the share subscription desk in 1844, 1845, and 1846, when the St Lawrence was the only through railway planned to run between Montreal and the Atlantic; how much less appealing must the project have appeared when, at the end of construction, the line faced competition from an extended Champlain and St Lawrence and the apparently threatening Montreal and New York?

Had the St Lawrence and Atlantic been finished when the new St Lawrence canals were opened, the two routes might easily have been integrated as a unified transportation system, and commercial success would perhaps have followed. But this is not certain and there are good grounds for doubt, as suggested above, that the system would have taken hold in this fashion. It was easy, perhaps too easy, to compare Montreal and its routes to the Erie Canal and New York in the early twenties without remembering that New York was a great port, a large city, and a major distribution centre even before the Erie Canal was begun.

This perhaps was the major weakness of the promoters of the railway. It is understandable that Portland should have wished to emulate the apparent success of Boston in overcoming its disadvantages compared to New York; and it is not difficult to see why Montrealers should have fallen prey to similar thinking. Although there was initially a general reluctance to purchase shares, in Montreal, and seldom wild enthusiasm, nevertheless some £200,000 was raised by Montrealers for the railway.

To Montrealers the major attraction of the St Lawrence and Atlantic was that when finished it would provide a winter outlet on the Atlantic. It would complete the excellent chain of canals along the upper St Lawrence between Montreal and Prescott and would make possible year-round trade with Europe at costs lower than charges on New York's canal or Boston's railways. One of New York's 'disappointed rivals,' Montreal would have its opportunity at last to become the emporium of trade for the Great Lakes basin.[85] The St Lawrence and Atlantic project seemed admirably suited for this purpose and for stimulating regional development in the Eastern Townships. For Montreal the railway provided an opportunity to acquire a minor Atlantic port far less powerful than Boston. Portland would be an outport, dependent almost exclusively on Montreal for trade with the interior. For Montreal's metropolitan aspirations the St Lawrence and Atlantic project offered brilliant hope.

These prospects were probably considerably improved by the railway's union, shortly after completion in 1853, with the Grand Trunk. Its fortunes became inextricably tied with those of another railway venture and its own strengths and weaknesses were obscured. It was probably soon forgotten that the St Lawrence and Atlantic had originally seemed a grand project, that it was a developmental as well as a portage railway, that it was to be Montreal's chief rail link to the sea, and that it was to have boosted the city's sagging prospects in the late forties.

The history of the St Lawrence and Atlantic before its absorption by the Grand Trunk is essentially a study of the Montreal business community's response to Boston competition for control of the St Lawrence trade. Although inspired by an American visionary, the Canadian part of the line had been created largely by Montreal businessmen, mostly leading general merchants who traded in the export staples from, and imports to, the west. Without their initial support for the St Lawrence and Atlantic the railway could not have been built. Notwithstanding the great importance of the provincial government's assistance, in the form of guarantees on bonds, Montreal private investment began the project, and Montreal businessmen directed it.

Yet there is little evidence that the St Lawrence and Atlantic was promoted for the entrepreneurial gain of a small group of the city's businessmen. It is probable that some made gains by buying and selling its shares, and it seems certain that a few, including William Workman, made substantial profits by buying shares when the railway was taken over by the Grand Trunk, when shares, previously selling at immense discounts, were valued at par.[86] Nevertheless, though available records do not permit a definitive statement about individual entrepreneurial gain in this company, there are no grounds for asserting that any fortunes were made — before the merger of 1853 — in the promotion of the St Lawrence and Atlantic project.[87] There are a couple of reasons why this should have been so. The most important was that by nature the railway was as near a community-wide endeavour as it was possible to make it. Most of the city's businessmen were involved in a major or minor way, as well as the municipality, the Seminary, a large number from Montreal's non-commercial groups, and many French Canadians. While it is probable that many shares were in default and many more changed hands it is surprising how constant, through 1851, that broad support continued to be.[88] It may be naïve to assert that such a breadth of participation and concerned scrutiny in the company would have prevented profiteering altogether, and it would certainly have tended to make any huge entrepreneurial rakeoffs less obvious. Possibilities of dishonesty abounded at every turn, and there is at least the possibility, if no evidence, that some were utilized.

10

Western railway projects and rivalries 1846-53

I

In the midst of excited discussion and capital construction around the St Lawrence and Atlantic during the late forties and early fifties, the railway idea was adopted as the solution to other transportation problems facing Montreal. A longstanding difficulty had been the impediments to navigation on the Ottawa and upper St Lawrence rivers, and of these the Lachine rapids only a few miles upstream from the city was the most difficult barrier to shipping. That obstacle and the inadequacy of the Lachine Canal gave rise to a project for a Montreal and Lachine railway.

Soon after its completion in 1848, this short, seven-mile railway was to become the basis for two extension lines, one south, the Lake St Louis and Province Line, and the other west, the St Lawrence and Ottawa Grand Junction. The former, examined later, was designed to provide Montreal with yet another outlet to the northeastern United States. The latter, a forerunner of the Grand Trunk Railway, was expected to extend the city's economic hegemony over the traditional Upper Canadian hinterlands. Just as the Lachine Canal a generation earlier had provided the vital link for a Canadian canal system along both the St Lawrence and the Ottawa-Rideau routes, the Montreal and Lachine Railway anchored the westward growth of Montreal's railway system in the forties and fifties. This chapter examines the Montreal business community's promotion of the two western lines, the Montreal and Lachine and the St Lawrence and Ottawa Grand Junction. The first was accomplished effortlessly; the second, though never constructed, was pursued actively long enough to provide an instructive example of Montreal railway entrepreneurship.

Between 1843 and 1848 the Lachine Canal, which had been completed in 1825, was being enlarged to make its capacity uniform with the great chain of canals then under construction along the St Lawrence. Though Montreal merchants anxiously awaited the completion of the waterway, a number of them were tempted to join Montreal to Lachine by a railway, for the advantages of railways were at that time widely advocated in the city. Whether or not the promoters of the Montreal and Lachine Railway already contemplated a broader scheme is not certain, but since the late thirties there had been serious discussion in Montreal of a western railway. In 1840 a large group consisting mainly of Montrealers had been authorized by the Special Council of Lower Canada to form a company to build a tramway from Montreal west to the provincial boundary of Pointe à Beaudet.[1] The way would cross the St Lawrence to Vaudreuil and proceed past Dickinson's Landing to Brockville or Prescott. Among the supporters of this abortive scheme was James Ferrier, a Montreal merchant who, six years later, was the leading promoter of the Montreal and Lachine Railway and its proposed extensions west and south.

An immigrant in 1821 to Montreal at the age of twenty-one, Ferrier, who was fresh from a mercantile training in his native town of Perth in Fifeshire, soon entered business in Montreal.[2] 'By industry and close attention he accumulated a fortune' Dorwin recorded, so that he was able to retire in 1836 and devote himself to various public activities and speculative ventures, including the Bank of British North America, McGill University, and municipal politics.[3] One eulogy somewhat extravagantly held that 'a full memoir of the Honourable James Ferrier would be the history of Montreal for a period of sixty years,' suggesting his importance in the local business world.[4]

Ferrier led the group of Montreal businessmen who petitioned the government in March 1846 for a charter to build a railway between Montreal and Lachine.[5] Supporting him were William Molson, William Dow, and Sir George Simpson, all three of whom had substantial interests in other railways, steamboats, and later in transatlantic shipping. They were accompanied by William Coffin, sheriff of Montreal, and Thomas Stayner, deputy postmaster general. Their petition, which proclaimed the utility of the proposed railway to Montreal and their readiness 'to subscribe the necessary funds for defraying the expenses of the work so that no delay may occur in carrying it into execution,' was quickly answered by the legislature granting them a charter in June.[6] The company was capitalized at £75,000 in fifteen hundred shares at £50 each, with authority given to borrow an additional £50,000. Stock subscription books were opened on 16 June, and within seven weeks all the shares had been taken up.[7]

By this time an impressive segment of the business community was behind the scheme, including John Boston, John Mathewson, John Torrance, J.G. Mackenzie, John Leeming, William Logan, James Logan, David Macpherson, Jesse Joseph, and Theodore Hart. Of these, only William Coffin and John

Boston, seigneur of Lacadie, were not in business;[8] the others were all leading figures in commerce and transportation. They were aware not only of the utility of a railway to Lachine but also of its value as a basis for further developments. William Molson, one of the leading figures in this promotion, was not then a shareholder in either the Champlain and St Lawrence or the St Lawrence and Atlantic and was able to participate freely in the new venture, committing to its success part of his large financial resources and his immense prestige in local business circles.

John Mathewson, another promoter, operated a small soap and candle factory in Montreal, he owned a large amount of property in the city, and was active in the affairs of the New City Gas Company and the Montreal Fire, Life and Inland Navigation Assurance Company.[9] John Gordon Mackenzie was a wholesale dry-goods merchant of long standing in Montreal. For eighteen years following his arrival from Scotland in 1811, he worked with Forsyth, Richardson and Company.[10] After establishing his own firm in 1829, Mackenzie became one of Montreal's most successful merchants, amassing a huge fortune. At the same time he developed interests in two banks, the Bank of Montreal and the City Bank, serving as director of both during the forties.

John Leeming was a Montreal commission merchant and auctioneer with wide-ranging interests. A prominent and popular lecturer in Montreal, Leeming gave learned talks to Montrealers on 'The Age We Live In,' 'The Origin of Drama and Remarks on the Genius of Shakespeare' and 'Money and Banking.'[11] He became bankrupt in 1849 and faded out of local affairs. Theodore Hart, like Jesse Joseph, was a local Jewish merchant. Though apparently less active in joint-stock companies in this period, Hart was active in commerce and shipping as a member of Benjamin Hart and Company, general merchants.[12] Prominent shipowners John Torrance and David Macpherson lent further distinction to the group promoting the Montreal and Lachine.

Many of these businessmen, who were joined by many associates as the project advanced to completion, were supporters of Montreal's other railways. Most of them were shareholders of either the St Lawrence and Atlantic or the Champlain and St Lawrence, and, since they were not likely to invest in an obvious competitor, both groups seem to have regarded the Montreal and Lachine as a complementary line.[13] This assumption held at least until 1850, when the St Lawrence and Ottawa Grand Junction received support from shareholders of both southern railways.

Since adequate finances to build the seven-mile line were assured, little time was wasted in starting construction, the first stage of which was completed on 19 November 1847, under the direction of Scottish engineer Alexander Millar.[14] The initial selection of an inferior route over an extensive and apparently bottomless marsh was a problem successfully overcome, but the railway required much work before it was completely and safely operational. Moreover, costs of construction and acquisition of a right-of-way had been higher than expected.[15] Thus more money was required. Although the company had been permitted to borrow up to £50,000, a petition by Ferrier to the legislature in March 1848 pointed out that the then depressed 'state of commercial affairs and – the scarcity of money now prevailing' did not permit the company to raise loans at the limited interest rate it was allowed to pay.[16] The company asked permission to borrow at a higher rate, to issue £50,000 worth of new common shares, and to convert the first issue to preferred shares with a guaranteed dividend of 6 per cent.

The bill embodying these recommendations was vetoed by the governor on the advice of the Colonial Office. 'Her Majesty has not been advised,' wrote the provincial secretary to the company, 'to confirm the act of incorporation proposed by the Legislature of the Province until the objections taken to the Act by Her Majesty's Government shall be obviated.'[17] Although not specified, these objections probably referred to details associated with the preferred stock, thought to be unacceptable because they were unworkable, irregular, or because they violated some principles of railway legislation which the Colonial Secretary was attempting to impose on Canada.[18] Six months later, however, the company submitted more suitable recommendations, and the legislature passed a bill to allow it to issue £40,000 worth of preferred shares at 8 per cent and debentures worth £50,000.[19]

The necessary improvements to the Montreal and Lachine were soon completed. It attracted a large passenger traffic, which, in the brief period from mid-April to the end of November 1848, amounted to 95,000 passengers. But it was not a profitable enterprise. The line was not competitive with canal barges for freight, and carried but 3,300 tons during the same period.[20] Its net profit that year was only £2500, a small return on an investment of £95,000.[21] There was barely enough revenue to pay dividends on the newly-issued preferred shares. As long as the railway remained just a portage line in competition with the Lachine Canal for bulk traffic, it would probably never be much more remunerative. Ferrier and his associates may have seen this problem from the beginning and have planned to make it a more extensive system.

II

In the forties and early fifties, one of the most important challenges facing Montreal in its ancient quest for commercial predominance was the need to improve transport links with its restive western hinterlands. The rapidly expanding settled distant regions of Upper Canada and the closer timber frontier of the Ottawa Valley were markets of great importance, while the flow of agricultural produce out of these areas yielded a rich reward. Since the early years of the century Montreal's growing range of banking, shipping, and insurance services, not to mention the growing number of commercial houses specializing in every major kind of trade, had deepened the city's commitment to the interior.[22]

The western areas of Upper Canada, however, were not to the same degree dependent upon Montreal for transportation. The interior province and its capital, Toronto, which was already emerging as the metropolis of Canada West, had, in the Oswego Canal, another outlet to the sea besides the traditional St Lawrence route.[23] Since 1845, when the United States drawback legislation was passed, Upper Canadian exports had been drawn through the Erie Canal system in ever-increasing volume. Another major threat was the Ogdensburg railway, the last link in Boston's push to the north; when completed, this line would strike a powerful blow against Montreal's western trade. The Ottawa trade might similarly be diverted by the Prescott and Bytown Railway, designed to link up with the Ogdensburg railway.[24]

A railway from Montreal deep into Upper Canada might well nullify these threats. As soon as possible Montreal needed a railway into the eastern section of that province, to Prescott, or to Bytown, or, if possible, to both. In his *Philosophy of Railroads*, the engineer Thomas Coltrin Keefer exhorted Montrealers to throw themselves behind the extension of the Montreal and Lachine west to Prescott. Such a line operating on a year-round basis, he pointed out, would provide farmers in the interior with an outlet for their grain and flour during the winter, when prices were highest. Montreal's citizens generally would benefit by lower food and firewood costs. Moreover, a railroad would liven up the 'Sleepy Hollow' country villages twenty to fifty miles back of the main towns along the St Lawrence. 'Nothing can be a more powerful antidote to this state of primitive but not innocuous simplicity,' for the railway was the greatest engine of progress of the age.[25]

Designed to serve both the St Lawrence and the Ottawa river systems, the railway was a reaffirmation of Montreal's interest in the Ottawa Valley. Though never a major Montreal investment frontier, the Ottawa had attracted some Montreal capital to various forwarding firms and to the supply of lumber camps.[26] Substantial quantities of Ottawa Valley lumber were handled at Montreal. Although forwarding from Montreal to Upper Canada by way of the Ottawa-Rideau route had declined during the late forties because of the availability of the St Lawrence canals, Montreal still traded strongly with the lower Ottawa Valley. A number of Montreal businessmen, Hosea Smith, David

Davidson, John Mathewson, John G. Mackenzie, James Torrance, and Henry L. Routh, were behind the Carillon and Grenville Railway Company which was chartered in 1847.[27]

Keefer's pamphlet extolling 'the civilizing tendency of the locomotive' was intended as advance publicity for the appeal by directors of the Montreal and Lachine to Montreal investors as well as to the provincial legislature. Legislative approval and wide financial support was needed for the scheme to construct a western extension to be called the St Lawrence and Ottawa Grand Junction railway.[28] The plan was to begin this new line north from Lachine across the island of Montreal to Rivière des Prairies, which would be connected by bridge to Ile Jésus. The island would be linked by another bridge to the mainland of Two Mountains county. From there the railway would proceed in a north-westerly direction to the Ottawa River, which would be bridged near Hawkesbury; proceeding westward the line would reach Prescott.[29] Thus a railway approximately 150 miles long would be thrust into the St Lawrence and lower Ottawa river hinterlands.

With the support of some municipalities along the proposed route,[30] Ferrier and other interested parties began petitioning for a charter for the St Lawrence and Ottawa Grand Junction in 1848. But aside from these importunate pleas — stated with a standard eloquence — there was a minimum of public interest in this project. Montreal newspapers carried little news through 1849 about this grandiosely-titled proposal to link the city with the interior by railway. When its charter was approved by the legislature in August 1850, little more than polite notice was taken of it in the Montreal press.

From the beginning the St Lawrence and Ottawa Grand Junction was dominated by the promoters of the Montreal and Lachine. The group empowered to build the western line included, besides Ferrier, Coffin, Stayner, and Mackenzie, the newcomers Peter McGill, Joseph Bourret, John Young, George Moffatt, John Frothingham, William Dow, and James Greenshields, all of whom were associated with either or both of Montreal's other two railway ventures, especially the St Lawrence and Atlantic.[31] These men, who were among the most prominent merchants, constituted an impressive list of promoters, a good sign indeed for this fledgling. By 1850, the St Lawrence and Atlantic, though far from complete, had its first section of thirty miles under construction and the promised support of the Guarantee Act after an additional forty-five miles were finished. The St Lawrence and Ottawa Grand Junction would be a most useful western feeder for the Portland line, and some day the two might be physically joined by a bridge across the St Lawrence.[32]

Yet the inactivity of these promoters following incorporation of the railway did not suggest serious intentions of moving ahead vigorously. No shares were sold, no detailed surveys were begun, and no publicity about the project was put into Montreal newspapers. Keefer's eloquent little pamphlet, which the directors commissioned him to write, appears to have been the sole evidence of their existence. One major reason for delay might well have been an anticipation of difficulties selling railway shares during Montreal's commercial depression of 1850. But even if they did not intend to build the line immediately, the securing of a charter (with its three-year time limit) was a good hedge against future vagaries of railway fortune. It was in fact a good bet, costing little to acquire and hold, that this charter would turn them a profit some day, whether on share dividends of capital gains, mergers with other lines, construction contracts, or land speculation.[33]

Aside from unfavourable business conditions, the St Lawrence and Ottawa Grand Junction was handicapped by its proposed route. Even in this early period of railway development when, because of its novelty, supporters were sanguine about its flexibility and ability to create traffic, the proposed route of this line was somewhat impractical. To cross from the island of Montreal north to the mainland was necessary if the railway was to cross the Ottawa River. But then to carry the line along the north shore of the Lake of Two Mountains and up the lower Ottawa River to Grenville, across the Ottawa to Hawkesbury, and west through the back regions of Prescott and Russell counties to Prescott, was a dubious scheme. While the north shore of the Ottawa would be a productive enough region of traffic, the area further west was questionable. This, at least, was the opinion of Casimir Gzowski, who in 1851 completed a light survey of both the St Lawrence and the Ottawa backcountry routes at the invitation of a group led by John Young. Gzowski concluded that a railway bordering the St Lawrence, shorter by fourteen and one-half miles and cheaper to build by an estimated £147,000, would also carry more traffic and prove to be more remunerative than a line further back from the river front.[34] That position was debated by Benjamin Holmes before the Standing Committee on Railways of the Legislative Assembly in 1851. Holmes considered the trade with the 'Lumber Districts of which Bytown is the Centre' as vastly more important to Montreal than the river commerce to Kingston.[35] He and others testifying before the committee supported the northern or Ottawa route for the proposed Grand Trunk Railway on the additional grounds that the towns along the St Lawrence were already well served by existing steamboat services.

The railway's promoters were not entirely inactive. During the period immediately after the charter was granted they made efforts to secure some initial commitment to the scheme from a number of municipal governments. In Two Mountains County a gathering in late December 1850 endorsed the railway, which together with the Montreal and Lachine was seen as a western extension of the St Lawrence and Atlantic. Those attending offered to take stock in the railway to the value of their lands required for the right-of-way, and they urged the county council to subscribe for £30,000 of the company's stock.[36] Similar support came several days later from the United Counties of Prescott and Russell in the form of a pledge to take £40,000 in shares. A similar amount was promised by the United Counties of Stormont, Glengarry, and Dundas, while the towns of Prescott and Bytown offered £7,500 and £15,000 respectively. A total of £132,500 was raised from these five municipalities alone.[37]

In response to these generous gestures the Montreal *Gazette* on 20 January called for a 'convention of all parties interested in the enterprise.' Despite the encouraging signs of Upper Canadian interest in the railway, however, the company's directors failed to utilize and expand it. During the early months of 1851, these men were preparing to build the Montreal and Lachine's southern branch, the Lake St Louis and Province Line, stretching towards Plattsburg, possibly showing their doubt about the necessity of connecting the St Lawrence and Ottawa to the Portland line. An additional barrier to action on the western line was the growing uncertainty about the suitability of the route chosen for drawing the Ottawa trade. Rhetorical estimates of the potential traffic from the back townships did not conceal from its promoters the fact that the expenditure of three quarters of a million pounds on this railway would need a good deal of traffic to justify. Moreover they might well have believed that their own line should wait until the route of the Grand Trunk was finally established.

The location of the Grand Trunk and the commencement of work on it in 1853 spurred the directorate of St Lawrence and Ottawa to act (their charter was about to expire too).[38] William Coffin, who had replaced Ferrier as head of the Montreal and Lachine and its branch railways in 1851, was the key figure in reactivating the St Lawrence and Ottawa two years later. In 1853 he and the other promoters, who included most of those associated with the project in 1850, decided to change the route of the railway by making Kemptville, rather than Prescott, its western terminus.[39] Thus, the railway would traverse the backcountry, leaving the 'Front' to be served by the Grand Trunk, and would draw traffic from the Ottawa Valley by linking with the Prescott and Bytown Railway.

Besides this intended alteration of its western terminus, there was a much more significant change in the project. Coffin, who by 1853 was bringing to completion the Montreal and Plattsburgh system, embracing the Montreal and Lachine, the Lake St Louis, and the Plattsburg and Montreal railways, now saw the St Lawrence and Ottawa Grand Junction as a feeder line. Thus an integrated system running from Kemptville − or perhaps from Detroit eventually − south to Plattsburg and ultimately to New York was being designed.[40] With its fulcrum at Lachine, seven miles up the St Lawrence from Montreal, this system threatened to divert much upcountry traffic from Montreal, the metropolis being outflanked ironically by one of its own former outports. This possibility would not have endeared the project to most Montreal merchants.

III

In the space of two years the St Lawrence and Ottawa Grand Junction had thus changed from being an extension of the St Lawrence and Atlantic into an adjunct of a rival to both it and the Champlain and St Lawrence. This change is an important reason why the owners of the latter proposed to build their own extension, the Montreal and Bytown, into the very region where the St Lawrence and Ottawa was to be constructed. When, in early 1853, plans to build the Montreal and Bytown Railway were known, the promoters of the St Lawrence and Ottawa line saw that they would be faced with a new rival for traffic. Efforts on both sides were redoubled, and, during the spring and summer of 1853, Montreal, the north shore, and eastern Upper Canada were treated to the unusual and entertaining spectacle of two groups of railway promoters vying for their approval.

For several months Montreal and the lower Ottawa Valley were immersed in a welter of controversy about the two railway schemes, expressed in newspaper announcements and editorials as well as at many public meetings. Although it was predictable that Bytown would shift its promised allegiance from the St Lawrence and Ottawa to the more direct Montreal and Bytown, and that most Montrealers would elect to do the same, it was not certain which line the region's municipalities would support. Ottawa Valley communities would be attracted to the Montreal and Bytown's route, which would proceed north from Montreal, across the island, across Ile Jésus, to the mainland, and on in a northwesterly direction to St Eustache. From here it would swing towards the Ottawa River, and through St Andrews, closely parallel to the river, on to Hull.[41] Besides offering the advantage of direct communications between Bytown and Montreal, this railway was very likely seen by some as the beginning of a much larger system which might extend east from Montreal along the north shore of the St Lawrence to Quebec.[42] Though its promoters made no statements about their plans to extend the railway west of Bytown, this possibility also was openly discussed in the lumber capital. In 1853, however, these were little more than dreams. The Montreal and Bytown was primarily designed to attach the Ottawa Valley firmly to Montreal and, in view of some of the railway's promoters, to the Champlain and St Lawrence Railway as well.

Behind the Montreal and Bytown scheme stood a number of Montreal businessmen entirely new to railway promotions in Montreal, many French

Canadians amongst them. Led by Alexandre Maurice Delisle, a prominent local Bleu politician,[43] this interesting group included other politicians, two bankers, and many merchants. Jacques Viger, the former mayor of Montreal, Benjamin Holmes, former cashier of the Bank of Montreal (1827-45), member of Parliament (1841-4), and alderman of Montreal, and Benjamin H. Lemoine, cashier of La Banque du Peuple, Jacob DeWitt, and William Workman were among the most prominent. Both Delisle and Workman had been directors of the Champlain and St Lawrence Railway Company since 1842. Delisle was later the chairman of the Board of Directors of the Champlain railway, in which he had £1000 invested, as well as £600 in the rival St Lawrence and Atlantic and a further £1000 in the City Bank. William Workman, a rich hardware merchant as we have seen, with £300 invested in the Montreal and Bytown, had nearly £5,000 invested in the Champlain and St Lawrence and many other financial interests besides.[44]

Supporting these leaders was a diverse group of French Canadian Montreal merchants who probably saw in the scheme an opportunity for them to extend their commercial influence into the developing region north of Montreal and along the north shore of the Ottawa River. Jean Bruneau, a director of La Banque du Peuple and of the City and District Savings Bank — as were so many others whose names follow — had apparently had commercial dealings in the Ottawa Valley for many years.[45] Although little is known of his business except that he had been a wholesaler of ready-made clothing and other dry goods, he was a comfortable if not wealthy man with a country house on the Lachine road in a huge and valuable tract of land worth an estimated £152.5 per arpent. An ambitious entrepreneur, he had been associated with the Banque des Marchands project. N.B. Desmarteau was a retailer of dry goods and shoes with two or three stores in the main business section of Montreal[46]; he and his partner, Louis Marchand, were shareholders and directors in La Compagnie du Richelieu and obviously saw new transportation ventures as promising. Pierre Jodoin, a dry goods wholesaler, owned the steamboat *Ste Hélène* in partnership with Maurice and Augustin Cuvillier and two Belleville and Gananoque merchants.[47] Also a director of La Banque du Peuple, Jodoin put £300 into Montreal and Bytown stock, the same sum that he had invested in the Montreal and New York. The Cuvilliers were large-scale auctioneers, usually of cargoes of incoming vessels from abroad. Maurice Cuvillier was a very substantial real estate developer; in 1850, he was advertising sixteen houses and five stores for rent in mid-town Montreal.[48] Hubert Paré was also a man of some consequence, although perhaps less so than the others. A grain merchant, he was a director of the Montreal City and District Savings Bank and of the Mutual Insurance Company and a substantial investor in the St Lawrence and Atlantic Railway Company.[49]

Jean-Louis Beaudry was perhaps the most prominent of the French Canadian businessmen involved in Montreal and Bytown. Beaudry's career in some respects parallels that of Masson, the titan of the French Canadian commercial community. He left his home, a rural parish north of Montreal, at the age of fourteen to work in a store, and in 1834 set up a dry goods business with his brother. He was very successful, and in 1849 he sold out his stock.[50] Retiring completely from business in 1862 and thereafter living off the rents on his many Montreal properties, Beaudry entered politics. An unsuccessful contender for an assembly seat in the provincial elections of 1854 and 1858, he emerged as a successful mayoral candidate in 1862 and, after holding office for four years, was for the next eighteen years intermittently a major contender and again a successful candidate for the mayoralty. He was elevated to the Legislative Council of the Province of Quebec in 1867. Beaudry put £400 into the stock of the Montreal and Bytown Railway company and was immediately elected to the Board of Directors. He remained strongly committed to the idea of a Montreal-to-Ottawa railway even after this scheme fizzled out in 1856.

Besides these promoters several French Canadian merchants and one or two professionals lent support, including Olivier Berthelet, a former MLA (1832-4) and Montreal city councillor (1840-2) a rich and influential man.[51] Joseph Bourret, a lawyer and recent former mayor of Montreal for four years during the forties had been a member, briefly, of the Legislative Council and later of the Baldwin-Lafontaine administration as commissioner of public works. For many years, 1846 to 1859, the year of his death, Bourret was a director of the City and District Savings Bank. Romuald Trudeau, merchant and director of La Banque du Peuple (1842-8), put in £100; Alexis Montmarquet, a director of La Banque du Peuple (1842-9) put in £300; while Tancrède Bouthilier, the collector of customs, invested £100 and P.J. Lacroix invested £300.[52]

French Canadians were a majority, by two to one, of the promoters of the railway and therefore far more prominent in this railway than in any other at that time. They were aided by merchants and promoters from other segments of the community. Besides Workman, DeWitt, and Holmes, there was John Leeming, the auctioneer, Theodore Hart, the general merchant and shipowner, Sydney Bellingham, a leading former Montreal newspaperman, public official, and later advocate of annexation, Augustus Heward, a leading broker, J.A. Perkins, a local commission merchant who had a substantial investment in the City Bank[53] and had been one of its directors in the late thirties and early forties, Ebenezer Tuttle, a stationer and director of the City and District Savings Bank, and Gotlieb Reinhart, a tavernkeeper and pork butcher; each of these businessmen invested £100.[54]

There is probably no single major reason why these individuals supported the Montreal and Bytown Railway. Many of the merchants hoped for improved trade with the region north of Montreal and in the farm country along the north shore of the Ottawa River, where most of the settlers were French Canadian. The line would also supply the lumber camps up the valley and convey a portion of the wood products down to Montreal. No less important, however, was the possibility – sometimes overlooked by railway historians – that the promoters were anticipating more lucrative and immediate gains. A number of them owned real estate in the eastern section of the city, where the company was authorized to build its terminus.[55] Jean-Louis Beaudry, Amable Prevost, Pierre Jodoin, A.M. Delisle, and N.B. Desmarteau owned small parcels of land in that area.[56] Theodore Hart held a larger number of properties, most of them in the more valuable central business district surrounding Place d'Armes. The extent of the promoters' interest in real estate values both inside Montreal and in the region through which the railway was to run is an important matter deserving further investigation.

Except for a handful of them, including Delisle and Workman, who were directors of the Champlain and St Lawrence, these promoters had no share in the management of other Montreal railway enterprises, although a few held railway stocks, sometimes in large quantities. The Montreal and Bytown scheme therefore represented the emergence of a new group of entrepreneurs in railway promotion, composed predominantly of French Canadian Montreal businessmen of minor, but not insignificant, stature in the city's economy. These dry goods merchants, shipowners, commission merchants and auctioneers were not prominent in other branches of Montreal business. Though not directors of the biggest banks – again with the exception of Workman – quite a few were on the board of La Banque du Peuple and the Mutual Insurance Company, enterprises in which French Canadians were the majority; several owned property, though not the most valuable urban real estate. Many were associated with other enterprises in which French Canadian businessmen were in the majority.

Minor businessmen in comparison to the mighty Scots and important Americans, these French Canadians were nevertheless participating actively in the far-reaching economic changes underway in their corner of the Province of Canada. They were aware of and accepted the financial and managerial implications of the joint-stock company; they possessed surplus capital, or at least expected to be able to meet the subscription payments of stock; they were motivated by optimism about this particular enterprise and probably also about the broad economic future of Montreal and the lower Ottawa Valley. This venture manifested the same spirit as the other railway companies in the late forties and early fifties – the quest for entrepreneurial gain or windfall profits in stock and real estate and for stronger metropolitan mercantile influence over the nearby lumber frontier. There is here little evidence of the 'mentalité' sometimes attributed to them, characterized by reticence, unwillingness to invest and accept the controls of joint-stock ventures, and failure to understand the implications of them. Montreal's French Canadian businessmen, in the Montreal and Bytown Railway Company, and in such other enterprises as La Compagnie du Richelieu, were demonstrating the same entrepreneurial capaicty as their more powerful Anglais counterparts.

There is little reason to believe that the climate of business opinion among French Canadians in Montreal and vicinity was much different than that among the English. The pages of the city's premier French newspaper, *La Minerve,* abounded with business advertisements of English as well as French firms. There were notices from all banks and railway companies concerning company meetings, calls on shares, dividends and schedule changes, and frequent reports and editorials on matters of current economic interest. During the spring and summer of 1853, for example, readers of *La Minerve*'s editorial columns were treated to very frequent and vigorously argued short treatises on the economic importance to Montreal of the Montreal and Bytown Railway and of the mooted Victoria Bridge. There was a certain ethnic or national purpose to the selection of these two specific questions for prolonged and frequent treatment: they might both contribute to the development of the city's eastern, largely French Canadian, section. The proposed route of the Montreal and Bytown would carry it into the city along St Denis Street, while the Victoria Bridge, it was argued, should be built from the same general area of the port to the south shore via St Helen's Island. Point St Charles, at the westernmost end of the port, was the intended, and ultimately the chosen, terminus of the bridge.

The Montreal and Bytown line, was not only hailed as a harbinger of economic growth for the city but was seen also as a weathervane of the entrepreneurial spirit of the times. Allowing the truth of the rumours that Delisle and Beaudry were serving their own real estate interests by promoting the Montreal and Bytown, *La Minerve* reminded its readers that the city's interests were also being advanced, 'bien ignorant celui qui ne comprend pas cela.' One could hardly expect otherwise:

Ce serait ridicule d'attendre que les hommes désintéressés dans une pareille entreprise prissent l'initiative et se donnassent le trouble que se sont donné MM Delisle, et plusieurs autres directeurs de la compagnie du Bytown. Quand il s'agit de protéger nos intérêts communs, doit-on attendre les suggestions et les services des étrangers? L'esprit d'entreprise ne doit pas être aveugle, et tout homme qui mérite de citoyen entreprennant n'entreprend rien sans être convaincu qu'il obtiendra des résultats avantageux.[57]

It is doubtful that a more forthright defence of current entrepreneurial practises could be found in the columns of the most business-oriented of Montreal's English-language newspapers.

French Canadian railway enterprise was not confined to Montreal. The Montreal and Bytown was very strongly supported in the rural districts through which it was to run. Individuals and municipalities subscribed to large blocks of shares. Other schemes were being advanced in other sections of Canada East: Quebec City promoters were just then discussing the idea of a railway along the St Lawrence north shore.[58] In the late forties a group led by Barthelémi Joliette had built a short and successful railway line from Lanoraie to Industry Village a few miles downriver from Montreal. In 1853, up the St Lawrence in Vaudreuil County an active group that included French Canadians was promoting a railway from the river to Vankleek Hill and eventually to Bytown.[59] The 'philosophy of railroads' had clearly taken hold in French Canada too in this early period of railway development in British North America.

IV

Reflecting the local enthusiasm for the Montreal and Bytown was an *Ottawa Argus* editorial of early 1853, which asserted that the town's commercial interests lay not so much in being served by a tramway to Montreal, for which the St Lawrence and Ottawa might have been adequate, but in ensuring that western trade was funnelled through its portals.[60] But the railway would not satisfactorily serve Bytown's needs, because, though it would use the Prescott and Bytown to reach the lumber capital, its main track would go through Kemptville, and eventually would reach Georgian Bay. 'As far as Bytown is concerned,' commented the *Bytown Gazette* a few weeks later, 'a more effectual way to ruin its trade, and to transfer its business to Kemptville and the interior could not be devised than to follow the Route now proposed as that of the St Lawrence and Ottawa Grand Junction Railway.'[61] The valley required a railway that touched the river at its 'most important points ... in order that the Lumberer may use it in bringing up his men and supplies to the various places which are used as Depots of the trade, pre-eminently chief amongst which stands Bytown.'[62]

If Montreal railway interests had any remaining doubts about which of the two lines Bytowners preferred, events such as the meeting of 28 February would have clarified the picture. Resolutions unequivocally favourable to the Montreal and Bytown were passed, and the rival scheme was condemned. Those assembled agreed that 'to make the Terminus of an Ottawa railroad from Montreal at

Kemptville, would neither embrace the Ottawa trade, nor reward the enterprise of its projectors in as great a degree as to place such a road at or through Bytown.'[63]

The Montreal and Bytown also attracted support from a number of intervening counties and townships along the Ottawa's north shore. In Two Mountains, however, municipal backing was not won without a considerable battle against supporters of the rival St Lawrence and Ottawa. Contention was sharp, because the prize was not just financial backing but also survival, because in the spring of 1853 the Montreal and Bytown project came up before the legislature for a charter.[64]

The new directors of the St Lawrence and Ottawa laboured long and hard to place it in Montreal's railway future. Besides William Coffin, the directorate now included Luther Holton, Peter McGill, John Young, Charles Wilson, William Molson, John Torrance, William Dow, David L. Macpherson, and David Davidson. McGill, Young, and Molson were especially knowledgeable about railways and had been recruited to lend strength to the company's appeal for financial backing.[65] With the assistance of engineer Thomas Keefer, they argued their railway's case in a special pamphlet.

Whereas the Montreal and Bytown would carry only a small passenger traffic, and the lumber trade would not bear the high railway rates, the pamphlet argued that the St Lawrence and Ottawa Grand Junction would draw agricultural exports from a productive region along its route. In the back sections of the counties fronting on the St Lawrence between Lachine and Kemptville was a growing agricultural frontier with a population approaching 180,000, which neither the Montreal and Bytown nor the Grand Trunk would serve adequately. North-south lines, such as the Prescott and Bytown and another railway from Brockville, would siphon much traffic from these back areas off into the United States. But the St Lawrence and Ottawa, reaching directly into these areas, would funnel their produce into Montreal and in this way confirm the city's hold over its hinterland.[66]

The rival railways were vying for financial support from the municipalities. From Two Mountains alone the St Lawrence and Ottawa was seeking £100,000 in the form of share purchases. By the late winter of 1853, however, Coffin and his associates must have known that their chances were dubious. Unfavourable letters appeared in Montreal newspapers during February and March from Two Mountains and other places in the vicinity. Although the Montreal *Gazette* clearly favoured the Montreal and Bytown scheme, it published letters defending the rival railroad.[67] But in this newspaper debate it became clear that many Montrealers feared the latter would divert western trade from Montreal to

Lachine and to the Plattsburg railway.[68] Although by 1853 the Montreal business community wanted to encourage lines to all points of the compass, it was of crucial significance to them that these lines radiate from Montreal.

While the dispute continued in Montreal, the County Council of Two Mountains decided to commit itself to buying shares in the St Lawrence and Ottawa. From Hawkesbury a month earlier the company had received news that the people of the locality, who once were favourable to the St Lawrence and Ottawa, were now indifferent between the two lines, as long as the town got railway service.[69] Loyalty to the scheme withered, and as the measure before the Two Mountains County Council was defeated in April prospects for success of the St Lawrence and Ottawa fast waned.

The decisions by other municipalities to purchase Montreal and Bytown shares accelerated the decline of the St Lawrence and Ottawa. In June 1853 Terrebonne County Council decided overwhelmingly to purchase £100,000 equity in the former on condition that Two Mountains do the same,[70] and that two branch lines be built within the county. A few weeks after the Terrebonne decision the Montreal City Council committed itself to support of the Montreal and Bytown on the recommendation of the finance committee.[71] (The fact that Mayor Charles Wilson was a director of the St Lawrence and Ottawa Grand Junction Railway Company seems to have made little difference because the council decided to favour the rival scheme instead.) By early July opinion in Two Mountains also clearly favoured the Montreal and Bytown, and even some municipalities west of the Ottawa River formerly behind the St Lawrence and Ottawa, such as the United Counties of Prescott and Russell, had gone over to its rival.[72] The St Lawrence and Ottawa by now was a quickly dying idea and with a Montreal decision, ratified by voters in a special plebiscite in September, the Kemptville line was dead. No more was heard of this somewhat visionary proposal.

Its failure was not simply a question of the strength or weakness of the railway alone but to some degree at least dependent upon the comparative viability of the rail empire of which it was an integral part. The Montreal and Lachine, which had fostered the St Lawrence and Ottawa scheme, was not an established or profitable railway. And while it had completed a southern branch to Plattsburg in 1853, it was not yet a demonstrably profitable enterprise. On the other hand, the Montreal and Bytown, besides its other advantages, had the backing of leading men in the Champlain and St Lawrence.[73]

v

The middle and late years of the previous decade had witnessed the promotion of three railways south and east to the Atlantic coast: the St Lawrence and

Atlantic, the Champlain and St Lawrence, and, most recently, the Montreal and New York. By early 1853, both the first and last-named of these railways had potential links with the west, the former via the Grand Trunk, and the latter via the St Lawrence and Ottawa Grand Junction. Up to this point, the Champlain and St Lawrence had no connections with railways running inland from Montreal. Moreover, it was clear that because the two inland lines were wedded to its competitors, the Champlain and St Lawrence was in danger, since the new railways were indeed intended to strangle it. To thwart these designs and guarantee traffic on its main line, the Champlain and St Lawrence would require its own feeder west of Montreal, the Montreal and Bytown project. The rivalry of the earlier railways for control of the Montreal-to-tidewater rail traffic was thus inexorably carried inland.

To pre-empt as much of the trade of the interior as possible for their own railway was the purpose of each of the three competing Montreal groups. This form of commercial warfare, enhanced by the new technology of the railway, succeeded the competition between Montreal and New York for commercial control of the Great Lakes basin, based upon strategically located canals. Earlier still, the rivalry between different groups for control of the fur trade had enlarged the field of battle to nearly half the North American continent by 1821. For Montrealers, then, there was nothing new in this kind of fight. Some of them might have seen it before; most had heard of it from old Nor'westers; all felt instinctively that it was necessary for survival.

The failure of the St Lawrence and Ottawa Grand Junction can be seen as both cause and effect of the poor fortunes of the Montreal and New York line. Without its own western feeder, the latter would have had to compete with the thriving Champlain and St Lawrence system that linked Montreal to Boston, or with the St Lawrence and Atlantic, soon to be finished, joining Montreal to Portland. The traffic on the Montreal and New York was mounting, but in the summer of 1853, it was still approximately only half the volume carried by the Champlain and St Lawrence.[74] With the advent of the Grand Trunk-St Lawrence and Atlantic system, it was clear that most rail traffic would be carried over this thousand-mile integrated route. Therefore the days of the Montreal and New York were numbered already, for it was only a matter of time before it would be made obsolete by the great Grand Trunk. In the late summer of 1853, when Coffin announced that the St Lawrence and Ottawa Grand Junction Railway Company had decided not to build its line, and that henceforth the rivalry between his group and the Montreal and Bytown was at an end, he was — perhaps knowingly — pronouncing the death sentence for the Montreal and New York.[75] Conversely, the defeat of the St Lawrence and Ottawa Grand Junction may well have been partly a result of the comparative weakness of its parent railway.

Before turning to an examination of the Montreal and New York Railway, of which the St Lawrence and Ottawa Grand Junction was the western extension, some salient points in the development of the latter should be considered. Although only an unrealized scheme, its brief and unfulfilled promotion provides an instructive example of Montreal railway enterprise. The St Lawrence and Ottawa Grand Junction was designed with two ends in mind. First, it was a defence against the Boston competition threatening Montreal's ancient hegemony over the upper St Lawrence. Second, it was intended to protect the Montreal and New York against the schemes of its rivals. The proposal to build the St Lawrence and Ottawa Grand Junction was hence an example of both vigorous metropolitan mercantilism and entrepreneurial élan to defend the metropolis and to ensure success for the Montreal and New York Railway. The pursuit of municipal endorsement by both the St Lawrence and Ottawa Grand Junction promoters and the opposing Montreal and Bytown company points up not only the intensity of the struggle between two groups for the control of the same region and for the crucial financial support municipalities were able and willing to provide. While the former lost the contest because of the more suitable route of its competitor, the battle between their connecting railways for the control of traffic from Montreal to the seaboard continued unabated.

11

The Montreal and New York Railway 1849-53

I

While promoters of the Montreal and Lachine Railway were engaged in wordy battles with the Montreal and Bytown during 1853, they were just beginning to enjoy the fruits of a three-year effort to build a southern branch to their main line. This extension from Caughnawaga, joined by a railway car ferry to Lachine on the Montreal side, was first named the Lake St Louis and Province Line and, together with the Montreal and Lachine, quickly became known as the Montreal and New York Railway. It was designed for two purposes. One was to give Montreal another outlet to the south – the third one projected, none of which were complete in 1849 – on the west side of Lake Champlain to Plattsburg, the trade centre for Clinton and Essex counties of upper New York State. The other, and primary, purpose of this southern extension was to join up with the Northern or Ogdensburg railway, and in this way secure for Montreal its long-sought western line, albeit one built through the United States. With this railway Montreal would be provided ultimately with a direct route to New York City as well as to Boston, because Plattsburg was the intended terminus of a railway from Whitehall, New York. The promoters hoped that the city of Montreal would also be able to outflank its rivals by tapping the Northern, which was intended to intercept its trade with the Great Lakes hinterland. And by means of the western feeder, the St Lawrence and Ottawa Grand Junction, for which they were then battling, they would be in an even better position to compete with the northern New York line to Plattsburg.

Even before the Montreal and Lachine Railway was completed, a group of Montrealers, including John Young, Harrison Stephens, Luther Holton, Theodore Hart, and Olivier Berthelet, petitioned the government in July 1847 for a charter to build a railway, to be called the Montreal and Great Northern

Junction,[1] south from St Lambert, across the St Lawrence from Montreal, to link up with the Ogdensburg. Even though this scheme, which presaged the bitter rivalry that developed between two railways running from Montreal to Lake Champlain, was not pursued, it is evidence of continuing interest by local businessmen in establishing a viable southern railway that would solve the city's nagging transportation disabilities.

The Lake St Louis and Province Line Railway Company, perhaps inspired by this former venture, received a charter in April 1848.[2] Its promoters included Hosea B. Smith, John Mathewson, John G. Mackenzie, James Torrance, and Andrew Gilmour. All except Smith and Gilmour were directors or leading shareholders in the Montreal and Lachine, which was still headed by James Ferrier, who also became president of the new company. Andrew Gilmour was a Montreal agent for the great timber shipping firm of Pollock and Gilmour, while Smith was a local crockery merchant with interests in La Banque du Peuple.[3] Its connections, still informal, with the Montreal and Lachine were clear. Besides offering the advantage of a through connection with Boston, and ultimately New York, over the northern New York and Vermont network, this railway south from Lachine, if completed soon, might well prove more attractive as an outlet for exports from the St Lawrence than either of its two rivals, the Champlain and the Portland line. Goods arriving at Lachine could be shipped south immediately without having to pay Lachine Canal tolls. Moreover, the region west of the Richelieu would be opened up and a considerable railway passenger traffic from Montreal, either south to Boston or west to Upper Canada, would help to make the line repay its promoters. And to balance this downward traffic, there would be a comparable volume of passengers and goods moving north, the latter destined for Montreal and Lower Canadian markets. At this early stage, however, there was little of this speculation about traffic potential, and the Montreal newspapers said little about the new railway venture.

The new company whose name was later changed to the Montreal and New York was capitalized at £150,000 in three thousand shares of fifty pounds each, and was given permission to borrow an additional £75,000. It was authorized to build from Lake St Louis (the wide section of the St Lawrence River between Lachine and the Cascades) to a point near the New York State town of Mooer's Junction. But construction on it was delayed, partly, it would appear, because the Plattsburg and Montreal railway with which the Montreal and New York was intended to connect was not yet complete, and partly because sales of the company's shares, begun in November 1849, were not going well.[4] Moreover, the first tangible signs of opposition appeared from the Champlain and St Lawrence, the railway most threatened by the parvenu Montreal and New York line. In April 1849 the Champlain and St Lawrence secured a renewal of its lapsed charter to extend its rails south to Rouses' Point to meet the Northern.[5] Worst of all was the news that the owners of the Northern — probably already committed to the Champlain and St Lawrence as their northern extension — were opposed to a linking up.[6] Prospects for the success of the grand scheme were greatly reduced, if not altogether destroyed, by that refusal.

II

Ferrier and his group, however, decided to build their southern extension to Plattsburg, a thriving town on Lake Champlain. Despite the refusal of a connection with the Northern, the Montreal and New York could now be viable in any case. Although Plattsburg had no railway connections yet, it possessed excellent steamboat communications with every other major port on the lake, including Burlington, the terminus of both the Rutland and the Vermont Central railroads, which connected with both Boston and New York.[7] And Whitehall, at the southern tip of the lake, was the terminus of another railway connecting to New York. Thus connections with Atlantic centres were assured. With that promise, and the visions of their own feeder railway from the west — the St Lawrence and Ottawa Grand Junction, chartered in 1850 — Ferrier and his associates determined to move ahead. Already there were promising signs of support in the counties of Beauharnois and Huntingdon through which the line would pass.[8] With this aid, and renewed efforts to bolster sagging share sales, which stood at only some six hundred, the Montreal and New York Railway could be completed.

Before starting construction, the directors sought formal amalgamation of the Montreal and Lachine and the Lake St Louis and Province Line Railway companies as the Montreal and New York, to confirm the informal relationship existing between them since the beginning, and changes in the charter to permit them to slightly alter the railway's route.[9] As it stood, the charter specified that the Lake St Louis and Province Line railway was to terminate in either Huntingdon or Beauharnois counties but within three miles of the boundary between them.[10] This provision, apparently designed to keep the railway from infringing upon the domain of the Champlain and St Lawrence only a few miles to the east, the company found "so narrowed and restricted [the railway] as to render it probable that [it] cannot be made to join any railway in the United States.'[11] And they requested that the charter be changed to allow the adoption of any route through the two counties.

The Champlain and St Lawrence reacted sharply. Though the government had refused to grant the change, the Champlain's directors pointed out in a strongly-worded petition that the owners of the Lake St Louis and Province Line intended to evade the ruling on its southern terminus 'by [making] a strained and forced construction of the charter.'[12] The alleged transgressor did not reply, and presumably its 'plotting' soon ceased.

The objections raised by the Champlain and St Lawrence to an invasion of their 'territory' by the Montreal and New York, are relevant to public policy and railway development in Canada at the beginning of the railway age. Why should the legislature have permitted the development of two competing railway systems, the Champlain and St Lawrence and the Montreal and New York – or three, if the St Lawrence and Atlantic were counted? The first two were certainly in pursuit of the same traffic and were built only a few miles from each other. Was this duplication of facilities acceptable from the standpoint of the needs of the Canadian or Montreal community at that time? Should not the government have been concerned about the possibility of a waste of resources? From a certain point of view the answer to both questions is affirmative, but the contemporary attitude was more nonchalantly permissive than in the mid-twentieth century. Governments in both Canada and the United States, while by no means unconcerned with the need to regulate railways, apparently did not consider it within their purview to develop the sort of comprehensive and long-range railway policies that would have made it possible to mitigate or obviate altogether the worst abuses.[13]

The thrust south to Plattsburg required the co-operation of that northern New York town. Early in 1851 the New York State legislature chartered the Plattsburg and Montreal Railway Company to build a line from Plattsburg to the international boundary at Mooer's Junction, where it would join the Montreal and New York.[14] Although the Plattsburg and Montreal would, in fact, cross the Northern, there was little chance of the two being connected. Nonetheless, the Plattsburgers had everything to gain from a connection with Montreal, for it implied that would perhaps their town might become a major entrepôt because of its strategic position, at least until the railway were extended further south along the west shore of Lake Champlain to Whitehall. However, dependence upon Montreal had its price, for the Plattsburg group were unable to control or even to influence the decisions of their sister railway company. In the end they were abandoned by the Montrealers, as circumstances drastically changed in the mid-fifties.

This estrangement was, however, some years in the future, and in the late winter of 1851 prospects for the Plattsburg line appeared to be very promising. Preliminary arrangements between the Canadian and American sides of the system were completed in March and the way was clear for construction to begin.[15] But the Montreal and New York had some financial difficulties to overcome first. The sale of shares in the Lake St Louis and Province Line

Company had not gone well since the subscription lists were opened in 1849. While it was true that the Montreal and Lachine and the Lake St Louis and Province Line were known now as the Montreal and New York, the two companies maintained separate corporate identities; indeed the union was not completed until 1853.[16] Of the authorized three thousand shares in the Lake St Louis and Province Line Company, only 654 were sold by the time construction was to begin, a not very encouraging response from Montrealers to the opportunity to build a New York connection. While some supporters held considerable numbers of shares, such as William Dow with fifty, Robert Anderson, a successful crockery merchant, with forty-six, William Molson with thirty, and James Ferrier with twenty-two, only small numbers were sold to the other shareholders, who included only a few of the Montreal commercial establishment. Though many of its most prominent members were supporters of the sister line, the Montreal and Lachine,[17] far fewer of them were behind the southern extension, either because of doubts about its viability or, more likely, because they were already shareholders in one or both of the two lines it would compete with.

Its shares were difficult to sell, and it was also difficult to collect payment on those that had been sold. In April 1851 a decision of the Board of Directors of the Lake St Louis and Province Line to call in two instalments on the shares, each of five pounds, elicited such a poor response among the shareholders that the decision had to be rescinded three weeks later and the call lowered to one instalment per share.[18] James Ferrier resigned from the chairmanship of the Board during that period, perhaps because of the railway's poor finances, which would make his task extremely difficult. He was succeeded by William Coffin, a Montreal lawyer, who was given in advance of £5000 honorarium in return for securing the completion of the railway within one year.

Since 1830 Coffin had risen quickly in the Montreal legal profession and in the public service. Although sheriff of Montreal from 1841 to 1852, Coffin, like Keefer, was something of a 'philosopher' of railways. In 1848 he wrote *The Canal and the Rail: Three Chapters on a Triple Project,* an important pamphlet on Montreal's transportation problems.[19] His first chapter was an argument for a canal from the St Lawrence to Lake Champlain, a theme advanced a decade later by John Young. But the next two chapters, which comprised most of the pamphlet, were concerned with railways. A shareholder in the Montreal and Lachine,[20] he argued cogently for the extension of this railway, first by a branch line west to Prescott, and second by an extended Champlain and St Lawrence south to the United States. The first proposal was very similar to the route the St Lawrence and Ottawa Grand Junction railway was to follow. With this pamphlet, and his reputation as an official and lawyer, Coffin was well qualified to head the railway at this critical stage.

He lost no time. He went to Plattsburg to complete arrangements for co-operation between the two railways.[21] Once it was decided that the railway company itself would build the line, subcommittees were appointed to handle various aspects of construction, such as ties, grading, fencing, and land acquisition. The Board of Directors of the Montreal and Lachine Railway 'pledge[d] itself to contribute all possible assistance by the issue of Bonds or otherwise to secure the completion of said enterprise.'[22]

The connection between the Montreal and Lachine and the Lake St Louis and Province Line was essentially financial. The Montreal and Lachine, by two of the acts effecting its incorporation, had been authorized to borrow up to £100,000.[23] In the 1849 Act, the company was permitted to sell £40,000 more shares, and these had been duly issued as preferred stock with annual dividends fixed at 8 per cent.[24] The Lake St Louis and Province Line, by its original Act of Incorporation, had been authorized to borrow £75,000, besides the £150,000 share capital, which was expansible by an additional £50,000 to £200,000.[25] Because of the fact that the sale of shares for the railway had faltered, it was necessary to borrow heavily by selling bonds. The directors of the Montreal and Lachine, arguing that the southern extension would greatly enhance the value of their line, convinced many of the preferred shareholders to convert their shares to company bonds. But the Lake St Louis and Province Line bonds were apparently much more difficult to sell. The latter company therefore used them as collateral for loans from the Bank of Montreal, which agreed to sell them for the company in London.[26]

From these financial transactions there were sufficient proceeds to complete the thirty-mile Canadian half of the railway to Plattsburg. Construction was begun in July 1851, and by early autumn of 1852 both the Canadian and American sections of the system were complete.[27] Rolling stock was purchased and arrangements made for through service between Plattsburg and Montreal. The Montreal and New York, and the Plattsburg line as it came to be called, jointly purchased a car ferry to cross the St Lawrence between Lachine and Caughnawaga.[28] At the southern end, connections with New York were assured by the steamboats of the Champlain Transportation Company, which connected with Burlington and Whitehall.

III

The railway was opened on 20 September 1852, and service began on a regular through basis between Montreal and Plattsburg. Judging from the daily published traffic returns of the Montreal and New York, however, it was not booming in the spring of 1853, since its traffic lagged well behind that of the

Champlain and St Lawrence, which offered through connections between Montreal and the eastern American seaboard after the completion of the extension to Rouses' Point in 1851. This service was not provided by the Montreal and New York until one year later, and at first not on a year-round basis. Most important, however, was the fact the Champlain railway's connections with Boston and New York took less than a day, a service the Plattsburg line, with its cumbersome steamboat bridge across Lake Champlain, could not match. In 1853, the first full season of the new line's operation, profits were small. Net profit was only £3700, approximately 1½ per cent on the £250,000 investment.[29] By contrast, the Champlain and St Lawrence in 1852, the first full year of its own through system, earned a profit of £15,289, or approximately 5 per cent on the £343,827 investment for the thirty-mile extension from St John's to Rouses' Point.[30]

Competition between the two railways became increasingly vigorous after the Montreal and Plattsburg system went into operation. In 1853, both railways began slashing freight and passenger rates in order to attract business;[31] by the autumn of that year the rate war had apparently become so serious that both were threatened with ruin. But the published daily freight traffic returns in the Montreal *Gazette* during the spring and summer of 1853 suggest that the Champlain and St Lawrence had, on the average, three times the freight volume of the Montreal and New York.[32] Although there is no certainty that the same discrepancy existed in passenger traffic on the two lines, there is a strong likelihood that it did, in view of the fact that the Champlain and St Lawrence was part of a through railroad system that offered prospective passengers service between Montreal and New York city in nineteen hours,[33] and probably equally efficient passenger service to Boston. Thus it must have been evident that in the course of time the Champlain and St Lawrence would be victorious.

On the other hand, the latter company obviously feared that, although the Plattsburg and Montreal railway was not at that moment a match for the Champlain and St Lawrence, it might soon become one. Since late 1852, efforts were being made to establish rail connections with centres south of Plattsburg. This would decrease reliance on Lake Champlain steamboats, which were wholly under the control of the Champlain Transportation Company,[34] and would obviate the costly and time-consuming trans-shipment from rail to boat and then back to rail at Burlington or Whitehall. Freight charges could be lessened and profits increased. Since January 1853, a survey had been in progress over the some ninety miles between Whitehall and Plattsburg and in May the *Whitehall Chronicle* announced that the terrain surveyed so far was found to be more suitable than expected.[35]

Hence the Champlain and St Lawrence and its connecting New England system were in danger of strong competition from a new railway network west of the Richelieu River and Lake Champlain. The owners of the American portion of the system were probably just as keenly interested in crushing this potentially dangerous competition, as were the proprietors of the Champlain. Burlington businessmen, whether involved in the railways or not, would also have been seriously worried by the threat of Plattsburg becoming a major rival railway entrepôt. Though the attack on the Plattsburg and Montreal railway by the Champlain and St Lawrence was carried out in Canada, it would have had the support of the latter's southern sister railways. It was very likely an international endeavour to crush the Montreal and New York railway before it could become a serious competitor. Indeed, the American interests were probably far stronger, because the interests of the average Montreal merchant would have been better served by two competing railways than by a monopoly.

A drastic move to eliminate the rivalry by closing the Montreal and New York was soon underway. This was accomplished by the simple device of leading shareholders of the Champlain and St Lawrence buying up the shares of the Montreal and New York company on the Montreal stock market where, at that point, they were selling at a discount of 17½ per cent.[36] Offerings normally exceeded demand, and it was not difficult to secure many shares.[37] It is not clear whether these purchases were sufficient to produce a majority holding, though a takeover might have been aided by shareholders and some directors of the Montreal and New York choosing to side with the Champlain and St Lawrence, as was alleged later by the injured Plattsburg interests.[38] William Molson was one who in the crunch preferred the better connected and more soundly financed Champlain and St Lawrence. Indeed, he seems to have been that line's veritable agent; in January 1852 he had held only thirty Montreal and New York shares, but by March 1854, when the battle for control was over, he held 198 of the 654 shares issued by the company.[39]

What followed is shrouded in mystery. With the same group controlling the majority of shares in both Canadian lines, two main options were open: either to maintain the two railways and try to keep freight rates at profitable levels, or, more sensible from a strictly economic viewpoint, to close out the weaker one, the Montreal and New York. But the second option was far from easy to accomplish, first, because of the financial obligations of the Montreal and New York in bonded debt, amounting to more than £100,000 and, secondly, because of its obligations to Plattsburg and Montreal, laid down in the agreement of 1851, to operate the tracks between Montreal and Plattsburg as one railway. This agreement was interpreted by the Americans as a commitment by the Canadians to continue operating their line indefinitely. Closing down the

Montreal and New York was obviously more than a simple case of desertion. It was tantamount to murder, because the abandoned Plattsburg would be left with a railway to nowhere. But should the Montreal and New York Railway go bankrupt, presumably those obligations could be eliminated. There is some evidence to suggest that in the autumn of 1853 the directors of the Champlain and St Lawrence set out to accomplish the bankruptcy of the Montreal and New York Railway.[40]

As the rivalry mounted, the Champlain and St Lawrence clearly demonstrated its ability to damage the Montreal and New York. Its own southern connections were with the Vermont railways, the Vermont and Canada, the Burlington and Rutland, and the Vermont Central, the first and last of which were controlled by Boston interests. During the summer of 1853 there were moves to consolidate these and other upper New England railways into an integrated and unified system.[41] In June, W.R. Lee was elected president of the Vermont Central as well as of the Burlington and Rutland, and it was reported that the Boston-owned Northern would include directors from these railways.[42] In the autumn, steps were taken formally to amalgamate the Central and the Rutland.[43] Their collective strength was impressive by comparison to the Montreal and Plattsburg system, which was barely finished and not yet able to offer through rail links with New York.

Efforts by the Vermont railways to control all forms of transportation in this region further weakened the competitive position of the Montreal and New York railway. Because they were able to influence the Champlain Transportation Company from which the Burlington and Rutland had purchased its entire fleet of vessels on the Lake, the Montreal and Plattsburg companies were forced to buy their own steamboat, the *Francis Saltus*, in 1853.[44]

Soon even the *Francis Saltus,* the last vestige of Plattsburg's transportation independence, was brought under attack. Without this steamboat, Plattsburg would be dependent upon the Champlain Transportation Company, which had bought back its fleet from the Burlington and Rutland Railway. Though an independent business, the former was probably more subject to the blandishments of the powerful Vermont railway interests than the comparatively weak Plattsburgers.

During the winter of 1854 the Montreal and Plattsburg system continued to operate, but it was increasingly apparent that a crisis threatening its very existence was imminent. The residents of Plattsburg heard in January 1854 of the probable merger of the Montreal and New York and the Champlain and St Lawrence.[45] But Montrealers assured them that no merger was pending and that none would be made without their concurrence. And yet, according to the Plattsburgers, the Montreal group controlling the destiny of the two hitherto rival companies were arranging for the amalgamation they had publicly denied. Realizing that the major result of this union would be the abandonment of the Plattsburg section, that town launched a vigorous counter attack by suing the Montreal and New York railway in a Montreal court and by petitioning the Canadian legislature to prevent the amalgamation. For two years they effectively prevented the legal merger of the two companies by such petitions.

First, however, the Plattsburgers remonstrated with the Montreal group. The Canadians, whose merger had been completed and needed only the sanction of the legislature to be made legal, soothed the complainants with an arrangement for pooling the train services. But in Plattsburg – now extremely wary of the wily entrepreneurs from Montreal – this was construed as a ruse, and suspicions were confirmed by new evidence of Montreal knavery, the seizure of the *Francis Saltus* by the Champlain and St Lawrence during the winter of 1854. William Molson, as vice-president of the Montreal and New York railway company, gave possession of the steamboat – then at Burlington for repairs – to an agent of the Champlain and St Lawrence railroad. Whatever the legal right of the Montreal and New York to take possession of a steamboat owned jointly by itself and the Plattsburg and Montreal Railway, the act was interpreted in Plattsburg as a seizure aimed at making their system, which relied upon the steamboat, inoperative. The city's businessmen were outraged.

They immediately took reprisal by seizing all the line's available rolling stock, which they threatened to keep until the steamboat was returned.[46] It soon was, but only after a New York court issued an order to that effect. The damage done by the complete cessation of railway service between Montreal and Plattsburg, however, could not be easily remedied, even by an appeal to the Canadian courts for payment of damages. As far as Plattsburg was concerned, the wilful destruction of their railway to Montreal could only be prevented by an appeal to the Canadian legislature not to allow the amalgamation of the Champlain and St Lawrence and the Montreal and Lachine, a bill for which came before the house in the fall of 1854.[47] Petitions against amalgamation, interpreted as the prelude to abandonment of the Montreal and New York, came from Clinton and Essex counties in upstate New York, where so much was expected from this railway, and from the Huntingdon County towns of Napierville and Laprairie, where similar hopes had been held.[48] Other petitions came from Montreal and New York bondholders and shareholders worried about the safety of their investments under the proposed new arrangements.

Probably the most eloquent and cogent petition to the legislature came from the 274 Plattsburgers led by J.B. Bailey. All were shareholders in the Plattsburg and Montreal railroad; they pleaded that they had invested in the company after being convinced by the 'eloquent arguments' made by visiting Montrealers about 'the advantages of the enterprise, the promotion of trade, social intercourse, and the kindly interchange of international feeling and friendly relations.'[49] They had trusted in the good faith of the Montreal group and in their intention to complete the contract for running the two connecting railways as one system, which, up to the autumn of 1854, had been operating successfully more than one year. Just when 'the receipts of the Roads were constantly increasing ... and the prospects of future business were of the most cheering character,' the unified system was being scuttled.

The petition by Bailey and his friends asserted that the amalgamation was 'illegal, unauthorized by the charters granted ... against public policy, injurious to the Citizens of Montreal, fatal to the investments made in good faith ... [and] destructive to the friendly intercourse which should subsist between neighbouring nations.' They were petitioning not only that the legislature refrain from confirming the amalgamation of the two Montreal-based railways, but also for such 'legislation as shall compel the Montreal and New York Railroad Company to re-open their communications and perform their solemn obligations and contracts in good faith.'[50] The allegations of perfidy against the Montreal and New York company, Bailey asserted, were not meant to apply to all directors; James Ferrier, William Coffin, J.G. Laviolette, and Colonel J. Scriver, were exempted from any imputations against their character. Indeed, they had 'acted throughout this unpleasant affair, with a nice sense of honour and good faith worthy of all praise.'

Although Plattsburg and its sympathizers could not forestall an amalgamation indefinitely, the formal union of the two companies was prevented for the time being. In delaying approval the provincial legislature was probably acting upon the recommendations of its Standing Committee on Railways, Canals and Telegraphs, before which most of the discussions took place and the allegations by Bailey and other petitioners were made. Since there is no documentary information on this question one can only surmise from the failure of the legislature to pass the bill that the committee recommended against it.

The Montreal and Plattsburg railway never revived its brief and modest commercial function after the season of 1853. Although complaints by its shareholders and bondholders and the 274 Plattsburg petitioners prevented the formal amalgamation of the Champlain and St Lawrence and the Montreal and New York, this combination of forces could not compel performance of the contract to operate the railway. They might have secured satisfaction from the Canadian courts, but only after costly and lengthy litigation. With the Act of the Canadian legislature of 1856 to amalgamate the Champlain and St Lawrence and the Montreal and New York to form the Montreal and Champlain Railway Company, the hopes of ever reviving the Plattsburg to Montreal system were forever dashed.[51] Since 1854 the connection had been broken. In 1856, the legal union was simply a confirmation of corporate decisions taken two years earlier.

IV

An assessment of the earliest Montreal railways to the south must consider several questions, such as the utility of the lines that were built to the economic life of the city, and their profitability to the entrepreneurs who promoted them. To these questions only tentative answers can be offered because of the virtual absence of statistics. In general, the utility of the lines seems to have been minimal. For the reasons noted above, the Lachine Railway attracted mostly passenger traffic, while the extension southward was designed to draw traffic from the western hinterland over its tracks. The railway to Plattsburg was of relatively little value to Montreal because it duplicated existing services to the east of Lake Champlain. It was the product of overly optimistic entrepreneurial expectations of high profits from heavy traffic in Montreal and upstate New York, to be realized once rail connections were completed to Whitehall at the southern end of the lake. It was built in the hope of besting a railway system that had been under development since the mid-thirties, and though this might now appear unrealistic, optimistic scheming was characteristic of the railway age everywhere in North America. The comparatively low traffic returns for the summer of 1853 showed that Montreal merchants felt themselves better served by its competitor.

Though evidence is sparse, it seems that the promotion of ordinary and preferred shares and debentures of the Lachine Railway to build the sister Montreal and Province Line railway was designed to be profitable. Prices of shares on the Montreal exchange would indicate that shareholders made few gains, and, since there were no large shareholders in the line, except at a late stage when amalgamation, not capital gains on shares, was the object, no one could have profited much in this area. The gain might have come from connections with contractors, but of this there is no evidence. More likely, however, was the possibility of profiting from the amalgamation of the two companies, only one aspect of which was the elimination of competition. Some of the large shareholders in the Montreal and New York railway stood to benefit considerably from the upgrading of the value of their shares, because of the terms of the merger which gave them par value. Moreover, not only individual entrepreneurs but also financial institutions with which some of the railway's directors were associated might have profited from the merger. The Bank of Montreal briefly held £100,000 in bonds in the Montreal and New York Railway. They would have been salable at a far better price after the merger than before.

The disappearance of the parvenu competitor to the Champlain and St Lawrence was unlamented by many Montrealers. For them it was a speculation that failed and its disappearance a positive benefit in immediate financial terms and in long-run quasi-monopolistic advantages. As merchants, some of them might have missed the rate war which gave them lower freight costs; as Montrealers, they might have regretted the loss of direct rail connections with Plattsburg and have even deplored the way in which the Plattsburgers had been let down. But Montreal businessmen were not simply merchants, they were also investors, not just public-spirited, honourable, and upstanding Victorians wanting to appear proper, but businessmen, who, appearances notwithstanding, had to know when to cut their losses. Similarly, once it was clear that the St Lawrence and Ottawa Grand Junction was outdistanced in importance and prestige by the Montreal and Bytown, the promoters cut short their efforts with finality.

With railways like the Montreal and Lachine and its extensions, tangible achievements, such as the number of miles built or the profitability of the extensions, were less important than the railway as an idea and its impact upon the climate of enterprise. The railway as an idea led to the promotion of companies not only to build railways but to build corporations, to muster capital, and to sell shares. Railway entrepreneurs like Ferrier and Coffin were seeking more than simply a transportation system, profits from which if forthcoming at all, would be over too long a term. The railway was for them an instrument of power and prestige for their commercial group, a source of strength and profit for the financial institutions with which they were associated, and beneficial to Montreal, from whose general prosperity they would all benefit.

This is not to suggest that Montreal businessmen were naïve boosters, for they recognized the limitations of Montreal's control over its hinterland. But they realized at the same time that the stakes in this commercial poker were high enough to warrant the risk of attempting a master stroke in constructing a brilliantly strategic railway. The legendary success of the Erie Canal may have been the single most influential transportation ideal in the mid-nineteenth century America. The Montreal promoters of the Montreal and Lachine Railway, with its extensions south in the Montreal and New York and its grandiosely titled western branch, the St Lawrence and Ottawa Grand Junction, were undoubtedly attempting to achieve such a coup. But at the same time they understood well the measurable, more immediate benefits of railway enterprise.

In some respects the Montreal and Lachine system and its rivals were failures. Yet, the price of failure was counterbalanced by their learning the limitations of railways. There was a growing awareness of what might be called the 'railway trap,' the mistaken belief that the railway was nearly infinitely flexible and that in railway development *panache* could outweigh experience, daring was a substitute for stability, and competition better than amalgamation. By 1854, although the death of the Montreal and Lachine empire was being lamented by some Plattsburgers in the railway committee of the Legislative Assembly, some Montreal entrepreneurs were already benefiting from their railway experiences.

PART THREE / INDUSTRY

12

The rise of Montreal as a manufacturing centre

The growth of large-scale industry in Montreal during the period from 1837 to 1853 is not commonly seen as an important aspect of the city's economic development in this period. In the concentration of economic historians on the importance of Montreal as the focal point of the 'commercial empire of the St Lawrence,' the growth of industry has been largely obscured.[1] The reason lies in the overwhelming importance of commercial activity in Montreal since its seventeenth century beginnings, and the transition from furs to wheat and flour as the primary staples of trade after the war of 1812-14 ensured the continuance of commerce as the centre of Montreal's economic life.

During the transition from one staple to others, the growth and change in transportation requirements in the St Lawrence stimulated the development of Montreal's first interdependent industries of shipbuilding and marine engineering. There occurred a conjuncture of favourable circumstances, including the geographical location of Montreal, the ready availability of domestic and imported material, the potential of a market for marine engines as wide as Montreal's expanding metropolitan reach, the proximity of an entrepreneurial and labour force specially experienced and skilled, and an adequate potential capital supply.[2]

Other industries were stimulated by one or more of these elements during the twenties and thirties, and, as the traditional brewing and distilling thrived, and the newer industries expanded, other enterprises appeared; among them, a rope works, a newspaper type foundry, and by the late thirties, ready-made clothing and shoes.[3] The optimism, prosperity, and expanding opportunity of the forties prompted further industrial growth in Montreal, including a significant expansion of the engine-building industry, along with an efflorescence of iron-using fabricating shops. The opening of the Lachine Canal in 1846 for industrial users of hydraulic power was thus a landmark, not the cause, of industrial development in Montreal. However, after this use of the canal was begun, the concentration of factories near it, the construction of larger buildings, and the attraction of even newer firms began to give the city for the first time the appearance of an industrial centre.

A striking feature of industrial development in Montreal during this period was the entrepreneurship that planned and directed it. The developers of industry throughout the first half of the nineteenth century, with very few exceptions, were not associated with the established mercantile groups in Montreal. This was not because of resistance on the part of merchants to the challenge of new opportunities; merchants were the important entrepreneurial element in the areas of finance and transportation as well as the active patrons of the shipbuilding and marine engine foundries. Merchants, however, might have refrained from direct involvement in industry because of the requirements of industrial management. The industrialist was then usually the sole owner, or one of a small group of owners. He was very often a former tradesman-artisan, some of whose attributes he retained long after he achieved success as a large-scale industrialist. Because of the relatively small size of most factories, his direction of affairs was so close that he was in many respects still the master craftsman, engineer, works manager, and possibly even chief salesman.[4] By the late forties some of Montreal's largest factories, engine works particularly, were organized in specialized shops which may have required some degree of hired management, but for the most part the owner himself seems to have directed operations daily. Corporation ownership and professional management were not leading features of many enterprises in Montreal in the forties and early fifties. Merchants, therefore, were excluded, except perhaps as promoters of industry, mainly because most would not have had necessary technical knowledge to manage the operation of even a relatively unsophisticated industrial enterprise.

Another reason for the general absence of merchants from industrial undertakings is that few would have wanted to invest surplus capital in such ventures. Any merchant with extra resources would not likely have been inclined to invest in fixed assets, returns from which would be forthcoming over a long time, in comparison with the customary ninety-day return on commercial transactions. Steamboats and later railways – in which many of the city's merchants put money – were indeed fixed assets, but since these were ventures under the day-to-day management of professional ship masters, and in most individual cases did not involve large amounts, they were not comparable with industrial entrepreneurship. While it would be unwarranted to assert that the avoidance of long-run investments was a universal practice or an article of faith for all Montreal merchants, the evidence during the forties would suggest that it was a practice or convention that most followed either out of habit or belief.

Industrial development required special skills and experience which, with few exceptions, could be supplied by experienced industrialists or artisans. Although Montreal had always had an inflow of fresh ideas and skills into its business community since the late eighteenth century, this infusion was nowhere more evident, both in size and in quality, than in the city's industrial expansion in the years from 1837 to 1853. It is impossible to determine the origins of most of the Montreal industrialists. The vast majority of them apparently were immigrants from England and the United States, mainly from Vermont and New York. Those whose origins are known evidently brought with them considerable experience and some capital. Very few were in the country long before they established their factories, because had they been present in Montreal beforehand, it is likely that their names would have been noted, almost certainly in Mackay's annual directory, from which very few escaped notice. Tested skill and adequate capital were two fundamental prerequisites for success, even on the industrial frontier which Montreal was in the early Victorian period. As in the fields of transportation, finance, and commerce, there were very few 'rags to riches' stories in Montreal industry. In the key industries of shipbuilding, marine engineering, iron founding, clothing, and flour milling the evidence clearly suggests that, with few exceptions, the firms that emerged as the most long-lived, the most profitable, and the largest had apparent advantages from the beginning.

While the following pages concentrate on the period 1837 to 1853, the years in which the growth of industry was most dramatically accelerated, developments from origins in earlier times must be covered not only for completeness, but also to make apparent the suddenness of change during the late forties and early fifties. It was in this period that Montreal truly became an industrial centre. From this time contemporaries began to note the similarities of Montreal's Lachine Canal sector with heavily industrialized areas of New England.[5] While commerce continued to be of primary importance in the economic life of the city, industry of all kinds was increasingly important as a substantial aspect of the Montreal economy. Montreal's industrial development was a metropolitan as well as an urban phenomenon, for it not only produced the transportation equipment with which Montreal's hegemony was cast over a wide hinterland but also provided an increasingly wide and complex group of goods demanded in that expanding market. Industrial growth made possible Montreal's adaptation to new requirements in its hinterland, and so enabled it to retain metropolitan dominance in the age of steam and iron.

II

The earliest and one of the most important industries to emerge in Montreal
during the first few decades of the nineteenth century was shipbuilding. From
about 1815 sailing vessels and steamboats were constructed in considerable
numbers in various yards, mostly at Hochelaga below the St Mary current. But
shipbuilding in Montreal never attained the importance it reached in Quebec,
where it was the staple industry employing some five thousand men in twenty or
more yards. In the forties and fifties Montreal built only a small fraction of the
number and tonnage of ships that Quebec did.[6] Montreal did not possess nearly
the geographical advantages of its rival. It was remote from tidewater, was the
entrepôt of only a limited quantity of the timber necessary for the construction
of the large ships, and until the early fifties was without a deep channel to allow
the largest ocean-going vessels to proceed downriver without difficulty.
Montreal, however, was well situated for the development of a special kind of
shipbuilding industry, for ships specially suited to the river systems that focused
on the city. These required schooners, sloops, barges,[7] and, above all, steamboats.
Lumber yards had sprung up at Hochelaga, downstream from the port near the
foot of St Mary's current. A supply of skilled labour at Montreal was available
among the immigrants from Britain, or in the Lake Champlain country which
had longstanding and continuing economic contacts with Montreal. Soon after
the first steamboat ran on the St Lawrence between Montreal and Quebec in
1809, Montreal's shipbuilding industry began in earnest.[8]

Ships were no doubt being built in the city long before 1815, but the first
known shipyard dates from that year. Thomas Munn established his yard at
Pointe à Callières immediately adjacent to the port on the Montreal riverfront.
For some years it was apparently the only one in the city, although at William
Henry (Sorel) ships were also built for the Montreal market. The precise number
of vessels Munn built at Montreal is unknown, but he was soon constructing
steamboat hulls, to be fitted up and readied for service by either of the two
major steam-engine builders.[9] He built at least two ocean-going barges of 800
tons each. Another yard, established in 1820 on a large tract of land at
Hochelaga, was the Montreal Shipping Company under the management of an
English naval architect, Farrington. Before the company went bankrupt in 1822,
it built two large ocean-going ships of 600 and 1000 tons and a large floating
graving dock for a Quebec shipyard. After the failure, Farrington moved to
Quebec, an act perhaps symbolic of the fact that it was there that large
ocean-going vessels would be constructed on the St Lawrence, while at Montreal
a more specialized industry would develop.

Of the other Montreal yards that sprang up during the twenties and thirties very little is known. Entry into the trade was apparently easy; capital requirements were limited, since most craft were built on contracts which called for payment in instalments as work progressed. Many of the smaller builders might well have been sailors on the beach for the winter, and their construction of a sloop or a barge was a form of winter employment combined perhaps with minor speculation. This pattern that obtained in the late thirties and forties presumably was also largely true of the previous decade.

Before the early thirties there are no reliable statistics of ship construction at Montreal. But later in the decade, the traveller J.S. Buckingham stated that in one shipyard alone sixty-one ships were built in 1825.[10] Since there were probably no more than a few steamboats built in Montreal in any one year during the twenties the overwhelming majority of these vessels were undoubtedly sailing ships, mostly of the small-river type of less than 150 tons. Nevertheless, large ships were still being constructed at Montreal shipyards as late as 1833, when fourteen square-rigged vessels averaging 460 tons were in progress.[11]

Though smaller numbers of ships were produced after the close of the twenties the industry was taking a new direction rather than dying. It was changing from a virtually sole emphasis on sailing vessels to the more complicated construction of steamboat hulls. As if to mark this transition, a new and specialized shipyard was inaugurated in 1828 at Hochelaga by naval architect James Johnston, in conjunction with a merchant named Handel who supplied the capital. Ships for ocean trade as well as inland traffic were built, but within a year or two, following bankruptcy and a new management, the work was increasingly oriented towards construction of river craft. In the early thirties this new yard came into the hands of Sheay and Merritt, the latter a practical shipbuilder from New York State, probably from the Lake Champlain area, and reputedly 'one of the best that ever came to Montreal.'[12] Both Sheay and Merritt had probably been in Montreal for a year or two previously, and they seem to have been well prepared for the management of their own yard. They began to build river steamboats and concentrated on this business for many years, although they also built ocean-going sailing ships. Their yard was the busiest in Montreal during the decade from 1835 to 1845, when they constructed ships and steamboats for most of the city's major forwarders and an annual quota of ocean ships in the 300-ton class.[13] Merritt became the sole owner in 1839, although it had already been popularly designated as Merritt's yard for at least two years. From then on Sheay's name does not appear on ship registry certificates. He seems to have been employed in the construction of ocean ships for Millar, Edmonstone and Allan.[14]

Other shipyards listed in the official government record of vessels constructed abounded at Hochelaga, attracted to the lumber yards there during the forties. The forwarding firm of Macpherson and Crane was then building their steamboats and barges, apparently at their own yard in Montreal, as well as at Kingston. William Parkyn, another prominent local shipbuilder, had moved to Montreal from Cornwall, England, at the age of seventeen in 1824,[15] and was for a brief time an associate of John Molson jr in the St Mary's Foundry.[16] Parkyn began building hulls for steamboats in the early forties at the rate of about one a year between 1843 and 1849, after which he left the business to establish another foundry on the Lachine Canal.[17] The presence of other shipbuilders who were in the industry for much shorter periods underline its transient character: James Campbell and Andrew Yale built a steamer in 1837 and a sloop the following year;[18] Joseph Lesperance, James Wiseman, Peter Graville, David Boss, and M. Cousineau were occasional builders of sloops during the forties, while Augustin L'Abbé, Thomas Boyd, Ferdinand Cantin, Michel Morissette, and Alexander Young occasionally built steamers, schooners, and barges during the same period. Although they might have leased shipyard facilities from larger builders, most of these small operators probably had their own.

The shipbuilding industry in this period was rather rudimentary. Quick and apparently easy entry, and exit, were among its paramount features. Easy access to the river, ready availability of building materials, and the generally expanding market for river craft were other basic attributes. Moreover, the technological requirements of shipyards were limited to the wood construction of sailing ships and the hulls and superstructures of steamboats. The engines and accompanying machinery were built at local foundries, where installation, final fitting up, and launching were completed. Towards the end of the forties Montreal's shipbuilding industry began noticeably to make the transition to this more advanced stage, but until then skill and experience with wood were more important requirements than capital, and there was apparently no reward for longevity or size. Total employment in the Montreal shipbuilding industry during the thirties and forties was probably substantial; precise figures are unknown and even estimates are difficult to make. The demand for labour varied as ship construction fluctuated with changing general economic conditions.

While engaged in constructing ships, none of the shipbuilders mentioned above were involved in banking, other transportation developments, or even in other industries. Also noteworthy is the fact that there were no French Canadians among the prominent builders until the mid-forties. The most important were immigrant Americans or British, and even among minor builders there were only a few French Canadians. Yet the major shipbuilder in Montreal at the end of the forties – and for at least a generation subsequently – was

Augustin Cantin, a French Canadian. One possible explanation for their absence is that the capital requirements, however limited, were too high. Or more likely, it might have been that the forwarders who purchased these vessels preferred to deal with builders of an experience which they esteemed and of a size that engendered confidence.

There is no ready explanation why Augustin Cantin should have become Montreal's greatest steamboat builder. But the few fragments available about his early business life supply evidence of entrepreneurial aggressiveness, foresight, and daring. He was the first shipbuilder to integrate the formerly divided operations of ship construction and marine engineering. He anticipated the shipbuilding industry's shift from Hochelaga to the Lachine Canal, a move suggestive of the impending change in construction material from wood to iron. Cantin's was the largest Montreal shipyard in the mid-forties, and indeed one of the largest industrial establishments on the Lachine Canal.[19] Soon after the enlargements to the old canal were under construction in 1843, Cantin requested permission from the Department of Public Works to breach the canal wall for an entrance into the shipyard and dry dock he intended to build there. A shipyard close to the port, with facilities to make major ship repairs, Cantin claimed, would be an immense benefit to inland navigation and trade.[20]

By 1843 he was at a relatively early but already successful stage of his long career. Born in 1809 at Cap Santé near Quebec, where he learned ship carpentry, Cantin had moved to Montreal in 1831 and worked in Millar and Edmonstone's yard, probably under the direction of Sheay and Merritt, the shipbuilders who later became closely linked with the Edmonstone-Allan firm.[21] Within a few years he began business on his own – or with Ferdinand Cantin, probably a relation – by building barges and small steamers. After abandoning this in 1834, for the next three years Cantin, still only in his twenties, lived in New York to learn the new building techniques used in the construction of American warships. From here he probably returned to Montreal and to Merritt's employ. At any rate, in 1841 he started his own shipyard near the first lock on the Lachine Canal. By 1843, his reputation among Montreal forwarders was well established, and a number of the most prominent strongly supported his application to build a dry dock to repair ships. 'No person,' they asserted, 'can afford us greater satisfaction in attending to that description of work in every respect, than Mr A. Cantin.'[22]

Cantin's new establishment began operations in 1846, and within a few years it was a sizable and varied shipyard busily building and repairing ships. The opening of the new yard marked a sharp upturn in Montreal ship production, and between 1846 and 1856 more than seventy ships were built there. Most were steamboats, but Cantin also constructed some of the sailing ships and barges still in extensive use on the St Lawrence.[23] He built all the necessary components of his steamboats, including the engines, at his works, which by 1856 covered fourteen acres and included two basins, a saw mill, and an engine foundry. He was constantly enlarging his establishment after 1846, by securing additional canal privileges and by purchasing along the canal's north side more land from the Sulpicians, who owned the vast St Gabriel farm bordering the canal west of Griffintown. In his dealings with the Department of Public Works, Cantin sometimes found his requests supported by eloquent testimonials. On his behalf in 1847 the future historian William Kingsford asserted that 'surely an enterprising British subject has a right to look to his government for assistance and protection in his undertakings,' a comment implying important assumptions about the role of government in Canada.[24] Further expansion and investment of £10,000 in 1850 in a new dry dock enabled Cantin to build larger vessels, including some small ocean-going steamships, and to operate more efficiently.[25] From this point he began to export ships abroad, although most were still sold on the domestic market. His production increased in the decade after 1846; seven steamboats alone were turned out in 1855, and between 200 and 250 men were regularly employed.[26]

By 1850 the shipbuilding industry in Montreal had attained the high degree of technical competence represented by Cantin's shipyard. In the preceding thirty-five years the industry had become highly centralized and efficient. Small shipbuilders continued to produce vessels, but the number of active builders had declined substantially, until by 1850 only three major yards were still producing ships in Montreal. By that time merely an occasional large vessel was turned out by the smaller builders. Rationalization was not complete by 1850, however, for marine engine foundries still existed independently of shipyards, and it was still possible for forwarders to contract for hull and engine separately. Hence the conditions still obtained for the existence of a separate shipbuilding industry. Yet the number of shipyards gradually waned, while Cantin's integrated operation expanded rapidly, probably because of the fact that he offered a complete ship unit. Perhaps also the size and vertical integration of his operations made them economically more efficient.

III

To a large extent engine foundries were adjuncts of shipyards and largely dependent upon the demand for steamboats. The early engineering industry in Montreal should therefore be examined in relation to shipbuilding, because it was in this context that foundries were begun and made their first contribution to the industrial development of the city. Although foundries produced other machinery, including stationary steam engines, later railway rolling stock, and, by the early fifties, locomotives, they originated and thrived in Montreal in conjunction with the local shipbuilding industry. They arose as part of the transportation revolution introduced on the St Lawrence by the *Accommodation*'s first voyage in 1809. The demand for steamboats on the upper and lower St Lawrence, the Ottawa, and the Richelieu increased during the thirties and accelerated during the forties, particularly after the completion of the St Lawrence canals. On the lower Great Lakes, steamboats for passenger travel and freight were in common use during the forties.[27] Montreal became the leading centre for the production of steamboats on the St Lawrence River because of the concentration of forwarders in the city. No other upper St Lawrence port produced as many steamboats and other vessels as Montreal yards.[28] As the marine engineering industry grew in Montreal after 1820, the city acquired a concentration of skilled and experienced entrepreneurs and artisans who formed the cadre that developed other industries in the late forties and early fifties. There was great interest and inventive talent in steamboat development, as evidenced by the number of patents taken out in the thirties and forties on engines, boilers, propellers, and paddle wheels.[29]

An examination of many contracts between shipowners or forwarders and foundries indicates that the overwhelming majority of the engines used on Montreal-constructed steamboats were built in Montreal.[30] Many steamboats constructed at William Henry were also fitted with marine engines from Montreal foundries, while as early as the twenties these establishments were building engines for upper St Lawrence steamboats and possibly for many Great Lakes vessels as well. The expansion of the engineering industry during the forties, stimulated the generally favourable economic conditions and the mounting volume of staples flowing from the interior, received an additional impetus by increasing demand for stationary engines for various industrial uses. Steam engines of standard kinds became increasingly available. By the end of the forties foundries in Montreal seem to have been producing fewer custom-built engines and more standard units. But the newer ones then being built at foundries on the Lachine Canal were apparently less specifically oriented to Marine engineering than the earlier foundries. With the rationalization of the shipbuilding industry and the expansion of Cantin's plant, the older marine engine foundries seem to have declined, to have been absorbed by others, or to have changed to the production of other kinds of machinery.

One of the earliest engine foundries in Montreal was established by John Ward in the autumn of 1819. Ward immigrated to Montreal from Vergennes, Vermont, in 1818, and his immediate prominence in the development of marine engineering is indicative of the importance of immigrant skills, especially

American technical experience and enterprise, in this industry. Long before the forties, Montreal was the scene of considerable American business activity, not only in the establishment of engine foundries but in industry and commerce generally.[31]

Ward first came to Montreal on an exploratory business trip in 1818. For a number of years previously he had operated his own engine foundry at Vergennes, where he built engines for Lake Champlain steamboats.[32] He had learned his trade in Elizabethtown, New Jersey, where his two brothers and his father operated an engine foundry. Ward apparently was well known in Montreal as a reliable engine builder. In August 1818 he received an invitation from Captain Sherman to manage his 'furnace establishment,' which built and repaired engines for steamboats on the St Lawrence.

The invitation to manage the foundry included the offer of a share in its ownership, and Ward went up to examine the place and to survey its potential local market. He quickly recognized the very promising future for a marine engine industry on the St Lawrence and saw that it could not be better located than at Montreal. He realized that steamboat traffic would grow with the increasing flow of staple goods from the upper St Lawrence, the prices of which he usually remarked upon in his letters. He well knew the trade between St John's and Lake Champlain ports, such as his recent home, Vergennes. On the Ottawa and even on the upper St Lawrence steamboats would inevitably soon come into wider use. Ward also felt that his own success was promised not simply by his experience and local repute but also by the advantages attached to the construction of steam engines on the spot specifically for marine use. Hitherto all of the engines for St Lawrence steamboats were imported, mostly from the Bolton and Watt factory which had the exclusive patent for their manufacture in Britain.[33] American marine engines were technically as good as the British and, though not as long-lived, cheaper. The high-pressure engine steamboats in use on the western rivers of the United States were especially admired by foreign visitors, and the general quality of American marine engineering evoked high praise from many. 'American river steamboats,' wrote the distinguished British naval architect, John Scott Russell, in 1841, 'stand in every respect, in science, in beauty, in magnitude, in speed, unparalleled by the river steamers of our own or of any other country.'[34]

Ward's impending entry into the already-initiated steam engine industry was thus not the result of especially brilliant foresight into the trends of transportation developments, but sprang from the desire and a well-proven ability to establish an efficient and profitable foundry. He was enthusiastic in his assessment of the future, and after a brief visit to Vergennes for business he returned to Montreal. However, he did not terminate his affairs completely in

Vermont, partly because he never regarded his venture in Montreal as anything more than a foray, or protracted entrepreneurial excursion, into the St Lawrence market. Soon he was learning as much as he could about St Lawrence steamboats, by observation and by talking to local shipbuilders and owners like John Molson and others about to embark on more extensive steamboat ownership. In August 1819, a year after his first visit to Montreal, he was awarded the contract to install an imported English engine in a boat being built at Montreal.[35]

Not long after he arrived in Montreal to settle, he purchased a one-twentieth share of the boat in which he had contracted to fit the engine. 'On returning here [from Vergennes],' he wrote to his father Silas in Elizabethtown, 'I have concluded to adopt the plan which you recommended of not attempting to start an establishment immediately but to wait a few months until I become better acquainted with the business and the people when I shall probably be able to do it to better advantage.'[36] However, in September 1819, it was clear that the English engine was not likely to arrive in Montreal before the end of the shipping season, and in early October Ward was commissioned to build one himself and immediately set about erecting a small foundry.[37]

Ward's plant was in a modest building near the port, not far from the future location of the Lachine Canal. He evidently chose this location with care. Proximity to the port, where iron and other imported components were unloaded, would have been a factor strongly influencing his decision. Ward soon imported tools, capital, and even skilled workmen – including his two brothers – from New Jersey. Soon after he decided to enter business on his own, he wrote asking his father to send him funds and skilled workmen.[38] About $150 would greatly help him in getting established, he wrote, enabling him to buy a turning lathe and a set of boiler tools. Since Ward preferred to remain free of partnership, the requested funds would allow him his independence. Before the end of the year his brother Samuel joined him, and the foundry was well along on building its first engine. Ward appealed for more workmen, good men, who, if unemployed in Elizabethtown, would be given plenty of work in Montreal. A further appeal for money, shrilly announcing that 'unless I receive some money soon I see but two alternatives, a British jail or a disgraceful retreat,' was answered within a few days by his father's remittance of $400.[39]

Thus was born the Eagle Foundry, probably the most important engine works in Montreal from the twenties to the early forties. After the first year and the early financial problems, the foundry rapidly expanded in the business of building and repairing engines, about which John Ward occasionally reported to his father. He built annually at least one engine and its fittings for steamboats, while repairing others. But in a few years he and his brothers were much busier.

In one twelve-month period from May 1822 to May 1823, they built four engines, as well as the machinery for a mill.[40] While John managed the foundry, brothers Samuel and Lebbeus, who joined in the mid-twenties, were contracting for new steamboat engines and repairing old ones up and down the St Lawrence. Besides Montreal steamboats, other boats being built at Sorel, Brockville, Kingston and Ernesttown were supplied with Ward's famous engines.[41] As far away as Toronto, Niagara, and Quebec the Ward reputation for excellent workmanship elicited patronage for the Eagle Foundry, in 1827 the Wards contracted to rebuild and install at Niagara the engine of the steamboat *Frontenac.*[42] At Montreal the Eagle Foundry got contracts to build most of the large engines for the new Molson and Torrance towboats.

Ward built and installed not only engines – probably the low-pressure type – but also the boilers and other devices, including the side paddlewheels, with which all St Lawrence steamboats were equipped. Ward's contracts usually gave only a bare outline of the specifications, describing merely the physical size and piston stroke of the engine, leaving the more minute details to further discussion. In the twenties Ward's engines were all custom-made for specific boats, but it is probable that as his business expanded he began to build and stock standard units. A more or less typical smaller engine built by the Wards had a thirty-five-inch cylinder with an eight-foot piston stroke; costing £2,000, it was installed in 1836 in a vessel being built by Campbell and Yale for Victor Chenier and Henri Monjeau of Longueuil, and Charles Boucher de Gosbois of Boucherville.[43] Engines were a large part of the total cost of a St Lawrence River steamboat, probably as much as three-fifths or two-thirds, depending on the size of the power unit. Payment was usually on an instalment basis as the work progressed, with the last payment due when the installation was completed. Ward's contracts usually gave him what amounted to a mechanic's lien on the boat, permitting him to sell the ship to recover his money; occasionally seizure was executed.

Despite mounting success during the decade following the opening of the foundry, John Ward's affection for Montreal and its people did not grow proportionately. Indeed, to him Montreal was a hateful place where, if one were not a 'Scotchman,' and especially if one were an American, there was considerable prejudice in business. Ward had never severed his own business interests in New Jersey, nor probably in Vermont either; 'and as I think New Jersey my home,' he wrote in 1822 to his father, 'I wish [my assets] to remain there.'[44] A year later he revealed that 'of all the places we have ever seen, New Jersey is rather the best to live in and the place we all wish to return to after we have supplied *John Bull* with all the steam engines that he wants ... The reason why we stay here now is because steam engines are wanted here more than in Jersey and there are fewer to make them.'[45] Not unlike many Montreal fur traders, Ward had come to Canada to prosper, intending to leave on retirement, they to Britain, he to his beloved New Jersey. Of course many stayed in Montreal, but more commonly not through prosperity but through failure to achieve it.

John Ward, anxious to return to New Jersey as soon as it was convenient, left Montreal in 1829. But he maintained an interest in the firm until November 1832, when he sold his share to Samuel and Lebbeus, who had been left in charge since his departure. By 1832 the foundry had come a very long way in size and diversity of production. In addition to marine engines, the Wards now produced barking machines for timber camps, leather rollers for local tanneries, metal punching machines, turning lathes, and iron wheels, and potash and sugar kettles. This variety of technical skills and productive flexibility provided alternatives during temporary declines in the demand for steamboat engines, such as occurred in 1829. The foundry was still in its original location near the Lachine Canal, but had been considerably enlarged since 1819. The plant had been expanded, and a new boiler shop built closer to the future canal. In sharp contrast to the basic investment of a few hundred dollars, the foundry in 1832 was worth well over £5,000, the sum for which John sold out his interest to his brothers. The former retired, not to Elizabethtown, but to Vergennes, where he re-entered the foundry business in a place where he felt confident of his reputation and free of discrimination at the hands of the Montreal Scots.

The Eagle Foundry continued building steam engines during the thirties. Its prominence was undiminished despite John's departure. Although he had left the city for good and no longer had a share in the foundry, John Ward appears to have maintained more than just fraternal relationships with his brothers and to have kept up other business ties in Montreal. Samuel paid him a ten-day visit in 1833, perhaps seeking assistance or advice in the management in the Montreal foundry.[46] Moreover, there seems to have been a regular exchange of skilled workmen between Montreal and Vergennes, as the labour needs of the two Ward foundries changed. In view of the scarcity of skilled workers, machinists, boilermakers, and fitters in Montreal, this partial integration of the work force benefited both foundries by ensuring the availability of workmen. Other more substantial business relationships were maintained. They are barely hinted at by the contract in 1844 by John Ward to purchase an engine from the Eagle Foundry for a steamboat he was having built.[47] Other evidence also suggests that, at least until 1846 he had continuing connections with Montreal, since he was then made an honorary director of the Montreal City and District Savings Bank.[48]

Vergennes shipbuilder George Brush was admitted to a one-third partnership in the Eagle Foundry in 1838.[49] Brush had moved north in the early thirties and served with the Ottawa and Rideau Forwarding Company, in 1834 becoming Kingston manager of the firm. Probably while there, if not earlier, he became acquainted with the Wards, who welcomed Brush's practical experience and business connections. Within seven years of his entry into the firm, Brush became its sole owner by buying out the remaining two-thirds Ward interest. Though they seem to have been vigorously in command of the foundry until at least the end of 1839, they perhaps, like their brother, pined for and returned to New Jersey or rejoined John in Vergennes.[50] Although Samuel and Lebbeus Ward had lived in Montreal longer than John, they participated only slightly more in the business and social life of the city. Lebbeus is listed as a donor to the Montreal Auxiliary Bible Society in 1835 and Samuel was a director of the City Bank from 1839 to 1846 and an elder of the American Presbyterian Church from 1841 to 1846 when he retired from the post, probably on the eve of his departure from Montreal.[51]

Brush maintained the Eagle Foundry on its established basis. He continued to produce marine engines as well as the considerable range of machinery turned out since the twenties. But more products were added, and his firm's advertisements in Montreal newspapers in the late forties announced both high and low pressure engines, mill gearing 'of every description,' double and single bark mills, bathtubs, pans and kettles of cast iron, bar iron, mill and jack screws, and iron tackle.[52] Operations, however, were not significantly diversified, nor was the foundry substantially expanded during Brush's ownership over the next few years, though probably efficiency was increased with specialization of functions by shops: pattern-making, blacksmith, fitting, moulding, boiler, and brass shops.

IV

The only other Montreal foundry in which marine engines were built was a smaller but somewhat older one than the Wards': the St Mary's Foundry, which dated from 1812, when John Molson sr, brought over John Bennet to install a Bolton and Watt engine for his new boat, the *Swiftsure*.[53] The foundry got its name from its location at the foot of St Mary's current, where Molson's brewery was located near the Hochelaga lumber and shipyards which extended further east along the St Lawrence.

The St Mary's Foundry for a time was integrated into Molson's business and operated as an adjunct of the brewery. But Molson began in the early thirties to rationalize his operations somewhat by putting his steamboats under the separate management of his St Lawrence Steamboat Company. About this time the foundry was sold or leased to Bennet and a partner named Henderson. Known thereafter as Bennet and Henderson's, or still as St Mary's, the foundry turned out a large number of engines. The exact nature of the continuing connections with the Molsons is not clear, but the foundry supplied many of the engines for Molson steamboats.[54] Impressive evidence of Bennet and Henderson's engineering competence lay in their building the engines for the *Royal William,* the first ship to cross the Atlantic solely under steam power. Their management of the St Mary's Foundry continued until 1845, when it passed back to the Molsons.

What induced Bennet and Henderson to give up business is not known; neither of them had been active in other Montreal business activity, an indication perhaps of limited resources. Whether they found that they were unable to compete with the Eagle Foundry in the Montreal market is not clear. The major reason for the change in ownership may have been the serious competitive threat that had recently arisen in the west end of the city with the establishment of Cantin's shipyard in 1843. Vertically integrated shipbuilding in one yard, from square timber and boilerplate to complete steamboat was beginning at Cantin's. Thus the change of ownership seems to have arisen from uncertainty in the industry, and it may be more a coincidence that other foundries were changing hands in these same years.

St Mary's Foundry continued in the Molson family, managed by John and William, sons of the family founder, John Molson, who died in 1835. They operated the foundry for some years by themselves with a series of partners. Soon after it was taken over in 1845, John Molson and William Parkyn formed a partnership to operate it. This arrangement was dissolved the same year and Parkyn ran the foundry for a time under lease.[55] This too was unsatisfactory; by 1850 the Molsons were back, probably reluctantly, by themselves in the foundry business. Much of the foundry at that date was devoted to the casting of railway car wheels for the St Lawrence and Atlantic Railroad. Molson was then involved in a bitter but losing struggle to protect the Canadian patent for the wheel he was manufacturing. His competitor was Samuel Bonner, an American newcomer to Montreal whose impending competition so frightened Molson that he fell back upon the arguments of Canadian patriotism in his petition to the government for protection.[56] Unable to compete effectively with other firms the Molsons sold the St Mary's Foundry in June 1852 to Warden King and George Rogers, the plant foreman. Instead of building marine engines or railway cars, however, the new owners concentrated on less prestigious, but apparently more profitable, casting of potash kettles, maple sugar coolers, and iron rails.

Samuel Bonner was not a newcomer to Montreal; he had been a resident of the city at least since 1837.[57] For a number of years before opening his own foundry, Bonner operated a small stove factory in Griffintown, near the canal, in partnership with William Hedge, another American who had an interest in early chemical production.[58] Although Bonner and Hedge sold their factory in 1843 to William Rodden, who expanded the plant considerably, Bonner remained in Montreal. In May 1845 he was ordained an elder of the American Presbyterian Church, (as much a tribal church for the Americans as the Scotch Presbyterian on St Gabriel Street was for Montreal's Scottish community). In 1848 Bonner was elected to the Board of Directors of La Banque du Peuple.[59] He was therefore very much a Montrealer, although perhaps not, in Molson's view, of the best sort. But Bonner did have some connections in the United States, and it was on these grounds that Molson appealed against American incursion. Sometime in the late forties Bonner had established or acquired an interest in a Plattsburg foundry and, according to Molson's allegations in 1850, was intending to move some of his equipment and workmen back to Montreal. There is no evidence to suggest that this competitive threat was ever carried out. William Rodden, who bought out Bonner in 1843, continued the foundry on much the same basis as before, although he might have produced an occasional stationary engine.[60]

By the end of the forties the marine engine industry had apparently reached a new stage. Hitherto, Montreal engine foundries had catered substantially to the shipbuilding industry and had supplied the St Lawrence builders with virtually all the engines installed. In addition, the foundries had begun the production of stationary engines, mills, and other machinery for the local market.[61] Until the forties, however, this was apparently supplementary to the main work of the engine founders, who, like the Wards, had begun producing engines in Montreal with the strict aim of building them for marine use. With the advent in the late forties of the integration of ship and engine building, the old marine engine foundries, St Mary's and the Eagle, were apparently unable to make the move forward to enlargement or integration, or, more surprising, to move laterally into making stationary engines and machinery. In the latter development new factories such as Bonner's and others located on the Lachine Canal after 1846 emerged as the most important, while the older foundries seem to have stagnated.

In view of the lack of adequate information, the reasons for the failure of the smaller industrialists to survive are far from clear. Aside from possible entrepreneurial incapacity, an external factor such as the opening of Lachine Canal to industry might be important not only because a new factory would normally make other similar works obsolete, but also because power there was no doubt cheaper and thus likely to lessen production costs.

V

It was natural that Montreal should have become a manufacturing centre. Besides the growth of industries oriented to a strictly local market, in the first few decades of the nineteenth century a number of small factories emerged producing various manufactured products easily distributed throughout its hinterland. Manufacturing, taken here to mean the production of standardized goods at least in part by machines, was limited to items that could be produced more economically at Montreal than elsewhere, by reason of location, raw materials, or tariff advantages.

Until near the end of the thirties, the city's manufacturing was small in scale and dependent mainly upon a very localized market. A small number of tiny factories produced carriages, confections, drugs and paints, rope, newspaper type, soap, and candles.[62] However, a small but significant clothing manufacturing industry was taking shape during the decade. Its growth was perhaps one of the major exceptions to the mainly local orientation of manufacturing in Montreal in this period. By 1838 there are indications that some items of men's street wear hitherto imported by wholesalers were being produced in Montreal. In 1839 advertisements for journeymen tailors were placed in Montreal newspapers, in May by Robert Norris, a retailer, and in November by Joseph McKay, possibly a tailor and manufacturer of ready-made clothing for some years. Merchants began to advertise Montreal-manufactured garments.[63]

The most successful and long-lived clothing manufacturers in this era were two English Jews, Edward and David Moss who arrived in Montreal in 1836. Almost immediately they began a large retail store and within a year were advertising ready-made clothing imported from England; they continued their retail trade until at least 1849. Probably sometime during the forties they started to manufacture their own merchandise by commissioning the production of garments from contractors, tailor-entrepreneurs who had the work done on their own premises or on the piecing-out system. At some point during the forties, however, the Mosses began fully integrated production in their own factory, which by 1856 was an immense establishment employing eight hundred people.[64]

Other aspects of the manufacture of clothing developed at the same time. By the thirties furriers were making coats, caps, and gloves. These included Green and Son, who began in 1832, and McDowell and Atkinson, who started a decade later. In the early fifties John Aitken and S.E. Scott were manufacturing shirts in Montreal.[65]

A number of important factors were associated with the development of the ready-made clothing industry. There would be limited economies of scale in a large plant, even after the invention of the sewing machine and the introduction of cheap hydroelectric power in Montreal at the end of the nineteenth century.[66] Probably the use of hydraulic power to propel sewing machines would explain the Mosses Lachine Canal plant, where garments were cut, sewn, and finished by hand. The Mosses may have had a clothing plant in the United States as well, for they boasted of an export trade worth £40,000 annually of 'American wares' to Australia.

There were other clothing manufacturing firms in Montreal in this era, but none of them were as large as the Moss plant. The next in size was one established in May 1854 by Macmillan and Carson, who employed forty-three workers and produced £10,000 worth of garments annually, £4,000 of it for export.[67] The other factories were probably then, as later, no more than lofts or garrets where a few tailors were able to produce garments as cheaply as they could be made in a shop of a dozen workers. Even after the introduction of the sewing machine, a small contractor could exist on the piecing-out system in which wages could be easily kept low. Thus the clothing manufacturing business was, in its earliest stage, an easy one to enter. An expanding population in Upper Canada during the thirties and forties created an enlarging market for clothing. Since the only appreciable difference between Canada and England in production costs of clothing would lie in labour costs, it was probably more economical to manufacture standard items of men's clothing for the Canadian market in Montreal.

The shoe manufacturing industry in Montreal developed from approximately the same general conditions, but with the added advantage that the basic material was produced locally, at the tanneries conveniently located outside the city in St Henri, where a substantial population of cordwainers lived. Montreal's first shoe factories were in production as early as 1819. Others were begun in the early forties. William Smyth began a small plant in 1843, and the partners Brown and Childs introduced sewing machines in their new factory in 1847. Both became large establishments in the fifties, the latter employing eight hundred workers in 1856.[68]

A number of small metalworking establishments sprang up in Montreal during this period. Among them was the Montreal Brass Works, started in 1851 by Robert Mitchell, a Scot, who had arrived in Montreal three years earlier. Making brass household fittings, Mitchell's firm thrived during the construction boom in the city in the early fifties. The Novelty Iron Works, established by Robert Gardner in 1850, turned out machinery for making candy, biscuits and confections, and later mixers, cutting machines, and bakery equipment.[69]

VI

While the first Lachine Canal was being planned and built during the early twenties, there was no discussion about using the hydraulic power there for industrial purposes, although the very first attempt to construct a canal had precisely this as a major object.[70] Following the completion of the canal in 1825 there was no rush of industry to its banks. Though there were one or two mills, such as Ogilvie's flour mill, which was established there in 1837, before enlargements were begun in 1843 the old canal did not attract industrial users of its power potential. However, industries did locate near the Lachine Canal especially its eastern end, close to the port of Montreal. Here in St Ann's Ward most of the city's small industrial establishments were built during the twenties and thirties, primarily because of the advantages of proximity to shipping.

The first serious plans to use the Lachine Canal's water for industrial purposes were made in 1844 by its engineer, A.E. Barrett. In his 1844 annual report to the Board of Works, he suggested that considerable revenue might be derived from leasing out canal sites for industrial purposes.[71] He pointed out that the exploitation of the power resources would be beneficial both to industry, which in the early forties was expanding at an increasing rate, and to the government, which would derive a revenue from the leases to help defray costs of enlarging the canal.

Industry would have been attracted to the canal's power potential for several reasons. Despite the general conditions associated with the use of water power for industrial uses, which made necessary a higher initial investment than for steam, the Lachine Canal was somewhat different. Here the government bore the cost of regulating the water flow, not only by building the canal but also by constructing the weirs and flumes into the individual sites. Additional advantages were excellent transportation facilities and proximity to associated or complementary industries, as in the case of shipbuilding and marine engines.

Soon after making his first suggestions to the Board of Works, Barrett laid out a rough plan of locations for mills, warehouses, and shipyards. The Board was favourable to the idea and planned to open the project by leasing twenty lots on the second basin, immediately above the canal's first lock. It was two years before practical steps were taken to implement these plans, but it is unlikely that much could have been done sooner, since the canal was still undergoing reconstruction until 1848. Although the works near the port were incomplete in 1846, they were probably in a sufficiently advanced state to allow the commencement of power development. There were, moreover, pressing appeals from a small but eager group of entrepreneurs interested in the project. These 'urgent applications, by certain parties' probably came from the millers and engine builders who bought up the first leases.

Barrett's specifications called for the allocation to each canal site of enough power to run four pairs of stones, or approximately forty-eight horsepower. These and other details were accepted by the Commissioners of Public Works and approved by the government in 1846. Soon arrangements were made to auction off the first sites on twenty-one-year leases for an annual rental of not less than the floor price of £107/10. Four lots were leased in November, another in January, and two more in May 1847. The remaining thirteen properties were granted by the commissioners 'upon the application of the respective parties.'[72] Public auctions were not held for these remaining lots, probably because there would not be sufficient competition and because applicants agreed to the upset price.

Most of the industrial establishments on this section of the canal were entirely new enterprises. Hence the opening of its power potential was not simply an advance in the industrial development of the city. It marked an entirely new departure in the city's economic history by making possible a rapid acceleration and diversification of industry there. It condensed within the seven years between 1847 and 1854 industrial growth which might never have occurred at all, or else would have taken much longer to develop.[73] The opening of the Lachine Canal to industrial use marked not only the development of Montreal as an industrial centre but also the advent of a new group to a position of stature in the business community. The changes after 1846 resulting from the exploitation of the canal, mark the sudden appearance of an industrial sector as an important part of Montreal's economic activity. The social consequences of the rise of manufacturing were reflected in a growing and changing population, the physical expansion of the city, and the development of the region bordering the canal, as well as by the rapid expansion of the labour force and the appearance of new elements within it.

One of the first to build a factory on the canal was Ira Gould, who put up a large five-storey grist mill and even larger storehouses in 1847.[74] A miller from Cooksakie, New York,[75] probably attracted to Montreal by British preferences on Canadian flour, Gould arrived in Montreal in 1843 to examine the power potential of the Lachine Canal. Whether he was responsible for initially sparking interest in its hydraulic potential is not known, but he was an aggressive early entrant to canal industry, and he later undertook the retailing of hydraulic power to others. He leased the first three lots on the canal and sufficient power for twelve run of stones. His investment of £37,500 in building and machinery suggests that he was already a highly successful miller. Next to Gould's mill was another built by James McDougall, also unknown hitherto in Montreal; his mill was one-third the size of Gould's and therefore probably represented an investment of some £12,000.

Iron foundries, however, were the dominant feature of canal development at this stage. One of the largest was E.E. Gilbert's Beaver Foundry. Of unknown origins, though probably Canadian, Gilbert applied successfully for three lots in October 1849, and a factory was soon erected, with £13,450 invested in land, buildings, and machinery.[76] The Beaver Foundry, which produced and repaired marine engines, was a substantial enterprise employing between sixty and eighty persons. The business expanded quickly, and so did Gilbert's ambitions. In 1853 he proposed to put up a factory for producing railway locomotives, but the project was never fulfilled. Gould sold out in 1856 or 1857 to Bartley and Dunbar.[77]

William P. Bartley and James Dunbar's St Lawrence Engine Works, established in 1850, was immediately next door to Gilbert's. Dunbar had been in Montreal since 1832, when he had some to the city from Scotland to assemble and operate some steam dredge machinery brought over to assist in harbour improvements begun that year.[78] Bartley's background, on the other hand, is not known. Theirs was a larger foundry than Gilbert's, producing a greater variety of iron machinery. In addition to its main business of building and repairing marine engines and ships, including a number of iron-hulled steamboats after 1854,[79] the foundry turned out mill machinery, boilers, cranes, windlasses, pumps, hydrants, iron castings, and forgings for railways, some of the rolling stock for which was built in the McLean and Wright factory nearby. Even before the amalgamation with Gilbert's foundry, Bartley and Dunbar's works were a sophisticated complex of specialized units, including a smithy, a foundry, and boiler, pattern, and finishing shops. In 1856, the factory employed 160 men and turned out an average annual production worth £40,000, nearly triple that of Gilbert's foundry.[80]

There were several other iron processing plants along this section of the canal. Of the several nail and spike factories, T.D. Bigelow's had been in business in Montreal since the 1790s and on the canal site since 1851.[81] By 1856 it employed fifty men in producing 1500 tons of nails annually. Thomas Peck's nail factory was much smaller in productive capacity than Bigelow's, but Holland and Dunn's was nearly as large. Peck, Holland, and Dunn had all been in business in Montreal for some years previous to their move to the canal in 1851, Peck since at least 1840 and Holland since 1844, when he petitioned the government for a patent for a new spike machine. Dunn had been in Montreal in 1835, when he had been one of the few English speaking promoters of La Banque du Peuple; he continued his interest in La Banque for some years and later helped to establish the Montreal City and District Savings Bank.[82] Near these iron works was a large sawmill operated since 1851 by Grant and Hall, who by 1856 were producing in excess of ten million feet of lumber annually.

In another factory nearby, Lyman and Savage produced paint, linseed oil products, and an assortment of drugs to the value of £30,000 annually by the mid-fifties.[83] The Lymans had long been in this business in Montreal. In 1803 the Lyman brothers, M.J. (a medical doctor) and Elisha, both of them recent immigrants to Montreal from the United States, began manufacturing some of the drugs they sold in their store. William Lyman, a son, along with William Hedge, succeeded to the business in 1819. Hedge, who retired in 1836, was later a partner with Samuel Bonner in a foundry business. William Lyman's brothers Benjamin and Henry joined the family firm after 1836. Between 1835 and 1851, the eve of its expansion in the canal sector, the company nearly doubled its assets from £4,000 to £7,250; this was doubled again, in the 1852 move to the canal, to an investment of £15,000 in plant and machinery.[84] Since 1835 the Lymans had begun to distribute their own products and imported manufactured goods, including a wide selection of medicines and surgical supplies, throughout the provinces. Branch outlets were set up in Quebec, Kingston, Bytown, and London, and a major warehouse at Toronto, which after a few years remained the only secondary distributing centre. The plant built on the canal in 1852 put out a wide range of items for domestic and industrial uses, including putty, paint, spices, and drugs; but the firm continued to distribute imported goods. At the same time the Lymans became the chief supplier of whale oil for lighthouses being built by the Montreal Trinity Board along the St Lawrence during the forties.[85] But William Lyman, the head of the firm in this period, was not among the most active or aggressive of Montreal's businessmen, judging from the fact that he was not diversified in his interests as were some of his fellow industrialists. His sole extramural business involvement seems to have been with the City Bank, of which he was a director for one year. Otherwise he appears to have kept very close to his drug firm. Perhaps because of this lack of business distractions, he and his brothers developed an impressively large business, one of the most long-lived in Montreal, under a single family's control.

Other factories and quasi-industrial establishments were set up on the first section of the canal. By 1856, there was another engine foundry owned by Milne and Milne, Tate's dry dock and shipyard, and the Berry sewing machine factory, none of whose owners are known.[86] By that date the total investment, based on the stated value of some factories and conservative estimates of others in the pamphlet prepared for the Grand Trunk opening celebrations, was approximately £250,000, or $1 million. The total number of men, women, and children employed varied considerably, according to the factory and industry involved and general economic conditions. In all, however, an estimated one thousand people were regularly employed at the factories on this section of the canal by 1855-6.

The second stage of development on the Lachine Canal had begun in 1851, immediately after the last lots on the section above were leased. The new section opened by the government was just below the canal's second or St Gabriel lock, so named because of its proximity to the St Gabriel farm belonging to the Sulpicians. The commissioners of public works in 1850 had seen that more power sites were in demand and asked the government for permission to lease the water power adjacent to any public works 'for a reasonable rate of compensation.'[87] Approval was given in August 1850, and preparations were made to lease more power sites by inviting offers in October through newspaper advertisements.

Two months later, John Young, on behalf of himself and a group of associates, including Ira Gould, the only additional person in the group who was specifically named, applied to the Board of Works for the whole power potential at the St Gabriel lock. 'The parties with whom I act in the project,' Young wrote in his petition, 'are anxious to have the entire control of the water power of this section of the canal.'[88] They offered to construct all the necessary flumes and to buy some of the still privately owned land on that section of the canal. The project had some merits, one of which would be saving the Public Works Commission the cost of auctioning the leases and the complications of dealing with a large number of lessees. The chief engineer of public works, Samuel Keefer, approved of the plan: 'it appears very desirable for the general interests of the country,' he wrote, 'to encourage the formation of such companies for the establishment of machinery and using the water power along the line of the canals, and it may even be desirable to give a *preference* to the application of companies over those of individuals, wherever, as in this instance, the company can offer satisfactory reference as regards their capital and capability of bringing the whole power into full operation.'[89] Keefer hastened to add, however, that, notwithstanding the usefulness of companies such as Young's, several previous applicants should have the opportunity of offering on the lots at a public auction. There would be seven lots, six to go at an upset price of £100 and the seventh, an island in the canal and suitable for a dry dock, at £150. Young was informed that the water lots would be sold at public auction, and in early January 1851 notices of the sale to be held early the following month were placed in Montreal newspapers.

The auction never took place. Years later, in 1887, a royal commission on the leasing of water power on the Lachine Canal, investigating the abuses of water privileges allegedly perpetrated by Young and Company, concluded that, despite Keefer's recommendations and the decision of the Board of Works, the leases had been sold privately to Young.[90] 'There is strong evidence to show,' they concluded, 'that the property was to be offered in such a manner as to prevent competition, and to enable [Young's] Company to acquire a full control of the water-power, or as stated in evidence by witnesses before us, it was arranged beforehand that this Company should obtain it, and the sale was a mere formality.'[91] Not only did Young circumvent the prescribed process for acquiring the leases, but he somehow secured them at a bargain price of £420 annually. Within a week or ten days he converted a bargain into a 'steal.' The auction for hydraulic power sites was supposed to be for five lots, each with four run of stones, or a total of twenty run. Keefer had strongly urged this limitation, until it could be determined to what extent the large quantity of water passing the locks would affect navigation. Nevertheless, Young managed to have his substantial but limited package transformed into a lease giving his syndicate control not only of twenty stone power, but 'the entire surplus water,' in other words the right to drain virtually unlimited amounts of water from the canal and implicitly the right to develop unlimited hydraulic power. Over the next thirty-five years, Young and his associates developed 120 stone power, which they subleased to various industries. The lease in which the abuse of procedure and the perversion of the government's intentions was accomplished was found to be legally void in 1853, but the attorney general east, Lewis T. Drummond, observed 'that it would be a harsh proceeding on the part of the Government to take advantage of this informality for the purpose of entirely annulling a contract entered into in good faith by the lessees.'[92] Though not a supporter of Hincks's policies, especially on railways, Young had been Drummond's colleague between 1851 and 1852 in the Hincks-Morin government as chief commissioner of public works, so that the recommendation for clemency is, in that context, understandable.

Little is known of the syndicate which so successfully enjoyed what it had set out to accomplish. Because of his active public life John Young's career is better known than that of his associate Gould. Young's activities embraced several facets of Montreal's economic existence during the mid-Victorian period, and especially dear to his heart was the improvement of Montreal's water transportation system, as his pamphlets and newspaper contributions amply demonstrated.[93] Thus it is not surprising that he should have taken a keen interest in the enlargement of the Lachine Canal and, incidentally, in its being utilized for industrial purposes. Gould had come to Montreal apparently with the sole purpose of investigating the canal's power potential, and having seen it he became one of its major enthusiasts. Indeed it is probable that Gould, rather than Young, was the real entrepreneur in the St Gabriel development and that Young's membership in the group was as much a result of his public prominence, useful in representing the syndicate more imposingly to the authorities, as it was of his personal entrepreneurial *élan*. The only other known participant in the venture was Jacob DeWitt, but it is unlikely that there were many more, because the necessary investment was limited to the relatively small amount required to build flumes.

The exploitation of the power potential at the St Gabriel lock took place as quickly as it had at the basin below four years previously. By 1854 the industrial development there had almost reached its full potential. The factories included the Montreal India Rubber Company, which mainly produced rubber footwear at the rate of one thousand pairs a month for the Canadian market; the plant and machinery represented an investment of £17,000 and 110 men were employed.[94] The owners are unknown. The cotton factory, opened in 1853 by Massachusetts-born Frederick Harris, with a capacity of fifteen hundred spindles and forty-six workers, produced cloth for denims and ticks as well as wadding and batting for the Canadian market.[95] A woollen factory owned by George W. Weaver was capable of producing sixty thousand yards of cloth annually, but was not in production until 1857; Weaver too is unknown.[96]

Several woodworking factories were located in this sector. Among them was John Ostell's shop, at which seventy-five men were employed making doors, windows, and all kinds of joiners' finishings, mainly for the Canadian market. In the lumber storage yard, which encompassed five acres of land with buildings and machinery, £20,000 was invested. Nearby, James Shearer manufactured similar woodwork at a slightly smaller plant employing fifty-five men; and at William Allan's chair factory twenty-five were working. McCauren's sawmill and Wilsie's barrel factory completed the inventory of woodworking establishments.[97] None of the owners are known; their names occur in no other aspect of Montreal economic development in this period, and they are among the substantial number of all but anonymous industrialists who were not actively involved in other business endeavours.

Several metalworking plants stood on the St Gabriel site. A large axe factory, planned by brothers Thomas and Robert Scott in 1848, was opened three years later on the upper location.[98] They invested an estimated £15,000 in buildings and machinery and employed seventy men and six boys in the production of some 120 dozen axes daily for the domestic market. The Scotts were probably Americans; they brought in a number of workmen from the United States to help begin their plant, and they complained worriedly to the commissioners of public works when a shortage of water in the canal threatened to force layoffs, which could mean the permanent loss of irreplaceable skilled men.

The Ogilvie flour mill on the upper section was not as impressive in size or capacity as Gould's mill lower down the canal, since it operated only five run of stones compared to Gould's twelve. Because of the family's later prominence, however, much more is known of its business origins than about other significant individuals and groups in the economic life of Montreal during the forties.[99] The Ogilvies had been milling flour in Montreal since 1837 in their small mill on the old canal. In 1852 James Goudie, an uncle who was a prominent Montreal miller, took Alexander Walker Ogilvie into partnership. They built a three-storey mill in 1852 to process flour and other grains. Although this firm was initially a smaller establishment than Gould's, the Ogilvie plant was later extended further and became the largest in Canada.[100]

The second phase of industrialization along the Lachine Canal, then, was completed by 1854 or 1855; it included nearly as large a capital investment and work force as that on the lower canal basin finished a few years earlier. An estimated £200,000 was invested in plant and machinery in this sector of the canal and some 930 persons regularly employed in the factories there.

A third development, at Côte St Paul on the north side of the Lachine Canal above the second lock, began soon after all of the mill sites below were taken up in 1854. Though the story of industrial growth there is outside the time-span of this account, its course shows that the pattern begun in 1846 continued for a decade more at least. Samuel Phillips Day, an English traveller in the early sixties, commented on the intensity of industrial development along the whole Lachine Canal.[101]

VII

The extent to which Montreal had become an industrial centre by the early fifties can be measured in a number of ways. The first and most apparent is in the scale of the factories established in the city, the amount of capital invested, and the number of jobs created. Within seven years after 1847 some £500,000, conservatively estimated, was invested in thirty industrial enterprises during the first two stages of the exploitation of the Lachine Canal's hydraulic power resources. Almost two thousand jobs were created in the factories along it, and suburbs were built exclusively as dormitory areas for an enlarged, and in many respects new, working class spread out near the canal beyond old Montreal. These jobs, it must be stressed, were in new industries and did not include the large numbers employed in Montreal's immense brewing and distilling industry which produced an estimated £750,000 worth annually by the mid-forties.[102]

The capital investment was very large in contemporary terms, but its importance lies also in the fact that most of it was undertaken by newly prominent industrialists who were also recent arrivals to Montreal. This capital was new investment, much of it probably derived from sources outside of Montreal. In this period, Canadian banks extended loans mainly for commercial purposes and only for short periods, except for occasional temporary financing for public works. Loans from merchants to industrialists possibly took place, and it may be that in more cases than the ones cited here, merchants invested in manufacturing. The absence of extensive records concerning these industries, however, permits only tentative conclusions on this subject.

The expansion of the labour force was an important economic consequence of accelerated industrial growth during the forties. The sudden creation of eighteen hundred new jobs had general economic ramifications. Equally important is the fact that with the technological sophistication of industry came the growth of a highly skilled labour force. Montreal industry was increasingly dependent on steam and iron; the number and proportion of skilled metal tradesmen including steamfitters, iron moulders, and machinists increased; craft unions in Montreal in some of these trades were among the first in Canada.[103] The census of Lower Canada in 1851 does not provide the information needed to establish the origins of the skilled workmen, but, though the frequent mention of American artisans should not be ignored, it is likely that most were British immigrants drawn chiefly from the industrial areas of England. The growth and sophistication of the Montreal iron-working industries at the end of the forties and early fifties made it possible for railways to supply some of their needs of rolling stock from local factories.

Although the ethnic composition of the new industrial work force is not ascertainable, the fact that the dormitory areas adjacent to the canal, St Ann's, Point St Charles, and Verdun, were overwhelmingly English-speaking districts implies that only a small proportion of the workers could have been French Canadian.

At the entrepreneurial level, only one of the thirty-odd industrialists on the canal, Augustin Cantin, was a French Canadian. The reasons for the near absence of French-Canadians is a matter for further study. Without more information one can only speculate that their absence may have been because they lacked technical competence or because their capital resources were insufficient. Both factors were no doubt important, but they should not be overemphasized. As is evident in the shipping industry, French Canadians were able to muster considerable capital, and in the case of the shoe industry they demonstrated high technical abilities. The answer then might lie in the size of investment commitment necessary for steam-and-iron industrial enterprise, in contrast to the relatively limited capital requirements of the shoe industry. Moreover, location on the canal, the scene of dynamic industrial change in this period, necessitated a commitment of twenty-one years, which might have deterred less well-endowed aspiring industrialists.

Another important aspect of the rise of industry in Montreal was the variety of industrial production, which ranged from the simple processing of staple products to the technically complex manufacture of sewing machines. Between these extremes, paints, chemicals, steam engines, edge tools, clothing, and many different types of machinery were being produced. Besides inventions for steamboat equipment, Montrealers took out sixty-eight patents between 1826 and 1853 for a wide variety of machines, propellers, farm equipment, furnaces, ventilators, weightlifters, and a multiplicity of other contrivances.[104] Though probably few of these inventions were ever actually produced, nevertheless they showed considerable local interest in and talent for building new mechanical devices. Montreal manufacturers became increasingly proud of their productions and by 1854-5 were aware of the city's importance as an industrial centre. Though they sent but a few examples of the city's manufactured goods to the Great Exhibition of 1851 in London, Montreal industrialists displayed more of their wares at the Provincial Exhibition of 1853. There was a Berry sewing machine, 'the gem of the whole Exhibition,' a variety of furniture and wood products from the Hilton, Ramsay, and McArthur and Ostell factories as well as heating and ventilating equipment from a number of small manufacturing plants.[105] Two years later, at the 1855 Universal Exhibition in Paris, Montreal manufacturers sent a large number of items, an overwhelming proportion of all the Canadian manufactured goods displayed there.[106] Many Montreal industrialists were represented, including Augustin Cantin, John Redpath, William Rodden, George Perry, M. Holland, P. Dunn, William Lyman, the Montreal India Rubber Company, John Ostell, Robert Scott, and J. and W. Hilton. In sending their exhibits to Paris, Montreal industrialists were displaying a new kind of confidence in their products and in themselves, which had mounted strongly over the preceding few years; that confidence must have been heightened by the impressive number of prizes their submissions received.[107]

Though most Montrealers undoubtedly continued to think of their city as primarily a commercial metropolis, some were becoming more sensitive to its increasingly pronounced industrial character. During the spring and summer of 1849, William Workman presided over the recently-formed Montreal Association for the Encouragement of Home Industry. Supported by Jacob DeWitt, a Montreal member of the provincial legislature,[108] and by David Vass, Workman argued for duties on 'manufactured articles, which to an extent are, and may still more become the proper subjects for affording employment to the domesticated industry of Canada.'[109]

When considering best how to prepare for Canadian participation in the Great Exhibition of 1851, Montrealers, viewing Montreal as Canada's industrial centre, designated their city as the location for a preliminary provincial exhibition.[110] After listening to speeches lauding industry by merchants, politicians, and industrialists, they struck a large committee consisting mainly of many of their own prominent citizens to organize the week-long exhibition which took place in October 1850.

The assumption that Montreal was the industrial centre of Canada strengthened over the next few years as the number and size of manufacturing establishments increased. By 1856, when the city was preparing to welcome the Grand Trunk Railway's completion, visitors to Montreal were provided with pamphlets describing Montreal's accomplishments in commerce and advantages for industry. The latter 'make this the best site for a manufacutring city in Canada, perhaps on the Continent.'[111] It was no idle boast but a confident statement of the considerable accomplishments in this area already and the expectation that more manufacturers would be attracted to Montreal in the future.

A final but highly significant aspect of the industrial development of Montreal is the participation of the provincial government. Its involvement in the changes discussed in this chapter was very considerable. The enlargement of the Lachine Canal was an integral part of the canal-building programme of Canadian governments since the union of the provinces, but in general the attitude, not often articulated, that governed relations between governments, liberal or conservative, and business in this period was one of beneficent encouragement. It was manifested in the way groups and individuals petitioned the government for measures and assistance of various kinds. Present-day rhetoric about 'free enterprise' obscures the real climate of enterprise in Canada in the forties and fifties. On the part of government it was not simply the attitude of 'defensive expansionism' described by H.G.J. Aitken,[112] but a belief in 'progress,' which in early Victorian England meant, above all, the growth of industry, celebrated so magnificently in the Great Exhibition of 1851 and echoed by Canadians in the provincial exhibition of 1850. In Canada the 'age of progress' was characterized by a pursuit of another form of material advancement, commerce, while industry, as described here, seems to have begun in some cases as an outgrowth of commercial activity.

13

Conclusion

Between 1837 and 1853 Montreal participated in the North American transportation revolution and experienced important changes within its business community. The city emerged from this brief but creative period as a dynamic entrepreneurial centre with leaders of its commercial fraternity showing their vigour and flexibility in erecting new corporations in a wide range of fields. Though rooted mainly in commerce, these men seized the opportunities provided by new technology and by generally favourable economic conditions. In establishing new shipping, railway, and industrial ventures, Montreal businessmen engaged in collective entrepreneurship, utilizing their own resources and, for railways, drawing capital as well from the public and from varied institutions while benefiting from government support.

To be sure, this theme was already familiar. Montreal had always led Canadian developments in finance and transportation, and its merchants had erected companies in both: its businessmen had always sought commercial empire. What distinguishes this period in the city's history from the immediately preceding years is the intensity and variety of activity, and, most important, the transformation of many Montreal businessmen into much more venturesome entrepreneurs. The period under study here witnessed the rise to prominence of several major figures in Montreal's financial, transportation, and industrial empire. The provincial government played a highly significant role, indispensable for the success of nearly all of the transportation and industrial enterprises developed in those years. By building canals and improving rivers, by providing guarantees for railways and subsidies for steamships and industrial sites, and by acting with general permissiveness towards the chartering of corporations – with little attempt to prevent duplication or socially harmful decisions – the government created vital conditions in which these enterprises might thrive. These were policies of a Canadian positive state, similar in many ways to

American state paternalism towards business in the same era. Montrealers were among the leading beneficiaries of Canadian state enterprise and investment because of the size and economic importance of their city.

The transformations in most aspects of economic life in Montreal during these years were accomplished by a relatively small group of businessmen, merchants, industrialists, forwarders and professionals, from all the city's distinct ethnic elements, some of which were beginning to merge in social as well as in economic life. The continuing preponderance of a small group of Scottish immigrants, several with experience going back to the fur trade, was evident. Yet prominent businessmen had emerged from other sectors of the community as well. The New Englanders were the most significant element which was active not only in commerce but also in key sectors of Montreal's rapidly expanding industrial sector. Throughout this period there was also strong business participation by French Canadians, who exhibited entrepreneurial vitality equal to that of the Scots and New Englanders. The theory that the ethnic proclivities or 'mentalité' of French Canadians made them unwilling or ineffective businessmen is not borne out by events in Montreal during these years.

Though few became titans in all fields, as did the city's Scots, followed at some distance by Americans, several of Montreal's French Canadians participated noticeably and very successfully during the forties in traditional commercial business as well as in the new industrial and transportation ventures of that era. A significant number were fully aware of the potential in the new technology of steam and iron and in the comparatively new forms of financing through joint stock companies; and many had enough capital to buy shares. What had happened to these 'non-commercial people?' To a very great extent the involvement of French Canadians was part of the expansion of bourgeois economic opportunity during the forties in Montreal, at the heart of the St Lawrence commercial system. Some of the French Canadian businessmen of Montreal and neighbouring villages now saw a chance to profit by the expected further growth of the city in shipping, railways, industry, and real estate. French Canadian merchants had always been at a substantial disadvantage in Montreal, whose essential economic function was to serve as an Upper Canadian port and an aspiring major outlet for Great Lakes exports. With few exceptions they had not ventured west, nor even, it seems, into the nearby Ottawa Valley timber camps, which provided an immense market for goods and supplies handled and financed at Montreal. The forties, however, for them as for their *Anglais* colleagues, were years of beckoning opportunities, and many were tempted to share in the prosperity. Their first attempts were limited, almost timid yet they became increasingly confident as this period unfolded and more daring entrepreneurial moves followed in the years to come.[1] The story of increasing

French Canadian participation in business during the nineteenth century has yet to be written. Studies of credit, capital formation, and investment zones will provide useful insights into French Canadian business behaviour in the nineteenth century.

The importance of these factors is illustrated by another reference to Montreal's New Englanders, whose economic importance in the city generally and as a powerful force by the forties in its wheat and ash trade gradually weakened as a result of the decline of American exports through the city. At the same time the increasing significance of imports as the leading sector of its economic life and the tendency for this trade to be concentrated in the hands of firms with both British and Montreal branches, also weakened the position of most Yankees, who may have had difficulty establishing sound transatlantic linkages and were facing a decline in their basic trade. They and the firms they founded were gradually absorbed into the business community, just as were enterprises initiated outside Montreal — the Champlain and the Portland railway lines and the Compagnie du Richelieu.

Montreal businessmen were prepared to make use of new instruments at the sacrifice of traditional ones. During the heyday of water transportation, the St Lawrence was the main channel for Montreal's trade. But the merchants saw nothing sacred about the river, for they were committed to the metropolitan mercantilism of Montreal more than to notions of British North American economic nationalism or, as the annexation crisis demonstrated, loyalty to the mother country. Although commerce and loyalty coincided during the earlier nineteenth century, by the late forties, when that unity appeared to be breaking down, the merchants were ready to supplement the imperfect St Lawrence with railways to American ports, and to integrate those lines into the expanding upper New York-New England traffic network. Any incipient Canadian nationalism in the 'commercial empire of the St Lawrence' was little felt by contemporaries, who viewed the river as merely a convenient transportation system. The vital question to Montreal businessmen was the viability of their investments in commerce, which meant ensuring a continuing flow of essential east-west trade to maintain the competitive strength of Montreal among rival cities on the east coast of North America. They realized in the late forties and early fifties that the north-south railways were admirably suited to the seaward journey.

As far as they were concerned with these strategic matters, Montreal businessmen were primarily interested during these years in improving the city's connections to the sea. This was the vital challenge. Outflanked by New York's Erie Canal for a generation, outmanoeuvred more recently by the United States Drawback Acts, and shattered by the withdrawal of imperial protection after

1846, the commercial fraternity realized that they had to reduce transportation costs between Montreal and the Atlantic. Equally important was the concomitant need to ensure year-round communications with overseas markets through a winter port. Only then would the long-sought hinterland be secure. Montrealers also recognized the need for improved shipping and railway communications with Upper Canada, but their financial resources and entrepreneurial energies were primarily utilized for the fight for metropolitan survival. Unique in North America at this time was Montreal's drive to the sea. Her rivals, especially Boston and New York, were actually on the Atlantic coast and thrusting efficient transportation systems into the interior. By the mid-forties Boston businessmen were performing prodigies of railway construction to link the city with the St Lawrence River.

Professor Creighton has argued compellingly that the Montreal merchants strove to control the trade of the entire mid-western region in the Great Lakes basin; whether it was British or American territory apparently mattered little to them by 1849. It was trade and its orientation to Montreal that they were pursuing through the forties and well beyond. Whether western commodities were destined for markets in Boston or New York was of little concern. They would funnel as much North American trade as possible through Montreal, whatever its destination, provided only that the city be kept an independent entrepôt, free of control from Boston merchants, bankers, and railway promoters. Supplying the British market, controlling the imports of British manufacturers, and attracting staples and western markets involved the commercial community of Montreal in an unremitting battle among North America's great cities for continental dominion. Montreal's major rivals were New York and Boston, and some Montreal businessmen surprisingly still thought they could equal those cities and eventually even surpass them. Railways were their great hope; railways would establish year-round connections with Europe, putting Montreal at last on an equal footing with its seacoast rivals and, most importantly, making possible the reduction of transportation costs on imported goods and exported staples through Montreal.

But Montreal had to remain independent of its competitors. Dependence upon railways, banks, shipping companies, and merchants situated in Boston or New York would mean eventual eclipse, because Montrealers would soon be reduced to the status of agents. And their opportunities for entrepreneurship in nearly all these fields would probably be far less substantial than if their city was the centre of control. Avoiding domination from United States centres suited their own personal interests and ambitions; it did not arise from any nascent nationalistic spirit. They were perfectly well prepared to use the northeastern United States as a land bridge to the Atlantic. This was not, then, a departure from the dream of establishing the commercial empire but the adoption of another means of reaching it. Even though it meant some degree of continental integration and linkages with rival cities, the primary goal was served nevertheless. And the integration with the American railway network was not necessarily a sign of actual or even potential weakness in the attainment of their goal, because Montrealers believed that they could enjoy certain benefits, such as more traffic, while still retaining the advantage of independent decision.

For Montreal, the interior lines of communication were well provided for by the vigorous government canal construction programme that by 1848 had at last removed navigational impediments in the upper St Lawrence River. With this comforting assurance the Montreal businessmen looked to the east as their most challenging transportation frontier. Some, of course, realized that Montreal's confidence in the improved upper St Lawrence transportation system was misplaced and that railways were needed in that region too. Most of the city's leading businessmen also understood that better transportation by itself would not ensure the fulfilment of their metropolitan aspirations and throughout the 1837-53 era there was an efflorescence of new and expanded commercial, financial, and industrial developments. The first and vital task, nevertheless, was clearly to establish more efficient links to the sea. The three railways built southwards are indicative of this broadly felt, sense of urgency. These railway lines and the other companies founded in that era also show the substantial vigour and sizable financial resources available in the embattled Canadian metropolis.

The fact that they had always pursued or dreamed of capturing the American market helps to explain why many of the Montreal merchants became quickly converted in the summer and autumn of 1849 to the panacea of annexation. Union with the United States seemed a perfectly logical and sensible solution. The merchants had never been nationalists and never would be — unless it was in their economic interest. It was because patriotism for Montreal merchants was traditionally but a reflection of their economic interests that annexation was an acceptable alternative. Their loyalism to Britain had been founded, largely though not entirely, upon financial considerations. Once the pillars of imperial protection were hewn down in 1846 and the implications of this for Montreal commerce became strikingly evident during the 1848 trading season, when there was a drastic decline in both imports and exports through the port, the city's merchants made the obvious, natural choice. The Annexation Manifesto, issued in October 1849, when it was clear to the merchants and small group of manufacturers in the city that the depressing commercial trend of the previous year was continuing, stated that political union with the United States would radically change the economic and political climate in the Canadas. Unfettered trade with the United States and the stimulus which that market would provide for Canadian manufacturers and merchants promised new vistas of prosperity for the Province of Canada in place of 'the universal and increasing depression of its material interests ... that afflict our country.'[2] During the summer of 1849 the Annexationist movement built up widespread strength in Montreal, and by October there were few dissenters to the Manifesto. Most of the major English-language newspapers, notably the *Courier*, the *Herald*, and even the *Gazette*, the principal organ of the city's commercial community, came out strongly in favour of the proposals to join Canada with the United States.

One can thus only agree with the statement that 'the rapid spread of the agitation had been largely due ... to the belief that the imperial connection was responsible for the depression of the colony.'[3] G.N. Tucker asserted that 'the arguments used on behalf of annexation were almost entirely materialistic ones,' and Creighton equated annexation with the continuing pursuit of an 'international commercial state.'[4] What should be added, however, is that the high drama of the annexation crisis, which passed so quickly, masks the fact that Montreal merchants had always been continentalists; their commitment to the trade along the St Lawrence–Great Lakes midcontinental axis made the border seem only an interference with their ambitions. In the continuing pursuit of the position as entrepôt to the west, they planned to build their railways towards the southeast, to the American Atlantic seaboard and the warmer water of year-round navigation. Such a connection would attach the staple-producing regions to Montreal by means of cheap efficient transportation to and from the great market for produce and suppliers of manufactured goods in Britain. The adherence of these western regions to a trading system dominated by Montreal seemed in 1848 and 1849 to depend on the continuance of British imperial preferences. Once the end of these supports spelled ruin for Montreal's trading system, the close ties with the United States, both west and east, led the commercial fraternity to embrace annexation.

Why did annexation to the United States, instead of other possible options, present itself as the panacea for Montreal's economic dilemma? Aside from the emotional atmosphere of outrage brought on by the British rejection and the satisfaction of cutting the imperial connection, there were substantial economic benefits forecast. The United States would provide a market for Canadian produce formerly sent abroad. But perhaps more important to Montreal merchants was the probability that in the new integrated economy Montreal and they themselves could prosper. Railway projects languishing for lack of sufficient local capital would be built by US investors, 'and railway enterprise in general would doubtless be as active and prosperous among us as among our neighbours.'[5] American capital would be poured into Canadian real estate and would double property values. And American capital would raise Canada 'where water privileges and labour are abundant and cheap' to an industrial nation 'enhancing the value of property and agricultural produce and giving remunerative employment to what is at present a comparatively non-producing population.'[6]

In their Annexation Manifesto, Montreal businessmen candidly described the climate of enterprise they had been attempting to create since the mid-forties. Railways and commercial expansion were only parts, albeit highly important ones, of the local economic environment of the forties. It included also the physical growth of the city, the initiation and expansion of all kinds of 'Public works and private enterprise,' and the creation of an industrial cluster in the city, one of the very places in the province where cheap and abundant water privileges and labour were in close proximity to each other and to a substantial local and potential foreign market. Industrial expansion, already underway in 1849 in a newly opened sector of Montreal's Lachine Canal, would bring immensely beneficial results for the entire city and especially for its economic leaders, who were not only merchants but also promoters of a wide variety of companies in railway, mining, banking, insurance, and gas, and often real estate developers besides. Commerce too would be enhanced because the wheat and timber staples formerly sold in Britain would find a market in the northeastern United States, which Montreal was in an excellent position to serve.

Businessmen of the time, as they do now, clearly assumed that economic growth required a positive state providing not only a helpful framework for enterprises but also deep government commitments to them. Yet, surprisingly, few Montreal businessmen became directly involved, in this period, in the politics of the Province of Canada. Many undoubtedly had extensive contacts with the politicians, and there is little doubt that major decisions, such as the passage of the Guarantee Act of 1849, were brought in with the strong 'encouragement' of aspiring promoters. The hard evidence of how influence was brought to bear on certain politicians and how the businessmen may even have helped to design certain legislation is lacking thus far. There were no doubt certain politicians who acted as sponsors of enabling bills for the whole range of companies begun in Montreal during this decade and a half. The MLAs for Montreal in this era, George Moffatt (1841-7), Benjamin Holmes (1841-4, 1848-51), Pierre Beaubien, Alexandre-Maurice Delisle (1841-4), C.C.S. De Bleury, John Young, and William Badgley, were in all likelihood extremely active in the legislature in committees and behind the scenes. So were James Smith, attorney general east from 1844 to 1847 and Francis Hincks, who, though MLA for Oxford, Canada West, was a resident of Montreal for most of the period; these men probably took an active part in many legislative discussions concerning Montreal companies, especially railways, and fostered them in any way they could. Further research might well reveal the extent of involvement by these or other politicians in the interstices of Montreal railway and other company promotions in this period, although to date there is no known body of evidence on this fascinating theme. Until it is found historians can only conjecture on the possible or probable connection of Montreal businessmen and the politicians.

Most changes in Canadian economic history have been brought about by adaptations of new technologies and by government policies specially tailored to suit one kind of enterprise or another. Both mechanical invention and generous government assistance were utilized successfully by Montreal businessmen, joined during this period by an emerging group of industrialists. Both groups added new dimensions of economic strength to Canada's major metropolis during a highly important era of transition.

Notes

ABBREVIATIONS

APQ   Archives de la Province de Québec

ASCM   Archives of the Superior Court of Montreal

CR   Chateau de Ramézy, Montreal

PAC   Public Archives of Canada

BRH   *Bulletin des Recherches Historiques*

CBD   *Canadian Biographical Dictionary and Portrait Gallery of Eminent and Self-Men, Quebec and Maritime Provinces volume* (Toronto, Chicago, New York, 1880)

CHR   *Canadian Historical Review*

CNR   Canadian National Railways papers (PAC, RG 30)

JLA   *Journals of the Legislative Assembly of the Province of Canada*

JLC   *Journals of the Legislative Council of the Province of Canada*

Montreal Directory (1841-2)   Robert W.S. Mackay, *The Montreal Directory for 1841-2; Containing First, An Alphabetical Directory of the Citizens Generally; Second, A Classified Business Directory, In which the Names of Subscribers Only Are Arranged Under Their Proper Business Heads; And, Third, A Directory to the Assurance Companies, Banks, National, Religious, and Benevolent Societies, and Institutions, And to all Public Officers, Churches, etc., etc., In the City* (Montreal, 1841 and annually thereafter)

Prov. Sec. Corres.   Provincial Secretary's Correspondence (PAC, RG4, C 1)

Stats. Prov. Can.   *Statutes of the Province of Canada*

TWO / THE BUSINESS COMMUNITY

1 See Cooper, *Montreal,* chap. 5, and 'The social structure of Montreal.'
2 Landes, *Bankers and Pashas,* chap. 1
3 PAC, Edward Murphy Papers, II
4 McCord Museum, McGill University, Jedediah Hubbell Dorwin, 'Antiquarian Autographs.' This is a collection of signatures and brief descriptions of a large number of businessmen with whom Dorwin was associated in the Canadas, the United States, the Maritime provinces, and Britain. Most autographs – many of which followed by Dorwin's brief but very valuable comments – are numbered. The Gates entry, however, is not numbered.
5 MacKay, *Montreal Directory* (1845-7), 64, 71, 80, 93, 161, 166, 211. These men are known to be of US birth either by membership in the American Presbyterian Church, by a notation to that effect in Dorwin's 'Antiquarian Autographs,' or by their signing a statement (published in the *Montreal Transcript,* 28 Nov. 1838) proclaiming loyalty to Britain by Montrealers of US birth.
6 But see Knowles, 'The American Presbyterian Church,' ·156.
7 Ibid., 238. See also McDougall, 'The American element.' Americans living in Montreal experienced social discrimination, according to Ward. PAC, Ward Papers, John to Silas Ward, 30 Oct. 1821 and 1 Feb. 1829. Among the reasons for this discrimination was the belief that many American criminals were taking refuge in Canada: [Auto] Biography of Harrison Stephens, 5, manuscript from Murray Ballantyne of Montreal. One indication of the contempt (or fear) felt by some Montrealers towards Americans in local business was expressed by R.H. Bonnycastle in his *The Canadas in 1841* (London, 1842), 76-7, quoted in Parker, 'The towns of Lower Canada,' 396: 'Amongst all these the shrewd and calculating citizen from the neighbouring republic, drives his hard bargain with all his wanted zeal and industry, amid the fumes of Jamaica and gin sling.'
8 See PAC, Jedediah Hubbell Dorwin Diaries, 1811-1883, 32, 34, 48, 54.
9 McCord Museum, McGill University, Bagg Papers, Letter Book, Oct. 1821-Sept. 1825, Abner Bagg to Howard White, 2 May 1822; Bagg to Richard P. Hart, Troy, NY, 29 Mar. 1822.
10 Ibid., Letter Book, Dec. 1819-Oct. 1821; Dorwin, 'Antiquarian Autographs,' passim
11 Goad, *Atlas,* plates 3, 4, 21
12 The foregoing information on John Frothingham comes from McIvor, *Canadian Monetary, Banking, and Fiscal Development,* 38; Lower Canada, *Provincial Statutes* (1833), c. 32; *Montreal Almanack;* MacKay, *Montreal Directory* (1840-8), passim; JLA (1834), App. S; (1841), App. C; *Montreal Transcript,* 15 Feb. 1840
13 Lynne, 'The Irish in the Province of Canada,' 79. See also Cooper, *Montreal,* chap. 14.
14 *Census of Canada* (1871), IV, 206; see MacKay, *Montreal Directory* (1842-53), passim; Pentland, 'The Lachine strike.'
15 *Census of Canada* (1851-2), I, 40
16 See Sack, *Jews in Canada,* chaps. 12-13.
17 Ibid., 70-1
18 Dorwin, 'Antiquarian Autographs,' 716; MacKay, *Montreal Directory* (1844-52); Goad, *Atlas;* Sack, *Jews in Canada,* 149-50
19 Prov. Sec. Corres., 151, (1846), 1037
20 MacKay, *Montreal Directory,* passim
21 Ibid. (1845-6), 221; (1852), 262
22 Ibid. (1845-6), 240-2; (1852), 280-4
23 The assertion that 'ce n'est qu'à partir de 1840 ou 1850 que les Canadiens français sortiront de l'ombre, qu'ils envahiront notamment pour y occuper la première place, le commerce des épiceries en gros': (Jean Bruchesi, 'Histoire Economique,' in Minville, ed., *Montreal Economique,* 29) is open to serious doubt. An examination of MacKay's Montreal directories reveals that very few French Canadians were listed either as 'Grocers, Tea and

Spice Dealers' or as 'Grocers, Wine and Spirit Dealers': MacKay, *Montreal Directory* (1845-6), 247-9; (1852) 291-2; (1854), 341-3. One contemporary noted, however, that 'the rise of [the] French element in wealth, business importance, and influence in trade in the city, since the establishment of the Banque de Peuple in 1834, and the change produced by the events of 1837, are wonderful to those who can remember their depression up to that time': Brown, 'Montreal fifty years ago.'

24 See Masson, *Joseph Masson:* Université de Montréal, Collection Baby, Boîte 124
25 His brother-in-law, Jean-Moise Raymond, continued the family business and was MLA for Huntingdon-LaPrairie from 1824 to 1837: Lefebvre, 'Jean-Moise Raymond.'
26 Auclair, 'Terrebonne,' 5. See also ASCM, Henry Griffin Papers, 3 Aug. 1838, 16163.
27 Turcotte, *Conseil Législatif,* 121. Masson also served concurrently as a member of the Special Court of Sessions which conducted Montreal civic government from 1836 to 1840 and was an alderman in 1843-4: Lamothe, *La Corporation de Montréal*, 205. City of Montreal Archives, Assessment Books, 1852 -
28 *Census of Canada* (1871), IV, 206
29 Sociologist Norman Taylor has recently argued that reluctance to relinquish personal control was one important consideration governing the unwillingness of certain French-Canadian industrialists to expand their factories: Taylor, 'The French Canadian industrial entrepreneur.'
30 CR, 827
31 *Montreal Transcript,* 18 Feb. 1837; Dorwin, 'Antiquarian Autographs,' 30; *Montreal Transcript,* 17 Mar. 1840.
32 Harvard University, Dun and Bradstreet Credit Ledgers, Canada, 5, 6, 7 (Montreal)
33 Prov. Sec. Corres., 151 (1846), 1037
34 See Ferrie, *Life;* Austin, 'Two mayors,' 8.
35 Campbell, *History of the Scotch Presbyterian Church,* 383; Taylor and Notman, *Portraits,* II, 343.
36 Dechêne, 'William Price,' 24; McGill University, European and North American Manuscripts, CH 341, S301, Griffin Papers, Folder no. 1
37 ASCM, Henry Griffin Papers, 4 Nov. 1841, 8047
38 PAC, Peter McGill Papers, 51
39 His bank book for the period 1835-9 shows frequent debit and credit entries, for very large amounts, and a balance always in excess of £30,000. Ibid.
40 Montreal *Gazette,* 29 Sept. 1860; Sarah Lovell, *Reminiscences,* 18-19. After 1853 bad times came upon Peter McGill. Although he was still a powerful man in the Bank of Montreal, his firm began to decline. Never free of huge debts to his former British partners, Gould and Dowie, McGill was forced in 1858 to transfer virtually his entire fortune to his creditors in order to secure release.
41 Denison, *Canada's First Bank,* II, 419; Audet, *Les Députés de Montréal,* 241
42 McGill University, Griffin Papers; *Pilot,* 10 May 1853
43 The City of Montreal property assessment records from 1852 are available in the Montreal City Archives at City Hall.
44 MacKay, *Montreal Directory* (1845-6), 224-228; (1852), 270-1
45 *Census of Canada* (1851-2), I, 406
46 MacKay, *Montreal Directory* (1845-6), 244-246; (1852), 290
47 Ibid. (1843-4), 269-271; (1852), 262
48 Ibid. (1843-4), 239; (1852), 262; (1843-4), 244-6; (1852), 270-1; (1843-4), 264-7; (1852), 281-4
49 Ibid. (1843-4), 269-71; (1845-6), 244-6; (1852), 290; (1843-4), 274-8; (1845-6), 250-3; (1852), 293-5; (1843-4), 264-7; (1845-6), 240-2; (1852), 281-4; (1843-4), 256-7; (1845-6), 236-7; (1852), 276-7
50 Out of five banks operating in Toronto in 1851, two were branches of Montreal banks: Masters, *The Rise of Toronto,* 18. Masters contends that this was only one aspect of Toronto's subordination to Montreal. Ibid., 19

51 Denison, *Canada's First Bank,* II, 9, 67. *Stats. Prov. Can.* (1847), 10 and 11 Vic., c. 116.
   The City Bank's capital, however, was reduced two years later to £375,000 as a result of
   heavy losses: ibid. (1849), 12 Vic., c. 185; (1843), 7 Vic., c. 66
52 Ibid., 10 & 11 Vic., c. 63; *Ordinances of the Special Council of Lower Canada* (1841),
   3 & 4 Vic., c. 37; *Stats. Prov. Can.* (1843), 6 Vic., c. 22. The company was renamed the
   Montreal Assurance Company in 1850: ibid. (1850), 13 & 14 Vic., c. 121; (1847),
   10 & 11 Vic., c. 79; (1847), 10 & 11 Vic. c. 80; (1847), 10 & 11 Vic., c. 83.
53 *Morning Courier,* 27 Feb. 1849
54 'Origins of the Montreal Board of Trade,' 28; Montreal Board of Trade, *Anniversary
   Volume.* The presidents from 1836 to 1871 included Jules Quesnel, Austin Cuvillier,
   J.T. Brondgeest, George Moffatt, Thomas Cringan, Peter McGill, Thomas Ryan,
   John Young, Hugh Allan, Luther Holton, Thomas Kay, Edwin Atwater, Thomas Cramp,
   and Peter Redpath. Ibid.
55 *Montreal Transcript,* 21 April 1838
56 Campbell, *The Scotch Presbyterian Church,* 99
57 Ibid.; Phoenix Assurance Company, *First in the Field,* 8-10; ASCM, Griffin Papers,
   11 Dec. 1838, 16382; *Montreal Transcript,* 13 April 1839
58 Campbell, *The Scotch Presbyterian Church,* 366-8
59 *Stats. Prov. Can.* (1841), 4 & 5 Vic., c. 90; An organization akin to a junior board of trade
   was formed in January 1841 for the 'mental improvement of the numerous and highly
   respectable body of young men engaged in counting houses and stores, and who are to
   become the future merchants in the city.': *Montreal Transcript,* 30 Jan. 1841
60 Prov. Sec. Corres., 151 (1846), 1027; Montreal *Gazette,* 15 April 1845; Prov. Sec. Corres.,
   127 (1845), 1386. These views were echoed by submissions from the Quebec Board of
   Trade and by Thomas Ryan, a Montreal shipowner. See also ibid., 149 (1846), 781.
61 Ibid., 884; 168 (1846), 2895; 156 (1846), 1595
62 *Morning Courier,* 15 April 1849
63 Ibid., 13 April 1850
64 Montreal Board of Trade Archives, J. and R. Esdaile Circulars 1848-1851; Montreal Stock
   Exchange, 'One hundred and thirty-two years of progress,' 1.
65 Evans, *Corn Exchange,* 2; Montreal Board of Trade, Council Minutes; Johnson,
   'The Montreal Stock Exchange,' 14; *Stats. Prov. Can.* (1849), 12 Vic., c. 194
66 *Montreal Transcript,* 18 May 1841; The association prided itself on the number and value
   of the books in its collection. Members were occasionally urged to contribute to the
   Library's book fund. Montreal *Gazette,* 14 Mar. 1849. There was keen interest in the
   library and in the type of periodicals placed in the reading room. See *Report of the Speeches
   and Proceedings at a Special Meeting of the Mercantile Library Association of Montreal
   Held on Monday Evening, April 8, 1850, to take into consideration the action of the
   Board of Direction in respect to the explusion of the 'Christian Inquirer' from the News
   Room* (Montreal, 1850).
67 Montreal *Gazette,* 6 Mar. 1845; 15 April 1845; 17 Mar. 1847; 3, 5 Jan., 23 Feb. 1849;
   11 Feb. 1850; 16 Jan. 1852. Lectures on topics of interest to businessmen were the most
   commonly offered. Some were published; see Montizambert, *Mercantile Law of
   Lower Canada.*
68 Walrond, ed., *Earl of Elgin,* 68

THREE / FORWARDING FIRMS ON THE UPPER ST LAWRENCE

1 Province of Canada, *Tables of Trade and Navigation* (1851), 19; (1852), 26; (1853), 26;
   (1854), 26
2 *Montreal Transcript,* 25, 27, 30 April 1839
3 Mackay, *Montreal Directory* (1845-6), 244
4 Patton, 'Shipping and Canals,' 499

5 The author uncovered no evidence on the extent to which any of Montreal's forwarders acted as 'an agent who performs services (as clearing of customs, receiving, assembling or trans-shipping or delivering) designed to assure the passage of goods of his principal to their destination:' *Webster's Third New International Dictionary of the English Language,* 3 vols., (Chicago, 1966), I, 896

6 In the mid-forties the large number of independently-owned sailing craft bringing goods to Montreal from the upper country were provided with towage upriver between the St Lawrence canals by three large steamboats: Prov. Sec. Corres., 140 (1845), 3175; the government of the province undertook to subsidize this service in 1849. Calvin, *Saga of the St Lawrence,* 117-130

7 Patton, 'Shipping and Canals,' 536-7

8 Taylor, *The Transportation Revolution*

9 Glazebrook, *Transportation in Canada,* I, 71; Croil, *Steam Navigation,* 317;

10 Legget, *Rideau Waterway*

11 Ibid., 318. The company was sometimes referred to as the 'Ottawa Line Company.'

12 CR, Mittleberger Papers, William Mittleberger (Smith's Falls) to Charles Mittleberger (Montreal), 10, 17, Dec. 1831

13 MacKay, *Montreal Directory* (1845-6), 25. Bernard was probably F.A. Larocque's principal partner in Larocque, Bernard and Company. Dorwin listed him as a dry goods merchant. McCord Museum, Dorwin, 'Antiquarian Autographs,' 503; Morgan, 'Steam navigation,' 372; Denison, *The Barley and the Stream,* 152

14 McGill University. European and North American Manuscripts, Ottawa and Rideau Forwarding Company, 1837. Other Montrealers included Adam Ferrie, Benjamin Hall, John Fisher, A. Venner, John Strange, Thomas McKay, John Redpath, Charles Mittleberger, and Thomas Phillips.

15 Ibid.

16 Glazebrook, *Transportation in Canada,* I, 78; Morgan, 'Steam navigation,' 372

17 *Montreal Transcript,* 10 Oct. 1839

18 Taylor and Notman, *British Americans,* III, 246; Dent, *Portrait Gallery,* III, 206. See also Rattray, *The Scot,* III, 731-2.

19 See Preston, 'The Port of Kingston'; Montreal *Gazette,* 27 Mar. 1845.

20 PAC Department of Transport A, Department of Marine, 1, Ship Registers, 175, 176, 205; see Montreal *Gazette,* 2 June 1845.

21 *Morning Courier,* 1 May, 27 June, 3 Aug., 14, 18 Sept. 1849; Dent, *Portrait Gallery,* III, 206; Whitton, *A Hundred Years A-Fellin',* 33

22 Currie, *Grand Trunk Railway,* 10; Skelton, *Galt,* 31

23 MacKay, *Montreal Directory* (1853), 131

24 Croil, *Steam Navigation,* 318; Montreal *Gazette,* 1 April 1845; Dorwin, 'Antiquarian Autographs,' 475

25 Dent, *Portrait Gallery,* II, 193. Professor Klassen's thesis on Luther Holton's business career should be consulted for further details; CBD, 343

26 The firm was known as Henderson, Hooker and Company. MacKay, *Montreal Directory* (1844-5), 90

27 Smyth, *'The First Hundred Years,'* 69; CBD, 344; Wallace, *Dictionary,* 326

28 Montreal *Gazette,* 1 April 1845, 15 May 1849, 6 Mar. 1850

29 PAC, Ship Registers 176 / 26, 61, 137; ibid., 175 / 128; *Morning Courier,* 17 Dec. 1849; Montreal *Gazette,* 16 May 1845; *Pilot,* 16 April 1853

30 Ship Registers, 176 / 112, 113, 124, 125, 137; *Morning Courier,* 16 Jan. 1850. See also MacKay, *Montreal Directory* (1852), 286. The steamboat *Ontario* owned by Hooker and Jacques was operated during the 1853 navigation season as part of Hooker and Holton's Montreal-to-Hamilton line: *Pilot,* 16 April 1853

31 Ship Registers, 176 / 10, 11, 25, 26, 37, 38, 61, 137

32 CR, Mittleberger Papers, William to Charles Mittleberger, 3 Sept. 1829; Ship Registers, 175 / 159, 162, 167

33 Montreal *Gazette,* 7 May 1845; *Morning Courier,* 12 May 1849
34 Richards 'The Joneses of Brockville,' 171; Sydney Jones resided in 1852 and 1853 at St Lawrence Hall, a Montreal hotel. MacKay, *Montreal Directory* (1853), 131.
35 In the spring of 1836, the firm concluded a contract at Montreal to have its boats hauled upriver from Split Rock to Pointe au Diable by men and horses. ASCM, I.J. Gibb Papers, 13 April 1836, 171
36 *Montreal Transcript,* 19 Oct. 1839; see Innis and Lower, *Select Documents,* 147-9.
37 MacKay, *Montreal Directory* (1844-5), 23, 88; (1852), 27; Gibb Papers, 11 Dec. 1843, 7186.
38 *Stats. Prov. Can.,* (1847), 10 & 11 Vic., c. 75, 78; Gibb Papers, 29 Dec. 1847, 10247
39 Dorwin, 'Antiquarian Autographs,' 53, 911; *La Presse,* 11 Nov. 1933
40 MacKay, *Montreal Directory* (1844-5), 72
41 See CR, Mittleberger Papers.
42 Ship Registers, 175 / 161-2; MacKay, *Montreal Directory* (1843-4), 268
43 Montreal *Gazette,* 29 Jan. 1847
44 *Morning Courier,* 5 Dec. 1849; *Montreal Directory* (1852), 186
45 *Montreal Directory* (1844-5), 173; Ship Registers, 175 / 109, 110, 111, 113, 120; 205 / 55
46 Ibid., 176 / 134, 141, 144
47 *Montreal Directory* (1844-5), 58; Ship Registers, 175 / 94; Montreal *Gazette,* 4 June 1845
48 Ship Registers, 175 / 146, 148, 164; see also *Montreal Directory* (1844-5), 85; (1852), 55, 157, 286, 287; Gibb Papers, 24 June 1839, 3051. Hackett was in partnership with George Dickinson. *Montreal Transcript,* 27 April 1837
49 Ship Registers, 176 / 109
50 Ibid., 175 / 156
51 Montreal *Gazette,* 3 May 1845
52 *Pilot,* 2 June 1853
53 Gibb Papers, 6 Feb. 1845, 7645
54 There were twenty-four such vessels registered at Montreal over fifty tons and approximately fifty vessels of less weight; See Ship Registers, 175, 176.
55 This subject requires further investigation in the Ship Registers of upper St Lawrence and Great Lakes ports.
56 Ibid., 176, passim
57 Keefer, *Canals,* 102
58 Luther Holton, however, retained a sufficient interest in the prospects for Atlantic shipping to invest in both the Canada Ocean Steam Navigation Company and the Oneida project; see chapter 5.
59 Merritt, *A Brief Review,* 5; Calvin, *Saga,* 117
60 Brown, 'The opening of the St Lawrence,' the 'American Line of Steamers, operated three steamboats between Montreal and Ogdensburg and Cape Vincent, New York, from 1853 or earlier. *Pilot,* 6 May 1853
61 *Stats. Prov. Can.* (1844), 7 Vic., c. 59
62 *Montreal Transcript,* 29 Dec. 1836; 17 Jan. 1837
63 Ibid., 29 May 1838; 18 June 1839
64 *Montreal Directory* (1843-4), 197
65 *Montreal Transcript,* 18 June 1839
66 Montreal *Gazette,* 5 June 1845; see McGill, Griffin Papers for a number of fascinating early marine insurance cases.
67 Prov. Sec. Corres., (1850) 282 / 1667

FOUR / SHIPPING ON THE MIDDLE ST LAWRENCE AND THE RICHELIEU

1 PAC, Ship Registers, 175 / 4, 35; 176 / 82
2 Cooper, *Montreal,* 12

3 ASCM Griffin Papers, 1 Sept. 1838, 16199
4 Ship Registers, 175 / 2, 15, 11, 30, 22, 44, 47
5 Ibid., 176 / 68
6 Ibid., 175 / 33, 56, 57, 58, 61, 143
7 Ibid., 176 / 18; *Pilot* 5 May 1853
8 ASCM, Griffin Papers, 3 March 1846, 21185; Prov. Sec. Corres. (1849), 266 / 2632
9 Ibid., 281 / 1540
10 Ibid., 266 / 2632
11 *Stats. Prov. Can.* (1849), 12 Vic., c. 193; Prov. Sec. Corres. (1846), 150 / 900 Ship Registers, 175 / 88
12 Prov. Sec. Corres. (1850), 281 / 1540; 216 / 2632
13 Ship Registers, 175 / 6, 34, 62
14 Ouellet, *Histoire Economique et Sociale du Québec;* see Jodoin et Vincent, *Longueuil,* chap. 23, and Couillard-Despres, *Saint-Ours,* 402-3.
15 Atherton, *Montreal,* II, 577.
16 Lower, *Assault,* 97; Lanctôt, 'Panorama historique,' 101-2
17 Innis and Lower, *Select Documents,* 247; Cross, 'The dark druidical groves,' 148-9
18 Parker, 'The staple industries,' 63
19 A list of steamboats that plied the Richelieu at various times during the mid-nineteenth century is given in Couillard-Despres, *Saint-Ours,* 402.
20 Jodoin et Vincent, *Longueuil,* 548; Ship Registers, 175 / 3, 8, 13; de Brumath, *Histoire Populaire,* 364
21 Other French Canadian entrepreneurs were attracted to this business (Jodoin et Vincent, *Longueuil,* 550), and both the Champlain and St Lawrence and the St Lawrence and Atlantic later put their own cross-river steamboats in service.
22 Ship Registers, 174, 175; see also Couillard-Despres, *Saint-Ours,* 402-403.
23 Université de Montréal, Collection Baby, Boîte 124; see A. Cartier, Joseph Cartier, Eustache Cartier files.
24 Ship Registers, 175 / 27
25 Ibid., 41, 68, 80, 83, 84, 86, 92, 118, 122, 158; 176 / 17, 51
26 Canada Steamship Lines, Montreal, Société de Navigation du Richelieu, Minute Book, n.p.
27 Wallace, *Dictionary,* 199; MacKay, *Montreal Directory* (1844), 94; (1853), 125. The Hudon firm became one of Montreal's largest wholesale grocery houses. Benoist, *Monographies Économiques,* 71; CBD, 238
28 Ship Registers, 175 / 85; 176 / 39
29 Quoted in Montreal *Gazette,* 19 June 1849. *Le Moniteur* commented unfavourably on the fact that although this was a French Canadian venture, Hudon had manned his vessel with English-speaking sailors. Hudon replied to this criticism with the statement that he hired the most suitable sailors he could find. Montreal *Gazette,* 21 June 1849
30 See Armstrong 'Jacques-Felix Sincennes,' *Dictionary of Canadian Biography,* X, 657; Société de Navigation de Richelieu, Minutes, n.p., n.d. See Ship Registers, 175 / 107; 178 / 2, 103.
31 *Stats. Prov. Can.* (1857), 20 Vic., c. 170
32 Lower, *Assault,* 108
33 Compagnie du Richelieu Minutes, 15 Feb. 1854, hereafter cited as 'Richelieu Minutes.' The company's minutes for this date contain a valuable summary of receipts, expenses and net profits annually from 1846 to 1853.
34 Société de Navigation de Richelieu, Minutes, 15 Feb. 1847
35 Richelieu Minutes, n.p., n.d.
36 Ibid., 10 Mar. 1848
37 *Dictionary of Canadian Biography,* Preliminary List of Quebec businessmen, 1851-1900 (typescript); National Harbours Board, Montreal, Trinity Letter Books, 156, Benjamin Holmes to Louis Marchand, 28 May 1852; Richelieu Minutes, 27 Feb. 1849

38 Richelieu Minutes, 28 Feb. 1850. Competition was so severe on the Richelieu, according to one author, that fares were repeatedly reduced. Wood, *All Afloat,* 149.

39 By early February 1848, Sincennes, who had begun by owning forty shares, held sixty-seven of the Richelieu's total of 130. Richelieu Minutes, list of share transfers, n.p., n.d.

40 Ship Registers, 175 / 107. The probability of a partnership with Mears is suggested by the fact that St Louis mortgaged the *Oregon* back to him on the very day that he bought the vessel from Mears himself. This was a complicated but not uncommon business practice in steamboat ownership on the St Lawrence at that time, as the ship registers show.

41 The uncertainty of the date of St Louis' purchase arises from the fact that the *Vulcan,* which was built in Brockville in 1841, was reregistered in Montreal in August 1851, with St Louis as subscribing owner. Its reregistration was not synonymous with a change of its ownership, which St Louis probably held before 1851. Ibid., 178 / 2; 175 / 73

42 Richelieu Minutes, 28 Feb. 1850

43 The ship registers list some of these vessels; see 175 passim.

44 Richelieu Minutes, 28 Feb. 1850

45 Ibid., 77

46 Ibid., 14 Mar. 1850; 18 Feb. 1851.

47 Ibid., 27 Feb. 1851

48 Ibid., 15 Mar. 1850

49 Ibid., 11 Feb. 1851; 18 Feb. 1851

50 Ibid.

51 Ibid.

52 Province of Canada, *Tables of Trade and Navigation* (1854), Table 11. It is difficult, if not impossible, to determine accurately the volume of interport traffic along the middle St Lawrence and Richelieu rivers and the place occupied by Montreal in that trade. Available statistics pertaining to the Richelieu provide information only about traffic through the Chambly Canal and at the port of St John; they tell nothing of the traffic in goods and passengers between the villages on the Richelieu and Montreal. The shipping firms' records on this subject have not survived. For valuable data on exports and imports through St John's for 1849, 1850, and 1851, see Andrews, *Report,* 427, and other tables in part 5. All data on canal traffic are drawn from the *Tables of Trade and Navigation,* Tables 9 and 11.

53 *Tables of Trade and Navigation* (1854), Table 11

54 Ibid. (1851-4), Table 11

55 Ibid. (1953), (1854), Table 11

56 Ouellet, *Histoire Économique,* 616

57 Richelieu Minutes, 12 July 1850; 6 May 1851

58 Ibid., 20 Feb. 1852

59 MacKay, *Montreal Directory* (1845-6), 61, 142; (1852), 33, 169

60 Lamothe did not advertise in MacKay's directory, but he was able to maintain a house separate from his place of business. Ibid. (1852), 137

61 Richelieu Minutes, 20 Feb. 1852

62 *Stats. Prov. Can.* (1847), 10 & 11 Vic. c. 64; Brown, 'The St Lawrence and Industrie Village Railway,' 40

63 Richelieu Minutes, 20 Feb. 1852; Brown, 'Industrie Village,' 40

64 Richelieu Minutes, 18 Feb. 1853

65 Prov. Sec. Corres., 278 (1850), 1225

66 Richelieu Minutes, 15 Feb. 1853

67 Ibid., 20 Mar. 1853

68 Ibid., 31 Mar. 1856

69 Ouellet, *Histoire Économique,* 104

70 Cook, ed., *French-Canadian Nationalism,* 85. Thirty years later, however, Laurent-Olivier David thought that there were five major reasons for this entrepreneurial backwardness:

the psychology of the people, historical factors, the absence of practical education, the ignorance and greed of French Canadian businessmen, and, finally, poor use of capital. Zoltvany, 'David' 429

71 Taylor, 'The French Canadian industrial entrepreneur.' Cf. Ryan, *The Clergy and Economic Growth.*

72 Dubuc, 'Problems,' 23

FIVE / OCEAN SHIPPING AND TRADE

1 PAC, Ship Registers, 175 / 18, 28, 91; 176 / 91; ASCM, Gibb Papers, 16 July 1846; *Morning Courier,* 22 Sept. 1849

2 *Morning Courier,* 27 Oct. 1849

3 All figures quoted here are taken from Patterson, *Statistical Contributions,* 21. The figures published in the Montreal Board of Trade's *Fiftieth Anniversary Volume* are considerably different from Patterson's but show the same degree of fluctuation, and the graphs based upon both sets of figures show the same contours. The same is true of the figures for total tonnage of ocean-going vessels.

4 Patterson, *Statistical Contributions,* 21. From a low of 14,441 tons in 1838, the shipping increased to 50,277 tons in 1841 and declined to 35,682 in 1843. Subsequently, it leaped upwards to 49,635 tons in 1844, to 63,381 tons in 1847, then fell to 37,425 in 1849. From 1850, however, tonnage reached the level attained in the mid-forties and averaged approximately 60,000 tons annually for the decade.

5 JLA (1849), App. B

6 Patterson, *Statistical Contributions,* 21

7 JLA (1849), App. B

8 Patterson, *Statistical Contributions,* 21

9 *Montreal Brokers' Circular,* 17 May 1851

10 *Montreal Transcript* (Supplement), 21 April 1838

11 Patton, 'Shipping and Canals,' 603

12 *Montreal Directory* (1843-4), 197

13 Fry, *Steam Navigation,* 263

14 Rankin, *History of Our Firm*

15 *Montreal Transcript,* 21 April 1838

16 Montreal *Gazette,* 23 Jan. 1845

17 Shortt, 'Austin Cuvillier,' 305; *Montreal Transcript,* 1836-9, passim

18 *Montreal Directory* (1853), 155

19 *Montreal Brokers' Circular,* 1848; *Montreal Transcript,* 12 Jan. 1837; McCord Museum, Dorwin, 'Antiquarian Autographs,' 278, 418. In March, 1841 Routh wrote to the directors of the Bank of Montreal to solicit an appointment as their New York agent. PAC, Minutes of the Board of Directors of the Bank of Montreal, 26 Mar. 1841, 384

20 Dun & Bradstreet Credit Ledgers, Canada V, Montreal, 1847-72

21 National Harbours Board, Montreal. Trinity Letter Books, B. Holmes to H.L. Routh, 7 June 1847

22 Prov. Sec. Corres., 105 (1844), 4 June 1844

23 McGill University, European and North American Manuscripts, CH 341, S 301, Folder no. 1; CH 377, S 337, Honourable Peter McGill, Legal Documents, 1854-7

24 Montreal *Gazette,* 29 Sept. 1860

25 Dorwin, 'Antiquarian Autographs,' no number

26 Campbell, *Scotch Presbyterian,* 509. He was one of the subscribing owners of the ship *Gypsy,* registered in Montreal on 2 June 1838, and his executors sold part of his estate on 17 Sept. 1838. See Ship Registers, 175 / 29; ASCM Gibb Papers, 17 Sept. 1838, 2433

27 The firm was Millar, Parlane and Company until 1831; see Campbell, *Scotch Presbyterian,* 385-6.

28 Dent, *Portrait Gallery,* II, 39; Jones, *Pioneer Shipowners,* 27.
29 Wallace, *Dictionary,* 7; Ship Registers, 175 / 20
30 Wallace, *Dictionary,* 518
31 Montreal *Gazette,* 27 Feb. 1865
32 Université de Montréal. Collection Baby, Gerrard Papers, Declaration of 25 Aug. 1816, signed by Samuel Gerrard, Robert Gillespie, Jasper Tough, George Moffatt, and John Ware (for William Finlay). Some of these changes can be followed in the Baby Collection II, C2, Boîte 59, Commerce, finance, affaires (1820-30)
33 ASCM, Griffin Papers, 16 Sept. 1842, 18,659.
34 Montreal Board of Trade, *Fiftieth Anniversary Volume,* 46; *Montreal Brokers, Circular* (1848); *Montreal Business Sketches,* 184; Shipping Registers, 175 / 14.
35 Collection Baby, Boîte 124, passim
36 Campbell, *Scotch Presbyterian,* 491-3. See Scottish Record Office. James Dunlop Papers, 1773-1815; Dorwin, 'Antiquarian Autographs,' 55.
37 *Stats. Prov. Can.* (1847), 10 & 11 Vic., c. 83
38 Ship Registers, 175 / 115
39 *Morning Courier,* 8 May 1849; MacKay, *Montreal Directory* (1853), 238; Campbell, *Scotch Presbyterian,* 491-3.
40 See JLA (1843), App. NN; The firm of John W. Dunscombe & Company, of which the principal partners were John William Dunscombe of Montreal and Joseph Leaycraft of Quebec, was bankrupt in the early forties with debts of £61,250. Nevertheless, Dunscombe was still in business as a general merchant in 1845. *Montreal Directory* (1845-6), 69. Likewise, George Rhynas, bankrupt at the same times, was still in business in 1845. Ibid., 177. For comments by a contemporary. Emery Papineau, on the extent of bankruptcies in Montreal, see Ouellet, *Histoire Économique,* 492-4.
41 JLA (1849), App. B
42 Lindsay, *Merchant Shipping,* II, 261 n; Dent, *Portrait Gallery,* II, 38-9
43 In his reminiscences, contained in a speech to the Young Men's Association of Montreal's St Andrews Church in February 1880 (Montreal *Gazette,* 7, 14, 21, 28 Feb. and 7 Mar. 1953), Allan recalled that his employment with the Millar firm was just an accident. However, the fact that Millar had an extensive shipping business in Montreal and was known to the Allans, suggests that Hugh's employment with James Millar had been prearranged.
44 Professor Fred Armstrong, Letter (xerox copy) from George Burns Symes, Quebec, to Millar, Edmonstone and Allan, Montreal, 10 Oct. 1843
45 Ship Registers, 175 / 20, 29, 36, 42, 64, 69, 81, 82.
46 Montreal *Gazette,* 1845, passim; *Morning Courier,* 1849, passim
47 Montreal Board of Trade, *Fiftieth Anniversary Volume,* 92
48 Armstrong, Letter (xerox copy) from Wills, Laird and Company, Glasgow, to Millar, Edmonstone and Allan, Montreal, 8 Sept. 1840; Barber and Norris to same, 18 Sept. 1841
49 Ibid., William Rae, London, CW, to Edmonstone, Allan and Co., 13 Feb. 1852
50 Montreal Board of Trade, *Fiftieth Anniversary Volume,* 92
51 *Montreal Brokers' Circular,* 17 May 1851
52 Montreal Board of Harbour Commissioners, *Improvement of the Ship Channel* 31-51
53 Ibid., 28
54 Ibid., 33
55 *Canadian Economist,* 16 May 1846, quoted in Innis and Lower, *Select Documents,* 188-9
56 Montreal Board of Harbour Commissioners, *Improvement of the Ship Channel,* 181
57 The Montreal harbour commissioners were concerned with the management of the port, which was defined in 45 Geo. III, c. 12, of the *Statutes of the Province of Lower Canada.* See also St Lawrence Municipal Bureau (Montreal), comp., 'The Harbour of Montreal.' The Montreal Trinity Board, on the other hand, had responsibility for lighthouses, beacons, and buoys in the St Lawrence between Montreal and Quebec. J.E. Hodgetts, *Pioneer Public Service,* 180

58 Wallace, *Dictionary,* 613 Turcotte, *Le Conseil Législatif, 137*
59 Ibid.; APQ, S Baldwin Papers, Boîte III
60 Prov. Sec. Corres., 151 (1846), 1037
61 Dorwin, 'Antiquarian Autographs,' 41; "Origins of the Montreal Board of Trade,' 28-9; *Montreal Almanack* (1839)
62 CBD, 172-3; He had married Margaret Hutchinson, widow of a wealthy grocer who died in 1817 or 1818: Dorwin, 'Antiquarian Autographs,' no number
63 Denison, *Bank of Montreal,* II, 421; *Montreal Directory* (1848); *Stats. Prov. Can.* (1847), 10 & 11 Vic., c. 79; Prov. Sec. Corres. (1845), 120-119; Terrill, *Chronology,* 117. A prominent Methodist, Lunn took great interest in elementary education: Lovell, *Reminiscences,* 15
64 National Harbours Board, Montreal, Harbour Commissioners Letter Books; *Stats. Prov. Can.* (1844), 8 Vic., c. 76
65 Montreal *Gazette,* 13 May 1881; Campbell, *Scotch Presbyterian,* 255; *Morning Courier,* 27 Oct. 1849. See also Dorwin, 'Antiquarian Autographs,' 249; Terrill, *Chronology,* 108
66 'Origins of the Montreal Board of Trade,' 28-29; *Montreal Directory* (1848); Denison, *Bank of Montreal,* II, 421; Lamothe, *Corporation de Montréal,* 204. He made one of the largest Montreal donations in 1840 to the Presbyterian College (later Queen's) which was soon to be established in Kingston: *Montreal Transcript,* 15 Feb. 1840
67 Denison, *Bank of Montreal,* II, 421; McGill University, European and American Manuscripts, CH 323, S 283, Montreal: Sale of Property, 1851
68 Turcotte, *Conseil Législatif,* 239; Frederick H. Armstrong, 'Charles-Séraphim Rodier,' *Dictionary of Canadian Biography,* X, 624-5; Wallace, *Dictionary,* 642
69 Lamothe, *Corporation de Montréal,* 200-204
70 Turcotte, *Conseil Législatif,* 239
71 *Stats. Prov. Can.* (1851), 13 & 14 Vic., c. 97
72 Dent, *Portrait Gallery,* III, 195. There are a number of useful biographical sketches of John Young in the several late nineteenth-century compendia of eulogies of important Canadians. Although none of his business records for this period have survived, some letters and a considerable collection of his published writings were discovered in 1969 in Montreal by Professor Brian Young of the University of Vermont. This material was deposited in the Queen's University archives. See G. Tulchinsky and B. Young, 'John Young,' *Dictionary of Canadian Biography,* X, 722-8
73 CBD, 347
74 Joseph Knapp might well have been a Chicago merchant, considering Young's trade to that city. In any case, he was a new or temporary resident of Montreal in 1852, and was listed in MacKay's directory as a general merchant who boarded at St Lawrence Hall, a local hotel: *Montreal Directory* (1852), 130
75 *Morning Courier,* 7 Jan. 1850; *Elgin-Grey Papers,* I, 367
76 McLeod, 'Montreal and Free Trade.' Young demonstrated the disabilities of the navigation laws by pointing out that his attempt to import three shiploads of sugar and molasses from Cuba to Montreal was hampered by the fact that no British ship could be found to load for Montreal and that the existence of the navigation laws prevented him from sending an order of fifty tons of pig iron to Chicago. *Morning Courier,* 18 May 1849
77 Montreal Board of Harbour Commissioners, *Improvement of the Ship Channel,* xii and xiii
78 See John Young, *Letters to the Hon. Francis Lemieux*
79 Harbour Commissioners, *Improvement of Ship Channel,* 198
80 Ibid., 208
81 JLA (1855), App. GG. Return to an Address from the Legislative Assembly on the 22nd instant, for copy of certain correspondence relative to Montreal Harbour

SIX / THE ADVENT OF OCEAN STEAMSHIPPING

1 Smith, 'The Post Office,' 365.
2 Lindsay, *Merchant Shipping,* II, 259; Taylor, 'Canada's Merchant Marine,' 26
3 Montreal *Gazette,* 13 May, 30 June 1845
4 The first two Allan steamships cost $250,000 each; Fry, *Steam Navigation,* 140. The large Montreal-Quebec and Richelieu River steamboats built in the mid-forties cost about $20,000 each; Richelieu Minutes, 1845-8
5 *American Railroad Journal,* 30 Nov. 1850, 759
6 Ibid.
7 Prov. Sec. Corres., see 1841-1850 registers of numerous petitions.
8 Montreal *Gazette,* 4 Sept. 1851
9 Tucker, *Commercial Revolution,* chap. 8
10 Côté, *Political Appointments,* 9. Young retained the post from 28 Oct. 1851 to 22 Sept. 1852, nearly eleven months, the normal tenure of holders of that office, since it was created in 1846.
11 Young, *Origin*
12 Montreal *Gazette,* 22 Sept. 1851
13 Queen's University Archives, Young Papers. In a letter to Young on 26 Feb. 1852, Thomas Ryan reported Cunard's terms, which stipulated a subsidy of £10,000 for ten years.
14 Young, *Origin,* 8
15 JLA. (1852-3), App. Q, Report of the Commissioners of Public Works for 1851. See also *Stats. Prov. Can.* (1852), 16 Vic., c. 9, which enabled the government to pay up to £19,000 subsidy annually for seven years.
16 Alexander Allan died in Greenock at age 73; Montreal *Gazette,* 7 Apr. 1854
17 Dow Brewery Limited, Montreal, Archives. Edmonstone, Allan & Company to William Dow, 8 Nov. 1854
18 Fry, *Steam Navigation,* 140
19 *Stats. Prov. Can.* (1854), 18 Vic., c. 131
20 Edmonstone to Dow, 8 Nov. 1854, List of shareholders
21 Campbell, *Scotch Presbyterian,* 565
22 Ship Registers, 175 / 176, 177, 178
23 Young *Origin,* 10-11
24 Young Papers, John Young to D. Bellhouse, 17 July 1852
25 Keefer, 'Travel and Transportation,' 142.
26 Ibid.
27 Campbell, *Scotch Presbyterian,* 381; McCord Museum, Dorwin, 'Antiquarian Autographs,' 231
28 *Stats. Prov. Can.* (1853), 16 Vic., c. 131
29 Also in the London group were Thomas Holdsworth Brooking, Robert Carter, and Mathew Hutton Clayton; *Stats. Prov. Can.* (1853), 16 Vic., c. 131
30 Williams, 'Merchanting,' 121
31 ASCM, Gibb Papers, 26 Aug. 1842, 5605
32 *125th Anniversary Volume,* n.p.
33 Lamont, *Statement,* (n.p., n.d.) 3; *Return to an Address, 3*
34 Young, *Origin,* 10; Lamont, *Statement,* 3, 4; *Return to an Address,* 4.
35 *Return to an Address,* 5
36 Young, *Origin,* 8-9
37 *Return to an Address,* 5; Atherton, *Montreal,* II, 578
38 Lamont, *Statement,* 4-6
39 Campbell, *Scotch Presbyterian,* 381
40 *Return to an Address,* 6, 8
41 Montreal *Gazette,* 6 April 1853

42 *Return to an Address,* 17-18
43 Ibid.
44 Young, *Origin,* 24
45 *Return to an Address,* 13, 15
46 Young, *Origin,* 23, 30
47 Lamont, *Statement; Return to an Address,* 39
48 Keefer, 'Travel and Transportation,' 143
49 Ibid. See Patton, 'Shipping and Canals,' 602-8
50 *Stats. Prov. Can.* (1854), 18 Vic., c. 45
51 JLA (1849), App. B
52 JLC (1853), App. 000
53 From available official statistics in publications of the Province of Canada no aggregate figures of shipping between Montreal and the Maritimes or lower ports could be found. *The Tables of Trade and Navigation of the Province of Canada* between 1851 and 1858 annually provided figures for shipping between Montreal (Quebec also) and 'British Colonies.' The pamphlet *Statements concerning Trade and Commerce,* 15, provides statistics of ships and tonnage (displacement) from 'Lower Ports' to Montreal between 1854 and 1862. These two sets of figures were compared for the year 1854 in order to secure an approximation of the proportion that 'lower port' shipping was of the total to Montreal from British colonies. The following are, therefore, only estimates for the years 1850 through 1853, while the figures for 1854 through 1856 are from the same source.

1850	70 ships	5980 tons
1851	69 ships	5970 tons
1852	63 ships	5800 tons
1853	82 ships	7210 tons
1854	78 ships	6949 tons
1855	107 ships	9721 tons
1856	114 ships	9548 tons

54 JLC (1854), App. 000
55 PAC, Dorwin Diaries, 100-47
56 See *Montreal Directory* (1844-5), 183; (1852) 240; *Montreal Transcript,* 21 April 1838
57 Ship Registers, 175-101, 162
58 Montreal *Gazette,* 29 Jan. 1847; *Montreal Directory* (1852), 240
59 *Pilot,* 26 April, 10, 14, 20, 25 and 26 May, 1853
60 See Borthwick, *Montreal,* 123; Smyth, *City and District,* 22; Campbell, *Scotch Presbyterian,* 436, 439. Information on some of William Workman's real estate holdings in Montreal was supplied in a letter to the author by Mr A. Podbere, 13 May 1969.
61 Ship Registers, 174 / 147. See *Montreal Directory* (1844), (1853). He was listed as a grocer in 1844 and a general merchant in 1853.
62 *The Ogilvies of Montreal,* 11
63 *Montreal Directory* (1844), 142; (1852), 165, 187
64 Ibid., 61
65 Ibid., 121
66 Ibid., 205, 211, 365. *Dictionary of Canadian Biography,* Preliminary List, Lower Canada Businessmen, 1850-1900. Renaud was a member of the Legislative Council for De Salaberry from 1856 to 1867, and a senator from 1867 to 1873; Johnson, ed., *Directory of Parliament,* 487. During the sixties Renaud became one of Montreal's most successful grain exporters. Benoist, *Monographies,* 161-3
67 *Montreal Directory* (1852), 222. Scott was prosperous enough as early as 1840 to be able to make a gift of £75, one of the largest donations of any from Montreal, to the new Presbyterian College soon to be established in Kingston, *Montreal Transcript,* 15 Feb. 1840. See Campbell, *Scotch Presbyterian,* 432; Dorwin, 'Antiquarian Autographs,' 718; *Montreal Directory* (1852), 49, 277; Chapman was also an early minor benefactor of McGill

University. See McGill University Archives, Henry Chapman File. Dorwin, 'Antiquarian Autographs,' 219½; *Montreal Directory* (1852), 126. Kay was president of the Montreal Board of Trade in 1859, John Smith a very successful merchant, Dorwin, 'Antiquarian Autographs,' 231; Campbell, *Scotch Presbyterian,* 381; Robert Esdaile was later a founder of the Montreal Corn Exchange; Campbell, ibid., 496-7

68 *Statements Concerning Trade and Commerce,* 15
69 PAC, Buchanan Papers, 28, 23575, A. Gillespie (Liverpool) to Isaac Buchanan, 5 Sept. 1863

SEVEN / THE CHAMPLAIN AND ST LAWRENCE

1 Wilgus, *Railway Interrelations,* 49; Montreal *Gazette,* 10 Sept. 1835, quoted in Innis and Lower, *Select Documents,* 202; Brown, 'The Champlain and St Lawrence Railroad,' 14
2 Brown, 'The Champlain and St Lawrence Railroad,' 14
3 Sandwell, *The Molson Family,* 104; see *Montreal Directory,* 1842-54, passim
4 Montreal *Gazette,* 3 Jan. 1831
5 Montreal *Gazette,* 27 Feb. 1865
6 Wallace, *Dictionary,* 518
7 Campbell, *Scotch Presbyterian,* 382; Montreal *Gazette,* 27 Feb. 1865
8 'Origins of the Montreal Board of Trade,' 27
9 *Montreal Almanack* (1829)
10 Ship Registers, 176 / 14; National Harbours Board, Montreal, Trinity Letter Books, 156, B. Holmes to J. Joseph, 14 Feb. 1848; Trinity Minute Books (1839-47), 319-21. See also *Canada Gazette,* 8 Nov. 1845, 2227, and Prov. Sec. Corres., Register of Petitions for 1847.
11 Audet, *Députés,* 243
12 See Shortt, 'Horatio Gates,' 35; Dorwin, 'Antiquarian Autographs,' no number
13 PAC, MG 24, D26, 51;
14 McGill University, European and American Manuscripts, ch. 334. s. 94. Estate of Horatio Gates and Company, 15 Feb. 1836
15 Denison, *Bank of Montreal,* I, 13; 'Origins Montreal Board of Trade,' 27
16 Wallace, *Dictionary,* 260
17 Ibid., 390-1
18 Ibid., 641; European and American Manuscripts., c. 353, s. 313, 'List of partners in Larocque, Bernard and Company.'
19 Campbell, *Scotch Presbyterian,* 388; Denison, *Bank of Montreal,* II, 421
20 *Statutes of Lower Canada* (1832), 2 Wm IV, c. 58
21 Prov. Sec. Corres., Register for 1846
22 Dorwin, 'Antiquarian Autographs,' 657 verso, 56, 911; *Montreal Almanack* (1829)
23 'Origins Montreal Board of Trade,' 27; *La Presse,* 11 Nov. 1933; Denison, *Bank of Montreal,* II, 421.
24 *Montreal Transcript,* 28 Nov. 1837; Dorwin, 'Antiquarian Autographs,' 668; ASCM, Henry Griffin Papers, 29 Feb. 1840, 16892
25 Denison, *Bank of Montreal,* I, passim
27 Faced with early uncertainty about the future of a railway venture, Montreal businessmen were not unusual in their reluctance to invest more than just a barely 'respectable' sum. See Johnson and Supple, *Boston Capitalists and Western Railroads,* 40-1, 41n.
28 Brown, 'Champlain and St Lawrence,' 14
29 Province of Canada, *Committee on Railroads, 1851,* 282-4
30 Ibid.
31 Skelton, *The Railway Builders,* 37
32 PAC, Baring Papers, I, 493
33 Lower, *Assault,* 97n.
34 Canadian National Railway Headquarters Library, Lindsay letters, 21

35 Baring Papers, I, 493. Brown's figures in 'Champlain and St Lawrence,' 35, are erroneous. He made the error of taking the percentage of dividend as the dividend itself. This resulted in his exaggerating the dividend by 100 per cent or more.
36 Lindsay letters, 1845-9, passim
37 Ship Registers, 176-17, 74; Lindsay letters, 1845-7
38 Montreal *Gazette*, 1844-5
39 See National Harbours Board, Montreal, Trinity Letter Books (1839-47), 425-32; Trinity Minute Books, (1839-1847), 333-5.
40 Kirkland, *Men, Cities and Transportation*, I, 160, 166
41 *Committee on Railroads, 1851*, 282; *Montreal Directory* (1840-4), passim
42 Wallace, *Dictionary*, 254
43 *Montreal Directory* (1844-5), 27
44 Smyth, *City and District*, 63; *Stats. Prov. Can.* (1853), 16 Vic. c. 103
45 *Montreal Directory* (1852), 352; *Committee on Railroads, 1851*, 284; *Stats. Prov. Can.* (1853), 16 Vic. c. 103
46 Dorwin, 'Antiquarian Autographs,' 747; PAC, Ruggles Wright Papers, 1840-2, passim; *Montreal Directory* (1847-8), 266; (1852), 353; Smyth, *City and District*, 14-15; *Committee on Railroads, 1851*, 282
47 Morton, *Sir George Simpson;* 266
48 Montreal *Gazette*, 17 April, 7 May, 26 June 1845
49 Prov. Sec. Corres., 150 (1846), 913
50 Bishop, *Publications*, 323
51 Metcalfe, 'William Henry Draper,' 159; Prov. Sec. Corres., (1846), 1704
52 Ibid. (1847), 1731
53 *Stats. Prov. Can.* (1847), 10 & 11 Vic., c. 121
54 Walker, *Daylight Through the Mountain*, chap. 6; Kirkland, *Men, Cities, and Transportation*, I, 173
55 Prov. Sec. Corres., 246 (1849), 332; *Stats. Prov. Can.* (1849), 12 Vic., c. 179
56 Prov. Sec. Corres., 277 (1850), 1185, 1347; JLA (1850), 59, 89
57 *Stats. Prov. Can.* (1850), 13 & 14 Vic., c. 114
58 Montreal *Gazette*, 12 Aug. 1850
59 Ibid., 22 Jan. 1851
60 Ibid., 13 Aug. 1850
61 *Observations on the Question of Bridging the River Richelieu; Statement of Facts Laid before Sir Allan N. MacNab*, 13-28
62 *Committee on Railroads, 1851*, 140
63 Ibid., 141
64 Baring Papers, I, 493
65 Tucker, *Canadian Commercial Revolution*, 235
66 *Observations on the Question of Bridging the River Richelieu*
67 Kirkland, *Men, Cities and Transportation*, I, 169-70, 174; Champlain and St Lawrence Railroad Company, *Annual Report*, 19 Jan. 1852, 24.
68 Vermont House of Representatives, *Journal* (1849), 349-54
69 Champlain and St Lawrence, *Annual Report*, 6.
70 Brown, 'Champlain and St Lawrence,' 40; Denison, *Bank of Montreal*, I, 72
71 *Committee on Railroads, 1851*, 282-4
72 Champlain and St Lawrence, *Annual Report*, 22
73 *Tabular Representation*
74 *The Railroad Jubilee*
75 Montreal *Gazette*, 15 Aug. 1851
76 *Elgin-Grey Papers*, II, 892, 895
77 Montreal *Gazette*, 6, 24 Oct. 1851

78 Champlain and St Lawrence, *Annual Report*
79 Montreal *Gazette,* 19 Jan. 1853
80 *Stats. Prov. Can.* (1852-3), 16 Vic., c. 78
81 Brown, 'Champlain and St Lawrence,' 45
82 CR, 104
83 *Stats. Prov. Can.* (1855), 18 Vic., c. 177
84 Stevens, *Canadian National Railways,* I, 33

EIGHT / THE ST LAWRENCE AND ATLANTIC: FIRST STAGE

1 See Montreal *Gazette,* 10 Mar. 1836, quoted in Innis and Lower, *Select Documents,* 203-4
2 Skelton, *Galt,* 18
3 See Taylor, *Journal,* 51-2
4 Lower Canada, *Ordinances* (1841), 4 Vic., c. 10; *Stats. Prov. Can.* (1841), 5 Vic., c. 47
5 Wilgus, *Railway Interrelations,* 57
6 See Kirkland, *Men, Cities and Transportation,* I, chap. 1.
7 Ibid., chap. 7; Chandler, *Henry Varnum Poor,* 13; Poor, *International Railway,* 31
8 Reprinted in *International Railway,* 142-53
9 Prov. Sec. Corres., 117 (1844), 3933 (No. 3760 included)
10 Ibid., 114, 3511.
11 Montreal *Gazette,* 18 Jan. 1845
12 Ibid., 11 Feb. 1845
13 Ibid., 25 Feb. 1845
14 Prov. Sec. Corres., 114 (1844), 659 of 1845
15 Montreal *Gazette,* 18 Mar. 1845
16 Poor, *International Railway,* 34-41
17 Montreal *Gazette,* 8 Mar. 1845
18 Ibid., 11 Mar. 1845
19 *Stats. Prov. Can.* (1845), 8 Vic., c. 25
20 Montreal *Gazette,* 11 Mar. 1845
21 McCord Museum, Dorwin, 'Antiquarian Autographs,' 155, 671
22 'Biography of the Late Harrison Stephens,' 5
23 Dorwin, 'Antiquarian Autographs,' 103
24 CBD, 347
25 John Shuter was Peter McGill's father-in-law; Campbell, *Scotch Presbyterian,* 383-4.
   Little is known of his business activities, although Dorwin claimed that he 'made a fortune'
   during the war of 1812; he subsequently retired to England, and on his death in 1847 left
   a substantial estate in Canada. Dorwin, 'Antiquarian Autographs,' no number; ASCM,
   Gibb Papers, 5 Nov. 1847, 10134
26 *Montreal Transcript,* 28 Nov. 1837; *Montreal Directory* (1845-6), 250
27 Denison, *Bank of Montreal,* II, 419
28 Prov. Sec. Corres., 114 (1844), 659 of 1845
29 J.T. Brondgeest, interestingly, was a businessman *cum* intellectual. He was president of the
   Montreal Board of Trade between 1841 and 1843; and before moving to Hamilton sometime
   between 1845 and 1847 he made several contributions to geological studies of Montreal.
   Morgan, *Bibliotheca Canadensis,* 50
30 Prov. Sec. Corres., 114 (1844), 659 of 1845
31 Ibid., 124 (1845), 859
32 See Morison, *Massachusetts,* chap. 15
33 PAC, Canadian National Railways, 146
34 Montreal *Gazette,* 18 Mar. 1845
35 Ibid., 25 Mar. 1845
36 *Stats. Prov. Can.* (1844), 8 Vic., c. 25

37 Montreal *Gazette,* 26 June 1845
38 Ibid., 12 April 1845
39 Ibid., 12, 28 May 1845
40 Ibid., 14 June 1845
41 Denison, *Bank of Montreal,* I, 401
42 CNR, 146
43 Ibid.
44 Skelton, *Galt,* 20; PAC, William Hamilton Merritt Papers, 19, Moffatt to Merritt, 11 June 1845
45 Montreal *Gazette,* 14 June 1845
46 Ibid., 6 Aug. 1845
47 CNR, 146
48 Montreal *Gazette,* 9 Aug. 1845
49 Skelton, *Galt,* 22
50 *Proceedings,* 4
51 Chandler, *Henry Varnum Poor,* 16-17
52 Skelton, *Galt,* 22
53 Morton, *Report,* 69-79. See also Gravel, 'Un Accord Historique,' for a restatement of this agreement.
54 The adoption of the wide gauge by the St Lawrence and Atlantic in 1847 was a major reason for the decision in 1851 to build the Grand Trunk railway on the same gauge: Currie, *Grand Trunk,* 57.
55 *Proceedings* (1846), 5
56 Ibid.
57 Ibid., 7
58 CNR, 148-55
59 Ibid., 151
60 *Montreal Transcript,* 4 Aug. 1846, quoted in Innis and Lower, *Select Documents,* 207
61 CNR, 149, 150
62 Montreal *Gazette,* 16 Jan. 1845
63 CNR, 148
64 CR, 827; Smyth, *City and District,* 14-15
65 CNR, 151, 152, 154
66 Campbell, *Scotch Presbyterian,* 432
67 *Montreal Directory* (1840-49), under 'Bank of Montreal'; *Lower Canada Almanack,* 138
68 CNR, 153
69 Rose, *Cyclopaedia,* 764
70 See McLellan, ed., *Journal of Thomay Nye.*
71 CNR, 155
72 Ibid., 153
73 Montreal *Gazette,* 24 Aug. 1846
74 The Bank of Montreal Directors' minutes for this period do not tell whose notes presented for discount were accepted. Loans extended were likewise unspecified. The City Bank records apparently are not extant.

NINE / THE COMPLETION OF THE ST LAWRENCE AND ATLANTIC

1 Skelton, *Galt,* 25
2 PAC, *Committee on Railroads,* (1851), App. B, 258
3 *Montreal Directory* (1852), 352; (1853), 391
4 Ibid., App. E, 282.
5 *Morning Courier,* 25 July 1849; Atherton, *Montreal,* II, 594
6 Smith, *Post Office,* 153 ff; McCord Museum, Dorwin, 'Antiquarian Autographs,' 670

7 Wallace, *Dictionary,* 527
8 Audet, *Députés,* 246
9 Denison, *Bank of Montreal,* I, passim; *Montreal Courier,* 13 Mar. 1849
10 Shortt, 'Currency and Banking,' 133
11 Smyth, *City and District,* 165; Cooper, 'Savings Banks,' 141
12 Prince, *Montreal,* 92; *Histoire de la Brasserie Dow*
13 *Committee on Railroads, 1851,* 249; *Morning Courier,* 24 Feb. 1849; Prov. Sec. Corres., 178 (1846), 3363; *Montreal Directory* (1847-1848), 261, 267; Prince, *Montreal,* 92
14 *Committee on Railroads, 1851,* 263
   Montreal *Gazette,* 7 May 1877
   Turcotte, *Conseil Législatif,* 153
15 *Committee on Railroads, 1851,* 248
16 Ibid., 263
17 Smyth, *City and District,* 33-4; Wallace, *Dictionary,* 390-1; CR, 812; Terrill, *Chronology,* 116; PAC, Ship Registers, 175
18 McGill University, European and American Manuscripts, CH 353, S 313, William Lyman and Company, Insurance and Financial Papers, 1835-1856, 'List of partners in Larocque Bernard and Company'
19 *Proceedings,* (1848)
20 Montreal *Gazette,* 11 Jan. 1847
21 Skelton, *Galt,* 24
22 Galt, *A Letter*
23 Proceedings, (1848), 5; Skelton, *Galt,* 23
24 *The Economist* (1847), passim
25 Prov. Sec. Corres., 114 (1844), 3511
26 Ibid. See Register of petitions 1845, 659, 859
27 Ibid., 195 (1847), 1999; 218 (1848), 874; 232, 2547
28 Stover, *American Railroads,* 24
29 Kirkland, *Men, Cities, and Transportation,* I, 210; Chandler, *Henry Varnum Poor,* 14
30 Morton, *Report,* 69-79
31 Canadian National Railways, Headquarters Library and Archives, Montreal. Notes on *Proceedings of the Annual General Meeting of the Proprietors of the St Lawrence and Atlantic Railroad,* passim
32 Prov. Sec. Corres., 198 (1847), 2225
33 Morton, *Gauge,* 69-79
34 Prov. Sec. Corres., 198 (1847), 2225
35 Montreal *Gazette,* 22 Sept. 1847
36 *Stats. Prov. Can.* (1847), 10 & 11 Vic., c. 65
37 Prov. Sec. Corres., 218 (1847), 3555
38 Montreal *Gazette,* 9 Oct. 1847
39 *Committee on Railroads, 1851,* 256
40 Careless, *Union of the Canadas,* 117.
41 Montreal *Gazette,* 22 Sept. 1847
42 *Proceedings,* (1849), 6. See also Montreal *Gazette,* 29 Dec. 1848; 18 Jan. 1849.
43 Ibid., 12 Feb. 1849. See also Choquette, *Saint-Hyacinthe,* 170-8
44 Montreal *Gazette,* 17 Oct. 1851; 14 Sept. 1852
45 Ibid., 9 Feb. 1849
46 JLA (1849), App. HH; Proceedings, (1849), 13
47 Prov. Sec. Corres., 249 (1849), 666
48 Montreal *Gazette,* 5 Jan. 1849
49 *Morning Courier,* 8 May 1849
50 Keefer, *Philosophy of Railroads,* 4
51 Montreal *Gazette,* 21 Feb., 13 April 1849

52 *Stats. Prov. Can.,* (1849), 12 Vic., c. 29
53 *Stats. Prov. Can.* (1849), 12 Vic., c. 176
54 *Montreal Directory* (1852), 333-4; *Committee on Railroads, 1851,* passim. Indeed, many of the members of the City Council in the late forties were shareholders in the St Lawrence and Atlantic at one time or another. For example, of the 1852 Council, the mayor, Charles Wilson, held six shares. From the East Ward, alderman F. Leclaire held ten shares and councillor Joseph Tiffin twelve. From St Mary's Ward, councillor Austin Adams held six shares; from Centre Ward, councillor Thomas Mussen held six; from St Louis Ward, alderman J. Grenier held six and L. Marchard two; from West Ward, alderman H.H. Whitney held four; from St Anne's Ward, councillor N.B. Corse held four; from St Antoine Ward, alderman O. Frechette held ten; St Lawrence Ward alderman J. Whitlaw held two and councillor R. Campbell held two.
55 *Morning Courier,* 25 July 1849
56 Ibid.
57 Ibid., 28 July, 2 Aug. 1849
58 Ibid., 2 Aug. 1849
59 ASCM Gibb Papers, 18 Feb. 1847, 9518; H. Griffin Papers, 27 Nov. 1839, 16771, 'Last Will and Testament of Benaiah Gibb'; *Committee on Railroads, 1851,* 251
60 CNR, 146-55, subscription, passim
61 *Committee on Railroads, 1851*
62 Massicotte, 'Antoine-Olivier Berthelet.' His father, Pierre Berthelet, had more than three hundred stoves for hire to Montrealers; Cooper, *Montreal,* 62
63 Turcotte, *Conseil Législatif,* 131
64 The city issued £125,000 worth of bonds (to be redeemed within fifteen years) which were exchanged for 5,000 preferred shares, Skelton, *Galt,* 25. The company realized only £102,739/14/6 from this transaction. Glazebrook, *Transportation,* I, 156
65 Montreal *Gazette,* 21 Jan. 1850. In 1857, Galt stated to a special committee of the Legislative Assembly that £20,547/18/11 was raised by the Company from the Seminary; yet the Seminary does not appear in the list of shareholders of the St Lawrence and Atlantic Railway of 1851.
66 Montreal *Gazette,* 21 Jan. 1850
67 *Committee on Railroads, 1851,* 17-18
68 Montreal *Gazette,* 28 Jan. 1850; 31 Jan. 1851
69 *Committee on Railroads, 1851,* 18
70 Stevens, *Canadian National,* I, 62
71 JLC (1853), App. VVV
72 *Committee on Railroads, 1851,* 18; Skelton, *Galt,* 26
73 Barings and Glyn, Mills and Company each purchased £50,000 at par and sold the remaining bonds at a premium which went as high as 4 and 5 per cent. The St Lawrence and Atlantic paid them a commission of 2 per cent. See PAC, Baring Papers, I, passim; F. Hincks to Thomas Baring, 25 April 1851.
74 Montreal *Gazette,* 23 Jan. 1852. See also Baring Papers, I, A.T. Galt to John Young, 18 April 1851.
75 Montreal *Gazette,* 21 Jan. 1850. The company accounts of 1849 showed £404, 7, 8 and £325, 6, 0 paid to Thomas Cringan and Theodore Hart, respectively, for 'agency' charges.
76 *Committee on Railroads, 1851,* 19; Montreal *Gazette,* 17 Oct. 1851; *Stats. Prov. Can.* (1850), 13 & 14 Vic., c. 116
77 Montreal *Gazette,* 27 Sept. 1836; Trout and Trout, *The Railways of Canada,* 52
78 See Crocker *Report;* Montreal *Gazette,* 21 Oct. 1851.
79 St Lawrence and Atlantic Railroad Company, *Memorandum;* Poor, *First International Railway,* 152
80 St Lawrence and Atlantic, *Memorandum,* 7-9
81 Montreal *Gazette,* April to August 1854, passim

82 JLA (1854), App. FF
83 An American group which began lumbering operations in 1853 near Sherbrooke shipped a large quantity of lumber to Portland over the railway. Parker, 'Staple Industries,' 83
84 Montreal *Gazette,* 31 Jan. 1851
85 See Albion, 'New York Port,' 602-9
86 JLA (1857), App. 6
87 Galt, who was so closely connected with the company from the beginning, appears to have derived a major portion of his financial rewards from the project from the salary attached to the office of president: PAC, Galt Papers, VII, A.T. Galt to Amy Torrance, 18 July 1853
88 *Committee on Railroads, 1851*, 244-65

TEN / WESTERN RAILWAY PROJECTS

1 Lower Canada, *Ordinances of the Special Council* (1840), 4 Vic., c. 41. The ordinance was affirmed in a slightly amended form by a statute of the Province of Canada in 1841. *Stats. Prov. Can.* (1841), 5 Vic., c. 49
2 Dent, *Portrait Gallery,* IV, 93
3 McCord Museum, Dorwin, 'Antiquarian Autographs,' no. 832; CBD, 245; Turcotte, *Conseil Législatif,* 291. See also Lamothe, *Corporation de Montréal,* 205
4 Penington, *Railways and Other Ways,* 150; Ferrier was a pillar of strength to McGill University during its early years. See Taylor and Notman, *British Americans,* I, 165.
5 Prov. Sec. Corres., 149 (1846), 858
6 *Stats. Prov. Can.* (1846), 9 Vic., c. 82. Several amendments were made in 1847; ibid. (1847), 10 & 11 Vic., c. 63.
7 CNR, 274
8 ASCM, Griffin Papers, 29 Feb. 1840, 16892
9 CR, 663; MacKay, *Montreal Directory* (1845-6), 279
10 Montreal *Gazette,* 13 May 1881
11 See *Montreal Directory* (1842-3), (1843-4), (1848); *Morning Courier,* 12 April 1849.
12 See Sack, *Jews in Canada,* 125; *Montreal Directory* (1845-6), 96.
13 Like the Champlain and St Lawrence, the Montreal and Lachine was built on the standard 4' 8½" gauge so that rolling stock from other lines could be accommodated. Though the St Lawrence and Atlantic by 1847 had opted for the wider 5' 6" gauge, its track was not yet laid, and it was possible the decision would be reversed.
14 Brown, 'Montreal saw its first train 100 years ago,' 9, 12.
15 For a small piece of land in Ville St Pierre, owner J.B. St Denis was paid £30: ASCM, Gibb Papers, 12 Mar. 1847, 9595
16 Prov. Sec. Corres., 216 (1848), 593
17 Ibid., 231 (1848), 2064
18 McLean, 'An early chapter,' 345. See also JLA (1847), 270
19 Prov. Sec. Corres., 243 (1849), 189; *Stats. Prov. Can.* (1849), 12 Vic., c. 177
20 Prov. Sec. Corres., 277 (1850), 1179
21 JLA (1849), App. S
22 See Ouellet, *Histoire Économique,* chap. 12
23 Careless, *Union,* 28
24 See Kirkland, *Men, Cities and Transportation,* I, chap. 6
25 Keefer, *Philosophy of Railroads,* 8-9
26 Rankin, *Our Firm,* 107; Lower, *Assault,* 96
27 *Stats. Prov. Can.* (1848), 10 & 11 Vic., c. 119
28 Prov. Sec. Corres., 246 (1849), 356
29 Ibid., 280 (1850), 1457
30 Brault, *Histoire des Comtés Unis,* 98
31 *Stats. Prov. Can.* (1850), 13 & 14 Vic., c. 113

32 John Young in the late forties put forward proposals to bridge the river from the port of Montreal to Longueuil: Keefer, *Report,* 1

33 In his *History of Canadian Wealth,* 165, Gustavus Myers advanced these reasons for the acquisition of many railway charters in Canada during the time of the 'inception of railroad power.'

34 *Report of the Committee on the Montreal and Kingston Section of the Canada Grand Trunk Railway* (n.d.), 9-14

35 *Committee on Railroads, 1851,* 121-4

36 Montreal *Gazette,* 6 Jan. 1851

37 Ibid., 8, 20 Jan. 1851

38 *Report of the Directors and Chief Engineer of the St Lawrence and Ottawa Grand Junction Railway Company,* 5

39 Montreal *Gazette,* 2 Mar. 1853

40 Ibid., 2 Feb. 1852

41 *Stats. Prov. Can.* (1853), 16 Vic., c. 103

42 In a letter to the *Gazette,* 2 Mar. 1853, William Workman vaguely hinted at another Atlantic outlet.

43 Jacques Monet, 'Alexandre-Maurice Delisle,' *Dictionary of Canadian Biography,* X, (Toronto, 1972), 219-20

44 G. Tulchinsky, 'William Workman,' *Dictionary of Canadian Biography,* X (Toronto, 1972), 717-18

45 CR, Mittleberger Papers, 4 Dec. 1830; *Montreal Directory* (1845-6), 65; *A Topographical Map*

46 *Montreal Directory* (1845-6), 61

47 Ship Registers, 175-140, 176-109; *Report ... Loranger,* 63

48 *Morning Courier,* 1 Feb. 1850

49 Smyth, *City and District,* 14-15; *Montreal Directory* (1844-5); *Committee on Railroads, 1851,* 244-65

50 Turcotte, *Conseil Législatif,* 172; *Morning Courier,* 21 Nov. 1849; Goad, *Atlas;* CBD, 78

51 Audet, '1842,' 236; Turcotte, *Conseil Législatif,* 149-50; Smyth, *City and District,* 14-15

52 *Report ... Loranger*

53 JLA (1841), App. C; *Montreal Almanack* (1839); *Lower Canada Almanack* (1840) 130; *Montreal Directory* (1842-3), 152

54 Ibid., (1844-5), 206; Smyth, *City and District,* 14-15

55 *Stats. Prov. Can.* (1853), 16 Vic., c. 103

56 Goad, *Atlas*

57 *La Minerve,* 6 Aug. 1853

58 Ibid., 9 June 1853

59 Ibid., 9 Aug. 1853

60 Reprinted in the Montreal *Gazette,* 2 Feb. 1853

61 Reprinted in ibid., 23 Feb. 1853

62 Ibid.

63 Ibid., 9 Mar. 1853

64 Ibid., 25 Mar. 1853

65 *Report of the ... St Lawrence and Ottawa Grand Junction Railway Company,* 12

66 Ibid., 13-40

67 See Montreal *Gazette,* 7, 14 Feb., 30 Mar., 4 April 1853

68 Ibid., 2 Mar. 1853. See also *Report of the ... St Lawrence and Ottawa Grand Junction Railway,* 7

69 Montreal *Gazette,* 16 Mar. 1853; ibid., 14 Feb. 1853
Ibid., 4 April 1853. Indicating an awareness of their importance to Boston's own railways which connected to Canadian lines, the *Boston Atlas* reported news of the railway decisions of such municipalities as Two Mountains.

70 Ibid., 17 June 1853.
71 Ibid., 24 June 1853
72 Ibid., 7, 13 July 1853
73 *Report ... Loranger,* 62
74 Montreal *Gazette,* May to Aug. 1853.
75 Ibid., 30 Aug. 1853

ELEVEN / THE MONTREAL AND NEW YORK RAILWAY

1 Prov. Sec. Corres., 147 (1847), 2122
2 *Stats. Prov. Can.* (1846), 10 & 11 Vic., c. 120. The bill was reserved and received Royal Assent on 15 April 1848.
3 *Montreal Directory* (1845-6), 192; Terrill, 129.
4 *Morning Courier,* 3 Nov. 1849; CNR, 387, 389
5 *Stats. Prov. Can.* (1849), 12 Vic., c. 179
6 Stevens, *Canadian National,* I, 37
7 See Crockett, *A History of Lake Champlain;* chap. 15
8 CNR, 387
9 Prov. Sec. Corres., 280 (1850), 1456
10 *Stats. Prov. Can.* (1847), 10 & 11 Vic., c. 120
11 Prov. Sec. Corres., 280 (1850), 1456
12 Ibid., 1831
13 McLean, 'Railway Policy'
14 Delaware and Hudson Railway Company, *A Century of Progress,* 175
15 CNR, 387, 27 Mar. 1851
16 *Stats. Prov. Can.* (1850), 13 & 14 Vic., c. 112; CNR, 387, 15 Jan. 1852
17 Ibid., 389
18 Ibid:, 387
19 Wallace, *Dictionary,* 147; Coffin, *The Canal and the Rail*
20 CNR, 389
21 Ibid., 387, 30 April 1851
22 Ibid., 12 July 1851
23 *Stats. Prov. Can.* (1846), 9 Vic., c. 82; (1849), 12 Vic., c. 177
24 *Montreal Courier,* 22 Feb. 1850
25 *Stats. Prov. Can.* (1847), 10 & 11 Vic., c. 120
26 *Counterstatement,* 26-27.
27 Montreal *Gazette,* 25 July 1851
28 Montreal *Gazette,* 14 Aug. 1851. See also ibid., 7 Jan. 1852
29 *Counterstatement,* 23
30 Brown, 'Champlain and St Lawrence Railroad,' 35
31 Brown, 'Montreal saw its first train,' 16
32 Montreal *Gazette,* April to Aug. 1853, passim
33 Montreal *Gazette,* 9 May 1853
34 Crockett, *Lake Champlain,* 270
35 Reprinted in Montreal *Gazette,* 17 May 1853
36 See Montreal *Gazette,* July to Sept. 1853, passim
37 Brown, 'Champlain and St Lawrence Railroad,' 45
38 *Petition of J.B. Bailey and others*
39 CNR, 388, 387
40 *Counterstatement,* passim
41 Montreal *Gazette,* 14 June 1853
42 Ibid., 25 June 1853
43 Ibid., 24 Sept. 1853

44 Crockett, *Lake Champlain,* 275
45 *Counterstatement,* 12
46 Ibid., 16-18
47 *Petition of J.B. Bailey and others*
48 *Counterstatement,* 4-5
49 *Petition of J.B. Bailey and others*
50 Ibid.
51 *Stats. Prov. Can.* (1856), 20 Vic., c. 142. See Delaware and Hudson Railway Company,
   A Century of Progress, for the subsequent history of this railway.

TWELVE / THE RISE OF MONTREAL AS A MANUFACTURING CENTRE

1 Even the latest work on the economic development of Lower Canada in the first half of the
   nineteenth century does little to substantially alter this emphasis; Ouellet, *Histoire
   Economique.* However, in his *The Elements Combined* (9), William Kilbourn points to the
   Lachine Canal as the 'birthplace ... [of] modern industry in Canada ... in 1846.'
2 Jean Bruchési, 'Histoire économique,' in Minville, ed., *Montreal économique,* 30. See also
   Jean Delage, 'L'Industrie manufacturière,' ibid., 195.
3 Denison, *The Barley and the Stream,* chaps. 7 and 8; Bruchesi (see n. 2) asserts that Montreal
   possessed nearly five hundred industrial establishments and thirteen hundred workers
   in 1830.
4 See S.G. Checkland, *Rise of Industrial Society,* 5
5 Cooper, *St. George's Lodge,* 33
6 Faucher and Lamontagne, 'Industrial Development,' 195; Hind, ed., *Eighty Years
   Progress,* 136; Ouellet, *Histoire économique,* 500
7 The vessel of 90 to 110 tons, sometimes possessing a single mast and sail and often called a
   Durham boat, was listed in official shipping registers and Montreal newspapers as a barge.
8 Wilson, 'The application of steam, 8
9 CR, 921. Undated and untitled newspaper clipping on shipbuilding in Montreal
10 Buckingham, *Canada,* 143
11 Montreal *Gazette,* 19 Dec. 1833, quoted in Innis and Lower, *Select Documents,* 247
12 Atherton, *Montreal,* II, 574; CR, 921
13 Ship Registers, 175, passim; CR, 921
14 Ibid.; *Montreal Transcript,* 21 May 1839
15 Prince, *Montreal,* 90
16 Montreal *Gazette,* 19 May 1845, advertisement
17 PAC, Lachine Canal, 9
18 Ship Registers, 175-24ff
19 *Montreal in 1856,* 41. See also Day, *English America;* 187.
20 PAC, Lachine Canal, August [in] Cantin to Hon. H.H. Killaly, president of the Board of
   Works, 13 Sept. 1843
21 Massicotte, 'Les Chantiers Cantin,' 509; CR, 921
22 PAC, Lachine Canal, Murray and Sanderson, Lonson Hilliard, Quebec Forwarding Company
   per Alexander Ferguson, Henderson [Starke?] and Company, Macpherson Crane and
   Company per H. Jones to Hon. H.H. Killaly, 30 Dec. 1844.
23 Ship Registers, 175, passim; *Montreal in 1856,* 41
24 Lachine Canal, William Kingsford to Thomas A. Begley, secretary of the Department of
   Public Works, 10 May 1847
25 Ibid., A. Cantin to T.A. Begley, 10 June 1851
26 CR, 921; *Montreal in 1856,* 41
27 Glazebrook, *Transportation,* I, 70-1
28 The production of vessels at Portsmouth, near Kingston, however, was considerable;
   see Ship Registers, 205.

29 See Province of Canada, *Patents,* I
30 A number of these contracts have been examined in the archives of the Superior Court in Montreal.
31 See Denison, *Bank of Montreal,* I, chap. 4. In *Canadian-American Industry,* authors Marshall, Southard, and Taylor point out that American enterprise was spilling over to Canada 'even as early as the 1840s.'
32 PAC, Ward Papers, 1818-37, John Dod Ward, Vergennes, Vermont, to Silas Ward, Elizabethtown, New Jersey, 16 Aug. 1818
33 Denison, *The Barley and the Stream,* 80. See also Wilson, 'The application of steam,' 69.
34 Quoted in Hunter, *Steamboats,* 61
35 Ward Papers, John Ward, Montreal, to Silas Ward, 9 Aug. 1819
36 Ibid.
37 Ibid., John to Silas, 10 Sept., 3 Oct. 1819
38 Ibid., John to Silas, 4 Nov. 1819
39 Ibid., John to Silas, 24 Dec. 1819; 14 Jan. 1820
40 Ibid., John to Silas, 29 May 1823
41 Young, *Great Lakes' Saga,* 17
42 Armstrong, ed., *Toronto of Old* (Toronto, 1966), 345; ASCM, Griffin Papers, 10 July 1840, 17145; 9 Nov. 1827, 7531; Montreal *Gazette,* 16 June 1831, quoted in Innis and Lower, *Select Documents,* 295-6
43 ASCM, Griffin Papers, 15 Aug. 1836, 14139
44 Ward Papers, 'I am not a Scotchman, a circumstance of no small importance with some of the wise ones here.' John to Silas, 30 Oct. 1821. Ibid., John to Silas, 20 May 1822
45 Ibid., 23 Nov. 1832
46 Ibid., Samuel to Silas, 20 Nov. 1833
47 ASCM, Gibb Papers, 6 Sept. 1844, 7580
48 Smyth, *City and District,* 15
49 CBD, 99
50 Ward Papers, Samuel to Silas, 30 Dec. 1839
51 CR, 77; *Montreal Directory;* Lighthall, *American Presbyterian,* 36
52 *Morning Courier,* 1 Nov. 1849; *Montreal Business Sketches,* 23-5. The Eagle Foundry was still in business in 1893 under the management of George S. Brush, who entered the firm in 1854. Montreal Board of Trade, *Souvenir,* 126
53 Denison, *The Barley and the Stream,* 62, 82
54 This firm built engines for vessels in Kingston. Calvin, *Saga,* 118. ASCM, Griffin Papers, 7 May 1832, 9837; Spratt, *Steam Navigation,* 12
55 Montreal *Gazette,* 10 May 1845
56 Prov. Sec. Corres., 284 (1850), 1879; Canadian Manufacturers' Association, *Industrial Canada* (1967), 241
57 *Montreal Transcript,* 28 Nov. 1837
58 *Montreal Business Sketches,* 12, 97
59 Ibid., 97; Lighthall, *American Presbyterian,* 36; *Montreal Directory* (1847-8), 267; Prov. Sec. Corres., 284 (1850), 1879
60 *Morning Courier,* 11 Jan. 1850
61 Ibid., 5 April 1849
62 *Montreal in 1856,* 36-49
63 *Montreal Transcript,* 16 May 1839; 23 Nov. 1839; 6 April 1837; 9 Feb. 1839
64 Sack, *Jews in Canada,* 157; *Montreal in 1856,* 46; *Montreal Transcript,* 1837; passim; *Morning Courier,* 26 Nov. 1849; *Commission to Investigate ... the Sweating System*
65 *Montreal in 1856,* 46
66 The sewing machine was invented in 1846 in the United States, and was quickly introduced in Montreal. A factory producing them was in operation by 1850, *Montreal Gazette,* 4 Oct. 1853; see Dales, *Hydroelectricity*

67 *Montreal Directory*, 1853, listed (290) under 'Clothing Manufacturers (by machinery)' the firm of Rogers and Doane; *Montreal in 1856*, 46
68 Benoist, *Monographies*, 231, 232; Montreal Board of Trade, *A Souvenir*, 123; Faucher and Lamontagne, 'Industrial Development,' 261; *Montreal in 1856*, 45
69 *Industrial Canada* (1967), 194, 223
70 Jenkins, *Montreal*, 98. See also Tulchinsky, The First Lachine Canal, 3-4
71 Dominion of Canada, *Report of the Royal Commission on the leasing of Water-Power on the Lachine Canal*, 8
72 *Ibid.*, 10
73 *Montreal in 1856*, 43
74 Ibid.
75 Letter from Mrs Catherine Clarke to the author, 19 Nov. 1969
76 Lachine Canal, E.E. Gilbert to commissioners of public works, 16 Oct. 1849. Gilbert claimed to be a relative of Luther Holton's; *Montreal in 1856*, 43
77 Lachine Canal, E.E. Gilbert, Application to lease island, 5 May 1853
78 Wilson, 'The application of steam,' 232
79 *Montreal Business Sketches*, 133-6; See Montreal *Gazette*, 29 Dec. 1848. The St Lawrence and Atlantic Railway purchased platform and passenger cars from this firm: CNR, 162-141; 163-234
80 *Montreal in 1856*, 43-4
81 Lachine Canal, Thomas A. Bigelow to Samuel Keefer, 17 Oct. 1850; Kilbourn, *The Elements Combined*, 4; *Montreal in 1856*, 44
82 Lachine Canal, Statement of leases of Lachine Canal, 6 Mar. 1857, 2; *Montreal Transcript*, 15 Feb. 1840; Prov. Sec. Corres. 94 (1844), 158. This petition is missing: the information was found in the index of petitions; CR, 827; Smyth, *City and District*, 15
83 *Montreal in 1856*, 44; Lyman, ed., *Genealogy*, 66; *Montreal Business Sketches*, 97-100
84 McGill University, European and North American Manuscripts, Ch. 353, S 313, William Lyman: Insurance and Financial Papers, 1835-56; *Montreal in 1856*, 44; *Montreal Business Sketches*, 13
85 National Harbours Board, Montreal Trinity Board Minutes, passim; *Montreal Directory* (1845-6), 284
86 *Montreal in 1856*, 45; PAC, Lachine Canal, Statement of leases on Lachine Canal, 6 Mar. 1857, 6
87 Dominion of Canada, *Royal Commission on Water-Power*, 13
88 Ibid., 35-6
89 Ibid., 36
90 Young purchased four building lots on the Lachine Canal from the Department of Public Works for £1140 in March 1851, one month after concluding the St Gabriel water-lot leases. It is not clear whether these properties were adjacent to the water-lots or elsewhere in the canal sector. In any case, Young, who was at this point at the height of his financial strength, appears to have bought the building lots privately. See JLA (1851), App. T.
91 Ibid., 17, 38
92 Ibid.
93 See Morgan, *Bibliotheca Canadensis*, 405
94 *Montreal in 1856*, 39
95 Ibid., 40; 'Le premier moulin à coton,' 700
96 *Montreal in 1856*, 40
97 Ibid., 41-2
98 Lachine Canal, Scott brothers to T.A. Begley, 17 Feb. 1852, 18 Dec. 1852.
99 Rattray, *The Scot*, III, 764
100 *The Ogilvies of Montreal*, 10. Another uncle was William Watson, since 1827 chief flour inspector of Montreal, a position of importance and still another relative, Mathew Hutchison, was also an official in the flour inspection department. Watson became wealthy

and left his entire estate to his sister's children: *Montreal in 1856,* 43; Stevens, *Ogilvie in Canada,* 20

101 Day, *English America,* 187
102 *Canadian Economist,* 8 Aug. 1846, quoted in Innis and Lower, *Select Documents,* 302
103 Logan, *Trade Unions in Canada,* 29
104 Province of Canada, *Patents*
105 See Hunt, *Synopsis,* 66-8; also *A Few Words Upon Canada; Montreal Gazette,* 4 Oct. 1853
106 JLA (1856), App. 46
107 *Montreal in 1856,* 40
108 *Morning Courier,* 27 July 1849
109 Montreal *Gazette,* 2 April 1849
110 Ibid., 27 Mar. 1850
111 *Montreal in 1856,* 37
112 Aitken, 'Defensive expansionism'

THIRTEEN / CONCLUSION

1 See Young, 'North Shore Railway.'
2 *Montreal Courier,* 27 Oct. 1849
3 Allin and Jones, *Annexation,* 353
4 Tucker, *Commercial Revolution,* 146; Creighton, *Commercial Empire,* 382.
5 *Montreal Courier,* 27 Oct. 1849
6 Ibid.

Bibliography

PRIMARY SOURCES

Manuscript collections
Archives de la Province de Québec
    Série AA, Baldwin Papers
Archives of the Superior Court, Montreal
    I.J. Gibb Papers
    Henry Griffin Papers
Canada Steamship Lines, Montreal
    Compagnie du Richelieu, Minutes 1845-56
Canadian National Railways Headquarters Library
    Letters from Commissioner of the Champlain and St Lawrence Railways,
    W.D. Lindsay, to various persons, 1845-9 (typescript)
City of Montreal Archives
    Assessment Books, 1852-
Chateau de Ramézy
    Manuscript Collection
Dow Brewery Ltd, Montreal
    Archives
Harvard University, Baker Library
    Dun and Bradstreet Credit Ledgers, Canada
McCord Museum, McGill University
    Jedediah Hubbell Dorwin, 'Antiquarian Autographs'
    Bagg Papers
McGill University
    European and North American Manuscripts
    Henry Griffin Papers
    Henry Chapman File
    Horatio Gates Estate

    Larocque, Bernard and Company
    Ottawa and Rideau Forwarding Company
    William Lyman and Company
Montreal Board of Trade Archives
    J. and R. Esdaile Circulars 1848-51
    Council Minutes
National Harbours Board, Montreal
    Minutes of the Montreal Harbour Commissioners
    Letterbooks of the Montreal Harbour Commissioners
    Minutes of the Montreal Trinity Board
    Letterbooks of the Montreal Trinity Board
Public Archives of Canada.
    RG 30, Canadian National Railways, Vols 146-56, St Lawrence and Atlantic Railroad Books of Subscription to the Capital Stock
    RG 30, Canadian National Railways, Vol. 387, Lake St Louis and Province Line Railway Minute Book, 1849-52
    RG 30, Canadian National Railways, Vols 389-90, Lake St Louis and Province Line Railway Stock Ledger, 1851-4
    RG 30, Canadian National Railways, Vol. 388, Lake St Louis and Province Line Railway Stock Journal, 1851-4
    RG 30, Canadian National Railways, Vol. 274, Montreal and Lachine Railroad Company, Journal and Stock Register, 1846-55
    RG 11, PW 5, Vol. 7, Lachine Canal
    RG 12, Department of Transport A, Department of Marine. 1, Ship Registers, 1787-1933, Vols 175, 176, 178, 205
    MG 24, D 12, Jedediah Hubbell Dorwin Diaries, 1811-1883
    MG 24, E 1, William Hamilton Merritt Papers
    MG 24, D 16, Buchanan Papers
    MG 24, D 27, Baring Papers
    MG 24, D 19, Ward Papers, 1818-1837
    MG 24, D 26, Gates Papers
    MG 24, D 28, Peter McGill Papers
    MG 24, D 8, Ruggles Wright Papers
    MG 27, D 8, Galt Papers
    MG 27, 1, E 10A, Edward Murphy Papers
    RG 28, Minutes of the Board of Directors of the Bank of Montreal (microfilm)
    RG 4, C 1, Provincial Secretary's Correspondence
Queen's University Archives
    John Young Papers
Scottish Record Office
    James Dunlop Papers, 1773-1815

Université de Montréal
    Collection Baby, II, C 2, Boîtes 59, 124
Professor Frederick H. Armstrong, University of Western Ontario
    Letters from various correspondents of Edmonstone, Allan and Co. 1840-56
Professor John I. Cooper, University of Guelph
    Notes on the John Frothingham Diaries
Mr. Murray Ballantyne, Montreal
    [Auto] Biography of the Late Harrison Stephens, Esq., as taken from his
    dictation by a reporter, with other incidents connected with his life
    (typescript)

Newspapers and periodicals

The American Railroad Journal
La Minerve
Morning Courier
Montreal Gazette
Montreal Transcript
Pilot
La Press
The Economist

Printed primary sources

1 / Government documents
Dominion of Canada, *Report of the Royal Commission on the Leasing of
    Water-Power on the Lachine Canal* (Ottawa, 1887)
Dominion of Canada, *The Elgin-Grey Papers,* 4 vols (Ottawa, 1937)
Dominion of Canada, *Censuses of Canada, 1665-1871* (Ottawa, 1876)
Dominion of Canada, *House of Commons, Commission to Investigate ... Whether,
    and if so, to what extent, the Sweating System is Practized in the Various
    Industrial Centres in the Dominion,* Sessional Paper 61 (1896)
Lower Canada, *Ordinances of the Special Council*
Montreal Board of Harbour Commissioners, *Official Documents and Other
    Information Relating to the Improvement of the Ship Channel between
    Montreal and Quebec* (Montreal, 1884)
Province of Canada, *Census of Canada* 2 vols (1851-2)
Province of Canada
    Journals of the Legislative Assembly (1846),
    App. R, Second Report of the Select Committee appointed to consider what
    general Provisions ought to be introduced into such Railway Bills as may
    come before the House during present or future Sessions ...

Journals of the Legislative Assembly (1849)

App. B, Board of Registration and Statistics. Appendix to the First Report, 1849. Trade and Consumption

Journals of the Legislative Assembly (1849),

App. HH, Statement of the Receipts and Disbursements of the St Lawrence and Atlantic Railroad ... 30 Nov. 1848

Journals of the Legislative Assembly (1849),

App. S, Statement of the Cost of the Montreal and Lachine Railroad ... Receipts and Expenditure ... Tonnage and Passengers ... 1 May to 31 December, 1849

Journals of the Legislative Assembly (1849),

App. Z, Montreal Brokers' Circular, March 25, 1849

Journals of the Legislative Assembly (1851),

App. T, Report of the Commissioners of Public Works, for 1850

Journals of the Legislative Assembly (1851),

App. DDD, Information ... in Reference to the Proper Gauge to be Adopted for Railroads ... in This Province.

Journals of the Legislative Assembly (1852-53),

App. Q, Report of the Commissioners of Public Works for 1851

Journals of the Legislative Assembly (1854-55),

App. CCC, Return to an Address Relative to the Contract Between the Government and Messrs McKean and McLarty for Ocean Steam Service

Journals of the Legislative Assembly (1854-55),

App. FF, Returns from Canal, Road, Railway, and Navigation Companies, nos 2, 5

Journals of the Legislative Assembly (1855),

App. GG, Return to an Address from the Legislative Assembly of the 22nd instant, Nov. 1854, for copy of certain correspondence relative to Montreal Harbour

Province of Canada

Journals of the Legislative Council (1853),

App. OOO, Imports and Exports with the Lower Provinces

Journals of the Legislative Council (1853),

App. VVV, Return of Sums Paid by Governments, and Correspondence Between Engineers and Other Officers Relative to Certain Rail-Roads

Province of Canada, *Proceedings of the Standing Committee on Railroads and Telegraph Lines; Together with the Minutes of Evidence Ordered by the Committee to be Printed, July 14, 1851* (Toronto, 1851)

Province of Canada, *Patents of Canada,* 2 vols (Toronto, 1860, 1865)

Province of Canada, *Statutes*

Province of Canada, *Tables of Trade and Navigation* (Quebec, 1851-55)

Province of Canada, *Canada Gazette*

Report of the Committee to Inquire Into the Transactions of the Montreal and Bytown Railway, prepared by Mr. Loranger (Quebec, 1856)

United States of America, *Report ... on the Trade and Commerce of the British North American Colonies* by Israel D. Andrews (Washington, 1853)

Vermont House of Representatives, *Journal* (1849)

2 / Other printed sources

A Few Words Upon Canada and Her Productions in the Great Exhibition (London, 1851)

A Topographical Map of the City of Montreal and Vicinity Showing the Line of the New City Waterworks (Montreal, 1854)

Annual General Meeting of the Proprietors of the St Lawrence and Atlantic Railroad for 1847 (Montreal, 1847)

Beckett, S.B., *Guide Book of the Atlantic and St Lawrence and Atlantic Rail-Roads, Including a Full Description of All the Interesting Features of the White Mountains* (Portland, 1853)

Brown, Thomas Storrow, 'Montreal fifty years ago,' *New Dominion Monthly*, 25 March 1870

Buckingham, James Silk, *Canada, Nova Scotia, New Brunswick and Other British Provinces in North America, with a Plan of National Colonization* (London, 1843)

Campbell, Robert, *A History of the Scotch Presbyterian Church, St. Gabriel Street* (Montreal, 1897)

Champlain and St Lawrence Railroad Company, *Annual Report of the Directors of the Champlain and St Lawrence Railroad Company, to the Stockholders, on Monday, 19th June, 1852* (Montreal, 1852)

Coffin, William, *The Canal and the Rail: Three Chapters on a Triple Project* (Montreal, 1848)

Counterstatement of the Plattsburgh and Montreal Railroad Company, Addressed to the Legislature and Public of Canada (Montreal, 1855)

Crocker, William P., *Report of a Survey of the Projected Line of Railroad from Stanstead to Montreal: With Estimates of the Cost of Construction* (Montreal, 1854)

Day, Samuel Phillips, *English America: or, Pictures of Canadian Places and People*, 2 vols (London, 1864)

Ferrie, Adam, *Life of the Hon. Adam Ferrie* (np, nd)

Galt, Alexander T., *A Letter to the Chairman of the North American Colonial Association* (London, 1848)

Goad, Charles E., *Atlas of the City of Montreal From Special Survey and Official Plans Showing All Buildings and Names of Owners,* 2 vols (Montreal, 1890)

Hunt, Robert, *Synopsis of the Contents of the Great Exhibition of 1851* (London, 1851)

Keefer, Thomas Coltrin, *The Canals of Canada: Their Prospects and Influence* (Toronto, 1850)

– *The Philosophy of Railroads, Published at the Request of the Directors of the Montreal and Lachine Railroad* (Montreal, 1850)

– *Report on a Survey for the Railway Bridge Over the St Lawrence at Montreal* (Montreal, 1853)

Lamont, Robert, *Statement of the Principal Circumstances Connected with the Establishment of a Line of Ocean Steamers Between Liverpool and Canada, and the Service Performed from May, 1853 to December, 1854* (np, nd)

Lower Canada Almanack and Montreal Commercial Directory (Montreal, 1840)

MacKay, Robert Stuart W., *The Directory of Montreal* (Montreal, 1841-53 annually)

McLellan, Hugh, ed., *Journal of Thomas Nye Written During a Journey Between Montreal and Chicago in 1837* (Champlain, New York, 1937)

Merritt, William Hamilton, *A Brief Review of the Revenue, Resources and Expenditures of Canada, Compared With Those of the Neighbouring State of New York* (St Catharines, 1845)

Montizambert, Edward L., *A Lecture on the Mercantile Law of Lower Canada* (Montreal, 1848)

Montreal Almanack (Montreal, 1839)

Montreal Brokers' Circulars (1848, 1851)

Montreal Business Sketches With a Description of the City of Montreal, Its Public Buildings, and Places of Interest, and the Grand Trunk Works at Point St. Charles, Victoria Bridge, etc., etc., Prepared and Published by the Canadian Railway Advertising Company (Montreal, 1865)

Montreal in 1856: A Sketch Prepared for the Opening of the Grand Trunk Railway of Canada by a Subcommittee of the Celebration Committee (Montreal, 1856)

Morgan, Henry J., *Bibliotheca Canadensis* (Montreal, 1867)

Morton, A.C., *Report on the Gauge for the St Lawrence and Atlantic Railroad* (Montreal, 1847)

Observations on the Question of Bridging the River Richelieu Above the Town of St John's for Railroad Purposes (Toronto, 1851)

Patterson, William J., *Statistical Contributions Relating to the Trade, Commerce, and Navigation of the Dominion of Canada* (Montreal, 1869)

Petition of J.B. Bailey and Others of Plattsburgh in the State of New York, Stockholders and Proprietors of the Plattsburgh and Montreal Railroad (Quebec, 1854)

Plan for Shortening the Time of Passage Between New York and London, With Documents Relating Thereto, Including the Proceedings of the Railway Convention of Portland, Maine, and the Charter of the European and North American Railway, with subsequent acts and resolves passed by the Legislature of Maine, and the doings of the Executive Committee in Relation thereto, Published by Order of the Convention (Portland, 1850)

Proceedings of a Special General Meeting of the Proprietors of the St Lawrence and Atlantic Railroad, Held in Montreal, 30th July, and the Report of A.C. Morton, Esquire, Chief Engineer (Montreal, 1846)

Proceedings of the Third Annual Meeting of the Proprietors of the St Lawrence and Atlantic Railroad, held in Montreal, on the 19th of January, 1848 (Montreal, 1848)

The Railroad Jubilee, An Account of the Celebration Commemorative of the Opening of Railroad Communication Between Boston and Canada, September 17th, 18th and 19th, 1851 (Boston, 1852)

Report of the Committee on the Montreal and Kingston Section of the Canada Grand Trunk Railway (np, nd)

Report of the Directors and Chief Engineer of the St Lawrence and Ottawa Grand Junction Railway Company, May 9th, 1853 (Montreal, 1853)

Report of the Speeches and Proceedings at a Special Meeting of the Mercantile Library Association of Montreal. Held on Monday Evening, April 8, 1850, to take into consideration the action of the Board of Direction in respect to the expulsion of the 'Christian Inquirer' from the News Room (Montreal, 1850)

Statements Concerning the Trade and Commerce of the City of Montreal, for 1862; being a reprint of three articles from the "Daily Witness" (Montreal, 1863)

Statement of Facts Laid before Sir Allan MacNab, Kt., Chairman of the Railroad Committee of the Legislative Assembly of the Province of Canada in Relation to the Application of the Champlain and St Lawrence Railroad Company for the Right to Bridge the Navigable Waters of Lake Champlain and River Richelieu, Between Rouse's Point and Isle aux Noix, and to Build a Railroad From the Said Bridge on the East Side of the River Richelieu to the Province Line (Toronto, 1851)

St Lawrence and Atlantic Railroad, Annual Reports (Montreal, 1846-53 annually)

St Lawrence and Atlantic Railroad Company, *Memorandum From a Meeting of the Board of Directors* (Montreal, 1852)

Tabular Representation of the Present Condition of Boston in Relation to Railroad Facilities, Foreign Commerce, Population, Wealth, Manufacturers, etc., etc.; also, a Few Statements Relative to the Commerce of the Canadas (Boston, 1851)

Taché, J.C., *Descriptive Catalogue of the Productions of Canada Exhibited at Paris in 1855* (Paris, 1855)

Taylor, Fennings and William Notman, *Portraits of British Americans with Biographical Sketches,* 3 vols (Montreal, 1865-8)

Taylor, Henry, *Journal of a Tour from Montreal thro' Berthier and Sorel to the Eastern Townships* (Quebec, 1840)

Walrond, T., ed., *Letters and Journals of James, Earl of Elgin* (London, 1873)

Warburton, Eliot, *Hochelaga; or England in the New World,* 2 vols (London, 1847)

Young, John, *The Origin of the Ocean Mail Steamers Between Liverpool and the St Lawrence and the Advantages of the Northern Route* (Montreal, 1877)

Young, John, *Letters to the Hon. Francis Lemieux, Chief Commissioner Public Works, on Canadian Trade and Navigation, and the Citizens of Montreal, on the Commerce of the City and the Means of Its Further Development* (Montreal, 1855)

SECONDARY SOURCES

Books

Allin, Cephas D. and George M. Jones, *Annexation, Preferential Trade and Reciprocity, An Outline of the Canadian Annexation Movement of 1849-50, With Special Reference to the Questions of Preferential Trade and Reciprocity* (Toronto, nd)

Anon., *The Ogilvies of Montreal* (Montreal, 1904)

Armstrong, Frederick H., ed., *Toronto of Old* (Toronto, 1966)

Atherton, William Henry, *Montreal, 1535-1914* 3 vols (Montreal, 1914)

– *History of the Harbour Front of Montreal Since its Discovery by Jacques Cartier in 1835* (Montreal, nd)

Audet, F.J., *Les Députés de Montréal* (Montréal, 1942)

Benoist, Emile, *Monographies Economiques* (Montréal, 1925)

Bishop, Olga, *Publications of the Government of the Province of Canada* (Ottawa, 1963)

Borthwick, John Douglas, *History and Biographical Gazeteer of Montreal to the Year 1892* (Montreal, 1892)

– *Montreal – Its History, To Which is Added Biographical Sketches With Photographs of Many of Its Principal Citizens* (Montreal, 1875)

Brault, Lucien, *Histoire des Comtés Unis de Prescott et de Russell* (L'Orignal, 1965)

Calvin, D.D., *Saga of the St Lawrence, Timber and Shipping Through Three Generations* (Toronto, 1945)

Canadian Biographical Dictionary and Portrait Gallery of Eminent and Self-Made Men, Quebec and Maritime Provinces Volume (Toronto, 1880)

Canadian Manufacturers' Association, *Industrial Canada* (Toronto, 1967)

Careless, J.M.S., *The Union of the Canadas, 1841-1857* (Toronto, 1967)

Chandler, Alfred D., *Henry Varnum Poor, Business Editor, Analyst and Reformer* (Cambridge, Mass., 1956)

Checkland, S.G., *The Rise of Industrial Society in England, 1815-1885* (London, 1964)

Choquette, C.-P., *Histoire de la Ville de Saint-Hyacinthe* (St Hyacinthe, 1930)

Cook, Ramsay, ed., *French-Canadian Nationalism, An Anthology* (Toronto, 1969)

Cooper, John Irwin, *Montreal: A Brief History* (Montreal, 1969)
- *History of the Montreal Hunt Club* (Montreal, 1953)
- *History of St. George's Lodge, No. 1, G.R.Q.* (Montreal, 1955)
- *Montreal, the Story of Three Hundred Years* (Montreal, 1942)

Cornell, Paul G., *The Alignment of Political Groups in Canada, 1841-1867* (Toronto, 1962)

Côté, J.O., *Political Appointments and Elections in the Province of Canada from 1841 to 1865* (Ottawa, 1918)

Couillard-Despres, A., *Histoire de la Seigneurie de Saint-Ours,* II ième Partie, *La Famille et la Paroisse de Saint-Ours, 1785-1916* (Montréal, 1917)

Creighton, Donald G., *The Empire of the St Lawrence* (Toronto, 1956)

Crockett, W., *A History of Lake Champlain: A Record of More Than Three Centuries, 1606-1936* (Burlington, 1937)

Croil, James, *A History of Steam Navigation in Its Relations to the Commerce of Canada and the United States* (Toronto, 1898)

Currie, A.W., *The Grand Trunk Railway of Canada* (Toronto, 1957)

Dales, John H., *Hydroelectricity and Industrial Development: Quebec, 1898-1940* (Cambridge, Mass., 1957)

Deane, Phyllis, *The First Industrial Revolution* (Cambridge University Press, 1967)

De Brumath, Adrien Leblond, *Histoire Populaire de Montréal Depuis Son Origine Jusqu'à Nos Jours* (Montréal, 1890)

Delaware and Hudson Railway Company, *A Century of Progress, A History of the Delaware and Hudson Company, 1823-1923* (Albany, NY, 1925)

Denison, Merrill, *Canada's First Bank, A History of the Bank of Montreal,* 2 vols (Toronto and Montreal, 1966-7)

- *The Barley and the Stream, the Molson Story* (Toronto, 1955)

Dent, John C., *The Canadian Portrait Gallery*, 4 vols (Toronto, 1880)

Easterbrook, W.T. and Hugh G.J. Aitken, *Canadian Economic History* (Toronto, 1956)

Evans, O.R., *Montreal Corn Exchange Association, 1863-1963* (Montreal, 1963)

Fry, Henry, *The History of North Atlantic Steam Navigation with Some Account of Early Ships and Shipowners* (London, 1896)

Gilbert, Heather, *Awakening Continent, the Life of Lord Mount Stephen, Volume I: 1829-91* (Aberdeen, 1965)

Glazebrook, George P. de T., *A History of Transportation in Canada,* 2 vols (Toronto, 1966)

Greig, William, *Hochelaga Depicta; or the History and Present State of the Island and City of Montreal* [Montreal, 1839], Facsimile (Toronto, 1901)

Hind, Henry Youle, ed., *Eighty Years Progress of British North America* (Toronto, 1863)

Histoire de la Brasserie Dow, 1790-1955 (Montréal, 1955)

Hodgetts, J.E., *Pioneer Public Service, An Administrative History of the United Canadas, 1841-1867* (Toronto, 1955)

Hunter, Louis C., *Steamboats on the Western Rivers: An Economic and Technological Survey* (Cambridge, Mass., 1949)

Innis, Harold A., *Essays in Canadian Economic History,* edited by Mary Q. Innis (Toronto, 1956)

Innis, Harold A. and Lower, A.R.M., *Select Documents in Canadian Economic History, 1783-1885* (Toronto, 1966)

Jenkins, Kathleen, *Montreal: Island City of the St Lawrence* (New York, 1966)

Jodoin, Alex et J.-L. Vincent, *Histoire de Longueuil et de la Famille de Longueuil* (Montréal, 1889)

Johnson, Arthur M. and Supple, Barry E., *Boston Capitalists and Western Railroads, A Study in the Nineteenth-Century Railroad Investment Process* (Cambridge, Mass., 1967)

Johnson, J.K., ed., *The Canadian Directory of Parliament, 1867-1967* (Ottawa, 1968)

Jones, Clement, *Pioneer Shipowners* (Liverpool, 1934)

Kilbourn, William, *The Elements Combined, A History of the Steel Company of Canada* (Toronto, 1960)

Kirkland, Edward C., *Men, Cities and Transportation, A Study in New England History, 1820-1900* 2 vols (Cambridge, Mass, 1948)

Kos-Rabcewicz-Zubkowski, Ludwik and William Ed. Greening, *Sir Casimir Stanislaus Gzowski, a Biography* (Toronto, 1959)

Lamothe, J.C., *Histoire de la Corporation de Montréal* (Montréal 1903)

Landes, David, *Bankers and Pashas, International Finance and Economic Imperialism in Egypt* (New York, 1969)

Legget, Robert F., *Rideau Waterway* (Toronto, 1955)

Lighthall, G.R., *A History of the American Presbyterian Church of Montreal* (Montreal, 1923)

Lindsay, William S., *History of Merchant Shipping from 1816-1874,* 2 vols (London, 1876)

Logan, H.A., *Trade Unions in Canada* (Toronto, 1948)

Lovell, Sarah, *Reminiscences of Seventy Years* (Montreal, 1908)

Lower, Arthur R.M., *The North American Assault on the Canadian Forest: A History of the Lumber Trade Between Canada and the United States* (Toronto, 1938)

Lyman, Arthur, ed., *Genealogy of the Lyman Family in Canada. Ancestors and Descendants of Elisha Lyman (No. 18), From the End of the 18th Century to the Present Time (1943)* (Montreal, 1943)

Macmillan, David, ed., *Canadian Business History, Selected Studies, 1849-1971* (Toronto, 1972)

Marshall, Herbert et al., *Canadian-American Industry, A Study in International Investment* (Toronto, 1936)

Massicotte, Edouard-Zotique, *Faits Curieux de l'Histoire de Montréal* (Montréal, 1924)

Masson, Henri, *Joseph Masson, Dernier Seigneur de Terrebonne* (Montreal, 1972)

Masters, Donald C., *The Rise of Toronto, 1850-1890* (Toronto, 1947)

McDiarmid, Orville J., *Commercial Policy in the Canadian Economy* (Cambridge, Mass., 1946)

McIvor, R. Craig, *Canadian Monetary, Banking, and Fiscal Development* (Toronto, 1961)

Minville, Esdras, *Montréal Economique, Etude préparée à l'occasion du troisième centenaire de la ville* (Montréal, 1943)

Monet, Jacques, *The Last Cannon Shot, A Study of French-Canadian Nationalism, 1837-1850* (Toronto, 1969)

Montreal Board of Trade, *Fiftieth Anniversary Volume* (Montreal, 1892)

- *A Souvenir of the Opening of the New Building, One Thousand Eight Hundred and Ninety-Three* (Montreal, 1893)

- *One Hundred and Twenty-Fifth Anniversary Volume* (Montreal, 1947)

Morgan, Henry J., *Sketches of Celebrated Canadians and Persons Connected with Canada, From the Earliest Period in the History of the Province Down to the Present Time* (Quebec, 1862)

Morison, Samuel E., *The Maritime History of Massachusetts, 1783-1860* (Boston, 1922)

Morton, Arthur S., *Sir George Simpson: Overseas Governor of the Hudson's Bay Company* (Toronto, 1944)

Myers, Gustavus, *History of Canadian Wealth* (Chicago, 1914)

Ouellet, Fernand, *Histoire Économique et Sociale du Québec, 1760-1850* (Montréal, 1966)

- *Histoire de la Chambre de Commerce de Québec, 1809-1959* (Québec, 1959)

Pennington, Myles, *Railways and Other Ways: Being Reminiscences of Canal and Railway Life During a Period of Sixty-Seven Years* (Toronto, 1894)

Phoenix Assurance Company Limited of London, *First in the Field* (Montreal, 1954)

Poor, Laura, *The First International Railway and the Colonization of New England: Life and Writings of John Alfred Poor* (Portland, 1892)

Porter, Marjorie L., *Plattsburgh 1785-1815-1902, Plattsburgh Barracks* (Plattsburgh, 1964)

Prince, Lorenzo, et al., *Montreal Old and New* (Montreal, 1913)

Rankin, John, *The History of Our Firm, Being Some Account of the Firm of Pollock, Gilmour and Co. and Its Offshoots and Connections,* 2nd ed. (Liverpool, 1921)

Rattray, William J., *The Scot in British North America,* 4 vols (Toronto, 1880-84)

Rose, George Maclean, ed., *A Cyclopaedia of Canadian Biography: Being Chiefly Men of the Time* (Toronto, 1886)

Ryan, William, *The Clergy and the Economic Growth of Quebec, 1896-1914* (Quebec, 1966)

Sack, Benjamin, G., *History of the Jews in Canada* (Montreal, 1965)

Sandwell, Bernard K., *The Molson Family* (Montreal, 1933)

Skelton, Oscar D., *The Life and Times of Sir Alexander Tilloch Galt* edited and with an introduction by Guy Maclean (Toronto, 1966)

- *The Railway Builders* (Toronto, 1916)

Smith, William, *The History of the Post Office in British North America, 1639-1870* (Cambridge, 1920)

Smyth, T. Taggart, *"The First Hundred Years", History of the Montreal City and District Savings Bank, 1846-1946* (Montreal, nd)

Spratt, H., *A History of Transatlantic Steam Navigation* (London, 1950)

Stevens, George R., *Ogilvie in Canada, Pioneer Millers, 1801-1951* (Montreal, 1951)

- *Canadian National Railways, Volume One; Sixty Years of Trial and Error* (Toronto, 1960)

Stover, John F., *American Railroads* (Chicago, 1961)

Taylor, George Rogers, *The Transportation Revolution, 1815-1860* (New York, 1968)

Terrill, Frederick William, *A Chronology of Montreal and of Canada from A.D. 1752 to A.D. 1893, Including Commercial Statistics, Historic Sketches of Commercial Corporations and Firms and Advertisements, Arranged to show in What Year the Several Houses and Corporate Bodies Originated* (Montreal, 1893)

Thompson, Norman and Edgar J.H., *Canadian Railway Development, From the Earliest Times* (Toronto, 1933)

Tombs, Laurence C., *The Port of Montreal* (Montreal, 1926, McGill University Economic Studies, No. 6)

Trout, Edw. and J.M., *The Railways of Canada for 1870-71, Showing the Progress, Mileage, Cost of Construction, the Stocks, Bonds, Traffic, Earnings, Expenses, and Organization of the Railways of the Dominion. Also, a Sketch of the Difficulties Incident to Transportation in the Pre-Railroad Days* [Toronto, 1871], Facsimile (Toronto, 1970)

Tucker, Gilbert N., *The Canadian Commercial Revolution, 1845-1851,* edited and with an introduction by Hugh G.J. Aitken (Toronto, 1964)

Turcotte, Gustave, *Le Conseil Législatif de Québec, 1774-1933* (Beauceville, 1933)

Vincent, J.L., *Histoire de Longueuil et de la Famille de Longueuil* (Montréal, 1889)

Walker, Franklyn, *Daylight Through the Mountain: The Life and Letters of Walter and Francis Shanly* (Toronto, 1957)

Wallace, William S., *Macmillan Dictionary of Canadian Biography* (Toronto, 1963)

Whitton, Charlotte H., *A Hundred Years A-Fellin,' Some Passages from the Timber Saga of the Ottawa in the Century in Which the Gillies Have Been Cutting in the Valley, 1842-1942* (Toronto, 1942)

Wilgus, William J., *The Railway Interrelations of the United States and Canada* (Toronto, 1937)

Wood, William, *All Afloat, A Chronicle of Craft and Waterways* (Toronto, 1915)

Young, Anna G., *Great Lakes' Saga* (Toronto, 1965)

Articles

Aitken, Hugh G.J., 'Defensive expansionism: the state and economic life in Canada,' in T. William Easterbrook and Melville H. Watkins, eds, *Approaches to Canadian Economic History* (Toronto, 1967), 183-221

Albion, Robert G., 'New York Port and its disappointed rivals, 1815-1860,' *Journal of Economic and Business Statistics* 3 (1931), 602-29

Armstrong, Frederick H., 'Jacques-Félix Sincennes,' *Dictionary of Canadian Biography* 10, 656-8 (Toronto, 1972)

- 'Charles-Séraphim Rodier,' *Dictionary of Canadian Biography* 10, 624-6 (Toronto, 1972)

Auclair, Elie J., 'Terrebonne, les Masson, leur Chateau,' *Transactions of the Royal Society of Canada,* 3rd ser., 38 (1944), Section I 1-15

Audet, Francis J., '1842,' *Les Cahiers des Dix* 7 (1942), 215-54

Austin, P.R., 'Two mayors of early Hamilton: Colin C. Ferrie and George E. Tuckett,' a speech before the Head-of-the-Lake Historical Society, 11 March 1955, (typescript)

Bladen, V.L., 'Construction of railways in Canada to the year 1885,' *Contributions to Canadian Economics* (1932), 43-60

Brown, George W., 'The opening of the St Lawrence to American shipping,' CHR 7 (1926), 4-12

Brown, Robert R., 'The Champlain and St Lawrence Railroad,' *Bulletin of the Railway and Locomotive Historical Society* (1936), 6-62

- 'Montreal saw its first train 100 years ago,' *Canadian National Railways Magazine* 33 (1947), 8-17

- 'The St Lawrence and Industrie Village Railway,' *Bulletin of the Railway and Locomotive Historical Society* (1947), 39-43

Buckley, Kenneth, 'The role of staple industries in Canada's economic development,' *Journal of Economic History* 18 (1958), 439-50

Careless, J.M.S., 'Frontierism, metropolitanism, and Canadian history,' CHR, 35 (1954), 1-21

Cooper, John Irwin, 'Some early Canadian savings banks,' *Canadian Banker,* 57 (1950), 135-43

- 'The social structure of Montreal in the 1850s,' Canadian Historical Association *Report* (1956), 63-73

Dechêne, Louise, 'Les Entreprises de William Price,' *Social History* 1 (1968), 16-52

Dubuc, Alfred, 'Problems in the study of the Canadian society from 1760 to 1840,' Canadian Historical Association *Report* (1965), 13-29

Faucher, Albert and Lamontagne, Maurice, 'History of industrial development,' in Jean C. Falardeau, ed., *Essais sur le Québec Contemporain* (Québec, 1953), 23-37

Gravel, Albert, 'Un accord historique,' *Mélanges Historiques Dans et Autour des Cantons de l'est,* 4 (1968), 1-4

Hamelin, Jean and Roby, Yves, 'L'évolution économique et sociale du Québec, 1851-1896,' *Recherches Sociographiques,* 10 (1969), 157-69

Lanctôt, Gustave, 'Panorama Historique de Saint-Jean,' *La Société Canadienne de l'histoire de l'Eglise Catholique* (1945-46), 93-104

Lefebvre, Jean-Jacques, 'Jean-Moise Raymond (1787-1843), premier député de Laprairie (1824-1838), natif du comté,' BRH 60 (1945), 109-20

'Le premier moulin à coton au Canada,' BRH, 39 (1933), 699-700

Massicotte, E.-Z., 'Un Philanthrope Canadien Français, M. Antoine-Olivier Berthelet,' *Faits Curieux de l'Histoire de Montréal* (Montréal 1924)

Massicotte, E.-Z., 'Les Chantiers Cantin à Montréal,' BRH 42 (1936), 509-10

McCalla, Douglas, 'The Canadian grain trade in the 1840s: the Buchanan Case,' Canadian Historical Association *Report* (1974), 95-114

McKee, Samuel jr, 'Canada's bid for the middle west. A quarter century of the history of the St Lawrence waterway, 1849-1874,' Canadian Historical Association *Report* (1940), 26-35

McLean, Simon J., 'The railway policy of Canada, 1849-1867,' *Journal of Political Economy*, 11 (1901), 191-217

– 'An early chapter in Canadian railroad policy,' *Journal of Political Economy* 6 (1898), 323-52

Monet, Jacques, 'Alexandre-Maurice Delisle,' *Dictionary of Canadian Biography* 10, 219-21 (Toronto, 1972)

Morgan, H.R., 'Steam navigation on the Ottawa River,' *Ontario Historical Society Papers and Records* 23 (1942), 370-83

Nelles, H.V., 'Introduction' to *The Philosophy of Railroads* by T.C. Keefer (Toronto, 1972)

'Origins of the Montreal Board of Trade,' *Journal of Commerce*, Series II, 55 (1927), 28-9

Parker, W.H., 'The towns of Lower Canada in the 1830s,' in R.P. Beckinsale and J.M. Houston, eds, *Urbanization and its Problems* (Oxford, 1968), 391-425

Patton, M.J., 'Shipping and canals,' *Canada and Its Provinces,* 23 vols (Toronto, 1914) 10, 475-624

Pentland, H.C., 'The Lachine Strike of 1843,' CHR 28 (1948), 255-77

– 'The role of capital in Canadian economic development before 1875,' *Canadian Journal of Economics and Political Science* 16 (1950), 457-74

Preston, R.A., 'The history of the Port of Kingston,' *Ontario History* 46 (1954), 201-17, and 47 (1955), 23-38

Richards, Elva M., 'The Joneses of Brockville and the Family Compact,' *Ontario History* 65 (1968), 169-84

Shortt, Adam, 'Founders of Canadian banking – Horatio Gates, wholesale merchant, banker and legislator,' *Journal of the Canadian Bankers' Association* 30 (1922), 34-47

– 'Founders of Canadian banking – Austin Cuvillier, merchant, legislator and banker,' *Journal of the Canadian Bankers' Association* 30 (1923), 304-16

– 'Founders of Canadian banking – The Hon. Peter McGill, banker, merchant and civic leader,' *Journal of the Canadian Bankers' Association* 31 (1924) 297-307

– 'Founders of Canadian banking – The Hon. Adam Ferrie, reformer, merchant and financier,' *Journal of the Canadian Bankers' Association* 32 (1924), 50-63

- 'Economic history, 1840-1867,' *Canada and Its Provinces* 5, 185-257
- 'Currency and banking, 1840-1867,' reprinted in E.P. Neufeld, ed., *Money and Banking in Canada* (Toronto, 1964), 132-48

Schumpeter, Joseph A., 'Economic theory and entrepreneurial history, in Ross M. Robertson and James L. Pate, eds, *Readings in United States Economic and Business History* (Boston, 1966), 101-10

Smith, William, 'The Post Office, 1840-1867,' *Canada and Its Provinces* 5, 365-404

Taylor, Norman W., 'The French-Canadian industrial entrepreneur and his social environment,' in Marcel Rioux and Yves Martin, eds, *French-Canadian Society* (Toronto, 1964), 271-95

Williams, David M., 'Merchanting in the first half of the nineteenth century: the Liverpool timber trade,' *Business History* 8 (1966), 103-21

Zoltvany, Yves-F., 'Laurent-Olivier David et L'Inferiorité Economique des Canadiens Français,' *Recherches Sociographiques* 10 (1969), 426-30

Unpublished theses and manuscripts

Cone, Gertrude E., 'Studies in the development of transportation in the Champlain Valley in 1876,' MA thesis, University of Vermont, 1945

Cross, Michael S., 'The Dark Druidical Groves: the lumber community and the commercial frontier in British North America to 1854,' PH D thesis, University of Toronto, 1968

Dechêne, Louise, 'William Price, 1810-1850,' L. és L. thesis, Laval University, 1964

Dictionary of Canadian Biography, 'Preliminary List of Quebec Businessmen, 1850-1900'

Dubuc, Alfred, 'Thomas Molson, Entrepreneur Canadien, 1791-1863,' Thèse de Doctorat, Université de Paris, 1969

Hopper, A.B., and T. Kearney, comp., 'Canadian National Railways: synoptical history of organization, capital stock, funded debt and other general information, as of December 31, 1961,' Canadian National Railways Headquarters Library, Montreal, typescript, 1962

Johnson, John S., 'History and organization of the Montreal Stock Exchange,' MA thesis, McGill University, 1934

Junkin, William R., 'The Port of Montreal,' MA thesis, Cornell University, 1930

Knowles, David C., 'The American Presbyterian Church of Montreal, 1822-1866,' MA thesis, McGill University, 1957

Klassen, Henry C., 'L.H. Holton: Montreal Businessman and Politician, 1817-1867,' PH D thesis, University of Toronto, 1970

Lynne, D.D., 'The Irish in the Province of Canada,' MA thesis, McGill University, 1960

McDougall, Elizabeth Ann, 'The American element in the early Presbyterian Church in Montreal, 1786-1824,' MA thesis, McGill University, 1965

McLeod, Paul, 'Montreal and free trade,' MA thesis, University of Rochester, 1967

Metcalfe, George, 'The political career of William Henry Draper,' MA thesis, University of Toronto, 1959

Montreal Stock Exchange, 'One hundred and thirty-two years of progress,' typescript

Parker, Keith A., 'The staple industries and Canadian economic development, 1841-1867,' PH D thesis, University of Maryland, 1966

St Lawrence Municipal Bureau (Montreal), comp., 'Chronological legal enactments pertaining to the establishment, growth and development of the harbour of Montreal,' 1959

Taylor, Norma Claire, 'The economic development of Canada's merchant marine,' MA thesis, University of Toronto, 1924

Tulchinsky, Gerald J.J., 'The construction of the first Lachine Canal, 1815-1826,' MA thesis, McGill University, 1960

Wilson, George H., 'The application of steam to St Lawrence Valley navigation, 1809-1840,' MA thesis, McGill University, 1961

Young, Brian, 'The North Shore Railway,' PH D thesis, Queen's University, 1972

Index